THE
RIP CURL
STORY

Tim Baker grew up as a landlocked surfer in the eastern suburbs of Melbourne and relied on the Rip Curl recorded surf report to find out what was happening on the coast. The first major sporting event he covered as a cadet journalist was the Rip Curl Pro, and the first brand-new wetsuit he owned was a burgundy-and-blue short-sleeved Dawn Patrol steamer. He is a former editor of *Tracks* and *Surfing Life* magazines, and has received the Surfing Australia culture award three times. His previous books include *Bustin' Down the Door*, *High Surf*, *Occy*, *Surf for Your Life* (with Mick Fanning), *Surfari* and *Century of Surf* (spot the recurring theme!).

FOREWORD BY MICK FANNING

THE

RIP CURL

STORY

TIM BAKER

EBURY
PRESS

EBURY PRESS

UK | USA | Canada | Ireland | Australia
India | New Zealand | South Africa | China

Ebury Press is part of the Penguin Random House group of companies whose
addresses can be found at global.penguinrandomhouse.com.

First published by Ebury Press, an imprint of
Penguin Random House Australia Pty Ltd, 2019

Cover photographs: front cover © Brent Bielmann; back cover © Ted Grambeau
Cover design by Alex Ross © Penguin Random House Australia Pty Ltd
Typeset in 12/17 pt Minion Pro by Midland Typesetters, Australia

Printed and bound in Australia by Griffin Press, an accredited ISO AS/NZS 14001
Environmental Management Systems printer

A catalogue record for this
book is available from the
National Library of Australia

ISBN 978 0 14378 887 4

penguin.com.au

'The Search is made up of many individual journeys, and the story of Rip Curl is made up of the personal journeys of many people. Mine is just one of them.'

Brian Singer

'It was a simple dream – to keep surfing, live at the beach, and somehow cobble together a livelihood that allowed for maximum surf time and surf exploration. That we managed to do so much more than that is testimony to the strength of that same dream that beats in the hearts of all surfers.'

Doug 'Claw' Warbrick

CONTENTS

FOREWORD
BY MICK FANNING

The following pages tell an incredible true story of how two mates started a surfboard company in a shed and grew it into one of the most recognisable brands in the world. It's a story of twists and turns that is both funny and real, documenting the journey they've endured to end up where they are today.

Rip Curl and its people have been a huge part of my life for two decades. From signing with them as an over-awed teenager to winning my first Rip Curl Pro as a wildcard, from overcoming injury and personal tragedy to winning world titles, from Search missions to remote waves right up to my retirement dinner at Torquay in 2018, they have been there through all the major milestones of my life. And we're not done yet.

Both Claw and Sing Ding know who they are as people, and that is reflected in the company that they have created, with the help of mates who became partners, and who all have their quirky sides.

Claw is the most passionate surfer I have ever met. I'll never forget him sitting with all the surfers in the competitors' area on

Réunion Island for the first ever Search event comparing scores and cracking jokes when people were way off the mark, as his predictions were pretty much on the money every time. The surfers walked away just mind-blown that a boss of the company would sit and engage in great banter for a whole day, clapping and jumping in his signature excited way.

Brian is more to the point, with quick, short and sharp conversations that hold a lot of meaning. He doesn't need all the fluffy stuff that goes into a conversation – he wants to get straight to the point and give his opinion or get an answer. Very rarely have conversations with him gone over the five-minute mark, but you always walked away clear on what was being said and he'd always finish with, 'If you need anything from Rip Curl, call me.' I really admired that about him.

Rip Curl is an incredible company that has stayed close to its roots, starting with surfboards and moving into wetsuits, which are still the world leaders today. The company has always tried to make surfing products for surfers, as this is exactly who they are, surfers first and foremost. All they've ever wanted to do is surf. These guys created the Search as their brand philosophy so they could keep surfing and going on surf trips for as long as possible.

'Never fighting the fun' is a brand principle that really shines through the company. Rip Curl's rule, that you can never get fired for going surfing, shows a deep respect for surfing and the beginnings they came from.

I don't know if there are enough pages to tell all the amazing stories and adventures in Rip Curl's evolution, but I'm sure this book will open your eyes and help inspire a sense of adventure and belief to just get out there and do it.

I hope you enjoy the story that follows, because the last 20 years of my experience with Rip Curl have been amazing, inspiring me to chase my dreams of becoming world champion and providing the support that is needed to do so.

To each and everyone that has been part of Rip Curl, this is a huge congratulations for creating a company that is truly for the surfers.

Cheers,
Mick

INTRODUCTION

It's 1985 and I'm a keen young cadet reporter for the Melbourne *Sun News-Pictorial* covering the big stories: fruit and vegetable prices, shipping movements and country lawn bowls results. But I have an audacious scheme to make this dull newspaper gig serve my salt-water kink.

I succeed in convincing my chief-of-staff to send me down to Bells Beach to cover the annual Rip Curl Pro. I'm ecstatic. This is something of a coup for a lowly cadet fresh out of high school, in an age when the paper's sports coverage rarely extends beyond footy, cricket, horseracing and the odd notable boxing bout.

I hightail it to Torquay in the mustard-yellow, vinyl-roofed office Cortina – with my meals, a cheap motel and petrol money covered for the Easter long weekend – barely able to believe my luck. The first person I run into is a police reporter from our sister afternoon paper the *Herald* (when afternoon papers were still a thing, before the *Herald* and *Sun* were merged five years later into – you guessed it – the *Herald-Sun*).

'What are you doing here?' I ask the police reporter, a little indignantly. 'I could file for the *Herald* if you need a story. And besides, you're a police reporter. What are you doing at a surf contest?'

He casts me a knowing sneer, and has a brooding, inner-city, post-punk air of menace about him that's weirdly out of place by the beach. 'It's a quiet Easter. Figured I'd come down in case there was a drug bust or a riot at the Torquay pub.'

Twenty-three years after the Bells Easter Rally was first staged, and 12 years after local wetsuit company Rip Curl tipped in a few grand to make the event professional, the world's longest-running surf contest was still regarded in some quarters as a potential crime scene rather than a major sporting event.

Fast-forward another 30 years and the Rip Curl Pro is now trumpeted as one of Victoria's six hallmark sporting events, promoted by Tourism Victoria alongside the Melbourne Cup, the AFL Grand Final, the Australian Open, the motorcycle Grand Prix and the Formula One Grand Prix. Today the surfing event is webcast live to a global audience of millions and beamed into millions more homes on cable TV. Thousands brave the frigid southern climes and line the clifftops and narrow ribbon of beach to soak up the action each Easter. The top competitors pocket hundreds of thousands of dollars in prize money and sometimes millions more in sponsorship deals.

The journey of surfing and Rip Curl, from marginalised counterculture ratbaggery to mainstream acceptance and respectability, has long fascinated me. And, in one way or another, I've been documenting it ever since my trip as a cadet to Bells Beach. As Rip Curl's 50th anniversary approached and I was commissioned to record the company's rich and colourful history, it seemed like the task I'd been training for my whole working life.

My police reporter colleague's hopes of unearthing disgrace-ful surfer behaviour were already, in 1985, a hangover from a bygone era. When the sleepy fishing town of Torquay, with its fibro cottages and tea-tree fences, came to prominence by hosting the 1970 world surfing titles, at which time Rip Curl was barely a year old, there were scandals aplenty. Drug busts, dust-ups at the Torquay pub and surfers expelled from the event for these and other misdemeanours.

The mid-'80s, when I pulled off my first of many surfing junkets in the name of gainful employment, were an intriguing transition period for surfing, Rip Curl and its storied Bells contest: a pimply adolescent taking its first tentative steps into the grown-up world, not entirely sure if it really wanted to leave its carefree, delinquent past behind but dazzled by the prospects of adulthood. Ratbag-gery was still in evidence, but for the most part it was carried out well away from the prying eyes of mainstream sports reporters.

The next year I managed to get myself down to Bells again for Easter, but this time I had an appointment with then *Tracks* editor Nick Carroll to be interviewed for a position as associate editor of the irreverent surf mag I had grown up devouring. While Occy and Tom Curren surfed a memorable semifinal in the Bells Bowl I was grilled by the crew-cut, chisel-jawed *Tracks* editor, his expression impossible to read behind his mirrored aviator sunnies. I was fortunate that his publisher had decreed they hire a 'proper' journalist who surfed a bit, rather than a proper surfer who wrote a bit, and I landed the job. I spent the next 13 Easters at Bells Beach, now well and truly immersed in the residual ratbag-gery that tradition demanded.

While the surfing world fixated on the passing parade of mighty surfing champions and their graceful exertions on Bells' wide, inviting walls, I was at least as fascinated by the jovial, knockabout, slightly mysterious characters at the helm of this lurching pleasure cruise. Rip Curl founders Doug Warbrick and Brian Singer, known to all as Claw and Sing Ding, came across as the kind of down-to-earth, blokey, salt-encrusted characters you could find around surfboard factories in grimy industrial estates all over the country – except that they presided over one of the most successful surf companies in the world.

Claw was the more public figure, a keen student of surf history and an unabashed fan of the thrust and parry of surfing competition, who grew so excited at key moments he'd literally bounce up and down on the spot. Brian seemed a little more private, but he had the vocabulary of a truck driver and a voracious appetite for wild times that friends spoke of in hushed tones. The other surf moguls I came to meet in the subsequent 30-odd years of surf journalism seemed more serious, driven, disciplined characters, but Claw and Brian gave the impression that their wealth and business success were some happy accident: that they'd simply been in the right place at the right time, had ridden the wave of surfing's rising popularity and had been conduits for the cosmic energy centre that Torquay represented to its first wave of counter-culture surf immigrants.

Certainly, Claw and Brian could play hardball; contract negotiations were almost a contact sport. But the serious business of, well, business seemed like little more than a practical necessity to allow the good times to continue to roll, like checking the oil and tyre pressure on their own global, pleasure-seeking surfari.

When I was editor of *Surfing Life* magazine in the early '90s, we published the work of a wildly talented cartoonist named Paul Collins, who produced an occasional series called, 'If surfers ruled the world'. In these politically incorrect scribblings, burly doormen ushered dishevelled surfers to the front of the queue at fancy nightclubs, flanked by buxom cocktail waitresses proffering free drinks. A traffic cop waived a speeding ticket for a wild-eyed surfer because the surf was pumping. A judge sentenced a surf-ski rider to death for cluttering the line-up with his wretched craft. These scenarios were the stuff of adolescent surf fantasy, but it seemed to me Claw and Sing Ding had succeeded in creating such a world, in their quaint coastal hamlet of Torquay and then in surf outposts further and further around the world. Like modern-day bushrangers, they generated their own folklore in which it was often challenging to sort fact from fiction. I've borne witness to enough of the more outlandish chapters to conclude that there is at least as much of the former as the latter.

In the fictionalised 2013 feature film *Drift* ('based on real events', it claimed), its star Sam Worthington declared emphatically, of the maverick beginnings of Australia's surf industry, 'You can't beat the man by becoming the man.' Claw and Sing Ding proved otherwise as they rode their way to the top of the heap and created a surfing lifestyle once unimaginable: luxury surf charters, heliskiing in Canada, the employment of countless other surfers who might otherwise have been deemed almost unemployable, an office culture that encouraged maximum surf time and wild partying. 'No one has ever been sacked from Rip Curl for going surfing,' is a proud company boast. In Torquay at least, surfers did rule the world.

I first met Claw and Brian at one of Rip Curl's now infamous Easter media nights. In its earliest iteration, this was little more than a gathering of senior Rip Curl management and the editorial staff of the major surf magazines around the company board table, followed by dinner at the nearby Chinese restaurant. That board table, littered with VB stubbies and bowls of chips, beer nuts and dips, became the scene of increasingly unruly behaviour and an ever-expanding cast until it was deemed prudent to move the annual event to a more capacious venue.

For me, media night climaxed one evening in the early '90s when a faux-military battle played out in the Rip Curl car park, which had been transformed into a war zone with army trucks and cosplay soldiers sporting imitation rifles, complete with blanks and pyrotechnics. The multitudes were then transported in the back of the trucks down to Bells Beach, armed with 'grenades' of Black Russians – a pre-made, sickly mix of vodka and Kahlua – which ensured the festivities roared on well into the wee hours down at the notorious Bells beer tent. I may have compacted several years into one, but in my blurred recollections, surfers in fluoro wetsuits and surfboards decorated with LED lights surfed the inky line-up while a chopper followed them with a spotlight. Another year's hijinks sound like the set-up to an implausible joke: a fire-eater, a samba dancer, a ladies' string quartet, a camel and a dwarf magician walk into a surf shop. Each year's media night tried to outdo the last until it was unsettling to contemplate where they could possibly go next. When Claw and Brian rode through the office on the back of two camels, it was safe to say we'd reached peak weird.

You could also discern how well the business was tracking by the largesse of media night. Another year in the early '90s, business was so buoyant that a loud and festive Sing Ding urged the assembled surf media to help themselves to whatever they liked from their retail store. It's been said that most sports journalists would compromise themselves for a cup of tea, though the going price was a little higher that year, as unsteady surf scribes made off into the night with great bundles of wetsuits and ski jackets piled high in their arms. The Rip Curl inventory system, not to mention its balance sheet, must have taken months to recover. The alarmed retail manager came to work the next morning and promptly rang the police to report the mysterious disappearance of thousands of dollars' worth of stock. Cops descended on Bells Beach sleuthing for clues and had to puzzle over the parade of surf media figures prancing about in expensive new Rip Curl gear.

Of course, we live in more sober times today, a fact which you sense aggravates Sing Ding and Claw no end. Who hired these bean counters who say we can't give half our stock away in the midst of a ferocious bender? Killjoys! And yet I suspect there are more cunning and calculating instincts at work beneath the surface of Rip Curl's bon vivant founders than they let on.

As their rivals Quiksilver and Billabong expanded their empires across the globe, floated on the stock exchange and made paper millionaires of even their janitors, it was easy to imagine Rip Curl as the most vulnerable and least robust of the so-called Big Three, with one foot still in its humble beginnings. Even when those publicly listed behemoths eventually teetered and toppled, their carcasses picked over by predatory investment funds, it was tempting to regard the Curl as the Stephen Bradbury of the surf industry, skating to gold-medal glory as more favoured competitors fell and spectacularly took each other out. The more accurate analogy might be that of the hare and the tortoise, the publicly listed surfwear giants sprinting to the lead then curling up for a kip, while Rip Curl plodded on, unwavering from its mission.

Of course, there is more to Rip Curl's enduring success than dumb luck or fortuitous timing or simple steadfastness. That 'more' will form a large part of this book. What are we to learn from the rise of the Curl, from garage start-up to shambolic cottage industry, to global empire with thousands of staff, 350 flagship stores (many close to prime surf breaks, but also in Paris, London, Buenos Aries – even Yalta on the Black Sea, for goodness' sake!), 8000 stockists across 20 countries and more world titles among its stellar team riders than any other surf brand?

The overarching question for me going into this book was 'How?' How have two mates founded a global surfing empire that has not only kept their youthful surfing dreams alive and offered escape from the nine-to-five grind, but also made them wealthy beyond their wildest imaginings and provided a livelihood for thousands of others?

We live in an age where we are encouraged to believe that if we dare dream enough we can all accrue a fortune while doing the things we love. But back in 1969? Sure, the Summer of Love and a psychedelic hippie idealism might have washed up on our shores from California, or more specifically stashed in the hold of several yachts sailed to Australia by various psychedelic, hippie, idealist Californian surfers. But that particular technicolour dream did not involve starting business empires, employing people, trademarking logos and registering business names, unless you consider the Brotherhood of Eternal Love a business.

Claw and Sing Ding were sufficiently tuned in to the times to recognise there was a future in this wave-riding lark and its accompanying youth revolution. And yet their entrepreneurial instincts set them apart from their peers, who were more interested in joining the Hare Krishnas and seeking enlightenment than dreaming up business plans.

If you go looking for the origins of this taste for commerce there are clues in their early family lives. Claw's dad was a cabinet-maker, a champion boxer and middle-distance runner, and not averse to taking considerable leaps of faith; he transplanted the family from his native Queensland to Melbourne to be closer to his wife's family, and founded a successful taxi empire. Sing Ding's father had a senior position as an accountant at Ford, and moved his family from Brisbane to Sydney to Ford's Geelong headquarters as his career blossomed. After a brief stint in beach-cleaning, Brian stumbled into school-teaching and got a plum posting to Lorne, where a young surfing phenom named Wayne Lynch was one of his pupils. It would have been a good if unremarkable life, teaching the sons and daughters of the fishermen and farmers of south-western Victoria.

Yet one chilly winter morning, Brian's restless spirit was drawn to the curious character in a dressing-gown eating a can of baked beans around the communal fire at Torquay back beach. In his early 20s, Claw fancied himself as a kind of 'noble, romantic beachcomber', in his own words, but the image of airy eccentricity was deceiving. He had tried his hand at tiny seasonal pop-up surf shops in bayside Brighton, Torquay and Lorne, screening surf movies, buying and selling surfboards and having a crack at anything that might turn a buck from the new craze of surfboard-riding. At that time, Brian was also experimenting with some informal surf commerce, and it didn't take too much encouragement from the bloke in the dressing-gown to ditch the teacher's chalk and team up in a loose business partnership.

It is remarkably easy to imagine Claw or Brian today in a similar circumstance to many of their salty old surf-dog mates they still knock around with, driving clapped-out HiAces or kombivans and shaping a few boards for cash, or skippering a surf charter boat somewhere in remote Indonesia, or permanently stationed behind the counter of a corner surf shop, doing the odd ding repair for beer money, perpetually sweeping sand out of the seagrass matting.

The Rip Curl logo – that stylised crest of a curling wave, the oceanic equivalent of the Nike 'swoosh' – has well and truly infiltrated mainstream consciousness. Who didn't witness three-time world champ Mick Fanning bumped off his board by a shark in the middle of a 2015 pro event at Jeffreys Bay, South Africa? Or his return the next year to win the event where he'd been confronted with his own mortality? Or marvel at Bethany Hamilton's remarkable return to elite competition and big-wave riding after losing an arm to a tiger shark? Or wonder at Tyler Wright's inspiring world title, even as she nursed her brother Owen through recovery from a serious brain injury from a wipe-out at Pipeline in Hawaii, or applaud Owen's own comeback to win the first event of the 2017 season after he'd missed a year of competition?

These stories have transcended surfing and have become touchstones for resilience, loyalty, kinship and victories of will over adversity. But these high-profile sporting fairytales form just the tip of the Rip Curl iceberg, a story whose true bulk and girth lingers below the surface. Let's take a closer look and see if we can discover what secrets lie beneath.

CHAPTER ONE

THREADING THE NEEDLE: A PRE-HISTORY

After a gruelling ocean voyage of some 20,000 kilometres over three months, all the way from Europe, it came down to this. A narrow 90-kilometre passage between Cape Otway and King Island was all early navigators had to aim for as they sought safe harbour in the Great Southern Land. When Matthew Flinders sailed through Bass Strait in 1799, he had proven that Tasmania, or Van Diemen's Land as it was then known, was an island, eliminating the need to sail around it and shaving some 40 days off the ocean voyage to the east coast of Australia.

But the faster route came at a terrible cost. By the mid-nineteenth century, pressure mounted to hasten the ocean voyage from England to Australia. Sailors would cut as close to Antarctica as possible, enduring wild seas and horrendous weather in an attempt to harness the Roaring Forties winds to catapult them towards the narrow entrance to Bass Strait. With a treacherous coastline of towering cliffs to their port side and a minefield of scattered islands and reefs before them, mariners referred to navigating the western entrance to Bass Strait as 'threading the eye of the needle'. The rugged cliffs of south-west Victoria were known as the Shipwreck Coast; the splintered timbers and stricken souls of around 700 shipwrecks were scattered along a 130-kilometre stretch of coast from Port Fairy to Cape Otway.

The wreck of the British barque *Cataraqui* in 1845 and the loss of nearly 400 lives on board led to the construction of the Cape Otway lighthouse, Australia's oldest working lighthouse. Mariners breathed a sigh of relief once they rounded Cape Otway and entered Bass Strait, the beam of the lighthouse signalling that the worst of the voyage was now behind them. On the eastern side of Cape Otway, where the ocean swells moderated, a series of seaside hamlets sprang up. Here, the daunting coastal cliffs gave way to green headlands, bays and undulating hills. Small farming and fishing communities sprang up in Apollo Bay, Lorne, Anglesea and Torquay, bolstered by large holiday crowds in summer.

Originally known as Spring Creek, Torquay was renamed after the kind of genteel English seaside holiday town the early settlers tried to replicate in their new homeland. The town was centred around the safe and sheltered front beach, and little attention was paid to the untamed back beaches. Bathing boxes were built along the foreshore, and residents and visitors would walk along the Esplanade dressed in their finery.

If you stand at Point Danger today and look south-west along the sea cliffs towards Bells Beach, you can feel the energy of this storied coast. The discovery of a 25-million-year-old fossilised whale skeleton at Bells Beach in 2009 by a morning beachcomber is a reminder of its ancient origins. Here those wild Southern Ocean swells achieve some kind of order as they comb the contours of the area's exquisitely sculpted surfing reefs. The concentration of surf spots within a few kilometres – Southside, Centre Side, Bells, Winki Pop, Boobs, Steps and Bird Rock, and the beach breaks of

Jan Juc, Torquay Point and Point Danger itself – has few equals along this country's 20,000 kilometres of coast.

Brian 'Sing Ding' Singer considers Torquay and the Surf Coast, and further west beyond Cape Otway, a 'global energy centre', one of a handful of locations in the world where a confluence of geographical traits and earthly forces produces a kind of adventure-sports hot spot. Similar energy centres include the ski fields of Chamonix; the North Shore of Oahu; Grindelwald, under the north face of the Eiger in Switzerland; and Machu Picchu. This indefinable energy on the Surf Coast, Singer says, explains why two of the world's largest surf companies, Rip Curl and Quiksilver, grew out of an otherwise unremarkable, sleepy rural village.

But the coast has another, longer history: it is also Wathaurong or Wadawurrung country, comprising a community of some 25 clans with a common language, spread throughout the Bellarine Peninsula and north as far as Ballarat. A large red ochre site near Point Addis is said to have provided an important commodity for trade, and the pigment was valued for ceremonial purposes. In the 1920s, a jarosite paint factory was established on the site. In one way or another, this region's influence has travelled the length and breadth of the country.

It was here where the escaped convict William Buckley found shelter and kinship with the Wathaurong community for 32 years in the 1800s, giving rise to the expression 'Buckley's chance'. Buckley made his home in a hut on the Karaaf River, now known as Thompson's Creek, not far from Torquay. While massacres by the early settlers on the Wathaurong people were widespread, Buckley was treated with great respect by the locals, who believed he was the reincarnation of an esteemed leader.

It was also along this coast that surfboard-riding first came to the frigid waters of south-west Victoria. In 1919, Louis Whyte, a wealthy Geelong businessman, holidayed in Honolulu with his wife, Marnie. Whyte learnt to surf from the great Hawaiian surfer and Olympic swimmer Duke Kahanamoku, from whom he also bought several boards and took them back to Australia. Whyte would have cut a striking figure driving his Rolls-Royce from his home in Geelong to his luxurious holiday home in Anglesea, with solid timber boards protruding from the back seat. He and his friends attempted to ride the boards on the gentle peelers of Lorne Point with varied degrees of success, between aperitifs and games of croquet on his expansive lawns.

In 1923, Manly surfer and swimmer Ainsley 'Sprint' Walker, the nephew of pioneer Sydney surfer Tommy Walker, was transferred from Sydney to Melbourne by his employer and took his surf-board with him. Walker had been a protégé of Duke Kahanamoku when he had visited Australia in 1914. An accomplished 50-metre swimmer himself, Sprint had taken up surfing largely because Duke's example convinced him it was the ideal companion training for swimming. But Sprint was disappointed to find most Victorian lifesaving clubs and ocean activities centred around the calm waters of Melbourne's Port Phillip Bay. He made lonely explorations to the open ocean beaches of Portsea and Sorrento before discovering the consistent waves of Torquay. Rather than lug his board to and from the coast, he would bury it in the sand until his next excursion.

Nineteen thirty-two saw the opening of the Great Ocean Road, a huge public program that employed returned servicemen after World War I. The winding road carved out of the sea cliffs would open up the Victorian west coast to tourism and subsequent surf discoveries.

By the 1930s, a growing cast of hardy characters was riding the waves of Torquay Point. A lifesaving club had existed at Torquay's sheltered front beach since 1922, but it wasn't until 1946 that the Torquay Surf Life Saving Club was formed to patrol the more treacherous waters of the back beach, becoming the first surf club in Victoria. Its establishment marked Torquay as the epicentre of surfing in the state.

THE INVENTION OF NEOPRENE

In 1927, chemical giant DuPont made a bold decision to fund what it called 'pure research', which was not aimed at any specific commercial outcomes, but to progress the study of chemistry. The company recruited a brilliant young chemist named Wallace Carothers, luring him away from his work in organic chemistry at Harvard University. Carothers suffered bouts of depression and was initially reluctant to accept the offer. He was known to carry around a capsule of cyanide with him, lest the depression become too much to bear.

Even so, Carothers went on to a distinguished career at DuPont. He was encouraged by his bosses to explore the possibility of creating a synthetic rubber, as increasing demand for natural rubber was pushing up prices, and in March 1930 one of his staff, Dr Arnold M. Collins, succeeded in isolating chloroprene, a liquid which polymerised to produce a solid material similar to rubber. DuPont initially marketed its discovery as DuPrene, and it found numerous applications as an insulant for telephone wires, and for gaskets and hoses in automobile engines.

Carothers is best known for his invention of nylon, which proved a gigantic windfall for DuPont, but despite a decorated career he continued to be plagued by depression. In 1937, the same year Carothers died by suicide, DuPont dispensed with the trade name DuPrene in favour of the generic neoprene. He could not have known then that these two inventions he oversaw would one day come together in the modern surfing wetsuit, an elastic nylon jersey, or lining, laminated to neoprene to make it more durable and easier to get on and off.

Demand grew for the use of neoprene in consumer goods like gloves and shoe soles, and the war effort exhausted the supply. It wasn't until 1951 that Hugh Bradner, a physicist at the University of California, Berkeley, dreamed up the notion that a thin layer of water trapped between the body and a barrier of insulation might help keep divers warm in cold water. Up until then, efforts to insulate divers against the cold had focused on keeping them dry. Bradner reasoned that the insulating properties of neoprene would quickly warm the water to body temperature. The wetsuit, as opposed to the existing 'dry suit', was born.

Bradner constructed the first neoprene wetsuit in his UC Berkeley lab and tested it by wading into the icy waters of Lake Tahoe. Encouraged by the suit's remarkable thermal properties, he started a wetsuit company called EDCO to try to monetise his invention, but discovered he made a better scientist than a businessman. Though Bradner sold suits to the US Navy, he concluded there wasn't much of a market for them and never patented his design. It was left to more canny commercial operators in the late '50s – the Meistrell brothers, who founded Body Glove, and Jack O'Neill, the one-eyed pirate entrepreneur behind the O'Neill brand – to refine and popularise the surfing wetsuit.

THE WORLD COMES TO TORQUAY

Adrian Curlewis had not survived the fall of Singapore, the horrors of Changi Prison and the Burma 'Death' Railway to have the Olympic organising committee disrespect the august organisation he had presided over for 20 years. As president of the Surf Life Saving Association of Australia, Curlewis had lobbied long and hard for surf lifesaving to be an exhibition sport for the 1956 Melbourne Olympics, showcasing all that was wholesome and noble about Australian youth. But the organising committee had snubbed his advances.

Curlewis was not a man to be put off by a setback. He'd been president of the SLSAA since 1934, interrupted only by his time as a prisoner of war. As a younger man, Curlewis had been one of the pioneer surfers of Sydney's Northern Beaches in the 1920s, but the harsh experience of his military service had hardened his attitudes and he was already concerned about the frivolous, pleasure-seeking attitudes of a new generation of young beach-goers. The International Surf Carnival was conceived to display to the world the skill, virtue and courage of Australia's volunteer surf lifesavers, and to blow a resounding raspberry to the Olympic officials who had overlooked this proud Australian institution. Surf lifesavers were invited from around the world to compete, and in attendance were 116 clubs from around Australia, as well as a large international contingent.

Torquay was chosen as the venue, as the oldest surf club in the state, and for its proximity to Melbourne. An estimated 50,000-strong crowd flocked to the popular holiday town, which at the time had a permanent population of just 1000.

What Curlewis could not have foreseen was that the carnival would introduce Australian surfers to the new lightweight balsa-wood surfboards brought by the US surf team, including Greg Noll, Mike Bright and Tommy Zahn. The new balsa boards allowed surfers to 'corner' or angle across the peeling wave, and manoeuvre deftly in and around the 'curl' of the wave. The young surfers of Torquay, and those who witnessed similarly earth-shifting surfboard-riding displays at Manly and Avalon in Sydney, soon wanted no part of the militaristic march-pasts and rescue drills of surf lifesaving. The boards were also light enough to be tied to the roof of a car or towed behind a bike on a 'board trailer', eliminating the dependence on a surf club to store equipment and ushering in a new era of surf exploration.

Modern surfboard-riding had arrived in Australia, and our beaches would never be the same. Torquay was ground zero for the revolution, where local board-builders and surfers were quick to emulate the equipment and feats of the Americans. Desperate to halt the decline of Australian surf culture into the hedonistic, rebellious teenage beach party celebrated in the US bestselling novel and box-office hit *Gidget*, Curlewis had unwittingly hastened the process. And when it came to hedonistic teen rebellion, the Torquay crew didn't need a whole lot of encouragement.

The notorious Boot Hill crew, a band of pioneer wave-riders including Rex 'China' Gilbert from the Torquay surf club, occupied a few adjacent sheds and shacks on the outskirts of the town. The Boot Hill crew's exploits were already legendary: racing cars along beaches or sending them hurtling off cliffs, wild parties with kegs of beer, the infamous kidnapping of a circus elephant, an annual black-tie dinner at the Torquay pub for which they arrived on the back of a garbage truck. All in all, the Boot Hill mob showed a wanton disregard for the kind of civic duty Curlewis hoped to instil in young surf club members. In 1967, Curlewis was knighted for his service to surf lifesaving and public safety, just as many of his traditional values were put to the sword in the Summer of Love's hot-blooded orgy of sex, drugs, rock-and-roll and freewheeling wave-riding, unconstrained by the strict moral framework of the surf clubs.

Perhaps it was the volatile, cold southern climate, the distance from major cities and the surfing mainstream, or the need to create their own entertainment, but Torquay had a way of attracting larger-than-life characters who didn't mind defying the status quo. There was less of a divide – more of an overlap – between the two tribes of beach users, surfers and surf lifesavers, than there was in other parts of the country. Perhaps because the local clubbies were already wild and loose enough in Torquay.

THE SINGERS ARE ON THE MOVE

Brian Singer looked out the window of the car at the flat, brown, featureless landscape and wondered where his parents had brought him this time. Major moves were part and parcel of the Singer family life, as his father Owen's career as a senior accountant for the Ford Motor Company required regular transfers for him to oversee the expansion of the iconic American company Down Under. The move from Brisbane to Sydney had not been so bad, though Brian missed the family holidays to Coolangatta, swimming in the turquoise waters of Kirra and Greenmount, falling asleep to the sound of waves after long days on the beach.

'Since I was a young kid living in Brisbane I loved going to the beach,' Brian now reflects. 'I would have been six or seven when we had our first holiday on the Gold Coast. That was my first connection with surf beaches – it was like a playground, just being allowed to roam along the beaches without adults.'

By 1953 the family had settled in Miranda in Sydney's south, only three train stations from Cronulla, where the colourful riot of beach action mesmerised the teenager: surfers riding 16-foot hollow plywood toothpicks, girls parading along the Esplanade, the cool older surfers holding court outside the milk bar.

But *this*? The move to Geelong four years later had been billed as another exciting family adventure, but staring out at the flat, dry plains between the old Essendon airport and Geelong, Brian felt only dread. As the eldest of three kids, at the age of 13, Brian experienced the sense of dislocation most acutely.

'I hated moving from Sydney, my friends and a big city. I was used to a fair bit of freedom,' says Brian. 'I remember driving from the airport down to Geelong. It was just before Christmas, one of those hot days . . . It was like we were going to the end of the earth.'

The saving grace was that Geelong was within striking distance of Torquay, which Brian already knew as the centre of surfing in Victoria and the scene of the International Surf Carnival a year earlier. On that first day, before they'd even had a chance to unpack boxes in their new home in the unremarkable Geelong suburb of Belmont, Brian had persuaded his mum, Jean, to drive him to Torquay to take a look. '[At first] we ended up at the front beach with no surf. I wasn't very impressed,' says Brian. 'Then we found the surf beach where the surf club is, and I thought, this isn't so bad.'

The family spent the Christmas holidays hanging around the camping ground behind the surf club, and Brian made the most of the consistent southern swells. In the wake of the International Surf Carnival, he got to experience the full spectrum of Australian wave-riding equipment, from the old 16-footers to the first balsa Malibu boards and the local efforts to replicate them in hollow ply, the Okanui. Torquay was already inhabited by an enigmatic surfing crew including board-maker Vic Tantau, Olympic wrestler Dick Garrard, surf club caretaker China Gilbert, jazz musician Owen Yateman and a mischievous younger generation of Torquay gremmies: Ray Wilson, Max Innes, Rodney Papworth, Barry Stach, Warren Evans, Kenny Baensch.

'Our relatives in Brisbane told my parents, "Whatever you do, don't let him join the Torquay surf club,"' says Brian. 'It was full of the Boot Hill crew, who were quite infamous around Torquay and beyond. Our escapades were mild compared to that crew.'

His parents managed to keep their increasingly surf-obsessed son's focus on his education until the end of high school, but his salt-water fever showed no signs of abating. He joined the surf club, borrowed whatever boards he could and, when he got a job as a lab assistant at CSIRO, saved up for his first board, an 8'8", second-hand Vic Tantau model, purchased for 30 pounds from gremmie Barry Stach.

The following year Brian began a science degree at Melbourne University. 'By then the surf bug had hit, and I wasn't all that keen on study. I struggled along for three or four years and only passed a year and a half [of that].' If the surf was on, he'd skip lectures, catch the train to Footscray and hitchhike to Torquay.

In summer, the Ocean Beach crew would roar down from the NSW Central Coast in an old hearse and add to the cast of wild surfing characters. 'John Monie [a future rugby league player and premiership coach] was the leader of the pack, and the only clean-living one. The rest of his tribe were a fairly wild bunch,' says Brian. Which meant they fitted right in at Torquay.

The question then became how to fund this surfing lifestyle. Brian began fixing dings in the family garage in Geelong, then answered an ad in an early issue of *Surfing World* magazine to become an agent for well-known Gold Coast board-builder Joe Larkin, earning three pounds per order.

Brian became a regular around the ubiquitous beach fires that kept surfers warm between surf sessions in the days before wetsuits. It was around one such fire on Torquay back beach that he first clapped eyes on an unusual character named 'Claw', with a shaggy Beatles mop top, thick-rimmed spectacles and a cheeky black-toothed grin.

ARCH WARBRICK STANDS HIS GROUND

Arch Warbrick had a problem. In fact, he had several. His dad was laid up in military hospital, his health ravaged by the effects of mustard gas in the Great War, leaving Arch's mum to care for four sons and a daughter on her own. In the 1920s, Arch and his siblings were reduced to wheeling a trolley around inner Brisbane, particularly on the mean streets of Fortitude Valley, scavenging for bottles and old bits of driftwood that could be sold for firewood.

His most immediate problem, though, was that a gang of street thugs wanted to deny them even this meagre income. The gang claimed their booty and the Warbrick kids trudged home, each quietly fuming. But Arch was especially livid. They would need to stand their ground. Remarkably, next time, Arch knocked the gang leader out, in the first public exhibition of what would become a famous boxing prowess. After that fight, the local coppers dragged Arch along to the police boys' club to ensure his pugilist instincts were given a healthy outlet. 'They watched him fight and went, "Well, we don't need to teach him much, do we?"' Arch's son, Doug 'Claw' Warbrick, recalls proudly. Arch would soon become a champion boxer and cross-country runner, with numerous state and national titles.

Some eight years later, under the headline 'Will Warbrick shake hands with Hitler?', Brisbane's *Daily Standard* speculated on the prospects of the local lad making the Australian team for the Berlin Olympics. Arch narrowly missed out, as there were only funds for one Australian boxer to travel to Berlin, but he maintained his reputation as one of Queensland's greatest all-round sportsmen of the day.

Arch enjoyed particular success in New Zealand, where he travelled with an Australian boxing team and lived for a couple of years to take up a land grant offered by the NZ Government to encourage immigration. There he discovered a family connection to the local Māori community. Warbrick is a famous name in New Zealand rugby; five Warbrick brothers were among the 'NZ Natives XV' that toured the UK and Australia in 1888, and all five are in the International Rugby Hall of Fame.

Arch returned to his native Queensland and worked in various jobs, often tough physical work – cane cutter, milkman, fruit-cart vendor, pineapple farmer – that served as training for his sporting endeavours.

In January 1943 the Brisbane *Truth* delivered this news: 'Ex-amateur boxing champion Arch Warbrick has won enough cups and medals in boxing and running circles to set himself up in the jewellery business. Mrs "W." added to the ex-champion's long list of trophies through the week when she presented Arch with a pigeon pair of twins.'

The boy was named Doug. His twin sister, Louise, only survived for two weeks, victim of an outbreak of gastroenteritis which had swept through Brisbane. Five years later, Claw's parents had another daughter, named Laurel Louise. Soon after, the family moved north to Maroochydore on what's now known as the Sunshine Coast, but then was simply the North Coast.

Arch Warbrick and his brothers became fixtures at the Maroochydore Surf Club. Arch was good mates with the club's surf boat captain, Jack 'Bull' Evans, later the founder of the famed porpoise pools at Snapper Rocks in Coolangatta. The surf boat crew had been rowing out to Mudjimba Island since the '30s with a couple of early solid timber surfboards, to ride the long lefts that peeled along the southern end of the island.

Claw's earliest memories are of the beaches of Maroochydore and Noosa, bodysurfing on his father's back or being pushed into tiny waves on the enormous timber surfcraft of the day. Soon he was venturing south with his father and sampling the waves of the

Gold Coast, and by the age of 15 was surfing seriously on whatever type of surfboard he could get his hands on. '[The year] '58 was pivotal for me, because I was riding any sort of board I could borrow, 16-foot toothpick, surf skis, solids. My dad and I made an eight-foot hollow,' recalls Claw.

HEADING SOUTH

Throughout the '50s the Warbricks had migrated back and forth between Queensland and Victoria, where the family of Doug's mum Jean lived. Eventually young Doug was sent to Brighton Grammar School in Victoria. It was a move that held less fears than it might have for a teen brought up on dreamy warm water and Queensland point breaks. His extended family had a long history of surfing in Victoria back to the 1930s. Claw had surfed Lorne Point and knew Torquay as the scene of the 1956 International Surf Carnival.

The Warbricks settled in Park Street, Brighton, on the corner of St Kilda Street, right opposite Brighton Beach and the cold grey waters of Port Phillip Bay. There always seemed to be a few aunts and uncles residing with them. Weekends and school holidays were spent in Torquay, and Claw discovered that rideable waves sometimes broke in the bay.

'We surfed a lot in Port Phillip Bay . . . You'd get a big sou'-west change once or twice a week, and when the wind was really blowing the whole north-east side of the bay would light up with short period slop,' says Claw. The wind swell would focus into a little patch of sand between the Brighton Beach baths and the pier. 'If the wind went to the south, the left break on the corner of the baths got clean and peeled along this sandbar for 50 metres.' On good days, it was even possible to shoot the pier, as long as you ducked your head.

As a goofy-footer, it was all Claw needed to develop a severe case of surf fever. Arch helped Claw make a small board trailer to allow him to wheel his board to the beach, then he was away. The bay had a surprisingly vibrant surf scene for a body of water that received no ocean swells. 'Dendy Street had these reefs and sandbars; there was Frankston pier; St Kilda pier had the best waves in the bay – I've seen overhead 300-metre lefts – and there was Middle Park, all the way down to Mornington and Williamstown. There was a vigorous surfing scene in the bay, a lot of camaraderie, but also some friction,' he says.

Claw sought out fellow surfers at Brighton Grammar, including Bells pioneer and future Victorian surfing champion Terry Wall and a charismatic character named Rennie Ellis, who would go on to become a renowned photojournalist of Australian beach culture; for Claw, Ellis was 'a free-minded, free-spirited person, [and] a bit of a mentor for me'. Other Brighton surfers included an artistic kid named Simon Buttonshaw; a stocky, talented surfer named Rod Brooks, also the son of a boxer; and aspiring surfboard shapers Pat Morgan and Max Davidson.

The Warbricks spent the Christmas holidays in a caravan parked in the camping area behind Torquay Surf Club. Arch knew local identity and Olympic wrestler Dick Garrard from his boxing days, so he had an in with the surf club crew. This might help explain why, on the first morning of their holidays, Arch was able to borrow a board from local hotshot Terry Wall.

'It was my first balsa board from Vic Tantau, and to put a nose rocker in it he'd cut a wedge out of the balsa and glued it back on at an angle,' Terry Wall explains. 'And Claw's dad asked if he could borrow this board. It was only a couple of weeks old . . . It was my pride and joy.'

'Somehow Arch got his hands on the board. The tide had come in and there was a heavy shore break,' says Claw. 'Arch goes out there, turns around in the shore break, takes off on a wave, straight down the mine, snaps the nose off the board.' Claw was horrified, but they paid Terry for the damaged board then fixed it up later. 'And I finally had a board I could surf on properly,' says Claw.

The family's fortunes flourished in the south. Arch started a taxi service and built the fleet of Warbrick's Taxis from one cab to 36, plus ran his own service station. Doug worked weekends pumping petrol and the station held the record for the most gallons sold in the Melbourne metropolitan area, largely because they were refuelling all of Arch's cabs. Arch later sold the business for a handsome profit.

Doug already had his sights set on Torquay as his permanent place of residence. The only question was how he'd finance a surfing lifestyle in this somnolent rural community. 'After high school it was, "Let's go surfing, do something entrepreneurial in surfing,"' says Claw. 'In the early '60s I was back and forth between Melbourne and Torquay, with a fair bit of Queensland mixed in with road trips up the coast.'

Surfboard shaper Pat Morgan played a major role in Claw's vision of a surfing life down at Torquay. 'I got a licence before the others. I used to pick up Rod [Brooks] and Claw and go down there on a Friday night,' says Pat. 'He's always been a nutcase. We used to pick him up at his father's house on the Esplanade at Brighton. It was a bit like the Addams Family house.'

Pat and Claw went on to make boards together and did the rounds of the few surfboard factories that sprang up around Melbourne, working for Max Gill, Peter Davies and George Rice, and under their own cheekily titled 'Dora' label. But both were determined to make Torquay their permanent home.

DISCOVERING BELLS

Claw didn't have his first Bells experience until 1961, when the beach was still a carefully guarded secret. An invitation was required from one of the regulars to even get in there. It was only weeks earlier that local surfer Joe Sweeney had hired a bulldozer to carve a road out along the clifftop to make Bells accessible by car. Joe had charged a select group of local surfers one pound each to use the new track to cover the hire of the bulldozer, and the hallowed surf break still had the air of an exclusive club about it.

Claw and a mate named Tony drove along the clifftop on a clean four-to-five-foot day and found only one other surfer at Bells, big-wave rider Marcus Shaw. 'Marcus was one of the ironmen of the day and he told us not to go out there, that it was big and danger-ous and there were sharks everywhere,' says Claw. 'Somehow Tony managed to get in an altercation and Marcus sent him in. He told me I'd be sent in too if I didn't behave myself. I didn't know what the required behaviour was. People rode waves together in those days, but Marcus was one of the first to adopt the "one man, one wave" ethos. He had right of way.'

Shaw put on a masterful display that made an impression. 'There was an extraordinary aura about the place, and to have one of the true legends of Bells Beach out there – his surfing was quite commanding,' says Claw.

Brian has a similar recollection of his first surf at Bells, in late '62, with the same imposing figure in the line-up. 'The first time I paddled out there it was quite big. It felt very threatening paddling over sets, quite intimidating, maybe six to eight foot,' says Brian. 'Marcus Shaw was out there, and I had trouble getting waves. On weekends it was not uncrowded, with 15 to 20 people in the water. Surfing was more concentrated around a few well-known spots, [with] fewer people but not so spread out.'

These were the pre-wetsuit days of fires on the beach and wearing footy jumpers in the water to try to stay warm. 'You'd cook yourself by the fire and dash out and catch a couple of waves, and come in and warm up,' says Claw. 'There was always a fire at the bottom of the stairs at Bells. I hardly ever went there [when] there wasn't a fire. It was just part of the culture and the lifestyle. And there were lots of great stories and banter around fires.'

Around the time Brian and Claw surfed their first waves at Bells, local surfers Vic Tantau and Peter Troy convened the first 'surfboard rally' there. Scheduled for December '61 at Bells, it was actually run in January 1962, and was won by Sydney's Glynn Ritchie, although some still claim Terry Wall was the rightful winner. The following year, under the auspices of the newly formed Australian Surfriders Association, the event was moved to Easter, where it has remained ever since.

The event gave Victorian surfing an annual focus and attracted more interstate surfers each year. The Victorian surfboard industry was beginning to take off and Claw did the rounds of all the surfboard factories, working his way up from sweeping floors to fixing dings, then from sander to glasser to shaper. The hands-on experience gave Claw a good overview of the surfboard business but he was already thinking beyond the building of surfboards and the geographical confines of Torquay.

'I could see the potential for growth in surfing by the time we started getting the movies from the US and *Surfer* magazine, and the Australian surf magazines and movies, and some rudimentary surf shops,' says Claw. 'It seemed something was happening. There were the board-makers in Brookvale and the southside of Sydney and all the other cities. Once we got foam, people started making surfboards all around Australia.'

In 1963, Claw opened a surf shop in Bell Street, Torquay, which was really not much more than a wire-mesh cage but gave him a taste for surf commerce. A year later he launched the Bayside Surf Centre in Brighton, in a tiny premises with cheap rent in Railway Arcade, close to the train station where passengers disembarked to go to the beach.

'It was a very sparsely stocked little surf shop. He had White Stag wetsuits from Sydney – Claw was the White Stag agent,' recalls Rod Brooks. 'He'd drive down to the ports in Melbourne and buy the American Levi's jeans from the US sailors, and bring them back to the surf shop and sell them for double the price. You could tell he was fairly entrepreneurial.'

Brian Singer, who was already buying, repairing and selling boards, was also on the lookout for opportunities to make a few dollars from surfing, and he and Claw bonded over their shared business instincts. The pair were eyeing the lucrative surf-movie-screening gig Peter Troy had secured, showing Bruce Brown's latest movies from the US. When Troy went off on his now legendary global surf travels, Claw and Brian began screening surf movies too. 'Sitting in the audience every night, we learnt the ebb and flow of a good surf movie, what made them laugh and what made them sit on the edge of their seat,' says Brian.

Claw convinced Brian that a livelihood from surfing was not such an outlandish ambition. 'His interest was in all things surf, and of course trying to make a dollar from it so you could get enough money to go surfing,' says Brian. 'He was eccentric, just a bit different, and he had the best knowledge of what was going on, including what was going on in California and Queensland. He was someone who was clearly not going to be interested in anything else.'

Claw, for his part, was pleased to have a reliable surfing buddy at a time when you still had to go looking for someone to surf with. 'I had this romantic notion of being a bit of a nomadic beachcomber,' says Claw. 'There weren't that many regular surfers around who were out there at every opportunity. You would have to drive around and find someone to go surfing with. Brian was pretty consistent in turning up when the waves were good. He had that entrepreneurial spirit. We were just like fellow travellers.'

Claw and Brian would only discover later that their uncles Ted Bellis and Bill Warbrick had worked together as linotype operators at the Brisbane *Courier-Mail*. Their jobs involved laboriously constructing the metal plates out of individual letters that each day's paper was printed from, a task that would eventually be made redundant by the onset of computers and digital printing.

Claw recalls long chats with Brian around fires and sharing a keg in the sand dunes at Torquay, discussing how to fund their lifestyles. In 1964, the Easter contest also served as the Victorian titles in the lead-up to the Manly world titles, and Bernard 'Midget' Farrelly was recruited as a special guest judge for the event. Claw says he still wasn't too sure about the whole concept of surfing competitions, but he put those reservations aside and picked the right time to have a good heat. 'The surf was pretty ordinary: south-east, small, high tide. We had eight-man heats – there were people going everywhere,' says Claw. 'I just kept taking off on lots of waves. I had no ambitions, it was a bit of a giggle. There were so many more accomplished surfers than me in [the heat].'

Claw made the semis, and while he doesn't recall surfing in a final, that was enough to make the Victorian team for Manly. 'They had a relatively large team in the opens. I scraped into that group and Brian finished with a similar placing, and then it became real,' says Claw. 'The world-title thing was big. I didn't have any ambitions or heat plans. I just went to go up there and meet all these characters.'

Brian has only vague recollections of qualifying for the Victorian team. 'I hadn't actually entered. I only got in because I had beaten a couple of guys who were already chosen. There were 10 or 12 in the Victorian team. I didn't realise at the time what a big deal it was,' he says. But by the time he got to Manly and saw 60,000 people packing the beach for the finals, he did realise. 'I can certainly remember Midget winning and I was stoked he won, and he won it with that famous cutback with his hands in the air,' says Brian. The experience would also stand them in good stead in the years ahead as their business ambitions expanded. 'Those Aussie titles were great times, and [it was] amazing to know a lot of surfers from around the country, and some of them became surf shop owners,' says Brian.

The first official world surfing titles brought them into contact with surfers from all over the world and opened their eyes to broader horizons. 'There were surfers, photographers, filmmakers, people involved in administration from all round the world, all in one place,' says Claw.

One of those photographers was a young surfer, John Witzig, who was already trying to carve out a niche for himself in the fledgling surf media of the day. John has fond memories of the Torquay surf scene of the '60s, from the time of his first visit to the Bells Rally in '63. 'It was just really fun. Everyone camped in the campground, and the pub was hilarious and just a livewire place,' says John. 'I met all the fabulous Boot Hill characters like Owen Yateman. Their stories were outrageous, they were disgraceful . . . They actually had battles with the police. They were really one of the reasons I was attracted to going down to Bells.'

John and Brian were both fascinated by the changing times. 'Brian was the first person I met in surfing who had a tertiary education,' says John. 'I have a clear impression of always thinking Brian was smart. I used to have great discussions with him.'

The highlight of the trip to Sydney for Claw was enjoying a session at Palm Beach on a long left in the middle of the beach with only one other surfer in the water. That surfer was Phil Edwards, widely regarded as the world's best at the time, who'd stepped aside from competition and served as head judge for the world titles. After the event, Claw joined a loose convoy of surfers who made their way up the coast in search of the relatively new surf discoveries of Crescent Head and Angourie on the NSW North Coast. He witnessed American Joey Cabell's celebrated surf sessions at Angourie, which many agreed represented the state of the art more vividly than the contest theatrics at Manly.

Brian wasn't so lucky. 'Terry Klemm [the Victorian surfboard-maker] talked me into going to Phillip Island,' says Brian. The decision still pains him today: 'I don't know how I got talked into going [there] instead of Crescent Head or Angourie.'

Significantly, Claw and Brian met many of the major players in the so-called Brookvale Mafia, the big surfboard manufacturers of the day. Successful surfboard businessmen like Gordon Woods and Barry Bennett fuelled Claw's belief that the surf industry had a future. 'For me the Brookvale Mafia are mentors. Gordon Woods appeared to me very businesslike and organised, and I drew a lot of inspiration from Gordon. Barry Bennett was this very deadpan Aussie,' says Claw. 'They were all tough with their workers: you had to do the job, and do the job right. Really good fundamentals – if a job's worth doing, it's worth doing well. Honesty and integrity. I'd pick their brains for anything.'

The Bells Easter Rally of 1965 has gone down in legend as the Bells event with the biggest waves ever, bigger even than those at the famed unveiling of Simon Anderson's thruster in 1981. It was an event Claw was relieved to be judging rather than competing in. 'The ground was shaking, you could hear the waves roaring out at Tubes at Point Danger,' says Claw. 'It was flat Good Friday morning, and by Friday afternoon it was six feet. Five-thirty Saturday morning, China Gilbert's on the phone. He's living at the surf club, and he's going, "You've got to see them, they're like mountains, they're like buildings."'

The event was won by Rob Conneely ahead of Nat Young, but Claw most vividly remembers two of the standout rides by fellow goofy-footers. 'The two most epic rides were Marcus Shaw and John Monie. They'd be calling them 20-to-25-feet waves,' he reckons, 'and they both had this great goofy-foot attack.'

That year, tragedy rocked Brian's family when his mother passed away. 'I was 21 and that was sort of the end of family life. Dad was travelling up to Ford in Melbourne and then he moved up there,' says Brian. 'The mother is usually the glue that holds a family together. Looking back on it, selfishly I wasn't considerate enough of my dad's situation. It must have been very difficult for him too.' But by now, even though he was still trying to finish science at Melbourne Uni, the surf was calling. Torquay increasingly became home.

There's a particular dynamic to Victorian surfing that often sees surfers torn between the career opportunities in Melbourne and the freedom and adventure on offer down the coast, and dedicated surfers resolve the dilemma any way they can. Claw worked for a time as barman and greenkeeper at the Torquay Golf Club, which allowed plenty of time to surf and had the added benefit of free meals in the club dining room, a perk Claw took generous advantage of. Brian found work flipping burgers and as a beach-cleaner, picking up rubbish and cleaning the campground toilets. His boss was Joe Sweeney, the man who'd first carved a road into Bells.

But Claw was determined to create his own business opportunities on the coast. He followed up the modest success of his Bayside Surf Centre and the Torquay surf shop by opening a summer surf shop beneath the Cumberland Hotel in Lorne, 40 kilometres south-west of Torquay, in the summer of '65–'66. Brian was his first employee.

'I was the manager and he'd come down on weekends, and I'd have to get off the couch and sleep on a little camp stretcher next to a 44-gallon drum of resin,' recalls Brian. Lorne had quite a hip Beat scene at the time, with the famous Arab Café, the Pacific Hotel out near Lorne Pier and the Wild Colonial Club on the beachfront staging live rock concerts. For two young surfers, there were plenty of prospects for fun and romance. But the shop was only a going concern in summer, and after the holidays ended it was back to Torquay to explore new ways of turning a buck.

BROOKO'S PLACE

Around this time, a group of young surfers moved in to an unfin-ished house owned by Rod Brooks, Claw's old mate from Brighton, with bare frames inside and blankets for walls. Conversations ranged from surfboard design to the Hare Krishna movement.

'All through the '60s, I had that house that I bought when I was 18 for $2000. Everyone would flop there until they got established,' says Rod, who was completing a cabinet-making apprenticeship in Melbourne and spending every weekend in Torquay. 'It was to lock-up stage. The thing was almost more than I could afford on my apprentice's wage. It was impossible for me to put lining on the walls or hot water, but it was better than a prefab.'

Brian recalls eating a lot of baked beans on toast, and listen-ing to three records on high rotation: Dylan's *Blonde on Blonde*, the Stones' *High Tide and Green Grass* and psychedelic rockers the Fugs. A little later they switched to Australian surf movie soundtracks. 'Whoever was up first would put on the soundtrack to *Hot Generation*, so that would get us all up and firing in the middle of winter,' says Brian.

'It wasn't a party house, but if someone was having a 21st we'd get kegs of beer and all the surf club crew would come,' says Rod. 'We were surrounded by paddocks, so we could pretty much do what we wanted. We always had a keg of beer going out the front.'

Terry Wall still holds fond memories of the rowdy household. 'It was bloody fantastic . . . In the winter there was a whole mob of people staying there – what a varied lot,' he remembers. 'Rod, who started Piping Hot and the Quiksilver wetsuit line, and ran the Quik Pro contests for many years and is an Australian Hall of Famer; Paddy Morgan, who was Rod's Scoutmaster and footy coach, was shaping boards and was recently inducted into the Shapers Hall of Fame at Huntington Beach; Claw and Brian; "Boots" Dowling, who moved to Noosa and ran a successful real estate company; Simon Buttonshaw, the artist who was Quik's creative guru; and Wayne Lynch, who was developing vertical and backhand surfing.'

The crew bonded over surf sessions in an era of experimentation and boundless opportunity. 'In those winters the crew surfed, there was nothing else in the town, and creative board designs and life ideas emerged,' says Terry. 'We huddled around the single bar radiator, and the vinyl record player returned to the same side endlessly. Dylan's epic "Sad-eyed Lady of the Lowlands" often played overnight. Plans were made for different surfing lives . . . There wasn't a lot of talk about starting an industry. I don't think it ever arose. Simon was the artistic member. He was quite a young guy, but a very spiritual guy. There was a lot of talk about morals and music. That house and those people for a couple of winters, it was a treasure. If you look at the success of just about all those people . . . There weren't too many [of us] who didn't have a crack at things subsequently.' Most of those friendships have endured, and the housemates have had a few reunions over the years.

Brian agrees there was no long-term vision of a surf industry or business. 'All the surfers I knew were the same – they didn't think further ahead than, "How are the waves going to be tomorrow?" and "Where are we going to go?" We were living in the present and taking opportunities as they arose,' he says.

Later, Claw and Brian shared another house in Riverside Drive, where they combatted the frigid Victorian winter by dragging a discarded telegraph pole into the house, sticking one end in the fireplace and gradually burning their way through it. 'We had the telegraph pole in the fire, [stretching] across the lounge room and sticking out the front door. We progressively dragged it into the fire as it burnt down over a few weeks, until we could shut the front door,' says Brian.

THE NOBLE ART

Claw and Rod Brooks also shared a love of boxing and would join Claw's dad, Arch, in trips to Melbourne's Festival Hall when a big fight was on, along with Pat Morgan and Brian. 'Any Queensland fighters in Melbourne would call for Arch,' says Claw, so they would often find themselves in the corner of the challenger from out of town. When an Indigenous fighter from Queensland beat the highly fancied Aldo Pravisani from Sydney on points, the crew found themselves in the midst of a full-scale riot.

On another occasion, when they'd scored ringside seats for a fight between Lionel Rose and Rocky Gattellari, Brian took a shine to an attractive woman sitting behind them. He couldn't understand why he was making no progress with his charm offen-sive until his friends pointed out that she was the girlfriend of champion boxer Johnny Famechon, who was sitting next to her wearing an ominous scowl. Illegal ringside betting was also rife and Brian was prone to have a wager, but things almost turned ugly on one occasion when he and the bloke he was betting with both claimed to have backed the winning fighter.

WE'RE TOPS NOW

When Nat Young emerged victorious at the 1966 world titles in San Diego, Australian surfing had officially served notice that it was leading the world. Australian surfers returning from California brought with them the influence of the emerging counterculture scene, but also a vision to forge their own surfing culture and style. Australian surfing was about to go through its most dramatic change since the introduction of balsa boards 10 years earlier.

In late '66 Brian decided to have one more crack at academia. He drove up to Melbourne to have an interview with his university lecturer about how he would mend his ways and attend lectures regardless of surf conditions. The swell had been up that morning, but thankfully the wind was onshore from the sou'-east so he wasn't missing anything. 'Halfway to Melbourne I could see these white fluffy seed pods coming from the north-west. I got out of the car and I could smell the nor-wester. I did a U-turn and went back to Torquay.' Brian reckons he could even now count on one hand the days when a strong sou'-easter has suddenly switched offshore in the middle of the day. That fateful change in wind direction spelled the end of his tertiary education.

But the tug-of-war between career and surfing would be resolved for Brian, at least temporarily, by a surprise job offer to take up a position as maths teacher at Lorne High School. Fellow surfer and schoolteacher Jeff Watt had finished third behind Rob

Conneely and Nat Young in the huge waves at the '65 Bells contest, and must have liked the idea of having another surfer among the staff at Lorne High School because he offered Brian the job despite his lack of teaching qualifications. The fact that Brian had studied maths and science at university was deemed adequate.

Brian's students included a freakishly talented goofy-footer named Wayne Lynch. 'Wayne just lived to surf. He was obviously a child prodigy from the age of 12 or 13. I used to stand at Lorne Point watching this young kid,' says Brian.

Brian shared a converted garage with Jeff, and remembers it as a magical time of fishing, surfing and teaching rudimentary maths to Years 7 to 10. But the world was changing fast and surfing was at the forefront of the looming youth revolution.

THE SUMMER OF LOVE

In the northern spring of 1967, hordes of young people began flocking to the Haight-Ashbury district of San Francisco in a spontaneous flowering of the counterculture or hippie movement. Inspired by the work of Beat Generation writers like Allen Ginsberg and Jack Kerouac, fuelled by the civil rights movement, women's liberation, the sexual revolution and opposition to the Vietnam War, and fed on a diet of New Age anti-consumerism and an embrace of psychedelic drugs and communal living, the Summer of Love saw tens of thousands of young people gather in parks and share houses.

The Haight-Ashbury's hippie newspaper, the *San Francisco Oracle*, announced: 'A new concept of celebrations beneath the human underground must emerge, become conscious, and be shared, so a revolution can be formed with a renaissance of compassion, aware-ness, and love, and the revelation of unity for all mankind.'

Even on the distant shores of Torquay, acid guru Timothy Leary's rallying cry to 'turn on, tune in, drop out' resonated with a younger generation already rejecting their parents' values. 'It had a big impact,' says Brian. 'Socially the world changed in that year from a fairly work-oriented, industrious generation, born of necessity after the Depression and World War II, and through the '50s and the accumulation of things: cars, washing machines, fridges ... There was quite a rapid change in the way the generation growing up saw their place in the world.'

The Beatles released their psychedelic masterpiece, *Sgt. Pepper's Lonely Hearts Club Band*. Anti-Vietnam and civil rights protests raged in the US. The contraceptive pill sparked a sexual revolution, and recreational drug use, most notably of cannabis and LSD, was embraced by the hippie movement as a tool of mind expansion and self-realisation.

Simon Buttonshaw was an early adopter of the counter-culture and became an influential artist responsible for much of the Torquay surf companies' most powerful imagery. In a 1978 interview in *Sea Notes* magazine he described the spirit of freedom that pervaded the Torquay surfing community. 'People no longer felt the need to lean on things they'd been brought up with,' he told John Witzig. 'They'd created for themselves a sort of semi-alternative lifestyle and philosophy and it was working for them. Different people viewed it from different ways and so you get some people taking a spiritual-type direction, you get other people thinking that it meant they could simply move to Torquay and have the same security that they had in Melbourne.'

Claw and Brian marked the Summer of Love by driving 2000 kilometres from Torquay to Noosa Heads in Brian's white Falcon station wagon, drawn to their own gathering of the surfing tribe on the long, gleaming walls of Noosa's mystical point breaks.

'Claw and I were quite different,' Brian says. 'We'd get in the car in Torquay and after half an hour he'd put me in the driver's seat, then I'd drive all the way to Queensland and he'd talk nonstop.'

Claw had good reason to be excited about their trip to Noosa. Ringleaders of the so-called Shortboard Revolution or 'involvement school' of surfing, shaper Bob McTavish and enigmatic Californian kneeboarder and inventor George Greenough, had taken up residency in the normally quiet Queensland beach town, and Claw and Brian were eager students. Nat Young had prepared for his world title campaign and developed his winning board 'Magic Sam' at Noosa the previous year, and the area's long, peeling points had become the ultimate testing ground for new equipment.

Brian had to return after a couple of weeks to his teaching job but Claw stayed for the winter. 'I spent the winter in Lorne teaching, surfing and fishing, and travelling up to Torquay on weekends to take up residence in Brooko's place with the rest of the crew,' Brian recalls. 'Although Lorne was far away from the emerging Summer of Love in San Francisco, the music and a few snippets of information were reaching that far.'

In Noosa, Greenough's long, raked fins and his wild surfing on extremely low-volume 'spoon' kneeboards fed into Bob McTavish's enthusiasm for shorter, lighter boards and vee bottoms. Coupled with the long, airbrushed walls of Noosa's famed point breaks, rapid advances were made in performance and equipment. Claw wasn't too far off the pace in the design stakes, with George Rice's early version of the vee bottom and a refined Bob Cooper fin. His progressive equipment earnt him entrée to the select clique, and he soaked it all up.

'It was a great winter for surf. We used to just hang out and go surfing – Noosa, the River Mouth, Alexandria Headland, Point Cartwright,' says Claw. 'Surfing was developing on a daily basis.

Bob was talking surfboard design and revolution and evolution, and George was a big contributor.'

At the end of the winter, Bob McTavish announced that he was heading to Sydney to create the 'revolutionary surfboard'. He had a lucrative new deal with Brookvale board-maker Denny Keyo. Claw sniffed opportunity and followed not far behind.

'I said to Bob, "I'll be driving back to Torquay to surf in the Victorian state round. I'll come through Brookvale." I'd always stop in and see Gordon Woods and Barry Bennett,' says Claw. 'I turned up there and saw the very first Fantastic Plastic Machine.' Keyo was unnerved by Bob's strange-looking creations, with extreme vees and rapidly shrinking proportions. 'Denny asked me, "Do you think Bob is crazy, Claw? They always told me not to employ him and he'd always leave whenever the surf was good."'

Claw reassured him they were onto something. 'I said to Denny, "They're going to change everything." . . . It was a social explosion, and people just embraced the shorter vee-bottom boards,' says Claw. He negotiated a deal to be the Victorian agent for the McTavish–Keyo collaboration and hit the road south with new business ideas fizzing in his mind.

Brian remembers Claw turning up at Lorne High School when he returned from Noosa, resplendent in the colourful hippie garb of the day and sharing the news of momentous surfboard design developments. Neither the school nor the local constabulary were thrilled by the appearance of this advanced guard of the counter-culture movement about to sweep the country. 'The local police sergeant didn't take kindly to Simon Buttonshaw and myself turning up in hippie gear,' says Claw. 'He drove up in a police van and said, "You freaks should get out of this place."'

Claw was happy to oblige, intent on hightailing it back to Torquay to workshop the business opportunities represented by the new vee bottoms. He had been running his seasonal pop-up surf shops for a few summers, but felt ready to take a bigger leap of faith. 'We were just scratching together enough to get to the next day or next week, to have enough money to go surfing when we wanted, and not have to turn up to work when the surf was great,' says Claw.

They recruited Terry Wall and opened the Bells Beach Surf Shop in a small petrol station owned by a local character called Mumbles Walker, opposite the Torquay pub at 42 Bell Street. 'Claw was always the thinker in the crew; Brian was the organised one. I don't know what the hell I did. We weren't a very serious crew, nor was it extremely organised,' says Terry. 'They formed a complementary duo, Claw being the creative and enthusiastic ideas man, Brian the frugal manager. Both had moved to Torquay and were willing to give anything a go in order to earn a crust – filling fertiliser bags in Geelong or fixing dings.'

A small ad in the local paper announced the arrival of the Bells Beach Surf Shop: 'Suppliers of the Best Surfboards and Equipment Available . . . Fashion Wear and the Works!' it declared. 'Buy your surfing equipment from your own club members. Proprietors: Doug (Claw) Warbrick, Terry Wall, Brian Singer – the most experienced surfers in the state.'

'The main product we had was the Fantastic Plastic Machine from Keyo Surfboards, shaped by Bob McTavish,' says Claw. 'What we had also was this incredibly influential, brilliant surfer in Wayne Lynch. Somehow or other we had arranged for one of the very first plastic machines to be for Wayne. I think it was number four. It arrived within a day of me driving back to Torquay. There was a bit of ceremony about it, people coming around to take a look. Wayne came up to Torquay and he went out at Bells or Winki, and surfed like no one had ever surfed before.'

Wayne's innovative surfing was the best possible advertisement for the new design. 'He surfed the board a lot up and down the Surf Coast, [and] a lot of surfers of the day saw him surf it . . . He had a local following,' says Claw. 'To me, Wayne had a powerful imagination for surfing.' The vee bottom allowed Lynch to lean the board hard over on a rail, come square off the bottom and drive vertically up the wave face, then carve increasingly radical turns up into and through the lip of the cresting wave. Wayne was able to surf the way he'd imagined surfing, turning constantly in and around the pocket or the curl of the wave, giving others a glimpse of the future.

In the stampede to embrace the new equipment, demand far outstripped supply, providing a crucial early business lesson. 'We had 100 orders in no time, but the boards never came. We stopped taking orders at about 200, but the orders went to thousands Australia-wide,' remembers Claw. 'Denny Keyo said, "We can't make them, we can't get enough blanks, we don't have a big enough factory, Bob doesn't want to use ghost-shapers."'

It was Brian's turn to travel up to Sydney and do a tour of the Brookvale surfboard factories to try to secure a supply of the new vee bottoms. His search led him to a progressive young shaper named Shane Steadman, who was ready and able to meet the demand for the new design. Stedman told them they'd need a name and decals for their boards, so as Claw, Brian and Simon Buttonshaw hung around the surf shop one afternoon they began brainstorming names. Simon had painted psychedelic artwork on Claw's first vee bottom from McTavish, and amid the bright colours and florid designs he painted the words 'rip curl, hot dog'. It was a bit of cosmic wordplay with the new surfing jargon of the day, and a variation of the mantra Bob had painted on one of his own early vee bottoms: 'hot kid, rip board'.

'Hot dog' had been a popular term in the US for years, but Claw and Brian liked the sound of 'rip curl', a more antipodean expression of this new style of surfing. Ripping the curl was precisely what Lynch had been able to do on the new equipment. The phrase neatly captured the moment surfing became 3D as surfers like Lynch harnessed centrifugal force to ride up and into the pitching lip of the wave.

The name stuck. Simon drew up some evocative artwork around the new name and Brian remembers going to see Jim the printer in Brookvale, who produced decals for every significant board-maker in the country. Claw and Brian were convinced they were well placed to cash in on the mounting surfboard revolution, but the pace of change made it difficult to keep up with design innovations.

'Vee bottoms went out of style as fast as they came in,' says Claw. 'Within months people started making progressive boards all over Australia. Inches were coming off every week. The old shapers were out of fashion overnight, the carpenters and cabinet-makers.'

'Everything was going short very quickly; all we were doing was trading in nine-foot things that nobody wanted,' says Terry. 'We didn't have a distinct place to do much in terms of repairs and storage. Brian had the master plan of buying a garage and putting it in the car park of the pub. I don't know if anyone was even asked. We bought this garage – it was painted black, and we painted flowers in psychedelic colours – but the bloody thing was too hot to be inside during daylight hours. That was where we put the increasing number of nine-foot relics that no one wanted, and where we did repairs. The garage was where a lot of the action happened.'

Claw had an early insight that the surfing industry would need to be about more than just surfboards, so they branched out. Much-sought-after American denim jeans like Levi's and Lee

Cooper were originally distributed through surf shops to try to retain their edgy youth-culture cool. If Claw couldn't secure stock he'd go down to the wharves in Melbourne when US Navy ships came in and buy second-hand pairs from the marines. But even these efforts couldn't keep the Bells Beach Surf Shop afloat.

'It petered out; we weren't making any money,' says Brian. 'For some reason, the whole thing came to a grinding halt and I was back teaching science at North Geelong High. It certainly wasn't as nice as Lorne but I do recall that the kids were great.'

'I think the whole of Brookvale got overwhelmed with the demand for these new boards,' adds Claw. 'And we spent too much time surfing and chasing girls.'

Terry moved to Newcastle at the end of summer to study for a PhD in chemical engineering, and went on to a distinguished career in science and academia. 'When I left we had a garage of longboard trade-ins that no one wanted, and XXS and XXL surf clothing that fitted no one,' he says. 'Not a resounding financial success. But the first Rip Curl boards had been made, Simon had created a great logo, working relationships had been created and a company was in the making . . . I figured it had been a nice time and said see you later, but Claw worked out there was some money owed to me and slung me 20 bucks.'

After that failed experiment, Terry figured it was time to get real and forge a legitimate career. 'The other reason I moved north was I couldn't see how I could live by the beach and make a living,' says Terry. 'The question we were all asking was, how can we live the life we want to live and still earn a crust in some way?'

CHAPTER TWO

RIPPING THE CURL: 1969–1974

As Australian surfing developed its own identity and a budding youth revolution swept aside old notions of how to live, the late '60s was the ideal time for the emergence of a home-grown surf industry.

John Witzig, one of the key documenters of the era, says, 'There was a disrespect of authority, a relative prosperity, the idea that we actually had something that was important and that we could be ourselves. The fact that kids could get hold of a car and move around – the moving around was enormously important . . . There was a whole finger to authority. The Vietnam War was totally pivotal. I was at uni and went to all the moratoriums. It was quite apparent that the government lied to you. It was a convergence of all sorts of things.'

After Brian returned to teaching, over the next couple of years he kept his habit of ditching school when the waves were firing. 'I'd always take pay day off because obviously I was pretty crook if I didn't turn up on pay day,' he says. And he wasn't without his reservations about his chosen profession. 'I loved the kids, but

I didn't think too much of the teachers,' he says. Brian noticed how many of his fellow teachers seemed to survive from pay cheque to pay cheque, and he already aspired to a less desperate existence. He also harboured a vivid memory of watching his dad commute to work: 'Seeing dad get in the car on a hot summer day in a suit in Miranda, I thought, shit, I never want to do that.'

So when Brian bumped into Claw walking down Gilbert Street, Torquay, in March 1969, he was immediately receptive to his friend's latest scheme. 'He said, "Do you want to make surfboards?" and I said, "Yes,"' Brian explains simply. Brian's qualifications for this bold new business partnership were compelling: 'I had a surfboard planer and a garage,' the latter of which was a wedding present from his wife's parents.

Brian had married his girlfriend Jenny seven months earlier. 'I met Jenny when I was down at Lorne in '67. She was teaching in the primary school but we didn't connect until later that year, and married in August '68,' says Brian. 'I was 24, she was 21. I moved from Riverside Drive from this fairly spartan share house with Claw and John Clarke to a house we bought up on the Great Ocean Road for $7,800. We had this great domestic situation, which was nice but quite a change. After I quit teaching to make surfboards, Jenny financed our living until Rip Curl started making a bit of money.'

Claw, meanwhile, had witnessed the cycle of surfboard design fashions, had been deeply influenced by the first generation of Australian board-builders in Brookvale, and was confident he was well placed to cater to the rapidly evolving tastes of Australian surfers. 'It was the start of the revolution,' says Claw.

They still had Rip Curl decals labelled '42 Bell Street' left over from their first foray into surfboards in 1967 so decided to stick with the name, and incorporated the company with an investment of $500 each. A young South African surfer named Andy

Spangler helped them chisel holes in the floor of Brian's garage to set up shaping and glassing stands. And, just like that, they were in business.

Claw thrived on the spirit of experimentation and did all of the shaping, while Brian had the dirty jobs of glassing, sanding and making fins. 'Laying up fins and having to cut them out with a Stanley knife just as the panel was gelling, emitting copious resin fumes, was the worst job ever,' he says.

Nonetheless, Claw says, 'There was probably more change and progression in the time I shaped surfboards than in any other time. After phase one of vee bottoms I only shaped modern shortboards. All the boards were already under eight feet.' Claw was heavily influenced by George Greenough's high-aspect, long, raked fins and his sophisticated understanding of bottom contours, as well as the innovative shapes of Ted Spencer, who spent plenty of time in Torquay and at the Hare Krishna community in nearby Aireys Inlet.

Nineteen sixty-nine was a great year for surf, and there was plenty of opportunity to test designs in quality conditions. Brian recalls 28 straight days through May and June of offshore winds and few surfers in the water mid-week. 'I'd come back from Bells, knock the fin off the board, move it a bit and go back to Bells to test the board,' he says. On 20 July 1969, the day Neil Armstrong and Buzz Aldrin walked on the moon, Brian recalls a perfect though grey day at Bells surfing with local surfer Charlie Bartlett. 'There were only two of us in the water surfing eight-to-10-foot waves lining up from Rincon right through the Bowl,' he says. 'We got out of the water and went straight home in time to watch their moonwalk on TV.'

The business was rapidly outgrowing Brian's garage. 'We only made three or four [surfboards] a week and we realised we needed to up the ante towards summer, so I found the old bakery to rent for $10 a week in late '69,' says Brian. The unused bakery on Boston

Road was transformed into a surfboard factory and showroom, with a glassing bay next door and a shaping bay out the back.

Sanding was done outdoors. It was the first job Brian delegated, and it's fair to say occupational health and safety standards were not too rigorous. Brian recalls one of their sanders, John Clarke, making a mess of a board. 'One day he's sanding and there's this big gouge sanded out next to the fin. I got pretty cranky,' he says. 'He started telling me how he got electrocuted and gouged the board. There was this six-foot-high fence next to us. He said, "There happened to be a guy walking by outside the fence, he jumped over the fence and knocked it out of my hand."'

Brian was sceptical about the far-fetched tale, figuring his sander was just making excuses for his botched work, but eventually had it confirmed many years later. 'Fifteen or 20 years later, I think I might have been at the pub, I got talking to a guy. I said we make surfboards, and he asked, "Did you have a place down at Boston Road? One day I heard this guy yelling out and I had to jump over a fence and knock this sander out of his hand that was electrocuting him." It was quite a revelation to me to realise the sander had been telling the truth all that time.'

There was a growing surfing industry in Torquay by this time. Fred Pyke had moved his surfboard business from Melbourne to Torquay in 1966. Pat Morgan followed suit in 1967, and was producing some beautiful boards with his innovative keel fins. Though profits were slim, the reward was the abundant, uncrowded surf.

Al Green was another young surfer with an entrepreneurial streak, who'd been working as a bookkeeper at a company called Australian Divers in Melbourne. The company had the Australian rights to the Aqua-Lung, developed by French diving legend Jacques Cousteau and engineer Émile Gagnan, and sold other diving gear including wetsuits.

Greeny had been trying to convince his boss at Australian Divers to branch into specialty surfing wetsuits without success. The old dive wetsuits were notorious among surfers for causing chafing under the arms and, more alarmingly, around the crotch, requiring the liberal application of petroleum jelly and/or talcum powder. 'I tried to talk them into making wetsuits for surfers, but the boss didn't want to know anything about surfers,' says Greeny. 'He called me into his office and said, "You ought to buy the stuff off me and go and make your own wetsuits,"' and so he did.

Greeny drove into Torquay with a bundle of brown-paper patterns and a stack of neoprene looking for partners for his new venture. 'I talked to Klemm Bell about it, I talked to Rip Curl about it. I went with Rip Curl,' says Greeny. He can't recall why he opted to go into business with Claw and Brian. 'I knew who they were, I knew them from being around, but not nearly as well as I got to know them,' he says.

Brian and Claw were by no means sold on the idea initially. 'At first, we said no. But then I started thinking, hang on, these wetsuits were going to advertise our surfboards,' says Brian. They decided to give it a crack.

'No one really had ownership of [the idea]; no one was really driving it,' says Brian.

'We made it up as we went along,' says Greeny.

Their early efforts were crude at best. The only neoprene rubber available locally was from a company called Leggetts in Clayton, in Melbourne's south-east, and the quality wasn't great. Finding sewing machines that could get a needle through the stuff was the next challenge. They eventually found a Pfaff 138 sewing machine that made a zigzag stitch after the seams were glued together.

The neoprene was cut out on the floor according to the patterns, then glued and sewn together. They only made one model: a short john, which had no arms and short legs. They installed the sewing machine in a rented basement near the pub and employed a few different people on it, but the process was painstakingly slow and running a business with three partners proved difficult.

'There were three of us at this stage, and it was a bit of a mixed-up jumble of who was doing what,' says Brian. They found a couple of local women who were happy to do the sewing for piece rates, but they soon realised they were going to need more help and more space. While the bakery remained the surfboard factory, they took the wetsuit operation to Claw's tiny one-bedroom flat on Zeally Bay Road.

By early 1970 it became clear that the three partners weren't going to be able to work harmoniously together. Some say Brian and Greeny were too similar, both straight-talking pragmatists. Greeny was already working on making board shorts and sheepskin ugg boots, and figured he'd go out on his own.

'We had a blue out in the yard and decided we and Greeny should go our own ways,' says Brian.

Greeny doesn't recall an argument. 'I don't think we ever really had a blue. I just wanted to get out. I didn't want to be the product manager, I wanted to be out and about ... We decided not to compete – that's the way we went,' he says. Their informal business relationships were dissolved amicably and Greeny moved on to his next business venture, the sheepskin work then Quiksilver board shorts. They remained friends, and Claw and Brian came on board as silent partners in Greeny's new business.

THE CIRCLE LOGO

The circular Rip Curl wetsuit logo has become one of the most beloved in surf culture, but there is no epic creation story behind it. The father of a mate of theirs, Brewster Everett, ran a business called Selex Decals, and Rip Curl required a specific type of label that would stretch with the neoprene. Brewster turned up with four designs for them to choose from, and Claw and Brian opted for the circular one with the suitably groovy font. No one paid too much attention to the little figures carting surfboards in the top right of the logo, which bore an uncanny resemblance to the poster for Bruce Brown's classic 1966 surf movie *Endless Summer*. In any case, Claw always said the figures were Australian surfers Chris Brock and Russell Hughes.

It didn't take Brian long to realise that the wetsuit business had legs, and was less work-intensive and more profitable than surfboards. 'Within the first year of [us making] wetsuits they'd overtaken surfboards,' he says. 'We were getting orders of 100 a week, making $10 a wetsuit. The penny dropped. This is the real deal. This is going to finance our surfing.'

Brian focused on running the business, and his management systems were simple but effective. 'You got an invoice book and a chequebook and a bank deposit book. With these three documents, you could run the whole show. People make it seem too hard,' says Brian. 'I admired Barry Bennett's surfboard blank business at Brookvale, so I just copied the layout of his invoice and statements when we had our own stationery printed.'

One of Rip Curl's first employees was a local kid Brian found sitting on the front doorstep of the bakery one morning before work. Brian assumed he was some kind of street urchin, totally forgetting that he'd placed a job advertisement in that morning's *Geelong Advertiser*. Gary Crothall was only 15 but was already sick of school, and keener on the idea of being a rock-and-roll drummer.

'I lived in Jan Juc and my mum said, "If you can find a job in

Torquay you can leave school," which was very nearly impossible,' says Gary. The rudimentary form of surf commerce being practised in the old bakery was his best hope of salvation. 'It was a scary interview. Brian was a maths and science teacher. I vividly remember him reading my report and shaking his head, but I got the job. I think they were probably desperate. It was my ticket out of Belmont High School.'

The youngster was fascinated by his new employers. 'I was really taken by Claw's eccentricity. He was always an interesting character to be around. Brian was a little bit more conservative, the more businesslike one. I call them the Lennon and McCartney of the surfing industry.'

Gary was put to work as a general roustabout at Claw's flat, where two women were now working on sewing machines full-time. His wage was $17.60 a week. 'The cheque bounced a couple of times,' he says.

The financing of growth was proving a constant challenge. Wetsuits were selling as fast as they could make them but that meant having to buy more rubber, pay more wages, hold more stock and wait to be paid by retailers. 'You had to drive to Melbourne to buy the rubber. They had a deal with the longer-term wetsuit-makers; if any newcomers came along they'd charge them double for the rubber,' says Brian. 'I'd write a cheque knowing I didn't have enough to cover it, then chase up retailers before the rubber cheque bounced. That went on for quite some years.'

The constant chasing of debt inspired a simple mantra when dealing with retailers: 'We give you wetsuits, you give us money.' And the surf shops eventually paid. 'Our bad-debt rate was really low, around 0.1 per cent of sales. You look at other industries where the bad-debt rate was a lot higher. All those people who looked down at the surf industry were way off beam,' says Brian.

One bloke they could count on to pay his bills was their good mate Terry 'Speaky' Lyons, who ditched a secure job with Telecom, the telecommunications giant that would one day become Telstra, to open one of Torquay's first surf shops. Speaky was delighted to have more products to stock, and even did a stint gluing up wetsuits himself in the Zeally Bay Road flat. At one stage, he was sharing a house with Al and Barb Green and helping them cut out Quiksilver's early board shorts.

'I must have been one of the first to sell their wetsuits there . . . I had access to stock, but it was pretty limited stock and they didn't stay on the shelf for very long,' says Speaky. 'I had board shorts and wetsuits both made in Torquay so that was ideal for me . . . I was offered a one-sixteenth share in Quiksilver. I said, "No, I'm going to be a retailer. You make the stuff and I'll sell it." Greeny went on to be fairly successful – he was flying up the front of the plane and I was still selling board shorts.'

Speaky managed to make a go of it, opening stores in nearby Belmont and Geelong in the ensuing years and still going strong today. 'Torquay was so seasonal. It was nowhere near what it is now. It was Christmas time then it was dead, and the Easter rally brought a few people in,' he says.

Brian and Claw soon realised they'd need yet more space and more sophisticated accounting methods. The old fibro house at the back of the bakery became available for rent so they took over the lease and turned it into their first real wetsuit factory and office. An old ramshackle garage next to it became the sanding and ding-fixing bay. 'We had a few different people around town sewing them up and then the house at the back of the bakery became available and that became the first wetsuit factory,' says Brian.

One of those people sewing wetsuits was Sybil Stock, who'd recently closed her drapery store in Torquay after 12 years. 'They came to see me and someone had recommended that I might like to sew their wetsuits,' recalls Sybil, now 87 and living in the Lions Village retirement home, just a stone's throw from the Rip Curl headquarters. 'Surf was up and they'd be gone. Claw would come down and he'd breeze in and breeze out, and if the surf was up, no work was done.'

'We had a big two-storey white house with a billiard room and they put their machines in that room,' says Sybil. 'We had to learn to sew rubber, and rubber wasn't easy to sew. It was terrible, I'd be up hours and hours trying to fiddle with them all. It was dreadful.'

At her peak, Sybil was doing around 100 suits a week, and her husband John made himself useful repairing the sewing machines when they broke down. 'Sparrow used to cut them, Gary Crothall used to bring them backwards and forward to me,' she says. 'They weren't just surfie bums, they were really hungry to make a go of it. A lot of the townspeople, they just thought they were surf bums, they didn't think they would ever make a go of that. We were thrilled to bits to think it went on.'

Next, Claw went looking for a local surfer called Butch Barr, an accountant fresh back from working for a mining company in New Guinea, to see if he was interested in doing their books.

'I was riding my bike along the Esplanade and Claw stopped me, and he said, "What are you doing?"' Butch recalls. 'I'd just come back from New Guinea, Bougainville. It was the wild west over there.' Claw offered him a job on the spot, and Butch joined the growing team installed at the Boston Road headquarters. Butch worked in an office in the fibro house and was handed the fledgling organisation's entire financial management system.

'It was like a petty cash tin. It was all pre-computers, a lot more pencil-pushing. Typewriters and carbon paper. There was no bank in Torquay. There was a general store. Milk was still delivered by horse and cart, says Butch. 'The early days, none of us had any money. For months on end we didn't pay ourselves because there was no cashflow. It was very hand to mouth. Did it matter? Not really . . . I had some money saved up from Bougainville. We were living the life we wanted to live.'

And if that meant your employer occasionally driving a car through the front wall of your office, well, so be it. The yard between the bakery and the old house out the back was notoriously boggy after heavy rain, and Butch recalls sitting at his desk one day when he heard a screech of brakes and looked up to see Claw hurtling towards him at the wheel of the company van. Claw hit the brakes, but that didn't stop him coming through the front wall.

ON THE ROAD

It was decided Brian should pilot their Transit van on the early sales runs up the coast, delivering stock to surf shops as he went. Rip Curl ran its first ad in *Surfing World* in late 1969 for their surfboards, and discovered that it opened doors when it came to visiting retailers with wetsuits too.

'We agonised over that ad for ages, just to get the feeling across,' says Brian. Under the heading 'The Dawning of Rip Curl Surfboards', it features a golden sunrise line-up shot of Bells Beach by Barrie Sutherland. 'Winter 1969 – crisp mornings, balmy days, clean fast surf,' the ad copy reads, though it's difficult to imagine by what standards Torquay's winter weather could be considered 'balmy'. 'Rip Curl Surfboards were born in the Bells reefs last winter. It was a groove for those involved in testing new designs and ideas. It still is. We know what we are doing and we will be around for a long time,' the ad boasted. 'Come along for the ride. All boards designed and shaped by Doug Warbrick and Brian Singer.' The ad gives their address as 5 Boston Road, Torquay, and lists only five stockists, four of them in Melbourne and one in Hobart.

Brian hit the road north in autumn 1970 with the first van full of wetsuits. 'When I said I was from Rip Curl, it was easy to get in the door as they'd already heard of us from our surfboard ads. I learnt the value of no cold calls.'

Brian would leave Torquay at midnight and drive through the night to Sydney. When he got to a new town he'd look up surf shops in the yellow pages. 'They came right before "surgical equipment",' he recalls. He'd often sleep in the back of the van, the wetsuits' thermal properties proving their worth as blankets. Brian loved life on the road.

'It was great meeting all the surf shop people back then: John Skipp in Wollongong, G&S in Bulli, Brian Jackson in Caring-bah, Tom Ugly's Surf Shop – they were one of the biggest wetsuit accounts – Byrne Brothers in Wollongong, Brothers Neilsen on the Gold Coast. In the city in Sydney, Tom Tsipris had General Pants, and bought out Surf Dive 'n' Ski from Barry Bennett and John Arnold. Tony Olsson had the Melbourne Surf Shop.'

Eventually, Brian realised it was too hard to carry sufficient stock in the van. 'So, I'd just go and take orders, and go surfing with the surf shop owners,' he says. He loved exploring the nooks and crannies of the east coast, and tried to teach himself to play guitar, but he was less keen on joining a certain surf shop crew who were fond of skydiving while tripping on acid.

His task was made easier by the fact that US wetsuit brand O'Neill was having trouble supplying retailers to meet demand. 'One standout was Ray Richards [in Newcastle]. He was very loyal to O'Neill,' Brian says. 'One time I called in there and he finally cracked it with O'Neill not supplying his orders, and he said,

"Okay, give me some," and then we had a great relationship with him and Val [Ray's wife] for years after.'

The Rip Curl range now consisted of short johns, long johns and long-sleeved jackets, which could be worn in combination with long johns for all-over warmth before there was such thing as a steamer. 'Long johns came into fashion, so I just got out some brown paper and wrapped it round my legs while wearing a short john and just drew pencil lines on it, and that became the pattern for the long john,' recalls Brian.

The next challenge was to find a sewing machine that could sew the full-length legs, a feat the old Pfaff machines couldn't manage. Brian eventually sourced an old 1910 Singer zigzag machine, which had been used to sew the flying boots of World War I pilots, from a diving wetsuit company.

The business was given another boost when the world titles, after having been staged in Manly, Peru, San Diego and Puerto Rico over the previous six years, were scheduled for Torquay in May 1970, with sponsorship provided by the unlikely alliance of the Victorian Government and Marlboro cigarettes. Meanwhile, issues around professionalism and competition were being hotly debated. 'People were saying, "Corky Carroll's getting paid $1000 a month to look like a kook on the back page of *Surfer* magazine,"' says Claw. 'The best surfers had given up career opportunities, and all of them questioned whether there should be a payback.'

Claw was watching the way the US surf industry had evolved beyond the essential hard goods of surfboards and wetsuits. 'We were already seeing the US industry going to apparel and using surfer endorsements and branding strategies, and they seemed quite powerful,' says Claw. 'South Bay board-makers were making hundreds of boards a week, but soft apparel you could sell to

Middle America. The Meistrell brothers, with Body Glove and O'Neill, were going strong.'

The international contingent brought a buzz to Torquay along with the latest in wetsuit designs from the US brands, including the first steamers. The idea of a one-piece, full-length wetsuit was a revelation. The old stiff rubber had made such an idea seem impractical, but new and more flexible rubber from Rubatex in the US, and later Sedo in Japan, opened up new possibilities. The imported rubber was expensive, but a vast improvement on the old Leggetts rubber.

'By this stage we realised some of the best neoprene in the world was coming out of Kobe in Japan,' says Brian. 'It was a factory owned by an old guy, Mr Sedo, who had made rubber bands during the Second World War. I made a lot of visits to Japan during this period and really enjoyed all of them, especially the challenge of dealing with the Japanese – the language, the culture were totally foreign but totally fascinating, and I must say they were very hospitable hosts.'

'The access to the Japanese stuff and a little bit of American neoprene was the real beginning of being able to make wetsuits specifically for surfers that could be designed to allow much easier paddling, which meant catching more waves. Basic but true,' recalls Ray Thomas, a local surfer who joined Rip Curl around this time. 'The effort to keep innovating wetsuit design at Rip Curl to make for a better experience in the water has never backed off since then.'

It didn't take long for Rip Curl to make the steamer its own. They even patented their underarm gusset, with Claw himself modelling the suit in the photo for the patent application.

Brian would spend hours fiddling with the layout of patterns on the neoprene to minimise waste of the expensive rubber, and would constantly refine patterns for comfort and fit. 'I'd sit in the water and come back, and within a day change the pattern to make it a bit better and have it in production immediately,' says Brian. 'We had a huge focus on product-testing that pervaded the whole company. Still today, if there's a problem with anything, we take it to the product manager and say, "This is not right. Why did it go wrong? Fix it."'

The world titles also opened up the concept of sponsorship or, at the very least, providing the top surfers of the day with free wetsuits in exchange for the exposure and credibility they would lend the brand. 'When we started in '69 they were lining up,' recalls Claw. 'When sponsorship came along, we looked after so many people. We had a lot of them on our books. I think you would have been hard-pressed to get someone like Nat Young to pay for a suit.'

Brian didn't see too much of the world titles firsthand, as he was busy back at Rip Curl HQ trying to keep up with orders. 'I was stuck in Torquay making wetsuits. The sewing machine kept breaking down and I was scouring around for more of them,' Brian recalls. He finally found a couple at a second-hand sewing-machine business in Melbourne, which was essential for finding spare parts when they inevitably broke down.

Claw was the Australian judge for the event and largely absent from work for the duration, particularly when the contest was moved down the coast to Johanna, on the western side of Cape Otway. The encroachment of an international contest into what was still a closely guarded surfing secret outraged some local surfers, including local favourite Wayne Lynch. It signalled the beginning of an influx of surfers to what would become known as the Surf Coast.

This pattern of migration from the cities to regional areas was mimicked around the Australian coastline. Sydney surfers flocked to the NSW north and south coasts, and Brisbane surfers were lured by the sublime point breaks of Noosa or the Gold Coast. Adelaide surfers began exploring the wave-rich west coast, and

Perth surfers headed south to the stunning waves of the Margaret River region. In many of these regional areas the appearance of surfers, with their long hair, dilapidated vehicles, apparent disdain for hard work, billows of mull smoke and rowdy social hijinks, made conservative rural communities uncomfortable. In Margaret River surfers were spat at in the street and refused service in petrol stations. The constabulary of Byron Bay and Coolangatta delighted in busting itinerant surfers for anything from vagrancy to faulty brakelights to possession of small amounts of pot.

A new style of surfing magazine had been launched soon after Rip Curl began life, a bawdy, irreverent newsprint journal called *Tracks*, and its hippie ethos and back-to-nature tone fuelled the rural migration. '*Tracks* was starting to talk about the country-soul thing . . . That [marked] the first big wave of surfers moving into Torquay to live,' says Brian.

The Torquay locals seemed more accepting of these strange new surfing immigrants, perhaps because they were running businesses, spending money in the town and offering employment where little existed. The surf club and the footy club provided social institutions where surfers rubbed shoulders with more conservative locals, and if the newcomers could win a paddle race or fill a slot on the half-back flank, all the better.

'A lot of the townsfolk got involved in the employment. We had this integration with the community,' says Claw.

'I never felt any antagonism. A lot of the older local women were sewing for us,' says Brian.

'It was a happy place, everyone knew everyone,' agrees Gary Crothall.

Perhaps if the good citizens of Torquay had known what went on behind closed doors and after hours they would have been more scandalised. One particular party on a farm in the early '70s has gone down in history as something akin to Torquay's own mini-Woodstock, with live bands, plenty of booze and weed, and an invitation that set the tone with a call to arms that eventually became a Quiksilver advertising slogan: 'If you can't rock 'n' roll, don't fucking come.'

Things got really interesting when some bright spark decided to try to get the most out of the residual hash oil stuck to the inside of a container by making a vat of hash-oil tea. No one had any idea of the potency of the brew and happily gulped it down by the mug-full. The party wound up fairly early, with most revellers passed out in fields gazing at the clouds. 'That party changed Torquay. Some people never recovered,' one partygoer tells me. 'Someone walked 30 kilometres to the Krishna farm out the back of Aireys Inlet and became a Krishna.'

But the migrations between Rip Curl and the nearby Hare Krishna farm were two-way traffic. 'Some of them would run off the rails and find Krishna to get back on their feet, and the final repository was Rip Curl,' says Brian. 'It was a pretty odd bunch. There were no thoughts of occupational health and safety. The factory inspector would come around every now and again, and there'd be open four-gallon drums of acetone in the surfboard factory. It would certainly not be regarded as a safe working environment today.'

Rip Curl developed a reputation for staging excellent parties, but only once the work was done. Brian and Claw were intent on making surf time and parties a priority, even when money was tight. 'Every Friday afternoon after work we used to get so pissed. We knocked off – that was the policy – and we ended up at the pub,' says Butch.

'Brian would go, "We don't have enough to pay you. We just have enough to buy a few slabs and have a party,"' recalls Steve Perry, another early Curl employee. No one seemed to mind too much. The reality of a job on the coast that allowed plenty of surf time was a dream come true for most employees, and the occasional delay in getting paid seemed like a minor inconvenience. 'Every month we'd get called up by the petrol station because we hadn't paid our bill,' says Steve.

These days Steve lives in a beautiful oceanfront home, a modern cubist timber-and-glass marvel set in landscaped Zen gardens and low coastal scrub, with spectacular floor-to-ceiling ocean views over Winki Pop. He's clearly done well out of the surf industry, having segued from his time at Rip Curl to a gig launching Oakley in Australia. He remains friends with accountant Butch Barr, who went on to similar success, making his fortune running Reef in Australia.

'If it wasn't for Brian and Claw I wouldn't have this place. They taught me how to run a business,' says Steve, regarding his opulent surroundings appreciatively. But when I meet him for our interview, Steve's doing it tough, battling throat cancer and suffering the effects of prolonged radiation and chemotherapy. The question of whether he was even up for the interview has been touch-and-go but he seems glad of the company, and stoked to see his mate Butch. As the stories flow, he becomes increasingly animated despite his ill-health. Sadly, not long afterwards, Steve succumbed to his illness, and was honoured at a mass paddle-out at Cosy Corner in Torquay.

Steve came to Rip Curl via an unusual employment history. 'I left school, joined the public service and became a customs officer. I had to park next to where they kept the sniffer dogs with my kombi and it was a party on wheels,' says Steve. 'I was down the coast every weekend . . . I had dealers come up and go, "I hear you're in customs, we need to have a talk." I went, this is crazy, what am I doing?'

Steve eventually pulled the pin on the career in customs and moved to Torquay. He picked up work on the Rip Curl night shift, newly convened in an effort to keep up with demand. 'Everyone was knocking off at five; you would turn up and someone would produce some drugs or booze, and it would turn into a bit of a party,' says Steve. He earnt $10 a week, and budgeted $2 for food, $2 for petrol, $2 for rent and $4 to party on the weekend. 'I didn't really drink back then, because the LSD was really good,' says Steve.

You could buy a house in Torquay for as little as $10,000 or rent one for $10 a week, and surfers would cram as many into a house as possible and pool their remaining funds for food and lifestyle. The old dear at Giddings milk bar, Molly Ross, would take pity on the impoverished surfers and buff them out with leftovers, and fruit and veg that was close to spoiling. The waves were free.

But there were still perils awaiting young surfers which threatened to shatter this idyllic existence. The Vietnam draft, the dreaded birthday ballot, was still in effect. Steve had become eligible when he turned 20 and was prepared to go into hiding to dodge the draft. 'I bought a car for 140 bucks, and we drove this old car to Margaret River, spent a couple of weeks at Cactus, and then ended up at Margaret. I didn't get called up so we came back,' he recalls.

Steve was welcomed back to Rip Curl and got a job on their newest product line, inflatable surf mats. The surf mat operation took place in the garage out the back of Brian's house in Jan Juc, and Ray Thomas headed up a group of misfits there. 'The surf mat crew were a strange mix,' says Ray. 'I had "Fledge", Greg Hill – he used to be king of Bird Rock, a great surfer; Anne Herriot, now Maurice Cole's wife; and "Pup", another good surfer. These guys were mostly on the dole in those days and just living the hippie surf life. It was my job to ensure that we had a certain number of mats made each week but, unfortunately, I was the only one who cared if we met the quota. Sometimes I was the only one to turn up at the garage ... which meant I sometimes worked into the night to get the quota finished.'

The surf mat crew often required a bit of a kickstart to get going in the mornings, the gurgling of bong water an almost mandatory prelude to the day's work. 'To get the other guys to work more often I had a house chillum,' says Ray. 'I remember one day after a big party at the "Rock", which was an infamous house just near Bird Rock, I had to wake up Fledge by getting my head though his bedroom window because he would not answer the door. I told him I had this block of the best hash, and if he did not get up and come to work he would miss out. That was the general type of incentive I used to get the others motivated too.'

Ray is a giant figure in Rip Curl's history, known variously as the King, the Dugong and the Pink Dugong, because he sunburnt easily. Brian used to pick up Ray hitchhiking when Ray was wagging school to go surfing. Later, when Ray had been expelled near the end of Year 12 for his repeated absences, Claw decided the young truant was Rip Curl material.

When Ray won $100 prize money in an early pro contest at Phillip Island he figured he could afford to surf for three months, paying $8 board a week at home. 'One of those onshore days Claw came down to the beach and hassled me to work for them,' says Ray. 'Claw said it was going to be onshore for days, so why not earn a bit of money in the meantime? That's how I started.'

Cheap Taiwanese imports eventually cruelled the surf mat market, but the locally made product's peculiar habit of blowing up like a beach ball when the ribs gave out might have contributed to its demise.

Ray managed the retail store on weekends until he moved to New Zealand. Steve Perry took over the retail store on weekends, and during the week he'd do the drive up to Melbourne to drop off wetsuits and pick up more rubber from Leggetts before the days of imported rubber. Weekends were busy in the shop. Many wetsuits were custom orders so surfers would come in to get measured for wetsuits or order boards, or pick up their new wetty or surfboard. As the retail trade grew, Steve would often be carrying large amounts of cash at the end of the day.

'I didn't want to have to go and do anything else, so I did everything I could to make sure there was enough money in that till to keep me going,' says Steve. 'If I gave Brian a bag of money he'd leave me alone.'

'It wasn't about ambition to make money,' says Butch.

'It was about survival,' says Steve.

'It was like a footy team,' says Butch.

Steve warms to the analogy. 'Brian was the coach: "We need a good week this week, we're skint."'

Quiksilver and Rip Curl enjoyed warm relations in those early days. If one was doing it tough the other might help them out. 'I'd phone Greeny for a loan one week, and then he'd ring me for a loan,' says Butch. They both knew what it was like to have creditors chasing them so they devised a kind of telephone code to reach one another. 'I had to let it ring three times and then ring straight back, and then he knew it was okay to pick up,' says Butch.

NEW ARRIVALS

One of Rip Curl's next employees would have a profound impact on the business, and the wetsuit industry as a whole. John 'Sparrow' Pyburne had been a grommet presence at Claw's first shop in Brighton, and had been surfing the wind swell between Brighton Beach pier and baths. In 1972, Claw heard Sparrow had completed a mechanic's apprenticeship and thought he might be handy tending to their temperamental old sewing machines. Sparrow, so named back in Brighton because of his skinny legs, didn't need much convincing.

'Those early days were for me the best time of my life,' he says wistfully. 'I'd cut neoprene at night and then go surfing all day. The girls would come in to sew and we'd pack our lunches and go to Winki.'

Sparrow exhibited an affinity for the craft of making wetsuits, and would become one of the most influential wetsuit technicians in the world. But his career had humble beginnings. 'I was cutting wetsuits, and there was a girl there called Sue and she was a dressmaker, and she showed me how to put two and two together to make a custom wetsuit, and from there I got involved in the patterns,' says Sparrow.

Maurice Cole was another young surfer drawn to the old bakery, originally in a short-lived role as a wetsuit gluer. It was here he met his future wife, Anne, who was sewing wetsuits. Maurice moved to Torquay in '71 and remembers being told that he was the 16th surfer to move to Torquay to live full-time. 'Every day you get up – oh, it's offshore. Shit, it's six foot. And whatever else you might have been thinking about was out the door, so you couldn't have a regular job,' says Maurice. 'We were the most unreliable people in the world. I remember trying to make $15 a week: $7.50 for rent, the rest would do food for the week, and I had 20 or 25c for pot on Friday night and Saturday night.'

Today, Rip Curl boasts that nobody gets sacked for going surfing, but back then if you didn't turn up for days on end there were limits to the policy. Maurice only lasted a week as a wetsuit gluer: 'The surf was really good so I didn't turn up to work, and one day Sing Ding paddled out and he went, "I guess you know you're fired," because I hadn't turned up for a while, because we'd had a really good run of surf. And I remember he went, "Fuck, how good are the fucking waves?" Like, it wasn't a drama.'

Even so, Maurice continued hanging round the bakery, watching Donny Allcroft shaping and Jim Pollock sanding, absorbing the fundamentals of surfboard production. 'There was nothing else to do when there was no surf,' Maurice says. 'Then Claw one day just said, "Hey, why don't you shape a board?" I got Donny to help me . . . Ray Thomas had that weekend off and a young Steve Perry worked that weekend and he sold it, so I made another one and I was up and away.'

Maurice teamed up with local standout Wayne Lynch as surfing buddies and a period of intense surfing, exploration and design development ensued. 'We worked out that between Portland and Phillip Island you can surf every day. The work level was pretty low – that's why there aren't a lot of boards from any of us from that time. I was too busy learning about surfing,' says Maurice. 'You've got to remember a lot of people were smoking and taking a lot of drugs in those days: acid, pot, hash . . . It was really relaxed.'

TODAY TORQUAY, TOMORROW THE WORLD

In 1972, Claw travelled to San Diego for the world titles as the Australian judge and team manager, along with a star-studded Australian team featuring Peter Townend, Mark Richards, Michael Peterson, Mark Warren, Simon Anderson, Paul Neilsen and a young Wayne 'Rabbit' Bartholomew. The event was the last of the big amateur world titles before the pro era began, and has gone down in history as a wild week-long party fuelled by copious quantities of illicit substances.

The world title was won by the largely unheralded Hawaiian Jimmy Blears in the men's and Sharron Weber in the women's, but for Claw the event was significant in opening his eyes even further to the international surfing scene. Like many of the Australians, he flew on to Hawaii where he witnessed firsthand the early pro events on the famed North Shore, the Hang Ten and the Smirnoff Pro-Am, both at Sunset Beach.

Long conversations with event director and mentor George Downing convinced Claw that this pro-surfing concept had a future, and he returned to Torquay in early '73 with a bold scheme to turn the Bells Rally into Australia's first full-blown pro event. 'He came back and said to me, "Do you want to do that?" It sounded sensible,' says Brian. 'Then we had to talk to Tony Olsson from the Victorian ASA [Australian Surfriders Association, now Surfing Australia], and convince him.'

It was already January, and Easter was in April, so there wasn't any time to waste. Claw and Brian ventured into Melbourne to see Tony at his Bourke Street store, the Melbourne Surf Shop. The Victorian ASA's offices were on the floor above, and Brian recalls sitting on a step in Tony's shop discussing their idea. Tony took a bit of convincing but was ultimately enthusiastic about the plan.

From the outset, they decided they needed to commit for the long term. 'I thought, if we have this once it will be a fleeting thing. We've got to do it for at least three years to get some momentum,' says Brian.

'It was going out on a limb a bit; we needed the weekend's trading to get over the line,' says Claw. 'Maybe we wouldn't pay the staff or pay ourselves for a couple of weeks, but it wasn't a huge financial commitment. We suspected it would work. We just thought it was important to have Rip Curl associated with this new movement.'

Butch, Rip Curl's beleaguered accountant, wasn't quite so sure. 'There was no money,' he says. 'The prize money came from the weekend's trading. We presented the winners with cheques and told them, don't try and cash them for a few days.'

Fortunately for Rip Curl, the Easter weekend crowds spent more than enough to cover the prize money. Bells also had the distinct advantages of a geography and road system that made it possible to charge spectators to attend. For years the gate takings from the Bells event had helped finance the Victorian team's travels to the national titles, and now that revenue helped make the country's first major pro event financially viable. The shire council pitched in by grading the Bells car park. Surfing's move towards professionalism was a hotly debated topic, even among the top surfers of the day who stood to benefit from it. But with amateur competition in decline after the '72 world titles, most were more than happy to jump on the bandwagon in pursuit of a livelihood from wave-riding.

Claw adopted George Downing's points-for-manoeuvres system, an early attempt at a truly objective judging system, as he'd seen firsthand the pitfalls of the old system. 'It was highly biased along national lines. You had coalitions of judges: judges would fall into line and judge under the Hawaiian style or under the Australian style. The perception was that it was kind of rigged.'

In George's system, points were allocated for each manoeuvre, with extra points weighted on wave height and manoeuvres considered 'radical'. Surfers could ride as many waves as they wanted, accruing points the whole time. Such rigorous methodology was a little out of step with the freedom-seeking, anti-establishment temper of the times, and organisers faced a tough sell at the competitors' meeting at the Torquay pub. Even so, most of the assembled surfing elite were prepared to get down and dirty in the competitive arena for a slice of a whopping $2500 in prize money, with the winner to take $1000. The competition ran over three rounds, with a leaderboard tallied at the end of each round.

Leading those who didn't listen was Michael Peterson, MP. 'Michael was there in body but maybe wasn't there in mind; he wasn't focused,' says Claw. Thus, the enigmatic and highly fancied Queenslander went out in the first round at six-foot Bells with an entirely wrong strategy for the new system. 'Michael went out and surfed three set waves from outside Bells reef and kicked out at the Bowl, rode his three waves and came in,' says Claw. 'Michael was enjoying that form of absolute dominance, and he's great at Bells. But on the leaderboard, dead bottom was Michael Peterson, and second bottom was Peter Drouyn, another great surfer. A big flaw with points for manoeuvres: it's an aggregate of everything you do, every wiggle you can call a defined manoeuvre and you get points. Michael was just stunned when he saw his name at the bottom. He asked three or four people what the fuck had happened. They were all staring at the board and the penny dropped for Michael.'

MP wouldn't stay at the bottom for long. 'He got the criteria and taped it to the dashboard of his car. From dead last in round one he scored nearly 2000 points in round two and the next round he won by a mile,' says Claw. 'He was a ferocious paddler and he started riding 13, 14 waves and doing every manoeuvre you've ever seen. He just blew everyone away.'

Michael took out the first Rip Curl Pro with the breathless quote, 'Jesus, I've won $1000.' The points-for-manoeuvres system was shelved after that bold experiment, but Claw still sees merit in it. 'We got the same winners by the way. It was put aside but maybe it wasn't that flawed because the same guys won.'

'MP had that figured out. He surfed like an over-amped gyro doing 10 manoeuvres a second,' Brian agrees. 'I can't remember there being too many internationals that first year, but it felt like a step forward for the business. And the parties were pretty big around Easter.'

Paul Holmes was a young travelling surfer and shaper from Newquay in England who'd been working at the Keyo and Farrelly factories in Sydney when he headed to Bells to check out the first Rip Curl Pro and landed a job scribing for the judges. 'There was a huge amount of excitement, everyone dug the concept,' says Paul. 'It was a week-long party with some surfing going on. I was in hog heaven, meeting all these surfers I'd seen in magazines – they were heroes, and I was having a beer with them.'

Holmes had left England in 1972 with the naive dream of somehow making a living out of surfing, and that first Rip Curl Pro set in motion a series of events that made that dream possible. He became a judge at the '74 Rip Curl Pro, then contest director of the Coke Surfabout in 1978, and went on to serve as editor of *Tracks* and then *Surfer* magazine in the US in the '80s.

'From the age of 18, I'd thought, there's got to be a way to make a living while living this lifestyle. How can you make enough money to pay the rent and surf when the surf was good?' Paul says. 'When pro surfing came along, I thought, here's my opportunity. People are going to get paid to judge, people are going to get paid to write about it. It was clear to us that this was something that was worth being pursued.'

The Rip Curl operation and its colourful proprietors also made a huge impression on a young Rabbit Bartholomew, who earnt a wildcard into the first Rip Curl Pro with a win in the Queensland titles, triumphing over the established Coolangatta pacesetters Michael Peterson and Peter Townend. 'I'd come on the radar with Claw and he was pretty impressed with the calibre of surfer I'd beaten,' says Rabbit. 'My first suit was a long-sleeved spring suit, and it progressed from there.'

What Rabbit recalls most clearly is the social scene around the event. 'I distinctly remember the parties before and after Bells each Easter. For the Easter break, all the rules went out the window, anything went,' says Rabbit. 'I remember walking into one party and Sing Ding was going off, the Rolling Stones were playing and he just seemed like a figure out of that whole scene, pure rock-and-roll. He was definitely the wild one.'

By 1974, Bells was an established part of Rabbit's seasonal migrations. 'The really great memories were going down in 1974 with Andrew McKinnon. I think I spent six weeks in Torquay and really got to know those guys,' says Rabbit. 'When I first met Claw I thought he was like Gyro Gearloose. I thought Claw was batty: this classic guy who'd turn up at Bells Beach in his thongs and socks – he still does it – twirling his hair, jumping up and down, and rubbing his hands.'

A BEER WITH TOMMY

It's well documented that Michael Peterson went on to thoroughly dominate the Rip Curl Pro for its first three years, and his lanky frame, wild mane and hyperactive laceration of the Bells Bowl became synonymous with the Rip Curl brand. Sadly, MP is no longer with us to explain his otherworldly command of the wide-open faces of Bells, as he died of a heart attack in 2012 at the age of 59. And he never had much to say on the subject when he was alive, struggling with schizophrenia and the effects of electroconvulsive therapy. But his younger brother Tommy is alive and well, and possesses a forensic memory of dates and details of this shadowy past.

Tom lives on North Stradbroke Island these days, but we arrange to meet for lunch at the Coolangatta Sands Hotel during one of his regular shaping stints. Tom's underground shaping career was catapulted into the spotlight by the patronage of another Rip Curl icon, Tom Curren, when Curren rode a tiny Tom Peterson–shaped Fireball Fish in huge Sunset-style rights on an early Search mission to Indonesia in 1994.

'A schooner of New,' are the first words Tommy greets me with when I arrive at the Sands front bar on a Thursday lunchtime. I'm more than happy to oblige. Tom's a masterful raconteur with incredible recall, and he takes his role as guardian of his brother's legacy seriously. He's even prepared notes, scrawled on the back of TAB betting tickets.

He remembers Mick's first trip to Bells in 1970 with shaper Joe Larkin and judge Terry Baker. 'Michael went down to Bells and came home two weeks later. He won the juniors and beat Wayne Lynch, so he was happy, and he turned up with this piece of rubber called a long john,' says Tom. The suit was a revelation, even during the Gold Coast's mild winters. 'While we were out surfing Green-mount in winter, he was surfing more hours than I was.

'Michael came home the next year with a new wetsuit. I said, "What are you going to do with the old one?" It was too long so out came the secateurs, and three inches came off the leg. I wore that wetsuit for a couple of years. Then Mick found out he was supposed to send his old wetsuits back.'

Mick liked the waves and country ambience of Torquay, and Bells became a regular extended Easter pilgrimage. Tom and their mum, Joan, accompanied Mick in '72 and a bond was formed with the Rip Curl crew. 'I still call Doug today Uncle Doug, and I call Singer, Singer. Uncle Doug's always been there if I need some help. I asked Singer for advice on a divorce once,' says Tom.

In Torquay back in the day, they met Sparrow and Donny Allcroft: 'Out the back they were sewing wetsuits. Mick shaped a board there, shaped a couple of boards.' Shaping boards specifically for the waves was key to MP's success, Tommy reckons. 'He made the equipment for the surf, same as MR [four-time world champion Mark Richards]. That's why they dominated Bells for so long. You've got to have area and volume to create speed.'

He remembers Mick leaving for Bells in '75, consumed with anxiety about the prospect of winning the event for the third straight year. 'He said, "If I win again they're going to hate me," and I said, "Go and win and make them hate you."' Tom went to North Stradbroke Island instead that year and won a local contest. 'It's the first time two brothers in two states have won two contests in Rip Curl wetsuits,' he says.

A handshake deal was struck to keep Mick furnished with new wetsuits in exchange for using him in Rip Curl ads. While the deal involved no money, Mick pocketed the lion's share of the prize money in the first three years of the Rip Curl Pro. But Mick was never keen on appearing in ads or fulfilling official duties as a sponsored surfer. 'Mick had a Rip Curl ad shoot. Come the day of the shoot, he's surfing at Angourie,' remembers Tom. 'I don't think he turned up to one ad photo shoot. Most of the time they got him coming out of the water. Flashing cameras at him is the quickest way to get rid of him.'

That handshake deal came to cover Tommy too, and continues to this day. 'Basically, from the time I was 17 to today – and I'm now 63, nearly 64 – I haven't bought a wetsuit and from 1988 I haven't bought clothes. And Mick was the same,' says Tommy.

'Mum was quite impressed with the Rip Curl company because they saved her a lot of money.'

Tom has countless memories of wild times with the Rip Curl crew over the years. He recalls swimming nude in Claw's pool at the tail end of a huge party, and Brian's habit of shunting parked cars up and down the street with his four-wheel drive. 'I've had so much fun with Brian, he's like an older brother because I've known him since I was 17,' says Tom. 'Brian would go down and drink with the boys from despatch because he used to say, "Without you we wouldn't be making any money."'

HITTING THE ROAD

There was no resting on their laurels after the success of Australia's first professional surf contest. Claw embarked almost immediately on a road trip with a kombi-load of wetsuits on a sales run to Western Australia for the Australian titles. Maurice Cole and a young Californian surfer, John Patton, went along for the ride. Typically, Claw retired from driving duties early on and put the unlicensed Cole behind the wheel. He rolled the kombi just outside Ceduna.

Claw was asleep in the back on a mountain of wetsuits with his feet protruding between the front seats. Patton was dozing in the passenger seat and Maurice's dog was at John's feet. Maurice reckons he hadn't seen another car for an hour and was amusing himself during the long, monotonous drive by flicking dog biscuits at Claw's feet, trying to get his dog to bite Claw's toes as he attempted to catch the biscuits in his mouth. Meanwhile, a howling, 40-knot cross-wind required a firm grip on the wheel. Distracted by his biscuit-flicking game, Maurice looked up to see a ute with a bunch of kids in the back appear suddenly out of a dip in the road. He swerved one way to miss them, overcorrected the other way, went up on two wheels then flipped and rolled down an embankment.

The crew were shaken but unhurt. 'We tipped it back up and drove it into Ceduna, and they fixed it all up,' says Maurice. But Maurice's dog took off into the desert, and despite their best efforts they could find no trace of him.

At Cactus they were hit by a wild storm as Claw slept in the van, and Maurice and John camped under a tarpaulin strung up with rope. They scored perfect waves at Caves, a quality right-hand reef break, where they ran into Hawaiian surf star Reno Abellira, the start of a friendship that served Maurice well on subsequent trips to Hawaii.

On their way back from Western Australia, they got word that a local farmer had noticed a dog waiting at the side of the highway where they'd rolled the kombi, day after day. He'd eventually taken it in, and when they tracked down the farmer Maurice and his dog enjoyed an emotional reunion.

INDONESIAN ENLIGHTENMENT

Brian celebrated the success of that first Rip Curl Pro with a trip to Bali with filmmakers Jack McCoy and Dick Hoole. The trip was an opportunity for Brian to reassess his life: Brian and Jenny had had a daughter, Samala, in 1971, but the demands of a growing business had taken a toll on family life, and the couple had separated temporarily in '73.

Alby Falzon's *Morning of the Earth* had come out the year before and blown surfing's collective mind. The stampede to Bali was well and truly on. 'Bali had a huge impact on me,' says Brian. 'There were quite a few drifters on the hippie trail from London to Australia, oil-rig workers from South East Asia, artists. It was quite a melting pot of unusual people, and such a spiritual place. And then throw surfers into the mix, and some surfers making a living through nefarious means.'

He recalls travelling out to Uluwatu in the back of a bemo, choking on fumes, and riding a motorbike while he sat on the nose of his board and the tail hung out the back. This was before there were any warungs at Uluwatu, when it was still a 30-minute walk in from the road and a careful dance down a bamboo ladder to paddle out through the cave. 'There were a few people, you were never surfing by yourself, but there were no warungs, no board-carriers, and one old local bloke who used to sit above the cave and watch for hours,' recalls Brian.

They surfed the empty waves of Balangan, paddled out to Kuta Reef, enjoyed the playful beach breaks of Kuta and explored the coast north up to Medewi. It may have only been a three-week trip, but Brian found it deeply transformative and struggled to adjust to normal life when he returned home. 'I was a bit shell-shocked afterwards, and suffering from the effects of the separation and thinking about things for the first time in my life.' He took a break on Sydney's Northern Beaches, soothed by the gentle strains of George Harrison's Hare Krishna album, *The Radha Krsna Temple*, and the hippie environs of Whale Beach.

The Rip Curl founders recall an unlikely meeting with the Hare Krishna leader Swami Prabhupada in Melbourne around this time, as they oscillated between entrepreneurship and the quest for enlightenment. The revered spiritual teacher's advice? 'Spend less time behaving like fish, and more time on self-reflection.' They took this to mean that the Swami deemed surfing a waste of time on the path to enlightenment, which pretty much spelled the end of their dalliance with the Krishna movement.

THE BEGINNINGS OF SPONSORSHIP

But the times, as Bob Dylan crooned, were a-changing. Professional surfing was gaining momentum, and in 1974 Claw was involved in the formation of the Australian Professional Surfing Association and voted in as founding president. A Sydney newspaper journalist, Graham Cassidy, succeeded in persuading Coca-Cola to stump up enough cash to run Australia's richest surf contest to date, the Coke Surfabout in Sydney, and suddenly there were two pro contests in Australia to lure the world's best Down Under.

A growing number of elite surfers were wearing Rip Curl wetsuits, often with distinctive colours that became their trademark, made as custom orders. Sparrow became the master of the tape measure, recording the dimensions of the world's best surfers and ensuring a fit to satisfy the most discerning surf star. 'I used to go up to Sydney with Claw and measure people up on the beach in front of everybody. It might have been a ploy of Claw's to capture the imagination of people,' says Sparrow.

As more international surfers were drawn to its annual event, Rip Curl got the chance to see its competitors' latest wetsuit designs up close. 'We had guys like [Hawaiian surfer] Rory Russell, they wanted to swap their wetsuits for our wetsuits. I thought, our wetsuits must be pretty good. That's when we started thinking our wetsuits must be up there with the world's best,' says Brian.

While the international contact was welcome, in other ways the geographic isolation had been a good thing for the business, promoting self-reliance and the development of their own business systems from scratch. 'We didn't know much about business, and I came to the conclusion that having that isolation and having to make things up from a common-sense point of view was a positive,' says Brian.

The identity of the first surfer to be paid to wear a Rip Curl wetsuit appears to have been lost in the mists of time: Nat? Midget? Wayne Lynch? Michael Peterson? MP might not have officially been on a salary, but in taking out the first three Rip Curl Pros he certainly became one of their chief beneficiaries.

'What I did know was that the market price for surfers was very difficult to judge,' says Brian. 'After a certain period in the mid-'70s when quite a few surfers started getting sponsored by different surf companies, a market was established so it became easier to establish the value of surfers.'

Wayne Lynch emerged from his self-imposed exile on the south-west coast to escape the Vietnam draft, and was lured out of retirement from surf contests by the professional era. Wayne showed he'd lost no ability or competitive smarts by taking out the '75 Coke Surfabout, while sponsored by Rip Curl.

It was inevitable that Rip Curl's success would attract competitors, and it wasn't long before veteran board-builder Fred Pyke secured the Australian licence for US wetsuit manufacturer Dive N' Surf, whose surfing wetsuits were marketed under the name Body Glove. Claw and Brian swiftly registered the name Body Glove in Australia, so Pyke was forced to use the rather less sexy Dive N' Surf for his suits, and wasn't too happy about it.

Claw's old Brighton buddy Rod Brooks, meanwhile, went into partnership with Pyke to try to modernise his operation. 'Fred was a bit resentful. He was from a different culture, and part of the reason why we only lasted three years was because I was more like [Rip Curl],' says Rod. 'Fred wouldn't spend a cracker on a new machine, you would fix up the old ones. But Fred was an excellent tradesman, one of the best I'd come across in my life.'

Rod left to start his own wetsuit brand, Piping Hot, in 1975, but he soon discovered that his old housemates made tough business competitors. 'We'd all grown up together, but they were formidable,' says Rod. 'They had the Bells contest. Lots of times we were catching up, and Bells would come along and then they'd take a giant leap forward.'

CHAPTER THREE

ON THE MOVE: 1975–1979

By 1975, the excitement many felt about the Whitlam Government's raft of sweeping social changes had given way to alarm at the nation's perilous economic state, with unemployment and inflation on the rise and a budget crisis looming. In this climate, one only had to utter the term 'regional employment' and various government bodies would fall over themselves to offer assistance.

At Rip Curl, the time had come to move out of their quaint but cluttered premises in the old bakery. To that end, Rip Curl secured a regional development grant, actually a low-interest loan, from the newly formed Victorian Economic Development Commission. The loan would allow them to construct a purpose-built factory, offices and retail showroom on Geelong Road (now the Surf Coast Highway), a high-profile position on the main strip coming into Torquay.

It might seem presumptuous for a young surf company to have imagined it would qualify for government support at a time when the establishment viewed surfers as drug-smoking layabouts. Maurice Cole had recently been busted for a small amount of hash, and the authorities had decided to make an example of him. Maurice was jailed for two years and stripped of his state title, confirming every parent's worst fears about surfing as a road to ruin.

But the Rip Curl chiefs seemed unburdened by self-doubt. 'We were the first loan under the scheme and the first one to pay it back. Some never paid it back,' says Brian. 'We felt we deserved it, being young and arrogant – "We've got a business, we're employing people. Why wouldn't we get it? Of course, we'll pay it back."'

Brian has only a vague recollection of the application process – 'I guess I must have filled out forms' – and of the subsequent send-off from the old bakery. 'We might have poured a few more four-gallon drums of acetone across the road and set it on fire,' he says.

Rip Curl's new headquarters opened in early '76 and was home to around 70 full-time staff who oversaw a retail store and wetsuit and surfboard factories, and the company's first designated warehouse and despatch facility.

Because they couldn't produce enough wetsuits to meet demand during winter, Brian was adamant they needed to introduce pre-orders or indent orders for wetsuits. The idea was to reduce their risk by offering retailers an incentive to lock in their orders earlier, giving Rip Curl more time to fill orders and allowing greater accuracy when forecasting production numbers. Rip Curl offered retailers a 5 per cent discount for pre-orders if they ordered at least 75 per cent of what they'd ordered the prior year. 'They said it would never happen, but within six months we introduced indents for wetsuits,' says Brian. 'It was another lesson that you can do all sorts of things that people reckon you can't.'

By 1976, Al Green was looking for active partners to help manage the growth of his rapidly expanding board shorts business, Quiksilver, and was looking to buy out his silent partners, Claw and Brian. Another young Torquay surfer, John Law, who'd finished third in the 1974 Rip Curl Pro, was eyeing a career in the surf industry rather than the uncertain returns of pro surfing, and jumped at the chance to buy in to Quik. Claw sold his shares to John Law for $13,000, and Brian swapped his 33 per cent share for a parcel of land.

Claw, Brian, Greeny and Butch Barr had bought 48 acres of land behind Bells Beach together a few years earlier. Butch had acquired the original Bell family homestead, Addiscot, as part of the deal, but Greeny had become frustrated trying to get council permission to build on his share of the land, so he and Brian agreed to swap it for Brian's shares in Quik. The two mates formalised the transaction without the help of lawyers, and with a written agreement on a sheet of A4 paper, which has since been lost. Brian still lives on that land today. 'We argued over the value of it: the relative value between the land and the shares,' says Brian. 'It was probably a few thousand dollars and we tossed for the difference. I can't remember who won the toss or any money being exchanged.'

FLYING HIGH

Brian had other things on his mind, chief among them learning to fly the company Cessna they had bought for $26,000 in the first flush of their success. They had already begun to detect an interesting counter-cyclical quirk to their business. When the economy took a downturn, business seemed to pick up: if surfers were short of work they surfed more, and while they might forgo the big-ticket items of new cars, houses or overseas holidays, they'd console themselves with the more affordable pleasures of surfboards and wetsuits.

The major impediment to Brian embracing the jetsetting lifestyle of a successful entrepreneur was his abiding fear of flying: 'I used to get scared flying, I would shit myself, so after I got back from Bali, I was driving back from Melbourne and I pulled into Grovedale [where the old Geelong Airport was] to get flying lessons.'

Once his hands were on the levers, Brian discovered a deep love of flying. 'When you're up there you're away from all the earthly problems, you've got to focus so you don't crash and burn,' he says. 'It was a great way to de-stress, just to go for a fly.'

Brian's second solo flight, in Ballarat, wasn't quite stress-free. 'I took off and couldn't get the thing down the first time due to strong winds. I went around again and thought, I'd better get it down this time.' Despite this tentative start, he and Claw were soon flying up to Canberra and Sydney for work, or up to the Gold Coast to chase a cyclone swell, or across to Phillip Island to score some offshore waves at Flynn's Reef in a sou'-easter.

'It was a six-seater so you could fit four guys plus surfboards, usually with Claw or Greeny and various mates,' Brian says. He can still remember the plane's call sign: Delta Papa Whiskey. 'You had to land in different spots because you would get stuck with bad weather. I landed in Mallacoota and Goulburn a few times and hung out until the weather improved.'

On one occasion, Brian crash-landed in a strong cross-wind at Phillip Island, finishing up nose-first in a ditch. Claw witnessed the ill-fated landing while waiting for Brian and Speaky to arrive at the island for the Alan Oke Memorial contest, which was then part of the pro tour.

'I went out to the airstrip near Woolamai to pick them up and there was an absolutely howling sou'-west wind blowing – treacherous cross-wind conditions,' says Claw. 'We were waiting in the little shed with a couple of other blokes, including world Formula One champion Jack Brabham, who had earlier put his twin-engine Piper Comanche down on the strip and said, "It's dangerous

Above: Claw: 'Me and childhood friend Dick Milledge with my first car, an EJ Holden, in Bell Street, Torquay, parked outside Dubby Davis's milk bar, circa 1961.'

Left: Brian: 'Me and Wayne Lynch around 1967 at Jan Juc, just prior to the shortboard revolution.' *Courtesy Rip Curl archives*

Brian poised on the nose on a little Lorne Point peeler in 1965, one of the first water shots taken by renowned local photographer Barrie Sutherland.

Claw: 'Noosa,1967: a beautiful national-park line-up shot by our friend Andy Spangler, with light crowds in the transition era just before the Fantastic Plastic Machines hit. We were blessed with endless carefree days like this, surfing uncrowded waves, and talking board design and performance between sessions.' *Andy Spangler*

Claw steering a big old longboard through his bottom turn on a small day at Rincon, the inside section at Bells, while Max Innes knee-paddles over the shoulder. *Barrie Sutherland*

Brian: 'My first trip to Bali in 1973 made a deep impression on me, as I think we did on the locals.' *Dick Hoole*

Claw: 'At the ferry terminal at Gilimanuk, en route from Bali to new surf discoveries in 1975, entertaining the local kids and considering getting into the local bucket business. I think I made the right decision to stick with wetsuits.' *Dick Hoole*

Claw: 'At Grajagan in 1975 before they built the camp, with friends Dick Allcock, Tony Ball and Terry Fitzgerald. We lived on rice and veggies, caught a few fish, and I found a freshwater creek to wash off in after long surf sessions. We were always aware there were creatures in the surrounding jungle: tigers, rhinos, pythons and monkeys. We made a hasty departure after six boatloads of pirates turned up and took all our supplies.' *Dick Hoole*

Claw: 'At Nusa Lembongan in the mid-'70s with Tony Ball and his Thai girlfriend, Carmel, Terry Fitzgerald, Dick Allcock and a few other colourful characters. We were among the first to surf Shipwrecks and Lacerations in the early wave of surfers to fan out from Bali to explore the surrounding wave-rich islands.' *Dick Hoole*

Claw: 'Enjoying a clean day in the playful lefts of Point Danger.'
Courtesy Rip Curl archives

No surfer better captured Rip Curl's maverick spirit in the mid-'70s than other-worldly Gold Coast talent Michael Peterson. *Dick Hoole*

Below: Claw: 'Two of our favourite team riders from the '80s and '90s, two-time world champ Damien Hardman and the original Searcher Gary Green, doing the same thing a decade later.' *Courtesy Rip Curl archives*

Above: Claw: 'Taking the *Corsair Express*, our first Rip Curl surf exploration vessel, across Port Phillip Bay to our favourite secret left. It really whet our appetite for boats providing the means to make new surf discoveries. Brian is at the wheel and I'm riding shotgun, with Mick Spitteri, unidentified and Damien Wilson along for the ride.' *Courtesy Rip Curl archives*

DAMIEN HARDMAN & GARY GREEN · VICTORIA

RIP CURL

ROCK SOLID SURFING

Damien Hardman flew the flag for Rip Curl on tour throughout the '80s and '90s with his ruthless competitive smarts and flawless technique. *Peter Simons*

Claw: 'The original Sumbawa boat trip in 1991 that led to the Search campaign. Brian conducts a little local commerce.' *Courtesy Rip Curl archives*

Claw: 'All aboard. From left, myself, François Payot, Marty Gilchrist and Rohan "Bagman" Robinson prepare to embark on that fateful boat trip.' *Courtesy Rip Curl archives*

François and Brian in a reflective mood in the afternoon glow, as the Rip Curl management team set sail for new and distant surf spots. *Courtesy Rip Curl archives*

Claw: 'On the bridge of the *Indies Trader*, the original Indonesia surf exploration vessel, with (from left) filmmaker Sonny Miller, three-time world champ Tom Curren setting the course, Brian enjoying the moment with a cleansing ale and myself at the wheel. An epic trip in 1994 that went down in surf exploration folklore.' *Ted Grambeau*

Claw: 'An equatorial, tropical-island version of *Reservoir Dogs*. The Rip Curl Search team go ashore on a remote Indonesian island near Macaronis to get the lay of the land. From left, Frankie Oberholzer, Chris Davidson, Brian, myself, Byron Howarth, Sonny Miller and Tom Curren (playing guitar), and our cook in the foreground (with coconuts).' *Ted Grambeau*

Claw: 'Tom Curren on the big day at Fish Bowls, riding the now legendary Tommy Peterson–shaped Fireball Fish. It seems a little uncanny that Tommy's brother Michael was such an influential surfer for Rip Curl in the '70s, and that 20 years later one of Tommy's boards inspired another Rip Curl icon, Tom Curren, to rewrite performance and design parameters in such dramatic circumstances.' *Ted Grambeau*

Claw: 'Tom Curren's celebrated first encounter with Jeffreys Bay in South Africa, the meeting of two mighty influences in surfing coming together in perfect synchronicity to register a moment of sublime surfing magic.' *Ted Grambeau*

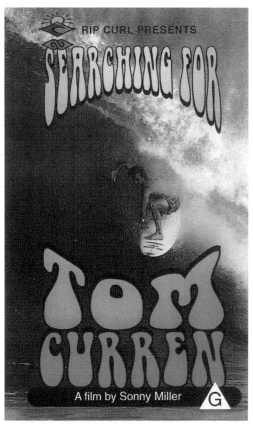

Searching for Tom Curren (1996) became one of the most celebrated surf movies of the modern era, featuring the cover shot of Curren straining to ensure his new tide watch is visible from the mouth of the barrel. *Courtesy Rip Curl archives*

Claw: 'At our informal management conference in Bali in the early '90s discussing the looming impact of Kelly Slater, the merits of the Search campaign, and the need to recruit the next generation, with (from left) François, Fred Basse, Brian, Neil Campbell, unidentified and Grant Forbes.' *Courtesy Rip Curl archives*

A very young Mick Fanning straight out of school and onto the Search, at the helm on a Maldivian boat trip, and en route to a decorated career with Rip Curl. *Ted Grambeau*

François Payot indulges in a little field research during a floating management meeting in the Mentawais. *Geni/Addiction*

Brian: 'Enjoying my annual trip to Galena, Canada, heliskiing deep in the woods.' *Mike Welch*

Samala Singer flying, in Chamonix, France, where she worked as an instructor and ski model in the mid-'90s. *Mat Lingren*

Dan Warbrick enjoying the steeps. He is now an accomplished photographer, and still shoots pictures for Rip Curl. *Kathy Brown*

The perks of the job: marketing chairman Neil Ridgway and creative director James Taylor deeply immersed in field research. *Courtesy Rip Curl archives*

Ted Grambeau's pioneering trip to Iceland yielded some of the most evocative wetsuit advertising images in history. *Ted Grambeau*

Mick Fanning scores a mysto wedging right barrel in Central America, during the *Missing* movie shoot.
Ted Grambeau

Mick prepares for the transition from tour competitor to full-time Searcher. Look closely at the baggage trolley, featuring a photo of Mick's Jeffreys Bay nemesis.
Ted Grambeau

Scenes from the Search: Mick and Matt 'Wilko' Wilkinson getting to know the locals on the road in Africa.
Ted Grambeau

Still dropping in at 70: Brian enjoys a recent Indonesian boat trip at Greenbush, Sumatra. *Eric Sonderquist*

Claw on assignment at Las Leñas, Argentina, testing the latest mountainwear range. *Courtesy Rip Curl archives*

What the Search is all about: Wilko, Gabriel Medina and Mason Ho clap eyes on a new surf spot for the first time.
Ted Grambeau

Rip Curl surf exploration vessel *Quest* stumbles on another alluring line-up in Indonesia. *Courtesy Rip Curl archives*

Born at Bells: the original line-up that inspired the birth of Rip Curl. From bouncing along the old clifftop dirt track, the Search has expanded to the far reaches of the surfable world.
Steve Ryan

today." . . . The initial landing looked good, then all of a sudden the plane veered violently to the right of the grass strip and into a large irrigation ditch, the plane coming to rest on its nose and the propeller ploughing the field.'

As they ran across to the stricken plane to see if its occupants were okay, the passenger door was flung open. 'Speaky came falling out only to be suspended in his seatbelt, hanging off the ground. The boys were concerned by this, but I could see they were going to be fine because Speaky was laughing his guts out,' says Claw. A subsequent investigation found the nose-wheel had seized, making steering on the ground impossible.

There were other trappings of success: a GT Falcon and a 16-foot motorboat they dubbed the *Corsair Express*, purchased to enable runs to the then semi-secret wave at the mouth of Port Phillip Bay. The Cessna also facilitated their other great extravagance, increasingly regular trips to Mount Buller to indulge their love of riding water in its frozen form.

THE ALPINE EXPERIENCE

Brian had been walking down to Winki Pop for a surf in 1970 when a friend, Randall Hawkins, a surfboard-builder from Frankston, called out, 'Do you want to go to Mount Buller?'

Brian's reply was quick and simple: 'Sure.'

'There's that opportunism again,' Brian says, pinpointing what he says is one of the defining traits of his career, a readiness to jump through windows of opportunity: Do you want to start a surf shop? Do you want to make surfboards? Make wetsuits? Sponsor the Bells Easter Rally? Go to Bali? Expand the business into the US, Japan, Bali, Europe, South America?

Buller was a recreational opportunity rather than a business one, but it has come to dominate Brian's life almost as much as the surf company he co-founded. He went up to Buller in the winter of 1970 with Randall and slept on the floor of the Monash Uni lodge. He loved the alpine lifestyle, and its parallels to the surf and beach scene. Within a year or two, Claw, Greeny and half the surfers in Torquay were regularly heading up to Mount Buller every time there was a decent dump, with Brian often flying into a little airstrip at the nearby town of Merrijig to reduce travel time.

By 1976, Claw and Brian were spending most of their winters at Mount Buller even as the business experienced rapid growth. 'Now that we had expanded our horizons the cost of our searching, thrill-seeking lifestyle was becoming hard to fund, so many of our crew looked for the cushy and prestigious jobs around the mountain,' says Claw. 'The most attractive of these were ski patrol or ski school.' It probably says much about the founders' contrasting characters that Claw chose the uncertain returns but fun, social lifestyle of a ski instructor while Brian opted for the regular income but sometimes gritty realities of the ski patrol.

'Ski patrol had the advantage of a regular salary whereas the ski school was based more on how many hours you actually worked, and where you stood in the ski-instructor pecking order,' says Claw. 'In those days it took years to get anywhere near the top bracket, which was populated with overseas experts, normally Austrians and French with some Americans. All the same, the ski-instructor community and lifestyle were a lot of fun and absolutely crazy. Every night at Buller there was a vigorous competition between the young hotshot Austrians and the suave Frogs for the affections of any girls daring enough to be out for the night.'

After their separation, Brian and Jenny had reunited and had a second daughter, Naomi, and soon after a son, Doji. 'I had a wife and kids, and as they grew up I couldn't afford to take them skiing.

I needed a lurk. Ski patrol paid a wage, an allowance for ski equipment and free parking on the mountain,' says Brian. 'It was great for the kids . . . They gained a hell of a lot of self-confidence when they realised they knew the mountain better than most adults and could ski as well as half of them.'

For 25 years, Brian served as part of Buller's professional ski patrol team, serving under its leader and his good friend Speaky. 'Brian would call me boss and people would look at me funny and go, "How can you be his boss? Isn't he the boss?"' Speaky recalls with a laugh.

Even now, 16 years after he retired from ski patrol, Brian still spends most of the winter at Buller, in a modern apartment next door to similar ones owned by Claw, the Perry family and Greeny. On the day I arrive in the late afternoon of a perfect winter day, after a week of the season's best snowfalls, Brian has spent the day skiing with Samala and Doji, and five of his grandchildren. Samala is a former national ski champion and the next generation look like continuing the family snow obsession. Even the youngest of Brian's grandchildren, Misty, at age four, could keep up with him on the slopes, he says.

Over the next several days, in sticky, windy, grey conditions, blighted by consistent drizzle, I have trouble keeping up with Brian myself, even though he has over 20 years on me and had a knee reconstruction 18 months before. If he gets more than 30 or 40 metres in front of me I can't see him or much else in the near-white-out conditions. And not knowing the mountain, should I lose him I suspect I will soon become lost in the howling gale. And then I'll be needing the ski patrol.

'Sorry if I'm slowing you down,' I offer apologetically when I catch up to him at the bottom of Shaky Knee's chairlift. I'm an intermittent skier, with maybe a dozen weeks under my belt over the past 30 years, rather than Brian's 50-odd winters in the northern and southern hemispheres, and my legs are burning after a few runs in the slushy conditions.

'No worries,' he says. 'It might be a different story if it was a powder day. There's no friends on a powder day.'

On the most miserable of my days at Buller, with 80 milli-metres of rain washing away much of the previous week's falls and the gale still whipping the mountain, I'm not sure I want to leave the warm comfort of the apartment at all. But even though he's here for the season, Brian's keen to go out for the first lift at 8.30 am, as he is every day. 'What else are we going to do?' he says. 'If you think about it, and um and ah, you'll talk yourself out of it. It's like going for a surf – you're always glad you went out.'

Brian has rescued plenty of people who've become lost and injured on the mountain, and he's been first on the scene of the occasional fatality. He says his experiences on the ski patrol have served as a healthy counterbalance to the challenges of the business world, where issues can feel monumental but are rarely life-threatening. Here he's just one of the boys, and there's an impressive spirit of camaraderie among the ski patrollers.

Brian recalls discovering the body of his mate Mick Thulke, a liftie who failed to report to work one morning. Brian skied to the bottom of the popular Federation run but was surprised to not find Mick at his regular post. 'I asked the guy at the top where [Mick] was, and he said he'd skied down ages ago,' says Brian. Brian went looking for his friend and found him off-piste among some trees, where he'd suffered a fatal head injury. 'He'd slipped down quite a long way,' says Brian matter-of-factly. The loss of one of their own sent shock waves through the close-knit Buller community.

A kind of black humour helps ski patrollers deal with the grizzly reality of their work. 'Don [Morgan] had a job where this bloke had skied into a tree. A really keen young patroller came along and they go, "What can we do to help?" And Don turns around and goes, "Dig a fucking hole." When there's a situation like that your emotions just turn off,' says Brian.

For most of his business career, Brian has spent two to three months each year at Buller, and most northern winters skiing in Chamonix, France, where he also owns a house. His children went to the tiny primary school at Buller when it only had seven students, and his second-eldest Naomi began her primary schooling in Chamonix, where only French was spoken.

Heliskiing in Canada has also become an annual ritual. 'Now we go to the same place with the same group of skiers and snowboarders from Buller and Thredbo, 30 people altogether, and that's incredible,' says Brian. 'You ski untracked powder the whole time. And we've got to know the guides there, they've become close friends. It's very physical and quite demanding. I'm not sure how many more years I'll be able to do it with my new metal knee.'

In our time at Buller I also accompany Brian to the annual ski patrol dinner at the Austrian-themed Grimus Lodge and restaurant, presided over by the gregarious Austrian proprietor Hans Grimus. Hans has been in Buller for over 50 years, having helped construct some of the first chairlifts on the mountain, and his Hotel Pension Grimus has been awarded Australia's best ski hotel eight times. Hans is dispensing schnapps amid the ornate carved wooden décor of his celebrated restaurant as keenly as ever, and the ski patrollers are his most beloved clientele. Sadly, a year later Hans died at the age of 78 after a protracted illness, leaving a gaping void in the Buller community. But on this evening, he is in great form despite his ill-health.

There's an elaborate ritual with incantations in German for every shot of schnapps thrown down, and the tales of wild times on the mountain in the early days are soon flowing: night-skiing by moonlight, facilitated by a borrowed snowmobile; herbal cigarettes ignited with flares when no one thought to bring matches on back-country runs; the patroller from the Western Districts farm arriving each season with a suitcase full of hallucinogenic mushrooms to dispense to anyone who was game.

This is not to cast aspersions on the professionalism and dedication of the ski patrollers today, but it's fair to say the same joie de vivre that gripped the old Boot Hill crew and attracted Brian and Claw to Torquay was just as alive in the thrillseekers of Buller.

PRO SURFING GOES GLOBAL

The Rip Curl Pro grew rapidly in its first few years. From $2500 prize money in 1973, it more than doubled in two years, offering $6000 prize money in the 1975 event co-sponsored by Surf Blanks, Midget Farrelly's surfboard blank business in Brookvale. In 1976 the prize jumped to $10,000, again co-sponsored by Surf Blanks and with Quiksilver now on board. 'Midget had won the very first world championship at Manly in 1964 and it was fitting that he was there for the birth of pro surfing in Australia as a sponsor, supporting our vision for the Rip Curl Pro,' says Claw.

The annual Bells event was starting to attract a more international field, drawn by the prospect of prize money at both the Rip Curl Pro and the Coke Surfabout, and the tantalising potential for an actual career in pro surfing. 'It seemed every year the shop was bigger, the contest infrastructure was bigger,' says Shaun Tomson, South Africa's top pro surfer of the day. 'Every year we used to love to go to Bells. It was so much fun surfing Winki Pop and Bells.'

Shaun had bought into the pro surfing dream, and had first been in Torquay as the youngest competitor at the 1970 world titles when he was just 14. By '75 he was trying life as a touring pro. He'd befriended Wollongong surfer and shaper Phil Byrne in Hawaii, and Phil was tight with the Rip Curl crew. 'He said to me, "There's this little company called Rip Curl and maybe I can persuade them to give you a free wetsuit," recalls Shaun. 'I went down there and met Claw and Brian and Sparrow. He measured me up and made me the first custom suit I'd ever had.'

The burgeoning scene of surf commerce, and Australia's loose and free-spirited surf culture, caught Shaun's imagination. 'Claw, Sing Ding, Sparrow, Greeny, Lawro, Boong – I was fascinated with the names. We'd surf all day and go to the pub and everyone would go to one person's house after the pub closed . . . We all surfed together, partied together, it was super pure,' says Shaun. 'Claw was such a stoked dude . . . He'd always rub his hands together and jump up and down. Singer was more analytical and standoffish.'

Shaun was struck by the cosy relationship between the two local surf brands. 'Quiksilver only made board shorts and Rip Curl only made wetsuits. There was such a friendship between these two brands because they were nothing then,' says Shaun. 'It was good to be there at the birth of the brands [which] paralleled the growth of pro surfing. They were both very focused on athlete sponsorship and involvement . . . They supported the surfers. They saw a simple equation: great surfers equal great sales.'

Shaun took the leap to the pro tour when it launched in 1976, becoming pro surfing's second official world champion in '77. 'My first Bells event was a revelation,' he says. 'Surfing in South Africa was starting to have a mainstream impact. We had the Gunston 500, but Australia had such a surf-educated population. When I got there, people knew about me. At home no one had even heard of me. I'd never seen a picture of me in a surfing magazine. I got off a plane in Perth and bought *Surfing World* and there were six pictures of me ... You realise surfing has this penetration of the culture.'

Tom Carroll had his first experience of Torquay and its emerging surf industry around the same time, journeying down for Easter with the Narrabeen crew in 1976 as a wide-eyed 14-year-old. 'I was such a grom. I was hanging out with Fatty Al [future Association of Surfing Professionals tour manager Al Hunt] and a few of the Narrabeen guys,' recalls Tom. He'd been hooked up with Rip Curl by his surfboard shaper, Narrabeen's Col Smith. 'I was just stoked to have one of their suits because all the best guys were in them,' says Tom.

Rip Curl and Quiksilver were still next-door neighbours on the eastern side of Geelong Road, and pro surfers would regularly walk from one premises to the other to collect their sponsored product. 'Sparrow measured me up and got me into a sharkskin long-sleeved spring suit with a front zip,' recalls Tom. 'Then Quiksilver offered me a clothing deal and I thought I was in, accepted by the club.'

Torquay's two home-grown surf brands were so cosy in these early days that Christmas parties were often an all-in affair. 'The Christmas parties in the old days were classic. Most of the people working there were women involved in the production of wetsuits. With the office and factory there were maybe about 50 people total,' says Ray Thomas. 'The ladies had voted in a rule that there were no partners, which meant they could let their hair down without being constrained by their partners or husbands. Everyone would get totally smashed and do some crazy stuff and usually Quiksilver had their party on the same night, so it was a big night in Torquay, with afterparties a mix of both companies.'

John Pawson was a top local surfer and son of the local publican, who tragically drowned surfing at Bells Beach in 1984. In a 1978 interview with John Witzig's *Sea Notes* magazine he was upbeat about the impact of the surf industry on the town. 'First of all, Torquay is a surfing town and all of those people, they came to Torquay to surf . . . before they ever considered setting up businesses,' said John. 'I don't know if they're getting rich but they're maintaining a lifestyle that's fantastic. Being able to travel two or three times a year, being able to hit the snow for the winter – I mean lots of them hit the snow for all the winter – and to go to Hawaii in the summer, and to be able to increase your business as well, it's just really good I reckon.'

THE SURFBOARD FACTORY

Claw had virtually given up shaping by '71 as the wetsuit business grew, and he shaped only the occasional board through to about '75. But surfboards had been Rip Curl's first product, and the surfboard factory remained the heart and soul of the business for many years.

Russell Graham grew up at Narrabeen and did his surfboard apprenticeship under the exacting tutelage of Midget Farrelly in Brookvale. In '74 he was offered a job glassing for Rip Curl and made the move south to Torquay.

'I got on well with Midget. I just followed what he did – I still do things the same way,' says Russ, who has a remarkable surfboard collection and an exhaustive knowledge of the Australian surfboard industry. 'Midget always drummed into me [that] it doesn't take much more effort to get it right . . . Ray Richards would come down from Newcastle on a Friday to pick up boards, and if they weren't polished right I'd have to fix them up and drive them up on Saturday.'

Russ was given free rein to run the Curl's surfboard program. He found the cold weather tough, but the consistently high-quality,

93

uncrowded surf soon won him over. 'After 12 months I went, "This is unbelievable."' He was soon well and truly embedded in the Rip Curl family; his wife, Barb, was one of Rip Curl's first wetsuit gluers.

His long-time collaborator at the factory was local shaper Doug Rogers. Doug grew up in Lorne, the son and grandson of fishermen, before the surfing bug sabotaged any prospect of him following in the family trade. Doug bought his first surfboard from Brian Singer and experienced his skill as a surfboard salesman firsthand. 'Brian was the consummate surfboard salesman. He said to me, "I've seen you surf, you're pretty handy. I've got a board that would really suit you,"' recalls Doug. 'I ended up buying this board from him but I didn't like it that much, so I decided I was going to make a board.'

Doug took to hanging around the old bakery to observe the manufacturing process, until Claw offered to sell him the materials he needed to make his own boards: blank, fibreglass cloth and resin. 'He said, "If you buy your stuff from us you can be my apprentice,"' recalls Doug. 'We were still in high school. We thought that we were big time: "We're apprentices to Rip Curl."'

Doug worked for Fred Pyke before opening the first surf shop on Geelong Road. In '75 he started doing some sanding for Russ and eventually shaped full-time at Rip Curl. 'One thing we always prided ourselves on: we'd never let a board out with anything wrong,' says Doug. 'The surfboard factory was the place to work because you had the flexibility of hours and we had plenty of fun. Crew from work would come down the back to de-stress.'

Pat Morgan, the old mate of Claw's from Brighton days, joined the factory in '76 and went on to a long career at Rip Curl. Pat had been running his own surfboard business for 10 years and was highly respected in the industry. Pat Morgan Surfboards, set up in an old butcher's shop just around the corner from Rip

Curl's old bakery, had been a model of efficiency, with a work ethic somewhat lacking in the less disciplined businesses around him. A non-drinker, Pat had married his schoolteacher girlfriend, Elaine (they are still together today), bought a block of land and built a house while the hippie era of the '60s and early '70s played out around him.

Pat had befriended the winner of the 1970 world titles, Rolf Aurness, and his father, star of the TV series *Gunsmoke*, James Arness. (Rolf had added a 'u' to his surname to distance himself from his father's celebrity.) '[James] said, "All the land behind Bells Beach and Torquay, I've seen what happened in California, you should buy some of this land." So, we did. That all came from James Arness.' Though few people got rich from surfboards, Pat would do very well out of land development in the decades ahead and had good reason to thank James for his prescience.

Pat was eventually drawn to the greater security of joining the Rip Curl empire. 'The Whitlam Government came in and they increased superannuation, and I worked out that the guys working for me were making the same money as me,' Pat says. 'I'd made 10,000 boards in 10 years, not making a lot of money, working seven days a week, and our kids were growing up. I rang Brian Singer and said how much I wanted to work for them. He rang back in 15 minutes and said yes. When I went to work for them they were getting rid of the competition as well.'

Pat had also worked in a furniture factory where they pumped out 40 bedroom suites in a week, so he knew about production efficiencies and ushered in a more professional approach to Rip Curl's surfboard program. 'Paddy started to get us a bit organised. He was a small talker but a big thinker,' says Doug Rogers. 'He had models in the '60s with a little logo for each one. Pat joined everything together and got it moving in parallel.'

'Pat was a real moderator. You had to put the logos in the same place on every board. At first I thought, I don't like this, then I thought, hang on, this works,' says Russ.

At the height of summer, they were doing 25 boards a week, maybe half that in winter. Russ recalls the parade of great shapers who came through the factory, particularly at Easter: Bob McTavish, Randy Rarick, Michael Peterson, Terry Fitzgerald, Ted Spencer, Mike Cundith, Ed Angulo. 'We got to meet a lot of really great overseas shapers, it was fantastic,' says Russ.

'There were always people coming in. I don't know how Russ got his work done. I think surfboard factories have always been like that, they've always been a meeting place,' says Doug. 'Monday to Friday was just flat knacker, and then I'd come in and work in the store on Saturdays because the shop was absolutely going gangbusters.'

Later, by the mid-'90s, as the business continued to grow, the decision was made to outsource surfboard production. 'The management of running surfboards is bloody hard. There's no money in it unless you're the shaper running your own business,' says Brian. Russ bought the old Watercooled factory up the road and continued making surfboards under licence for Rip Curl. His son Cory has continued in the family trade and Russ still glasses his son's boards today.

The surfboard factory trained up a lot of people who still work in the industry, and though rising costs and cheap Asian imports have made local surfboard production unviable for Rip Curl, Doug and Russ have nothing but fond memories of their time there.

'You didn't get a job at Rip Curl if you couldn't surf. Everyone was a surfer, everyone was keen. We all made a reasonable living out of it,' says Russ.

'And we always had surf time,' says Doug. 'We'd get free custom wetsuits. We were really looked after.'

'Brian and Claw have been fantastic, they've set my life up,' says Russ.

BACKDOOR MAGAZINE

Somehow, during Rip Curl's rapid growth, Claw and Brian found time to launch their own surfing magazine, *Backdoor*, to provide a southern alternative to the Sydney-centric surf media of the day.

'To some degree, [*Tracks*] was a Sydney surfing establishment view of surfing,' says Claw. 'That was a good thing, [but it presented] an opportunity for us to have a point of difference.'

Backdoor emerged from the creative soup of the Torquay surf industry in the mid-'70s, five years after *Tracks* had captured the zeitgeist with its lo-fi, newsprint, countercultural sensibilities. *Backdoor* was cut from similar cloth, black-and-white newsprint with a vaguely hippie aesthetic, but approached surfing culture from a southern coastal perspective. Central to the enterprise was an eager young journalist and surfer named Michael Gordon, son of a legendary newspaperman, Harry Gordon, and destined for an illustrious career as one of the country's top political reporters. Also in on the scheme were filmmakers and photographers Dick Hoole and Jack McCoy.

'It might have been at the Rip Curl Pro. All of a sudden we had these five people – someone's got a crazy idea, let's have a go at it,' says Claw. 'It might have been one of my crazy ideas. I might have picked it up from Dick or Jack or Michael.'

Whoever's idea it was, Michael was the driving force, the editor and linchpin of the operation. 'Michael was very professional and very astute, really driven, and wanted to spread his wings a little bit creatively. He had very high standards set by his dad and wanted to break out of the straight career in his dad's slipstream,' says Claw. 'We didn't know what we were doing but we had a hell of a lot of fun doing it for three or four years. I guess the ambition was to do 12 monthly editions but we were a bit more sporadic.'

These were the days of typesetting on bromides with a wax adhesive backing laid out on artboards – quaint and archaic by today's digital standards. 'I was hands-on throughout. We used to stick it down with wax. I was quite accurate at setting but we could all cut and paste,' says Claw.

Claw and Brian also saw value in having an outlet for their own team trips and the ability to piggyback projects on the magazine. 'It was a triple banger,' says Claw. 'We could provide Rip Curl surfers for Dick and Jack's movies, or the material would be presented to other people doing surf films, some could be used for *Backdoor*, and some for Rip Curl use. You got a number of uses from a trip up to the North Coast of New South Wales or Western Australia or Indonesia. They were some of my best times going on photo shoots.'

The surfer on the cover of the first issue of *Backdoor* was Rabbit Bartholomew, squatted casually in a Burleigh barrel, who went on the win the world title in 1978. 'Rabbit personified the Australian surfing spirit, he was a fierce competitor and a great character,' says Claw. 'He also represented our brand with distinction, and was instrumental in helping us with our assault on the USA,' adds Brian.

Jack McCoy also ran the Summer House restaurant in Torquay, which became the focal point of a riotous social scene. 'Jack and Tony Squirrel had the Summer House, quite healthy Australian coastal cuisine. It was just the place to be,' says Claw. 'The social atmosphere was spectacular, such an array of freewheeling, loose characters. The longer you stayed the more they misbehaved.'

Eventually, with the other careers of its creators demanding more time, *Backdoor* ran its course and printed its last issue in 1978, but it remains a fondly remembered slice of Victorian surfing history. 'I think everyone just lost interest a little bit – all the careers were taking off in different directions,' says Claw. 'Michael was pulled away to follow his own career, Dick went off to Byron Bay.' Jack McCoy, of course, became one of the most prolific and celebrated surf filmmakers of the modern era.

Michael Gordon went on to a decorated career as the chief political correspondent for Fairfax Media and, sadly, died of a heart attack during an ocean swim soon after his retirement, in February 2018. His funeral service was a veritable who's who of the Australian political and media landscape. 'Michael was clearly an outstanding journalist, which was evident at his funeral service – hundreds were there. It was just eulogy after eulogy. The first was from [former Prime Minister] Paul Keating. I was quite staggered,' says Claw. 'Many of his work colleagues brought up his love of surfing.'

SURFING USA

While Rip Curl's founders were becoming accustomed to the good life, their accountant Butch Barr had to sound the alarm bells, most dramatically in an urgent fire sale while they were off climbing mountains or heliskiing or surfing in exotic locales. When they returned, they realised Butch had sold their extravagant playthings to pay workers.

'We didn't have the cash to pay the wages,' says Brian. 'He'd say, "We're bankrupt," and we'd say, "No, no, no, we're not," and keep struggling along.'

Brian took the abrupt loss of his new toys in his stride. 'It was fun, but it was about that time I realised I wasn't flying enough each year to stay safe, and [they weren't] reliable without instrument rating,' says Brian.

One of the reasons for the critical cashflow issues was Rip Curl's bold expansion into the US. They were a little slower out of the blocks than their neighbours at Quiksilver, who had granted the US licence to champion Hawaiian surfer Jeff Hakman and his business-graduate buddy Bob McKnight in 1976. Hakman had won the Rip Curl Pro that year, and had been openly badgering Greeny for Quiksilver's US licence. Greeny famously challenged Hakman to eat a paper doily on the table in front of them to prove his commitment. Hakman obliged and, true to his word, Greeny granted him the licence. The story has gone down in surf industry folklore. 'I know it's true because I saw it, and . . . it wasn't just one of those little doilies,' says Brian. 'It was in Maxwell's Restaurant in Bell Street, owned by an old Torquay surfer named Max Innes. I was at a table adjacent to them and it got quite noisy. It took quite a while – he ate a bit then had to gulp down some water, then ate a bit more.'

The old bonhomie was still alive and well between Torquay's twin surf brands and, initially at least, the Quik crew in the US were a huge help to their compatriots. Quiksilver became Rip Curl's distributor in the world's largest surfing market, an arrangement that would seem unthinkable today.

Brian remembered how well their first ad in *Surfing World* back in 1969 had opened doors when he'd started calling on surf shops with their first wetsuits. 'So we had an advertisement in [US] *Surfer* magazine for four to six months before going over there,' says Brian. 'We didn't have any address on it but we were getting mail addressed to Rip Curl, Torquay, so we knew there was interest.'

Brian travelled to the US in 1977 and Jeff Hakman took him around to all of Quiksilver's biggest accounts. 'We travelled for a couple of weeks meeting all the retailers. There were 17 of them. They were very O'Neill-focused at that point, but we got orders from all of them and came back and got them made,' says Brian.

But Quiksilver was soon flat out meeting demand for its own products in the US and the cosy cooperation broke down. 'At some point, before any wetsuits were actually delivered, Quiksilver decided, we're not going to be your distributor anymore,' recalls Brian. Very quickly, Rip Curl had to find its own office and staff to keep the momentum going.

The man they found to head up their US operations was steeped in Californian surfing history. Don Craig was a well-known second-generation surfer who'd ridden for the prestigious Bing and Weber surf teams and whose father Doug was a founding member of the famed San Onofre Surfing Club. 'We found Don Craig, used his office in Newport Beach, got a telephone. It might have been the Quiksilver guys who introduced me to Don,' says Brian.

It was. Don had been working for an architect in Newport when he was approached by his friend Bob McKnight to become a sales rep for Quiksilver on a commission deal. Don thought it sounded too speculative to give up his day job, so he tried doing both.

'I tried to go out and sell at four in the afternoon but store owners were tired. I said, "I don't feel I can do it justice." I had a wife and kids at the time. It didn't feel secure enough,' says Don. 'They said, "Hang in there, we've got these guys who are our next-door neighbours in Torquay coming over too."'

When Claw and Brian next came to California, Bob introduced them to Don, hoping they could provide the young sales rep with a livelihood. Instead, Don ended up taking up the Rip Curl job with the promise of a regular wage. He went half-time with Rip Curl and half-time with the architect. 'We were like sister companies,' says Don. 'We set up a warehouse in Costa Mesa. We had a really fun relationship and it was great working together.'

'We wanted to follow our customers around the world. It was expensive exporting wetsuits to the USA due to freight and customs.

It was just an obvious move to set up an office on the West Coast,' says Brian. 'Claw and I had driven around California and had thought about Santa Barbara, because it reminded us of Torquay. But we figured Orange County had better access to staff, and the surf industry was all down that way and the magazines were there.'

Don's home became a halfway house for visiting Rip Curl surfers and staff. 'In the first two years, for 18 months of it I had someone from Rip Curl staying with me,' says Don. 'I got to know Wayne Lynch and Terry Fitzgerald, Derek Hynd, Steve Wilson, Butch and Chris Barr – they were all just great people. We had that common bond of surfing and they had a really good product.'

The timing was good. Australian surfing had risen as a world power and a source of innovation ever since the shortboard revolution of the late '60s. Steve Pezman was editor of *Surfer* magazine at the time and had witnessed the arrival of the Aussie brands firsthand.

'Before that, California saw itself as the most advanced surf culture. By the early '70s Australia had risen up the pecking order and was the equal of California . . . Everything started to swing to Australia influencing the mainstream trends within surfing,' says Steve. 'They moved into the market up here . . . and were accepted right away as a valid brand. Having a functional product as your base gives you validity. The thing with wetsuits is you have to be a surfer to need one.'

Bob Mignona was the advertising manager at *Surfer*'s arch rival, *Surfing* magazine, and he was desperate to try to land the business of this new Aussie start-up. 'When Quiksilver got here I knew McKnight, and I knew Jeff [Hakman]. I'd met Jeff in Hawaii, and they came to me to run all their advertising in *Surfing* magazine,' says Bob. 'We were really proud of the fact that they ran their first ads with us.'

Surfing was seen as the more youth-focused magazine, which had embraced the new pro era and its emerging heroes. But Claw felt an attachment to *Surfer* magazine, which he'd grown up reading as a portal to US surf culture. 'Claw was clearly a *Surfer* mag fan. My suspicion was he felt he could make an impact without having to compete with Quiksilver in our mag,' says Bob Mignona. He tried in vain to get Rip Curl's ad business but, even so, he warmed to these rough-hewn Aussies and their informal ways.

'Claw was incredibly knowledgeable about the sport. He was super connected to the top surfers,' says Bob. 'He had an incredible surfing pedigree, he had all the credentials of a Jack Shipley kind of guy [the Lightning Bolt co-founder and top contest judge of the day]. Jack knew everything about everyone. Brian was like a Harvard MBA. He was astute, he was really smart and when he got serious he got intensely serious, at times. If you start talking business he zooms right in. He was really intent on learning the craft of being a chief executive.'

After a year, it was decided Rip Curl needed a more prominent position and Don chose the old Del Cannon surf shop in San Clemente, close to one of Southern California's premier surf spots, Trestles Beach. 'There was still resin on the walls and floors,' says Don. 'I picked the location . . . Everybody had to park right there to go to Trestles.' The bold move angered the owners of some long-time local brands, who agitated for retailers to ban the upstart Aussies.

There was some seriously established competition to contend with, in the form of O'Neill and Body Glove. Don's strategy was simple. 'Customer service was a key thing for me,' he says. 'I learnt how to repair wetsuits. The knees would always wear out. I learnt how to cut out football-shaped patches and took the wetsuits to a shoe repair shop, and once he had enough he'd spend a day doing them. O'Neill took six weeks to get a repair back. I got it down to two weeks. I killed most of the retailers with customer service. I carried zippers with me. A guy comes into a shop while I'm there and goes, "My zipper just broke." I said, "Bring it in, I'll fix it for you." I knew I had a customer for life, and he'd go and tell his friends. Christmas Eve I'm dropping off wetsuits all the way down the coast. O'Neill ended up hiring more people in the area. They set up their own repair and distribution centre because I was basically outservicing them.'

Suits were still manufactured in Torquay and shipped to the US, but Don had the local knowledge to understand the nuances of different surf regions. 'All the suits coming from overseas, we'd unpack the boxes and then ship them out to the accounts,' says Don. 'The Santa Barbara guys wanted dark-coloured wetsuits, the South Bay surfers wanted colourful suits.'

Don reckons one of their big breakthroughs was what they termed 'dual density' wetsuits, featuring 3 millimetres of neoprene in the torso for warmth and 2 millimetres in the arms and shoulders for ease of paddling. Brian reckons the idea came from a grommet in a surf shop during a US East Coast sales run. 'Some young kid in the surf shop said, "Why don't you make the arms out of 2 millimetres to make it easier to paddle?"' recalls Brian. 'And I just went, dur! And that's how it started. In other words, listen to the customer.'

THE SHOP GROM

Sam George was an amped young Central California surfer who had seen Rip Curl's first ads in *Surfer* magazine, and when he walked into the Hobie surf shop and clapped eyes on one of the suits for the first time he had to have one. 'We were like, oh my god, here are these wetsuits,' says Sam. 'They made coloured wetsuits, which were forbidden in Santa Barbara. I took a lot of shit.'

Sam became an enthusiastic champion of the brand. 'I convinced the shop I worked for to carry Rip Curl wetsuits,' he says. 'That was how I got connected with Rip Curl. I got a custom suit. We were some of the earliest guys to start wearing Rip Curl and introducing them to a lot of areas outside Orange County.'

By 1979, Sam was the Western Surfing Association men's champion and wrote a polite letter to Rip Curl head office in Torquay, asking if he qualified for a start in the trials for the Rip Curl Pro. Before he'd even got a reply, he was on a plane to Australia for a six-week trip with $100 to his name, determined to at least see the famed Burleigh Heads and Bells Beach for himself. He lobbed at the Stubbies Classic on the Gold Coast without a spot in the event, just to soak up the pro-tour vibe. When the Stubbies finished, as surfers piled into vans or headed to the airport and travelled 2000 kilometres south, Sam stood by the side of the Gold Coast Highway with his surfboard and backpack and stuck out his thumb. A yellow Kingswood station wagon pulled over, and a friendly fellow with a Beatle mop top, Coke-bottle glasses and a grey tooth urged him to get in.

The driver was Claw. He offered the young American a lift to Torquay with one condition. 'He said, "We'll give you a lift, but there's a catch. We're servicing all of our Rip Curl accounts from Noosa to Bells." I got a tour of Australia that you could never get otherwise. We drove up to Noosa and all the way back and we stopped at all the surf shops,' says Sam.

Sam recalls having dinner with legendary surf adventurer Peter Troy on the Sunshine Coast, having thrilled to Troy's travel stories in surfing magazines for years. 'We didn't stay at hotels, we stayed at people's houses,' he says. He met a rollcall of significant shapers and surf shop owners all along the east coast. Sam rattles off the names: Hayden Kenny, Bob Cooper, Mike Davis, the Byrne brothers. 'And I just soaked in the stories.'

When they got to Bells, Sam managed to score some work in the Rip Curl store, given his retail experience back home. Claw let Sam sleep in the Kingswood, which had finally given up the ghost and was broken down in the front yard of Claw's home. 'After he had gone to work and the kids had gone to school, I would sneak into the house and have a shower,' says Sam. 'One day – it must have been school holidays – I got out of the shower and Claw's dad was there and he goes, "Who are you?" And Claw's daughter Tanya, who was really little, goes, "Don't you know? That's the man who sleeps in Daddy's car."'

Sam got into the trials and made it all the way to the final, his best result on tour, and immediately warmed to Torquay's rural environs. 'I immediately identified with it because it was like home, but the waves were better and the water was warmer,' says Sam. 'It was my surf dream way more than the Gold Coast. I identified with the topography. Being associated with Rip Curl made me feel like I belonged. Walking down those steps and hearing the music and the commentary – I don't think there's anything like that in pro surfing.'

And he could feel the buzz of the emerging centre of surf commerce. 'There was a feeling there that something was happening. It was all new,' says Sam. 'There were characters everywhere – Sparrow, Simon Buttonshaw. I got to stay at Pat Morgan's house behind Bells and talk about the keel fins. He let me ride one of them. I rode an eight-foot Pat Morgan keel fin at Bells. And this was all because of Claw. That drive with Claw was influential on my life as a surfer. Why did he pick me up? I think a lot of Rip Curl's soul is Doug Warbrick. There was something about Claw's passion.'

THE COMING OF CURREN

Rip Curl was still determined to crack the US market as Quiksilver had. But as the manufacturer of an essential piece of surfing equipment, the wetsuit, they were never going to sell to the inland masses as Quiksilver could with board shorts.

The prospects of making it in the US were given a major boost when Claw spotted and eventually signed a dazzling young talent from Santa Barbara, destined to raise Californian surfing out of its black-wetsuited, anti-contest, localised doldrums and elevate it back into a global surfing superpower. But the stunning natural talent and lofty ambitions of US surfing's next great hope were in stark contrast to his shy, retiring demeanour.

'I first met Claw at the Channel Island shop. He was on a road trip with Critta Byrne and Terry Fitzgerald,' says Tom Curren. 'They had wetsuits they were giving away and they gave me one . . . It was a jacket wetsuit, great for Santa Barbara,' he jokes in his deadpan manner.

For a young kid rising up through the amateur ranks, dreaming of a career as a professional surfer, the materialisation of this Australian surf brand proprietor and two sponsored team riders in his home town in the late '70s was a powerful omen.

'I was just starting out with the Channel Island team,' says Tom. 'Critta and Terry Fitzgerald I knew from my studies at surf movie high school. I knew their work.' He may have been starstruck by the Aussie pros, but the company founder also impressed with his mysterious ways. 'He was and still is an energetic, talkative fellow. He exhibits this unique body language,' says Tom.

Claw's role as talent scout had rarely been as important as when he got wind of this emerging wunderkind. 'I think we spotted Tom at 13 . . . People around the amateur surfing scene, particularly in California, and the magazines and photographers, were all talking

107

about him. We kept hearing these stories. It was almost like he was the messiah,' says Claw.

Of course, Tom was the son of a legendary figure in US surfing, Pat Curren, the big-wave rider and surfboard shaper who had become a shadowy, reclusive figure and was largely absent from Tom's own adolescence. 'We were dealing with Tom and his mum. She was a classic soccer mum, taking him to all the amateur contests,' says Claw, though Tom's famous father was a strong influence from afar. 'His dad used to make his own wetsuits – his dad was that sort of tinkerer,' says Claw.

Claw may have spotted his US surf star in the making, but under Tom's obligations as a member of the National Scholastic Surfing Association (NSSA), a strictly amateur body, Rip Curl would have to wait until Tom turned pro to sign their great American hope.

EUROPEAN BEGINNINGS

In 1979, Quiksilver and Rip Curl shared a booth at a large action-sports trade show called BOOT in Düsseldorf, Germany, manned by Brian and John Law, Greeny's partner in Quiksilver. Rip Curl had struck a distribution deal in France with a flamboyant French-man, Yves Bessas, who screened ski movies around the French snowfields and saw surfing as a logical counter-seasonal addition to his business.

'I was in the US and I got a phone call from a guy called Yves Bessas who was in the ski-movie-showing caper,' says Brian. 'He wanted to get the licence in France. He met me in a restaurant in Newport and he became the licensee in France. He was fairly avant-garde.'

Brian relied heavily on gut instinct when it came to appointing distributors or licensees. 'Ideally you go and spend time with your distributors, and I realised it wasn't any good having a distributor you didn't like hanging out with because you wouldn't go and hang out with them,' Brian says.

Yves was an alternative thinker, into the health and wellness movement before it was fashionable. His ex-wife Maritxu Darrigrand would go on to become head of Roxy in Europe. Yves employed a teenage surfer named Fred Basse to help screen movies around France. He became a key player in Rip Curl Europe.

'Yves had a guy working with him, Alan Teigen, but somehow Alan ended up being distributor for both Rip Curl and Quiksilver,' says Brian.

Yves earnt Brian's undying affection by taking him to Chamonix for the first time. 'I was due to stay for three days and I stayed for three or four weeks because the skiing was unbelievable,' recalls Brian.

This discovery probably did as much as anything to ensure Rip Curl's focus on the European market. The culture suited the Rip Curl founders down to the ground. 'We had also realised that the French and Aussies were in many ways very similar in attitude despite the language difference,' says Brian. 'We had some pretty interesting nights at the Düsseldorf boat show with our distributors in Denmark, France and Germany.' Supported by Australian Government export grants, Europe soon became a major region for the business.

THE SCHOOL OF LIFE

Peter Coles came to Rip Curl at this fascinating juncture in its evolution, as it was wrestling with the transformation from part of a cottage industry to a more professional outfit ready to expand internationally. Peter was living in Jan Juc and, like so many others before him, wondering how he might keep the surfing dream alive.

'I was not even 17 at the time, just finished high school. My father had a military background, a disciplinarian,' says Peter. His father spotted an ad for a job at Rip Curl in the *Geelong Advertiser* and dragged his son along to an interview. 'It was April 1979, and I walked in with the old man, spoke to the receptionist and waited for Ray Thomas,' says Peter. 'He was a big fella with a big beard, really intimidating. I said I was applying for the position you've advertised in the *Geelong Advertiser*. Ray said, "Sorry, I'm looking for a girl." I grabbed my dad and said, "Let's go." And Ray said, "Hang on, we'll give you a go."'

Peter imagined he might last a couple of months. 'I had a carpentry apprenticeship starting in a couple of months with International Harvester [makers of farm machinery]. They got into trouble and went down.' Forty years on, Peter is one of the Curl's longest-serving employees, most recently in the key position of Global Research and Development Manager for the wetsuit division. 'Ray put me into a workroom with Sparrow and I was his apprentice. I'd just take the rubber away in an old Holden ute down to the Torquay tip. I dumped tonnes and tonnes of neoprene offcuts, doing burnouts, before we learnt how to recycle neoprene,' says Peter.

The business offered him far grander opportunities in the years ahead. 'I'd landed in a company just starting to grow and develop,' says Peter. 'It was loose and organic. None of us really had any formal management training, but we all did a range of management courses. We hired more graduates but we always said you graduated from the school of life at Rip Curl.'

As the turbulent '70s drew to a close, it looked like Rip Curl had weathered the pitching seas in pretty good shape. Surfing had morphed from its countercultural, country-soul period to a growing professionalism in which surfers dared dream of viable careers pursuing their passion. Rip Curl had ridden this wave with a surfer's instincts, pushing things too far in one direction then coming back to what worked.

'Ten years after we began we started analysing what had made [the business] successful,' says Brian. They settled on four key factors: 'We worked hard, we knew the customer really well because we were the customer, and we must have been halfway smart. And luck – right place, right time.'

CHAPTER FOUR

FLUORO AND FLAMBOYANCE: 1980–1984

As the bright, shiny decade of the '80s dawned, optimism again gripped the surfing industry. The pro tour was growing, with a cast of impressive, articulate world champions in Mark Richards, Shaun Tomson and Rabbit Bartholomew, and surfing's appeal in Australia was spreading far beyond the coastal fringe.

'Surf was booming and we were booming,' says Brian. 'The '80s was a decade of fluoro and competition, certainly a turnaround from the mellow '70s. We were really starting to expand offshore.'

And so Rip Curl needed to move again. Claw and Brian had their eye on a large empty paddock opposite their existing position on Geelong Road with a view to building a grand new retail store, factory and corporate headquarters worthy of an international business. The only problem was the land would need to be rezoned from rural to commercial/industrial. Rip Curl was getting nowhere with the local council until the Geelong Regional Commission (GRC) became involved. By this stage, Rip Curl was a significant local employer in an area desperate for new employment opportunities, particularly for its youth. Claw and Brian were confident that council could be persuaded the surf industry represented the answer to the region's economic and employment woes, and dreamed up a vision for a surf retail precinct, complete with surf museum, to help their case.

The vision for a surf museum had been developed by Claw and Peter Troy during a three-day camping trip to Mudjimba Island on the Sunshine Coast, where Claw had recorded some of his earliest surfing memories. 'Peter had a lease on the island at that time. He was quite taken aback by my knowledge of the island and was somewhat incredulous at my stories of paddling over there towing a surfboard behind a 16-foot toothpick paddle racing board that had once been Peter's pride and joy,' says Claw. The pair established that Claw had somehow inherited the same board Peter had brought up from Torquay to Maroochydore many years earlier. 'Peter used to dry this board in the oven at the old Torquay bakery in pre–Rip Curl times. It's amazing how all the dots of surf history join up.'

'Brian and myself, Pat Morgan and a couple of other senior managers at Rip Curl had worked on the concept of the Surf Coast Plaza,' recalls Claw. 'We thought it would be a progressive thing for the surf industry of the area, and a good way to convince the Shire to rezone the land and support Rip Curl's plans to expand. We had an understanding that the development of surfing was more than an industry, it was more than a pastime. And we always put a lot of work and effort into trying to develop the whole surfing culture and lifestyle in a responsible way that would sustain into the future.'

'There was talk of us going to Queensland because there weren't enough people here for us to employ. That's when we realised employment was a big deal for the Geelong Regional Commission. And the wheels turned and they gave permission pretty quickly,' says Brian.

It was Pat Morgan who got the wheels moving so quickly. Claw and Brian were skiing in Mount Buller for the winter when Pat was tasked with sorting out the situation. Pat was invited to a council meeting and, shrewdly, he invited *Geelong Advertiser* journalist Gary Cotton, an old surfing buddy of Brian's from the early '60s, to document proceedings.

'Councillors were saying they didn't want factories in Torquay. I stood up and said, "Okay, we're moving to Queensland," and the next day Gary Cotton put it on the front page of the *Geelong Advertiser*,' says Pat. 'A guy from the Geelong Regional Commission picked up on the story and rang me so I went and saw him.'

Pat thought if they asked for a big block of land they might at least secure a smaller block, so he bedazzled the bloke from the GRC with Rip Curl's grand vision. Pat drew an elaborate design and described in vivid detail a complex similar to the Surf Coast Plaza that exists today, including surf museum, shops, cafés and restaurants, shade sails, landscaped gardens and boardwalks. 'I described what is there now, and this guy bought it hook, line and sinker, and he went and negotiated with John Spittle, the farmer [who owned the land],' says Pat. 'The GRC bought the land and rezoned it and built the museum. We got the block of land we wanted and some years later they built more shops along the front, next to the Rip Curl building.'

Pat Morgan was given the job of project-managing the build of the new complex. (His qualifications for the gargantuan task consisted of being a former cabinet-maker.) He engaged a Melbourne firm, aptly named Progress Builders, and oversaw the year-long construction. Claw and Brian made multiple changes on the fly, which presented a problem when the final building inspection was due. 'The building inspector came and I had to walk him through, and I did it so quickly that he couldn't comprehend what had been changed,' says Pat.

Then Pat had the task of filling the new premises with office furniture. Working to a tight budget, he found a place in Geelong that said they could provide everything for around $40,000. But Brian and Claw returned from their Buller trip with grander visions and took their business to an upmarket furniture store in Collins Street, Melbourne. 'Brian said, "We're going to have people from all over the world coming to talk to us, we have to have nice desks,"' Pat recalls. 'They spent a couple of hundred grand. I was just shaking my head . . . They had a big opening and what Brian said happened – people came from all over the world.'

'We wanted really good furniture. We wanted to dress the place up,' Brian says. The new showroom was a big step up from the shop over the road, and a world away from the old bakery. The premises included the largest surf shop in the Southern Hemisphere, with spacious office, factory and warehouse facilities for its growing workforce. With some substantial additions, they are still in the same premises today.

They saw the old place off with a monumental party that nearly got out of hand after some bright spark had the idea of billing it as a factory-wrecking party. 'A couple of the Rip Curl guys had put the idea to us, and we were aware that Quiksilver would do major internal restructuring of the building to suit their needs,' says Claw. 'We ran the party down the back in the dirty area where we glued wetsuits and made surfboards. The party turned out to be around Easter. I didn't think some of the guests would take the factory-wrecking idea so literally. Some of them went quite berserk, and damaged and broke a lot of things that we didn't intend to be damaged.'

It was mainly harmless fun, but there was a more sinister side to the occasion that caused some angst among the Torquay surfing community. 'I noticed that some of the Easter visitors seemed to be amped up on some new type of drugs that ... promoted aggression and even violence, which is a bit of a scary thing and something many of the Rip Curl crew and Torquay locals took note of,' says Claw.

'I went back the next morning and there wasn't one window that wasn't broken,' reckons Butch Barr.

The opening of the new premises was a more dignified affair. 1966 world champion Nat Young was flown in to officiate and a cast of local politicians and dignitaries, including local member and Federal minister Tony Street, were on hand for photo opportunities to show how they were supporting local business.

'It was a good party ... Even when they didn't have a lot of money they still did things well,' says Nat. 'I had to make a speech. I remember thinking that it was a big, impressive building and everyone was there who should be there. They really did become a force to be reckoned with.'

The Surf Coast Plaza included the Surfworld Surf Museum, now the Australian National Surfing Museum, and Geelong Road was renamed the Surf Coast Highway. Eventually, the local government area would become known as the Surf Coast Shire. The wild surfers of the late '60s and early '70s were gradually becoming respectable, in public at least.

In private, Claw and Brian were alarmed by the appearance of harder drugs in the surfing community, and saw it as a disturbing shift from the relatively benign, softer drug use of the hippie era. 'Generally speaking it seemed most people, including surfers, were using drugs like cannabis and hallucinogens as a mind-expanding and self-enlightenment experience,' says Brian. 'But it became apparent some people were using drugs, including harder drugs like heroin and speed and eventually ice, to just get stoned rather than as a search for self-enlightenment. We all vowed that if heroin turned up in Torquay we'd run [the dealers] out of town; however, by the time we realised, some of the people we knew were using and the horse had bolted. And at least one of our friends from that era subsequently died from a heroin overdose.'

'In my case, I privately clashed with a number of leading surfers and luminaries with respect to their reckless behaviour around hard and damaging drugs,' says Claw. 'This never seemed to have much positive effect. They just carried on, and there were many casualties.'

'Subsequently, cocaine arrived on the scene and surfers, along with many other sections of society, got stuck into experimenting with it but the vast majority soon realised it was a dead-end experience,' says Brian. 'Although authorities were saying it wasn't an addictive drug, there were relatively few people within the surfing community who abused it to the point of really harming their lives.'

THE MOVE INTO SURFWEAR

The first Rip Curl employee to move in to the flash new premises was the newly appointed 'product development manager', Doug Spong, an old mate of Claw's from Brighton days, who was tasked with broadening Rip Curl's product range.

Spongy remembers marvelling at Claw's early ambitions during their first surf trips along the Victorian coast a decade earlier. 'I remember driving in an old FJ Holden coming back from Phillip Island, and Claw was leaning back in his seat twirling his hair and going, "They're going to need bags to put their wetsuits in. They're going to need hats to stop them getting sunburnt,"' says Spongy. 'We really thought he was off the planet.'

Spongy had caught Claw's attention with some entrepreneurial flare of his own as a freewheeling traveller on the hippie trail through the '70s. Like most of the surfers who had begun to colonise Torquay on the weekends, Spongy was looking for a way to avoid going back to the city to do the nine-to-five thing. But rather than joining the cottage industry there, fate had other things in store.

Spongy recalls enjoying a post-surf kick of the footy with a couple of mates when a red setter ran off with their football. They managed to catch the wayward hound, found an address tag on its collar and returned it to its emotional owner. 'This Italian guy comes out in tears, drops to his knees crying, "My dog, you found my dog. I'll give you a reward. My father owns a shipping line. I'll give you a first-class trip anywhere you want to go."'

Spongy and his mates found themselves boarding the cruise ship *Achille Lauro* (best remembered for being hijacked by the PLO off the coast of Egypt in 1985) three days later bound for England, via Perth and Cape Town. 'On board it was hippie times,' Spongy says. In Cape Town, they went ashore, bought all the Durban Poison (a potent local strain of cannabis) they could afford, smuggled it aboard inside their underwear and were soon very popular with their fellow passengers. They had so much of the stuff that they had to bake two enormous chocolate cakes full of it and throw a party to get rid of it before they reached England.

Spongy and his pals funded a year-long surfari through Europe and Morocco by making leather sandals and bags, and selling them to the hippie stores in London or outside rock concerts. 'We'd be tripping and forget all about our stall, but we got to see Jimi Hendrix, The Doors, The Who,' he recalls.

Spongy wound up in Bali and saw surfers shipping home boxes of clothes to Hawaii and California to sell to fund their next trip, so he decided he'd give it a crack. He returned to Australia with a box of samples and landed a $10,000 order with Myer, which was then Melbourne's largest department store. Double Dragon clothing was born. Spongy did three runs to Bali, upping the ante each time, until his Balinese suppliers could no longer keep up so he took his business to India. The whole enterprise went belly up when his Indian supplier was running late with a big order and delivered the garments unfinished and unsellable. Doug was left with an $80,000 bank loan he couldn't repay and went looking for a regular job. He worked for a fabric company for a couple of weeks, donning a suit and tie in the city, but decided he couldn't cop it.

Claw figured Spongy had worked out the mysteries of Asian manufacturing and importing, and could be a handy asset. Claw had been heading up to the '79 Stubbies on the Gold Coast and suggested Spongy accompany him on the road trip so they could share the driving and workshop the prospect of him joining Rip Curl.

'So, I drove to Queensland, with him sleeping in the back. I had two pounds of dope stashed in the car. He would have freaked if he'd known,' says Spongy. Burleigh Heads was party central for the new pro tour and Spongy took to it like a duck to water. 'It was full tilt, it was all happening . . . Chicks, partying, drugs. I had an unbelievably good time.' Spongy's number-one partner in crime on the Gold Coast was another young, entrepreneurial surfer named Dave Cross, who had an insatiable appetite for wild times and would come to play a key role in the Rip Curl story.

Claw and Spongy drove home with a couple of swimsuit models from the contest presentation, dropped them off in Sydney and picked up pro surfer Jim Banks and photographer Aaron Chang for the trip to Torquay for Easter. It was at this point that Spongy was appointed product development manager, a role he took to with gusto, soon building up a large and profitable division in accessories and surfwear.

From the core business of surfboards and wetsuits, Rip Curl expanded into t-shirts, bags, hats, towels and even wallets, all designed in Torquay but often manufactured offshore, with a lot of visits to Asia to ensure quality control. Almost anything with a Rip Curl logo on it seemed to fly out the door of surf shops. Spongy recalls the ubiquitous nylon wallets with velcro as an especially profitable item. Board shorts remained off limits for the time being, the legacy of an informal understanding with their old Quiksilver mate Al Green that Rip Curl wouldn't make board shorts and Quiksilver wouldn't make wetsuits.

DAWN PATROLS, AGGROLITES AND INSULATORS

Rip Curl's flash new headquarters ushered in a more sophisticated approach to the business, the most visible manifestation of which was a new range of wetsuits with specific team riders and marketing campaigns to promote each model. This was a long way from the generic short and long johns the company had started out with a decade earlier.

Brian and Claw embraced the concept of product segmentation: coming up with different products to suit different types of customers, urged on by their new man in the US, Ron Grimes, who had a marketing background. 'We were in the boardroom of the new building and we had a blackboard, and on it was written, "New is better,"' remembers Brian. 'And that was Ron's idea. He'd say, "We need something that will excite the market in the US."'

'Ron, Brian and myself workshopped the idea of this new segmented wetsuit range with a few of our top people,' says Claw. 'Grimes was driving his business-school-graduate view, but Brian and myself had a vision of how we wanted our wetsuits to be perceived and how we wanted them to perform for our customers.'

'We wanted one for colder climates, the Insulator. The regular wetsuit was the Dawn Patrol and the competition model was the

Aggrolite, says Brian. 'It was after that we thought, who would best represent these three different types of wetsuits? It was quite a revolution in the wetsuit world.' They promoted Cheyne Horan as the Aggrolite guy, Rabbit Bartholomew for the Dawn Patrol and Wayne Lynch as the Insulator man.

Graphic designer Grant Forbes joined Rip Curl just before the launch of the new range, after having freelanced in advertising and graphics for various businesses in Torquay for the previous five or six years. His bold graphic style made an immediate impact and he was impressed by the young surf company's approach to marketing. 'I did a lot of work, under Claw's direction, on the look of the products,' says Grant. 'Ray Thomas and Sparrow were the skilled rubber guys, but Claw really drove the program. The marketing campaign was pushed heavily by Ron Grimes, who, though he didn't surf, was a very pushy but educated marketing guy. And I've gotta say, it was a brilliant campaign. I was really impressed with the thought that had gone into it and felt privileged to have the opportunity to pull all of the product graphics and advertising together. Phil Jarratt wrote all the copy, and that was great too.'

For Rabbit Bartholomew, the campaign captured the colour and individuality of the early pro era. 'That was totally Claw's idea. I remember Claw going, "You are definitely Dawn Patrol,"' says Rabbit. The fact that sponsored surfers were starting to earn a decent income made it all the sweeter. 'These companies got big enough that they could pay you. It went quite quickly. By the mid-'80s guys were making big money,' says Rabbit.

For Grant Forbes, the new campaign captured the emergence of a modern, more considered approach to the business even while aspects of the old shambolic, hedonistic approach persisted. 'In a lot of ways it was very, very sophisticated, and while it was just dripping with style, in just as many ways it was very, very loose,' says Grant. 'There were a few tangents, and some huge fun, but there was always a lot of intense discussion about product and marketing that usually dragged on into the night, because everyone wanted the best result. Incredibly passionate stuff. The company was very fragile though. It looked a million dollars from the outside but there wasn't too much effort put into the simple, boring business stuff that someone like Butch Barr, and Brian when he puts his mind to it, was really good at.'

RACEHORSES

In the early '80s, Brian discovered a new interest when Al Green managed to talk him into an exciting investment opportunity. The pair remained close despite their growing business rivalry and while they might have spent their working days trying to send the other out of business, at knock-off time they'd adjourn to the Torquay pub to solve the world's problems over a few cleansing ales.

During one such session, Greeny managed to convince Brian that it would be a prudent investment to throw in $3000 for a one-third share in a racehorse named Venus and Mars. Greeny had talked Brian into a few impulsive decisions, but this was taking it to a new level.

'A girlfriend of ours was Lesley Burroughs and she said, "I've got a horse I'm going to send to the yearling sales,"' Greeny recalls. 'I ran it by [trainer] Meggs Elkington. Meggs came along and had a look at him and said, "If you can buy him for 10 grand, I rate him as a racehorse. If you buy him I'll train him."'

When Greeny went looking for partners to help buy the horse he applied a simple strategy. 'Who will I get? Whoever I'm drinking with. Brian must have been around when it went down,' says Greeny.

True to his word, Elkington prepared Venus and Mars, and it went into the Australian Derby in Perth at 3–1 odds. It was an exhilarating first outing for Brian when the horse came home by a short neck over 2400 metres, giving him a taste for racehorses that continues to this day.

'Because we'd won the Australian Derby, blokes who'd been involved in horseracing for years talk to you as though you're a guru,' says Brian. 'It blew me away. This was my first horse – I knew nothing, and then these old guys thought I was some kind of know-it-all. It was bizarre.'

Brian recalls a lavish dinner out with his fellow owners with a huge cast of hangers-on, before they bailed out for a more private celebration at their hotel and then a wild party back in Torquay. His winnings did not last long, however. 'I was stupid and blew some of it on a couple of other horses. Then I thought I was going to be a genius at currency-trading and lost it all,' Brian says ruefully.

Greeny and Brian have maintained a keen interest, and sizeable investments, in racehorses. 'We didn't go silly but we always kept an interest. We were working, that was the priority. Horses were a good spectator sport and a bit of fun,' says Greeny.

TOUGH TIMES IN THE US

While Claw and Brian had seen Quiksilver rocket to riches in the US, the pace of their own growth seemed sluggish by comparison.

Don Craig had done a good job getting the brand into shops and servicing retailers and customers, but there was a sense that, honest and dependable as he was, he perhaps wasn't the guy to achieve the kind of growth they knew was possible in the US. Claw and Brian had taken a gamble on a smooth-talking businessman named Ron Grimes, a non-surfer, as the new US boss.

The cost of shipping and import duty was making suits too expensive, so the decision was made to manufacture in the States. 'They decided they wanted to set up a factory over here, five or six years into it. I didn't have any production experience. We were at about $3 million [in annual sales],' says Don Craig. 'They hired Ron Grimes from a racquetball company. He had brought it from $3 to $15 million, and that's what they wanted to do.'

A group of Rip Curl's best seamstresses, aptly named 'the six-pack' by Ray Thomas, were sent from Torquay to California for a couple of months to teach the local workforce how to make wetsuits to Rip Curl's exacting standards, and Ray Thomas and Butch Barr oversaw the new factory in Oceanside with the mission of making the American operation self-sufficient.

Ray and Grimes did not exactly hit it off. 'With Claw and Brian, outside of work you could call bullshit on them as much as you want. In the US they are always submissive to the boss. I'd never been to the US before,' says Ray. 'He was supposed to have a factory for me, a green card, a car and somewhere to live. I got there and he had nothing. He took me to lunch when I first got there and proceeded to tell me, "When we get a factory I want you to run all the shipping and despatch." I laughed at him. I said, "I can get on a plane and go home now. I work for Brian and Claw." He said, "You can't say that to me." He had a spit of the dummy. It was a bit of a volatile start.'

After the first 'six-pack' of Australian seamstresses trained the Americans, another six came over. Once they left, Ray was on his own. 'The six-pack girls did a great job and had an experience they would not have had. I know the ones with husbands and kids had to do a lot of negotiating with their partners. It was also an extra responsibility for me to make sure they were set up with accommodation and transport, and felt comfortable being there. I remember we had such a great mix of nationalities among the staff. White and black Americans, Samoan, Mexican and even a Russian. We had a real great team and used to have regular tearoom parties where the ladies brought in heaps of food of different origins and I would buy the booze myself as Ron Grimes did not appreciate my methods of building some team spirit. My job was to get the factory up to self-sufficiency in 12 months, which we achieved.'

Barb Williams had been working at Rip Curl since 1979 and was one of the first machinists to go over to the US, leaving her husband and children behind for 12 weeks. 'He didn't like it at first but he had his sister there so everything was okay,' says Barb today, now 80 and living in Echuca. 'I loved every minute of it. I wouldn't have changed it for the world. Ray was a really good boss, he always made sure that everything went well. There were always parties at the factory . . . Another six girls came over after we came back. They all enjoyed themselves, they had a lot of fun. There were some young ones and they knew how to have fun.'

One of those 'young ones' was Heather Beggs, now Jennings, who was 21 when she got the call-up, and left back in Torquay a boyfriend who is now her husband. 'We all lived together. It was always somebody's birthday. I know we had a lot of parties. That's how I remember it, lots of parties,' says Heather. 'We were always partying with Ray or going out to dinner with him. For those three months I don't think we were very sober. We definitely had a good time . . . One of the girls that we went with, Rosalie, she found a husband there. We were there for three months and she married him before we left, and they live in Geelong.'

Heather recalls seeing David Bowie in concert, visiting Disneyland and road trips down to Mexico. 'That was an eye-opener,' she says. The six-pack girls might have had a good time, but they did get the job done. 'I remember teaching this Mexican woman to sew and she had no English, it was basically sign language,' recalls Heather. 'The next year I received a Christmas card from her and I had no idea what it said.'

Rip Curl also bought the premises of the recently defunct Richard Nixon Museum, next to their existing retail store near Trestles in San Clemente. The museum was just a short hop from Nixon's beachfront presidential retreat known as the 'Western White House'. Claw recalls a tense meeting with Nixon's associates to negotiate the sale of the building. 'Brian and myself went to meet with some of Nixon's old cronies from the Western White House,' says Claw. 'These stiff-shirted right-wing types were more taken aback by our wardrobe and demeanour than anyone I'd ever come across before, but they seemed solely driven by money and prepared to talk any deal with us whatsoever. They talked a whole lot of long-winded bullshit and I remember at one stage teeing off with [former US President] Dwight Eisenhower's favourite driver inside the museum. I thought that would be the end of that but they wanted to do a deal.'

Don Craig remembers carting away old framed photos of the disgraced president and boxes of unsold golf balls emblazoned with his name, the market for Nixon merchandise thoroughly soured by the Watergate scandal. 'The locals had their noses out of joint. There was a newspaper article about how bad it was that these Australian surfers had bought the museum,' recalls Brian. 'We were looking at the place and we had access to it overnight so we had a bit of a party there among his old photographs, golf clubs and memorabilia.'

Ron Grimes was responsible for the launch of the Dawn Patrol, Aggrolite and Insulator in the US, but things did not quite go to plan. 'He set up a warehouse and we introduced the new suits and they put them in all the ads,' Don says. There was only one problem with this bold new marketing initiative. 'They didn't realise they had $700,000 worth of wetsuits that were all of a sudden obsolete. Everyone wanted an Aggrolite, a Dawn Patrol or an Insulator, in the new colours,' says Don. The backlog of old stock created a huge headache for the US business, and Grimes' management style was causing some anxiety back in Torquay.

Butch Barr was sent over to try to clean up the mess. 'When I went over there the whole company was in peril of going broke because the US had bled money,' says Butch. 'Within two weeks we cut expenses by 47 per cent. It was ridiculous what they were spending money on. It was a tough year or two. Grant Forbes came over and we worked our arses off and we changed the work ethic to more of an Australian one – work hard, play hard. One thing Torquay taught us all was that we had to juggle lots of balls. I could make wetsuits from start to finish, I could fix a sewing machine. That's when America started doing quite well.'

But the fallout left a sour taste for Don Craig, who'd stuck it out during Grimes' ill-fated reign. 'I was due a raise but they said, "We can't afford to pay your raise, we've got all these issues." I left in '85–'86, after eight or nine years in total,' says Don, who wound up working for O'Neill.

In the meantime, Bob Mignona had finally convinced Claw and Brian to advertise in *Surfing* magazine after a raucous sushi dinner in Costa Mesa with the founders. 'I was a don't-give-up kind of guy. I wanted Rip Curl's advertising because in the surf world globally Quiksilver and Rip Curl were the two leading new surf brands,' says Bob. But he could see that Rip Curl was doing it tough in the US.

'Butch came in and had a much better handle on the sport and where it was going,' says Bob. 'They went through a period when Brian and Claw were coming here a lot because now they were risking their whole American enterprise. With the population and the coastline, they should have been able to do five or six times the business they did in Australia.'

CURREN TO THE RESCUE

Rip Curl had one ace up its sleeve that should have ensured its success in North America. Tom Curren was an extraordinary natural talent who had all the attributes to make him the perfect figurehead.

'Stealing market share from O'Neill was going to be really hard. Americans were all into localism, black wetsuits, white boards,' says Paul Holmes, who was editing *Surfer* at the time. 'I think there was a great deal of resistance to these upstart Aussies who had the audacity to come up with coloured neoprene. The only thing that saved them was Tom Curren. That's what held it together for them, that longstanding relationship with Tom Curren. He had that Californian personality.'

'Tom Curren had a mystique about him and I think that played an important part for Rip Curl. He captured the interest of guys who weren't interested in pro surfing,' says Sam George.

As Tom eyed a pro career, his long-time shaper Al Merrick helped him negotiate with potential sponsors. 'There was kind of a nationalism thing made at one point by O'Neill about why I should go with an American company rather than an Australian company,' says Tom. 'That didn't matter to me because I had a real admiration for the Australians anyway. O'Neill, they were trying all kinds of different things with the wetsuits and it was a bit over the top. Rip Curl wetsuits were seen to be less experimental and the team was doing well in those wetsuits. Everybody had those suits – MR, Michael Peterson, Rabbit, Cheyne. Everybody noticed. We noticed that in Santa Barbara. They were dominating the sport.'

Tom had won a world junior amateur title in France in 1980, a harbinger of the deep affinity he would develop with French beach breaks in the years ahead, before taking out the open amateur world title in 1982 on the Gold Coast. When he turned pro in 1983, he signed with Ocean Pacific surfwear and Rip Curl wetsuits. 'We comfortably sponsored him alongside OP for a decade or more,' says Claw.

Tom Curren was a different kind of pro surfer. There was none of the rock-star posturing of Rabbit, or the emerging Aussies Gary 'Kong' Elkerton or Mark Occhilupo. Tom married his French surfer girlfriend Marie-Pascale when they were both still in their teens, kept a low profile, and shunned the pro-tour party scene and the media as much as his growing profile would allow.

Curren said all he needed to say in the water, his point-break-honed lines perfectly adapting to the beautifully crafted second-generation thrusters made for him by Al Merrick. The potential of the shortboard revolution of the late '60s, the aggression of Nat Young and Michael Peterson, the looseness and imagination of Wayne Lynch, the laser focus and steely competitive psyche of Rabbit and MR: all converged in the technically flawless and unflappable performances of the young Californian.

By the time Tom Curren arrived in Torquay for the first time in 1983, anticipation was high to witness Rip Curl's latest high-profile signing firsthand. And he did not disappoint, opening up a strong lead in the Australian Grand Slam as a rookie before he even got to Bells.

'I think it was the second-last stop on that leg, and I'd done well at Cronulla and Burleigh,' says Tom. Like many great surfers before and since, he initially struggled to come to terms with Bells' wide-open spaces and long walls. 'Bells was tricky because it just takes a while to get used to and I was riding a pretty small board. I didn't map out the line-up too well and I kept getting caught inside.'

What he remembers most vividly is the free surfing of the young South African sensation Martin Potter and the gritty, explosive performance of Gold Coaster Joe Engel, who advanced all the way through the trials to win the event. 'Martin Potter was doing aerials that year in free surfs, coming through Rincon straight to the bowl and doing airs and making them,' says Tom. 'I surfed Winki Pop against Joe Engel in the semis . . . Joe was really hard to stop when he got going.'

Tom embraced the rural surrounds and rugged coast of Torquay. 'It felt very much like home. It kind of reminded me of Santa Cruz,' says Tom. 'I had good results and had a lot of experience in colder water so I knew I could do pretty well.'

Staying in the home of his new sponsor imparted some important skills. 'I stayed with Claw and I got to learn how to navigate the TV, to try and see all three weather reports and surfing news reports. You had to navigate between the three channels and get all three reports on one TV. He would time it really good,' says Tom. He was less successful at emulating Claw's uncanny knack for predicting local surf conditions. 'The weather systems – I still don't understand how they work when they come around Tasmania, and how Claw can predict what's far away over there in Perth when he's reading these maps. I didn't figure it out then and I still don't understand.'

Regardless, Bells Beach would become a happy hunting ground for Curren in the years ahead, as he claimed the Rip Curl Pro title twice, in 1985 and 1990, helping propel him to three world titles. And no surfer would become more synonymous with the brand in the decade ahead, or more revered on both sides of the Pacific Ocean. Nonetheless, Curren's universal appeal didn't manage to bring an end to Rip Curl's challenges in the US.

THE TALE OF THE ILL-FATED CROKIES

One surfing accessory that met an untimely end was an innocuous product: sunglass straps fashioned from neoprene offcuts. It was really just a handy way of using scrap rubber, but Claw took a bunch of them along to a trade show to see if they'd sell. 'I don't think we'd sold many,' says Brian. 'That's when I got a letter in Torquay from a legal firm in New York.'

The lawyers represented a company in the US that had been producing similar sunglass straps out of neoprene called 'Crokies' that their client had patented in the US. The curt letter demanded that Rip Curl cease and desist from manufacturing their own sunglass straps.

'It wasn't long after that I headed off to America with Speaky,' says Brian. The old ski buddies headed to Jackson Hole to chase fresh powder runs, and found themselves enjoying a beer in a little one-pub town called Wilson, where they met a guy from the local ski patrol there. 'This bloke said, "I make Crokies and we're suing these Aussie guys,"' says Brian. 'Anyway, I strung him along for a couple more beers then told him the story.'

Without the involvement of any lawyers, for the cost of a few beers, Brian and his new American buddy managed to resolve their differences and Rip Curl agreed to cease production of the offending product. 'It was a good lesson in what you can achieve just by meeting someone face to face without any lawyers,' says Brian.

Rip Curl's neoprene offcuts wound up as stubbie holders, until new recycling technologies allowed them to be repurposed as shoe material.

WINDSURFING

When windsurfing boomed in the mid-'80s, Rip Curl turned to Pat Morgan to launch and run a windsurf division. He was a keen sailor after all, and his son Brendan was a windsurfing champion. As well as shaping sailboards and overseeing the development of windsurf-specific wetsuits, masts and sails, Pat's job also meant running the short-lived Rip Curl Wave Classic. A windsurfing contest would hopefully lend them credibility in the emerging sport, just as the Rip Curl Pro had a decade earlier.

Someone dreamed up the idea of offering European retailers a free sailboard if they attended the event, in an attempt to woo the booming European market. The boards were the new lighter wave-sailing models they'd developed for local conditions, almost unseen in Europe. No fewer than 40 shop owners took up the offer, mainly from surfless Germany, seriously testing the production capabilities of the new division, not to mention the capacity of Torquay to accommodate competitors.

'All these people came from all over the world to Torquay. We were flat out trying to get them accommodation,' says Pat.

'Everyone in Torquay had to put clean sheets on their spare beds,' his wife, Elaine, chips in.

But the free sailboards proved hazardous for the European retailers, who were unaccustomed to the latest in local design advances. 'In Europe they were all riding big, long sailboards. We'd just started riding the short wave-jumping stuff,' says Pat. 'All these mad Germans came and picked up their boards and went out at Point Danger, and hit the bottom and knocked their fins out. It was horrendous,' says Pat.

Even so, the event was considered a great success. 'That got windsurfing going for us. I think we ran it for three years,' says Pat. Though windsurfing quickly came and went as a significant part of the business in Australia, it did help Rip Curl grab a toehold in the next major market it had in its sights.

THE FRENCH CONNECTION

In 1980, Victorian surfing champion Maurice Cole was not long out of prison, having served two years for a relatively minor bust for possession of hash. He'd cut a deal to plead guilty and had expected to walk free on a good behaviour bond, but instead found himself made an example of, serving the toughest sentence for the charge in Victorian history, most of it in maximum security at the infamous Bluestone College, Pentridge Prison.

Maurice was stripped of his Victorian title by the sport's governing body, the Australian Surfriders Association, eager to distance itself from the dreaded surfer-druggie stigma. The ASA's hard line meant Maurice was ineligible for day release to compete in events while he was inside. Even so, a year after being released, Maurice had again won the Victorian title and managed to qualify for the Australian team to compete in the world titles in the sleepy, little-known surf town of Hossegor, France.

Maurice found himself trudging over the vast sand dunes of Hossegor's La Gravière beach – named after an old gravel pit – to a scene that would profoundly change the course of his life, the evolution of French surfing and Rip Curl's business. 'There were just teepees everywhere, spitting A-frame barrels, and not a soul out,' Maurice gushes with barely diminished awe even today, nearly 40 years on.

Maurice describes his sprint down the beach as 'like a scene from *Chariots of Fire*', with imaginary stirring music to accompany his slow-motion dash towards the ocean. 'To this day it is still the best day's surfing of my life,' says Maurice. 'I surfed for seven hours. At one stage my hair was dry for about four hours because I was so dialled in, just getting barrel after barrel.'

He was soon joined by several of his compatriots, some a little worse for wear after a big night sampling the local red wine but all similarly transported by the surreal vista before them. Maurice recalls a hungover Rabbit Bartholomew doggedly dragging his board over the dunes and breaking into the same *Chariots of Fire* sprint at the sight of the pumping line-up.

'What ensued was the most perfect day of surfing any of us had ever experienced . . . We surfed our brains out, the tube-riding got deeper and deeper as the afternoon wore on,' Rabbit recalls in his memoir, *Bustin' Down the Door*. 'The day had a profound effect on all of us. Never in our wildest dreams could we have imagined such perfection in Europe.'

Towards the end of the life-altering session Maurice noticed for the first time that a large crowd had gathered on the beach to watch. When he finally came to shore he received a hero's welcome, with resounding applause and cheers. Maurice recalls one elderly French woman gasping breathlessly, '*C'est quoi? C'est quoi?* What is it? What is it?' He realised they'd been mystified by his Houdini trick of disappearing inside a wave only to reappear as if by magic 30 or 40 metres down the beach in a shower of spray.

That epic session placed Maurice at ground zero for the birth of the French surfing industry. Looking for a fresh start after his bitter prison experience, still seething at his treatment by the ASA, and sensing opportunities in business and the uncrowded surf, Maurice and his wife, Anne, soon relocated to Hossegor. 'To come here was such a relief. We were still looked down on [in Australia], but here the French went, "This guy is a little bit eccentric, he must be an artist!" he says.

Rip Curl had already begun to make some tentative inroads into the European market under a distribution deal with French ski-movie-maker Yves Bessas. But by 1982 the French franc had fallen and the Australian dollar had risen to a point where there was simply not enough of a margin in it for the French distributor. Brian and Claw were still adamant that France and Europe represented new and exciting markets, and saw similarities between the semirural surf towns of Torquay and Hossegor. The idea of being in the right place at the right time as surfing boomed again was irresistible, so they decided to head over to start their own company in France.

Maurice, meanwhile, had set up a surfboard factory in an industrial estate in the back blocks of Hossegor, wrestling with the formidable challenges of sourcing blanks and fibreglass in a country that had no surfboard industry to speak of. Fortunately, he'd befriended a well-connected young architecture student, François Payot, who was keen to find ways to support himself and his surfing obsession on the coast rather than having to pursue an architecture career up in Paris.

The story of how this unlikely collaboration kickstarted the great European surf boom demands close examination. I fly to France in October 2017, just as the annual Quiksilver Pro has drawn to a close in those same epic La Gravière beach breaks, the final won in spectacular fashion by Rip Curl's Brazilian world champion Gabriel Medina. His semifinal victory over Hawaiian champion John John Florence is the latest instalment in an intriguing new rivalry, and Gab takes the win in a rapid-fire exchange of mind-bending aerial manoeuvres.

The contest is all over by the time I get to town, the crowds gone and the pro surfers already heading to the next event, the Rip Curl Pro, in Peniche, Portugal. I like it this way, to see a surf town return to normal, the crowds thin, the surf empty. Hossegor quickly begins to feel like a ghost town as more and more businesses – shops, bars, restaurants, hotels – begin to pack up for their winter hibernation. By day two I am literally the only guest in the historic Hôtel le Mercedes, which had been teeming with World Surf League staff just a day earlier.

There are fears locally that a new WSL schedule might mean an end to their autumn contest in prime surf season. The October time slot stretches the summer season out, and without it business may draw to an abrupt close at the end of summer.

Maurice Cole moved back to Australia in 1995 but still comes over for an annual shaping stint, and his boards remain in high demand. He picks me up for a surf at La Gravière – it's four to five feet, sheet glass, not too many people out, and at 62, after surviving cancer and several business disasters, Maurice is still a busy and imposing presence in the line-up, picking off set waves, chatting animatedly in French with old friends and driving smoothly over the pulsing waves in a stoic tai chi crouch. Afterwards he takes me for a drive through the vast surf industrial precinct just inland from town. We call in to the local surfboard factory where he makes his boards, Surf Odyssey, and it could be in a similar industrial precinct in the back blocks of surf towns the world over: the racks of boards with handwritten orders taped to them, the small cell-like shaping and glassing bays, and rudimentary construction of four-by-twos and gyprock.

Maurice seems profoundly at home in France, even though he hasn't lived here for 20 years. Every afternoon around four o'clock when he takes a break from shaping, he brings out a selection of local cheeses, a bottle of red wine and enjoys a thoroughly European afternoon tea with whomever else is on hand.

Maurice stays at François's immaculately restored French farmhouse in the countryside just outside Hossegor. The opulent spread is decorated with homewares, sculptures and artworks from François's global travels, particularly from Bali. The timber outbuildings have been fashioned into an exclusive yoga retreat, favoured by the well-to-do housewives of the region. The original ancient bare wooden beams of the farmhouse are still exposed, as a counterpoint to the luxurious interiors. The website for the yoga retreat, translated from French, declares poetically, 'The room decoration of the Audine farm reflects the exotic memories collected during the multiple and real (or imaginary) journeys of its hosts. Their desire was to create for you a world of peace, comfort and softness. During yoga retreats, this dream setting will make it easy to mingle with surfers and Buddhas, gathered into African fragrances.'

When I visit, François is away in Paris, but his influence looms large in the story of Rip Curl Europe. He is still the only major shareholder in the parent company aside from Claw and Brian, and tales of the dashing bon vivant and ladies' man with extensive business interests in restaurants and yoga retreats around the world create a larger-than-life, semi-mythical persona.

On my flight over, I watched Baz Luhrmann's spectacular adaption of the F. Scott Fitzgerald classic *The Great Gatsby*, the tale of the elusive millionaire playboy who stages outrageous parties in the decadent New York social scene of the Roaring Twenties and boasts of an aristocratic family background and past military glory. In François's absence, as tales of his largesse, his family connections, his taste for exotic women and his acts of generosity abound, I come to think of him as a French surfing Gatsby. But in his case the aristocratic background and heroic military history are entirely genuine. Who is Payot?

'Have you met François yet?' his former business partner and long-time right-hand man Fred Basse asks me.

I say no.

'Good luck,' he says with a grin.

FINDING FRANÇOIS

It is difficult to gain an audience with the mysterious Monsieur Payot. He is based in Paris because his daughter Dune has been unwell and he has devoted himself to her recovery. But he arrives in Hossegor unexpectedly for the funeral of his aunt and, amid his busy schedule, Maurice manages to arrange for us all to meet up for breakfast at the farm. Joining us is Fred Basse, the yin to François's yang: a quiet, sober presence and the perfect foil to François's volatile energy.

Over coffee and croissants, we cover everything from the history of surfing in France to Maurice's prowess as a debt collector, to how the surf industry lost the plot in the 2000s. It's an animated, wide-ranging conversation dominated by François's dry wit and candid observations in his thick French accent and lyrical English-as-a-second-language.

The popular version of surfing's beginnings in France is suitably glamorous. In 1957 Hollywood screenwriter Peter Viertel was in Biarritz for the shooting of the film version of the Hemingway classic *The Sun Also Rises*. Viertel, a keen surfer, saw the unridden waves of La Grande Plage in front of his hotel and wired home to the US for his surfboard to be sent. The locals were mesmerised by his wave-riding and were eager to emulate his feats. He taught a handful of locals to shape surfboards and left his board behind when he returned to the US. French surfing was up and away.

Unlike surfing's evolution in California or Australia, the sport did not become the preserve of penniless beach bums and drifters but attracted the sons of the aristocracy. The surfing clubs that were formed were more like exclusive country clubs than the working-class surf lifesaving clubs or rebel board-riding clubs of Australia.

The second generation of French surfers in the '60s combined these highborn beginnings with a new bohemian, hippie aesthetic, like suntanned Beat poets, cashed-up Kerouacs on surfboards. In the late '60s, visiting surfers from abroad began discovering that Europe indeed offered abundant, uncrowded and powerful surf, bringing modern shortboards and selling them to the locals when they left. Australian stars Nat Young and Wayne Lynch blew through town with filmmaker Paul Witzig, shooting the transition-era classic *Evolution*, which showcased the new shortboard-surfing and the sublime French beach breaks to equally stunning effect.

French surfing's focus began to drift north from Biarritz to the pounding surf of Hossegor, which had been unsuited to the old longboards. French surfers began to realise the prodigious inheritance of their waves and enjoyed the means to fully indulge them, funded in large measure by their familial inheritance.

François Payot was the son and grandson of doctors, expected to follow in the family trade. He grew up mainly in Paris but began surfing on a plywood bellyboard during family holidays to Hossegor when he was 13. His mother was from Hossegor and his grandmother had built one of the first houses in what was then a sleepy rural village. 'All in this area the people were scared of the sea so all the native villages are inland,' explains François.

The coastline here is known as la Côte Sauvage, the Savage Coast, and was avoided by the locals until Parisian holiday-makers started enjoying its gentler moods in summer. François was one who fell heavily under its spell, so much so that his decreed path into medicine was soon sabotaged by his salt-water obsession.

'My mother took me out of medical school because they say I spend too much time at the beach and not enough time at the university,' he says. He switched to architecture, which he could study in Bordeaux, much closer to his beloved waves of Hossegor. 'Now the real surfing time start, we start to have long blond hair, flannel shirt, and around the neck we have Moroccan stones, like hippies,' he says.

Hossegor became the focus for this new generation because of what locals call 'la Gouf', an enormous underwater canyon that funnels Atlantic swells straight out of deep water at the beaches of Hossegor. What had been a source of fear for the locals became a magnet for surfers. 'Australian or American surfers, they arrive in London or Amsterdam, they will buy a van, they will pass here August–September, they will go to Morocco for winter and then they will go back to their country at one stage and it was where we start to buy the surfboards from them before they leave,' says François.

François earnt his first surfboard in a game of cards. 'Gin rummy, I was a good card player. I win the game and with the money I buy a board,' he says. He scored a summer job managing one of the surf clubs where local surfers left their boards, and his entrepreneurial instincts revealed themselves. 'I am the first to have the idea to rent surfboards, and I make more money than I can imagine,' he says. 'At university we have no money, so that was my first surfing business.'

Along the way, François found time to complete his compulsory French military service for two years, serving as a paratrooper alongside the Italian army in conflicts in Africa. It was a million miles away from the bohemian French surfing lifestyle of the late '60s and early '70s. Though François doesn't like talking about his military days, shadowy rumours of his heroics abound, and he does admit the experience served him well when he went into business.

'It was quite an exciting experience. Now there is no military service,' says François. 'You learn to be a leader, how to take good decisions. When I employ people, to me it was a positive if the guy had been at the army. I knew if I say do that, they do that.'

In 1979, during the French national titles in Hossegor, François met another young surfer with an eye for business. Fred Basse was a former junior French surfing champion who had a part-time summer job screening surf and ski movies with Yves Bessas. François loaned Fred his prized board for the final, Fred finished second and a friendship was forged.

It was a meeting that recalled that of the Rip Curl founders back in Torquay 16 years earlier. François was the dreamy visionary like Claw, and Fred was the straight-talking pragmatist like Brian. The pair clicked. Both were looking for ways to stay at the beach rather than get a regular job in the city. In many ways, the beginning of Rip Curl in Hossegor feels like a replay of events in Torquay, in a parallel universe, as a new generation discovered wave-riding and threw off the conservative shackles of their expected paths in life.

Fred made the French team for the 1980 world titles, where he met Maurice Cole and shared that epic session at La Gravière. I ask François what Maurice's contribution to the French surfing industry has been. 'His contribution to the industry? Nothing. He is a nightmare to do business with. His contribution was to the skill of surfing,' François says. 'When you are in business with Maurice, one day you are the richest man in the world and the next day you are bankrupt,' he says, laughing.

When Maurice decided to open Hossegor's first surfboard factory, he couldn't even speak the language and had no idea how to navigate the administrative maze of starting a business in a foreign country. François took pity on him and decided to help out. 'I was thinking it was a good idea for four or five months to help him to run the business,' says François. 'It was not really difficult so we started that. I didn't get paid. That was a good excuse for me not to work as an architect. I never think it was a business. We have no money. I help Maurice for this six months and after I go back to my study.' Though this is how François imagined things would play out, he never did go back to university.

Instead, François helped Maurice register his wittily titled business Aussiegor, and began managing the factory while Maurice shaped. Maurice reckons he had been trying for months to get his business application through the maddening French bureaucracy. When François got involved and had a few well-chosen words to the right people, it was resolved within 24 hours.

When the French franc was devalued and it became unviable for Yves Bessas or Alan Teigen to import Rip Curl products, Maurice and François filled the breach. Brian and Claw flew over to explore starting up their own company in France, and in the meantime Maurice's business gave them a platform to continue importing product to try to service the growing demand. 'We did it as friends to keep it going, and Rip Curl said to us, we're going to set up our own company, and here was this tiny little company [Aussiegor] that had maybe 20,000 francs to its name,' says Maurice.

'Brian say, "Do you want to import Rip Curl?" and I say, "No, we have no money, and not possible, but with your money and my work we can do something great,"' François recalls. François, Brian and Claw hit it off immediately and Rip Curl agreed to a joint venture with him to set up a European operation based in France. 'I was a surfer too, we were magical people. The surfing world was quite far from Europe, but when a magical person meets a magical person they get along,' says François. 'They offer me a salary, I never get a salary in my life. It must have been about $2000 a month, so that was changing my life.'

François says he instantly felt like Claw and Brian were kindred souls. 'It was natural – they were a bit older than me, more experienced on life – but we fit well together. The spirit of the style was: we work in surfing, we are rebels,' François says. 'Brian is normal,

Claw is not so normal. The first time I meet Brian he come with his family, he was a totally normal guy. We are surfers, we share the same thing. Claw was more original, the way he dress, but like we say, we were in a world where there were so many different types of characters I'd not really be surprised.'

François called in Fred Basse to help and they formed a company, cheekily called Frogs, with Rip Curl owning 50 per cent, François 40 per cent, and Maurice and Fred 5 per cent each. They started in a tiny office in town with broken windows and no heating, building their own racks out of scrap timbers. 'At the beginning of Rip Curl, I was alone. I do everything. This gives you a legitimacy later on – you ask them [your staff] to do something you have done. I know what you do because I did it,' François says.

The timing, again just like Torquay back in '69, was impeccable. European surfing was about to boom and its sister sport, windsurfing, was already going through a massive growth spurt, providing another ready market to be tapped into.

'So, the real start of Rip Curl like it is in Europe, it was not because of a vision, it was the fact of the French devaluation,' says François. 'At the same time the windsurfing grow, so what was a niche market, surfing wetsuits, have another market on the side in windsurfing. And windsurfers start to discover surfing, which open the minds of millions of people in Europe about surfing [who] use the same product as us. And at the same time, they start to want shaped sailboards, and that meant we had a lot of interest from outside this area.'

François's parents, having watched careers in medicine and architecture fall victim to their son's surfing addiction, were not exactly thrilled at his venture into the wetsuit business but remained supportive. 'They were quite suspicious but at least they give the money to pass the first year, and then I think they were quite proud,' says François. 'My father the first year lent me 20,000 francs for the first season, and that was enough to pass. We pay him back quite quick.'

But growth was so rapid that by their second year they needed more financing than François's father was prepared to stump up. 'The French bank don't know surfing . . . You have to convince the parents, the bank, the administrators that there is a market around,' says François. 'When you say you are in business and you are in shorts and t-shirt the banks don't trust you. The Australian company was obliged to put some money in the bank for us because we need 1.6 million franc, around $250,000. We grow really quick. When the market start to explode you face new situations every day which make it exciting. We were lucky as a business to be at this time where everything was new. We were stoked by a new wetsuit, stoked by a new invention. Like kids you have new toys every day.'

Rip Curl made an immediate impression at the European action-sports trade shows, where surf was still a novelty. Most Europeans equated surfing with sailboarding, and Maurice's wave-sailing boards were seen as revolutionary. 'When we started doing trade shows, we had three square metres next to the toilet,' says Maurice. 'We had all the Rip Curl sailboards, and no one had ever seen foiled sailboards. All of a sudden, from this tiny little stand, we sold them all, we sold 30 of them. Everyone wanted one, all the guys, all the world champions. We became overnight sensations – "There's this guy, this crazy Australian" . . . And the partying, that was the thing that set us apart. We were drinking and partying.'

The European expansion was aided by Australian Government export grants that helped subsidise Rip Curl's forays into new international markets. Within a few short years, the city of Hossegor, like Torquay before it, began to cotton on to the notion that these long-haired hippie surfers were employing people, spending money in the town and attracting more visitors to the area. By 1985, finance from the city enabled Rip Curl France to build its own factory in the Soorts, inland from the town centre, where land was cheap. It was an investment that would pay off handsomely for the city in the years to come.

'You have to convince everyone, then everybody follow. You have to convince the region that it will be a good tourist attraction. You bring something new to the traditional world,' says François.

Despite the economic benefits, the old guard of Hossegor, the conservative farming community and wealthy Parisian holiday-makers, remained shocked by the young, drug-smoking surfers drawn to their town. If Torquay in the early '70s had been wild, Hossegor in the '80s was not far behind.

'When we came along we were surfing hard, we were really passionate about what we did and we partied exactly the same way,' adds Maurice. 'I didn't have time for business. Every time the surf stopped or the wind stopped you had to go out and party and have a good time. We were burning the candle at both ends. There was a lot of sex and drugs, and a fair bit of rock-and-roll.'

François always took a pragmatic attitude to the hard-partying culture of the surf industry, particularly as the business grew. 'You can party all the time, go crazy, but if you have a meeting at nine o'clock in the morning then you are at your meeting fresh,' he says. 'Your lifestyle must not be a danger to your business. If you employ 50 people, that's 50 families to feed.'

Gradually, the locals were won over, and the conservative elements claimed their new vagabond businesspeople with pride. 'Hossegor was just a summer village totally asleep the rest of the year, so in fact we bring some activity,' says François. 'So they don't really trust us but they don't really have opposition, and after when they see we bring good image they start to be really proud of us and the city help us to do the factory. The bank manager bring some of their customers – "Look, we are working with people who don't even have a tie and a shirt, they are in shorts and thongs, so we are really open-minded because we work with these people.'"

But there was still a ragged edge to doing business with the Curl, particularly if you didn't pay your bills on time and they called in the wild, colonial ex-con from Australia to heavy the accounts department. Maurice recalls a large retail chain failing to pay him for some sailboards. He found out the name, home address and phone number of the head of Accounts and comprehensively put the wind up him. 'I knew what I was doing because I used to collect debts when I got out of jail with the Pentridge collection agency, another whole fucking story,' Maurice says, laughing. 'These people had never come across anything like us ... In my broken French I'm starting to say, "I want to talk to you. Me, Maurice Cole, needs to talk to you, Pierre. It's going to be between you and me." He didn't know where I was going ... "You are now going to give me your promise, your word, that the cheque is going to be in the mail very quickly," and he went, "Yeah, yeah, yeah." And I said, "Good, because if the cheque isn't in the mail I'll be coming to this address and it'll probably be two o'clock in the morning and I will fucking collect the money."'

As expected, the accountant, now thoroughly freaked out, rang Rip Curl's accounts department wanting to know who this lunatic was, threatening to come to his house in the dead of night. They had the response scripted perfectly. '[Our accountant] went, "What? He called you? Oh no! Oh no! What did he say? Oh no. You mean ...? He's not! He's going to come through your door at two o'clock in the morning? That's what he used to do. That's why he's living in France." We got the fucking cheque the next day,' Maurice recounts theatrically.

Maurice's reputation as Rip Curl's resident debt collector soon spread, with sometimes unintended consequences. On another occasion Maurice and François were travelling to a trade show when they decided to call in on one of their retail accounts. 'We want to say hello to them to be nice … We arrive and we say to the seller, "Is the owner of the shop here? We are coming from Rip Curl to say hello to him,"' says François. The shop attendant delivered this news to the owner, who looked dismayed and scurried off. 'And he come back to us and he say, "I know I didn't pay on time. Here's the money … Sorry, sorry. I promise you I will never be late again." We go to be nice to the guy!' François exclaims, as he and Maurice crack up.

Rip Curl Europe was about to explode to the point where it would help prop up its parent company when other regions, most notably the US, went through tough times. 'The time go too quick, I was living for the day,' says François. 'I would not say I have the vision of the market going big. I have no vision. I don't care. I know that we are growing. What was important was that we could live, we could make money, we could help kids to live their passion.'

Amid all the feverish surfing, partying and business growth, it took several years to formalise Rip Curl's French business. In a pattern that would play out often in his roller-coaster business life, Maurice sold his share to Fred for around $25,000, a year before it would have been worth many times that amount. Maurice had got into a spot of bother with an enormous tax bill and needed the money in a hurry.

When I call into the Surf Odyssey factory to say goodbye to Maurice before leaving for Portugal, to trace Rip Curl's European expansion, there's a major swell due to hit within 48 hours.

Maurice, at age 62, in remission from cancer, struggling to stay afloat financially, awash with orders, is finishing off an eight-foot gun for himself to tackle La Nord, the legendary outer sandbank, in a couple of days.

'Someone asked me, doesn't it ever get to you that everyone else made millions and you made nothing?' Maurice poses. 'And I said, yeah, but no one else ever lived my life and I'm still here and I think I'm still relevant, I'm still shaping, I've got so many new things to come.'

Despite their wildly different experiences in business, Maurice and François remain the best of friends. 'We've always had each other's backs when shit goes down,' says Maurice. When Maurice was diagnosed with cancer, he needed a guarantor for a $100,000 loan to get treatment in the US. François didn't blink. 'I was really embarrassed. I had no money. I'd lost everything with BASE [a failed Australian surfboard business]. I said, I need someone to guarantee me for 100,000. And he looked at me, and he said, "You write the letter and you take it to Monica [François's personal assistant] and you get better. Now, when do we go surfing?"'

CHAPTER FIVE

BOOM AND BUST: 1985–1989

By the mid-'80s the great surf boom was showing no signs of slowing down, both in Australia and around the world. The big surf companies were growing well beyond their core markets of diehard surfers as the beach look was eagerly adopted by the masses from the suburbs. The big three Aussie surf brands – Quiksilver, Billabong and Rip Curl – rode the wave of their new mainstream cool to previously unimagined success.

'I think it was the very strong competitive instincts that all three of the companies had that helped to forge the surf industry in Australia,' says Brian. 'It's just like going for a surf with your mates, you've got to try and outfox them to get the wave.'

At Rip Curl, the boom manifested in events like media night, an annual party on the Thursday before the Easter weekend that grew more elaborate each year. 'Bells was getting pretty big and we realised the surf media weren't really being looked after that well, and we just wanted to do something for them, and it took on a life of its own,' recalls Brian.

'One of our objectives was to get a bit of feedback from the surf magazines on how our advertising campaigns and teams were being received and the general beat of the jungle,' says Claw.

'I don't know if a lot of that happened on the night because everyone got too pissed,' adds Brian.

Newly employed graphic designer Neil Campbell witnessed the escalating mayhem of media night firsthand. 'I remember the first media night. Brian said to go down the pub and buy a case of beer and invite the magazine crew around. And then it took off and became a massive media event,' Cambo recalls.

'They used to get a bit wild. The old office used to have a sauna. God knows what went on in there,' says Shayne Paterson, who was in charge of Rip Curl marketing and promotions during these intoxicating times. 'I have a clear memory of driving Brian home in my station wagon and he refused to get off the roof. There were no real drink-driving rules down there. Those guys ruled Torquay. There was probably only one cop in town. It was crazy times . . . a no-rules society.'

Shayne had started in Rip Curl's Sydney office as an office manager in 1982, doing everything from despatching orders to measuring up team riders and making wetsuit repairs. In 1985, she was transferred to Torquay to take over the marketing job, as well as serving as Claw's PA. At the time, she was dating John Howitt, the owner of Peak Wetsuits, a new budget brand based in Sydney – the business equivalent of sleeping with the enemy. 'I think Brian and Claw thought, let's get her out of there,' she jokes. Shayne was the first woman to hold a senior management position in the business. 'The company had a concrete ceiling. It was very blokey,' she says. Even so, she thrived on the informal Rip Curl culture. 'The camaraderie of that business, it was like a family. I still feel a part of it, I've never lost touch with anyone,' she says.

Though the workplace was great, going to a country town from the Northern Beaches of Sydney was hard. Shayne at least found some sisterhood and solidarity when Quiksilver's head of marketing, Rikki Jansen, also moved from Sydney to Torquay. 'We lived in this farmhouse in Grossman's Road, the scene of many a party,' says Shayne. 'One year I had [team riders] Rabbit, Nick Wood, Gary Green and Stuart Bedford-Brown staying with me, and I had girls climbing through the windows at midnight. It astounded me how these girls would throw themselves at these surfers.'

This was surfing's rock-and-roll period, when celebrities gravitated to the surf scene like moths to a flame. Footballers and rock stars in particular seemed drawn to Rip Curl's party culture. Australian Crawl, one of the top Australian bands of the era, even came on board as co-sponsors of the Rip Curl Pro in 1984. 'The social scene was incredible. With my business card I could get into any nightclub,' says Shayne. 'We hung out with the guys from Dire Straits ... We'd take those guys surfing and go and see them in concert. I measured up Australian Crawl one day and fitted them out with custom wetsuits.'

The other highlight of the Rip Curl social calendar was the annual Christmas party, though securing venues became increasingly difficult as their reputation spread. 'We were kicked out of a few restaurants in Torquay. At one time, we were banned from every restaurant from Torquay to Geelong,' says Shayne.

Pat Morgan was a rare sober presence amid the mayhem. 'I remember one time we went to this function venue in Geelong. There must have been 150 people, all came charging in at once. They'd all been drinking on the bus,' says Pat. 'The band started up full blast. The bloke from the conference centre nearly had a heart attack. He could see it was already out of control. He was running around trying to find the owner, and he asked me if I was the owner.'

There's a good chance Pat Morgan remembers things about Rip Curl parties lost to all other human memory. 'I was going to write a book and do 50 copies and charge those blokes 100 grand each, because I was the only one who was sober the whole time,' Pat jokes.

Jamie Brisick was a young Californian pro surfer who joined Team Rip Curl during these heady times. As a grommet from the woeful closeouts of Zuma Beach, west of LA, Jamie had developed a deep fascination with Australian surfing, and Rip Curl was his portal to this land of perfect waves and larger-than-life characters. 'Rip Curl was so synonymous with Australia, and Australia was so alluring,' he says.

When Jamie first found himself in Torquay for the Rip Curl Pro he could scarcely believe his luck. 'I was with Wes Laine and Willy Morris and we stayed in the trailer park. We went to this event at the Torquay pub and I remember getting more and more drunk. All my heroes were there, Simon [Anderson], Derek [Hynd], it was amazing to be among them. They were taking a piss in the stall next to me. It was like a Woodstock event. Torquay was bigger than I expected, way more of an event than I imagined it would be.'

Claw made a particularly powerful impression. 'Claw was bobbing on his feet, he was like a seal with that clapping going and that snaggletooth. He was so animated. He was so cool and loose and fun,' says Jamie. 'It was almost like he was winking at us, going, "We're just a bunch of dirtbag surfers and we're doing cool stuff all over the world." There was a sense of this scam we're on and it's going to be done soon so let's have fun with it . . . Go out the night before a contest? Of course you do. Rip Curl weren't opposed to that. They weren't trying to turn us into these robotic uber-athletes. They wanted it to be fun.'

THE ACCOUNTANT AND THE ART SCHOOL GRADUATE

The mid-'80s also signalled the arrival of two characters at Rip Curl HQ who would each make an impact in their own ways. One was graphic artist Neil Campbell, filling the imposing art-room shoes of Grant Forbes, who had moved to the US to shore up the troubled North American operation. The other was Rod Adams, who had originally come to Rip Curl as an auditor working for PricewaterhouseCoopers. Rod was so taken with the place he tossed in his promising career at one of the world's largest accounting firms to become Rip Curl's accountant.

'Early on, we were not totally responsible all the time, but we had the advantage of strong people who would step in to fill the void,' says Claw. 'The first one of these strong men was Butch Barr. Effectively, he was manager of finance and operations, and had his turn as CEO of Rip Curl USA. And the next big one was Rod Adams, who took a wide range of responsibilities.'

About a week after Rod started, one afternoon Brian asked him down to the surfboard factory at the back of the building to grab a few four-litre cans of acetone. 'He proceeded to tip it across the Surf Coast Highway, which was two lanes across, and then set fire to it,' says Rod. The rite of passage harked back to the early days at the bakery, and meant Rod had been accepted into the fold.

The Rip Curl crew soon realised there was some benefit in having a non-surfer on the team. 'I remember one day in the first two months of being there, the paymaster was stressing because there was surf,' says Rod. 'He went, "I can't pay people and go surfing." He abandoned it and I sat there until 4 am having no idea how to use this system, but I got everyone paid . . . You just can't walk out and not pay people.'

At times, Rod's work ethic was at odds with the party culture of the place. 'We had a party in the tearoom once and they wouldn't leave, so I got a fire hose onto them,' says Rod. 'I had to come back the next morning and clean it up.' On another occasion, when revellers were reluctant to call it a night and vacate the reception area, Rod turned a fire extinguisher on them.

'In the early days we had to be creative with our finances to fund a rapidly growing business and which at one time was losing money. We just worked bloody hard to make it work,' says Rod. 'I think they thought I was a workaholic, but I just enjoyed it so much. I enjoyed the cut and thrust of the business and making a difference every day. That's what drove me.'

Neil Campbell couldn't have been a more different kettle of fish – the loose, anti-establishment art guy who flew the flag for the company's bohemian beginnings. 'It got very, very corporate. Rod Adams, he was the Black Adder, he was our nemesis,' says Cambo. 'Brian loved him. Mr Bean, we used to call him. I used to have issues with the accounts department.'

Cambo was a country boy who'd moved to Geelong to study art at Deakin University, discovered the waves of Torquay and never left. Doug Spong had asked him to paint a surfboard for him in the splattered style of artist Ralph Steadman, mimicking the famous image of Hunter S. Thompson spectacularly throwing up into a toilet from his gonzo classic, *Fear and Loathing in Las Vegas*. Spongy was so impressed with Cambo's effort he offered him a job.

Cambo was thrown in the deep end, handling most of the design and advertising work in close collaboration with Claw. The art room became a haven for the free thinkers and misfits in the organisation. Cambo recalls his fellow artist Silas Hickey 'burning incense and playing weird music'. Even so, the work always got done. 'We were busy all the time, maybe a bit lacking direction, but I really liked that. I don't like too much oversight,' says Cambo.

He was acutely aware of the company's financial travails as they rode the roller coaster of boom and near-bust through the late '80s. 'It always seemed to be ballooning and collapsing,' says Cambo. 'One thing was going particularly well while something else was struggling. Domestically we did really well, but America was sucking. But there was always a great buoyant feeling – let's carry on regardless, let's book another trip because tomorrow it might end.'

One of Cambo's legacies was collaborating with local filmmaker Peter Kirkhouse on a series of Rip Curl videos as VHS boomed in popularity. Their gritty grunge aesthetic banished any perceptions of the Curl growing too corporate, and foreshadowed a move away from the '80s focus on surf contests. 'PK and I started doing *Savage Cuts* and *Rubber Soul* in the late '80s – '86, '87. That really started to change things. I always had the idea that the contest thing wasn't that big a deal.'

Cambo was also close to Rip Curl's all-conquering child star of the '80s, Nick Wood, who created a record that stands to this day, as the youngest surfer to win a men's major pro-tour event. Nick, the godson of Mark Richards, caused a sensation by winning the Rip Curl Pro in 1987 at the age of just 16, defeating the reigning two-time world champ Tom Curren along the way.

'Nick Wood was staying with me when he won Bells. I could see it was going to be difficult because he was so shy,' says Cambo.

Shayne Paterson remembers sharing the same concerns for their pubescent surf star, who had already developed an appetite for the frenetic tour lifestyle that would harpoon his boundless potential. 'I had to drag him out of bed and take him down to the contest the year he won it. He nearly missed his heat,' recalls Shayne. 'He was just a really shy kid, and I don't think he could handle the fame. It's a bit of a shame that back in the '80s they didn't have the resources to educate these kids.'

SPONGY MOVES ON

With the growth opportunities of the surf industry came ever-expanding workloads, in what was still a lean operation. As head of surfwear, Doug Spong was doing a loop through Hong Kong, Seoul, Taiwan and California four or five times a year, with two or three trips to Europe on top of that, and was largely left to run his own show. 'I didn't get daily direction, I only got direction twice a year, on a ski trip or surf trip,' he says.

His product range grew so vast that Accessories was cleaved off as a separate division under the direction of Pat Morgan, a development Spongy did not entirely approve of. 'I knew I needed a decent budget to get anywhere, if I was ever going to get a pay rise,' Pat says. 'Doug went away on a buying trip, so while he was away I moved in to his office. He went ballistic when he got back.'

By 1988, Spongy had built surfwear into a large, profitable division and wanted to buy in to the business, but Claw and Brian weren't having it. Burnt out from the workload and constant travel, Spongy walked away. 'I go, "Fuck this. I'm selling my house in Torquay and I'm moving to the Gold Coast. I'll be a cleaner at night and go surfing all day,"' Spongy says. Eventually, he was lured back into the surf industry at Billabong on the Gold Coast in the '90s, and successfully ran their accessories program under his own company, Thin Air. Billabong purchased the business from him for $30 million when they went public in 2000. Spongy used the windfall to launch his own surf label, Cult, which enjoyed rapid growth before he fell foul of an expensive divorce and the Global Financial Crisis. He lost the lot.

Today, Spongy lives in a modest canal home in Broadbeach Waters. He's working on a memoir of the jetsetting surf entrepreneur who made and lost several fortunes, a wild tale of perfect waves, opium dens and first-class travel. Spongy says he's still getting used to turning right into Economy when he gets on a plane rather than left into First Class.

About the only trapping of his former high-rolling life that's survived is a luxury fishing boat. When we catch up, Spongy's just returned from a fishing trip to Airlie Beach in north Queensland with his two old mates from that improbable cruise-ship voyage all those years ago. The fishing trip was dubbed The Red Dog Tour in honour of that mad red setter that pinched his football and launched the whole outlandish adventure.

THE MOVE INTO BOARD SHORTS

Before he left Rip Curl, Spongy could see that Rip Curl's move into board shorts was imminent. 'There was no written agreement [with Quiksilver] regarding board shorts and wetsuits. It was two friends adhering to an unwritten understanding,' says Spongy.

The man who eventually ushered in the move into board shorts was Grant Forbes, when he returned from his stint rebuilding the US business and took over surfwear. 'I recognised that we weren't going anywhere in the apparel business if we couldn't make shorts. I started making 'em,' says Grant.

Quiksilver responded by moving into wetsuits around the same time, and competition intensified between the two surf brands, although old friendships endured. 'One day Brian's walking around the corridors all day going, "Fucking Quiksilver". A quarter to five he picks up the phone and goes, "Greeny, what are you doing? You still going skiing on the weekend? Okay, see you down the pub,"' recalls Steve Perry.

Rod Brooks, who sold his own wetsuit business, Piping Hot, during the late-'80s credit crunch, introduced the wetsuit program at Quiksilver. 'By the time I came along Rip Curl had started making board shorts so Greeny said, "All bets are off, we'll make wetsuits as well,'" Rod says. 'I set about putting the first range together . . . Socially we still got on famously, but there was a period there from the '90s onwards when it became very competitive.'

The growing rivalry meant surfers who had been sponsored by both brands now had to choose between them. Two-time world champ Tom Carroll had sidestepped the looming conflict a couple of years earlier, in 1986, by defecting from Rip Curl to O'Neill. 'It was hard to go to an American company back then, but I felt I was going to get better support, because Curren was so prominent [at Rip Curl],' says Tom. 'Doing the sponsor change when they supported me and I loved the product was especially tough.'

Brian Singer remembers Tom flying down from Sydney and inviting them out to dinner to break the news. 'He was a real gentleman about it,' says Brian. A couple of years later Carroll made history by signing the first million-dollar endorsement contract in pro surfing, albeit over five years, when he became 100 per cent sponsored by Quiksilver.

LA BRADERIE

In 1986, Rip Curl Europe had opened its wetsuit factory at Soorts-Hossegor. Around this time, two staff members, manager Cécile Lormeau and wetsuit cutter Nicolas Lartizien, were sent to Torquay to learn the art of wetsuit-making from the man who had become the guru of the craft, John 'Sparrow' Pyburne.

'At that time, we were not trusting Asia to make us the suit and Rip Curl wanted to control its productions,' says Fred Basse. 'It was a beautiful operation, giving us a strong credibility in the market. We produced most of the wetsuits for the European market, we were doing custom-made suits and offering a quality aftersale service.'

They also opened their first Rip Curl store in downtown Hossegor. 'During the winter '85–'86, François went for a sales tour in Europe for four days,' says Fred. 'We were speaking about opening a shop at that time. In three days, with a trainee working with me called Pierre Agnes, with no money at all, we built a complete shop. It was the first Rip Curl–branded surf shop.' Pierre Agnes would go on to a distinguished career in the surf industry, rising to Quiksilver Group CEO, before he was tragically lost at sea in a boating mishap in early 2018.

But these new ventures stretched resources, and the French operation soon found itself with a serious cashflow problem. The European business was still highly seasonal and in the winter months revenue slowed to a trickle. 'One day we were broke, so we say we have to create something to get cash,' says François.

They staged a huge warehouse sale to shift surplus stock and aimed to make 300,000 francs over four days. 'In fact, we make 300,000 francs in two hours,' says François. The Easter sale became an annual tradition, as essential to the European business as the Rip Curl Pro back in Torquay. The sale, known as the *braderie* (clearance sale), was so successful it soon attracted other surf businesses to the area. Today there are 57 board-sport-related businesses in the Soorts, the greatest concentration of surf shops in Europe and possibly the world, and the Easter sale generates around three million euros. Police are required to direct traffic, parking is a nightmare and crowds flock from nearby Spain to stock up on discount surf products. Land in the area has skyrocketed in value.

When the *braderie* started, credit cards weren't common and Eftpos didn't exist so sales were almost all in cash. 'We realised we were getting serious when you have an armoured car with security guards pull up to look after the cash,' says Maurice Cole.

Buoyed by this success, François was inspired to sponsor a surfing contest in Hossegor. The Lacanau Pro had been running since 1979 just north of Hossegor, and Europe was a growing presence on the world tour. The first Rip Curl Hossegor Pro in 1986 wasn't part of the ASP (Association of Surfing Professionals) tour, but by 1987 François had taken the role of President of ASP Europe, upgraded his event to world-tour status and founded the European Professional Surfing Association to run a local circuit for European surfers.

François had a broad vision of what was required to nurture a healthy surfing industry and took on the role of president of SIMA (Surf Industry Manufacturers Association) in Europe, started a surfing magazine, *Trip Surf*, so there was some competition for the existing magazine, *Surf Session*, and initially distributed other brands like Billabong and Mambo to promote competition. He started his own print factory and took on most of the printing for the local surf industry after discovering a local surfer was pirating Rip Curl t-shirts. Rather than reporting him to the authorities, François set him to work in a legitimate business. They called the silk-screening company Toads, a play on its parent company Frogs.

'If I grow the whole market I grow my business. You need competition, you need a free press, you need a sport,' François says. 'I didn't know how much turnover we do or how many people we employ. I measure success by the perception of my brand.'

The strategy worked: the business grew, staff numbers soared and a sponsored local surf team was put together. Christine Pourtau, known universally as Kiki, was one of the first employees in 1985, handling invoicing and accounting, and has been with Rip Curl ever since. Then there were five or six staff. Today there are more than 100 working out of the Hossegor headquarters.

'I was called in just to replace a girl who was on holidays and that was 33 years ago,' Kiki says, laughing. 'François and I were friends to start with so it was complicated to see him as a boss . . . He's not patient, he's not a guy who likes to wait for you to understand.'

Even so, she recalls those early days with great fondness. 'They kind of do it for fun. It was just a good opportunity because François was an architect, he just had the opportunity to surf, to party, to be at the beach, to have a great time with his friends,' says Kiki. 'There were drugs everywhere, [the employees] were shoeless, but they worked hard. Once, a guy came to the office to sell shoes to show his collection but then he saw that they were all shoeless so he left.'

Gilles Darque, known as Keke, was one of the first sponsored Rip Curl Europe team riders, and eventually segued into a role as a sales rep and team manager. He now works as sales manager for technical products and is in charge of 'core distribution' to specialty surf shops. Kiki and Keke make a great double act, frequently cracking each other up with their nostalgic memories.

'I was a team rider and came to the warehouse and took my stuff and she would say, "You take all that stuff, for what?"' says Keke. 'I came with Patrick [Beven] and Miky [Picon] with a shopping trolley in the warehouse and we took this and this and this. We have no money but you can take everything you want. So many things. Kiki would say, "What are you doing? You're going to sell to your friends."'

'We were in the family, even the team riders, we were part of a family. We used to do custom wetsuits in your own colours. They had a book with all your measurements.'

The woman who took those measurements was wetsuit manager Patricea Dohen, who is still wielding the Rip Curl tape measure at Hossegor. Through Keke's translation, she tells me the factory was unlike any other workplace she had seen.

'In the factory people are working with no shirts, no shoes, music blaring. People say, what's up? This is a crazy place,' says

Patricea. 'At the beginning, the guys would come at 10 and have a shower after surfing, and if there were waves they would disappear and wouldn't work. And in the winter, it was a party. I said to my mother, "This factory will close, nobody wants to work." There are two people cutting and one says there's waves and you could hear machines going off and then there was no one there. In the end, only girls and dogs are at the factory and all the boys go surfing.'

The Hossegor office became famous for the number of dogs that accompanied their owners to work. 'When you start at Rip Curl they say, "I'm Guille, my dog is . . ." They have two names,' says Keke. 'When they go surfing there are plenty of dogs waiting for all the guys, dogs everywhere.'

Soon, our conversation is joined by Rip Curl Europe's first accountant, Mado Ustarroz, who has been here since 1987. 'I was working for an auditor, and a guy said to me, "They are looking for an accountant in a surfing company." I said, "Do they smoke joints? I don't think I want to work here," she says. 'I got a short contract for three months. My mother said, "How is the work?" I say, "They are very strange. I don't know if I'm going to stay."' That was 30 years ago.

'When I came here they had no accounting system, I think the computer was broken. I had to put in place all the organisation,' Mado says. 'I think we sell a dream. When we had meetings with the bank everyone was happy to see us because we were in t-shirts and they are in suits and ties. We are a dream for them.'

The Hossegor crew inherited their Torquay counterparts' taste for merging work and fun. 'By Friday afternoon there was *apéro* [drinks],' says Mado. 'I had to stop that because on the Friday afternoon they work drunk and no work gets done.'

The warm reminiscences flow as we stand around the old cutting table in the now largely idle wetsuit factory. Rows of sewing machines lie dormant, used only for the odd repair or novelty custom jobs, like Australian team rider Matt Wilkinson's range of whacky European-inspired wetsuits. These old hands miss the smells, the noises, the bustle of a working wetsuit factory, the visits from team riders getting measured up, the intricacies of custom jobs. There's a book of each team rider's vital statistics, 15 measurements from neck to ankle, and their specified colours.

The measuring-up process was an intricate and even intimate process. There's a rapid-fire volley of conversation in French and near-hysterical laughter. I look to Keke for a translation. He explains that current Spanish sales manager and former European champion Pablo Guttierrez was the youngest surfer on the team when he joined at just 15. 'Patricea was the first to touch his balls,' Keke announces with a wicked grin, setting them all off again.

François inspired enormous loyalty among his staff and his flamboyant business style permeated the company. 'If you have a big, big trouble you call François for help and he will always say yes. He has a social side, he has a humanity, it's very important,' says Keke. 'François say, "Oh, you are alone for Christmas. Come to the farm." Always helping.'

Mado concurs. 'He's charismatic so you want to follow him, even if I don't know where.'

But he could also be a tough and volatile taskmaster. 'Sometimes yelling and the next day he's super cool,' says Keke.

'He says, "I don't pay you to have problems, so bring me solutions,"' adds Mado.

Now François is not so hands-on in the business, they lament the fact that the younger generation at Rip Curl are largely unaware of his legacy. 'Most of the crew now don't know him but for most of the generations his influence was huge. The new crew are like, who is this guy with the pink pants?' says Kiki.

There's an enormous warmth for their Australian parent company and its eccentric founders, who still make quite an impression whenever they come to town. 'We organise a party for the new warehouse and there are very important people there, and there's Claw in socks and slaps [thongs],' says Keke, laughing. 'We are still a family with the Australian people, and the rest of the world, Brazil and Hawaii. If you need anything, no problem.'

I comment that Patricea is like the Sparrow of Hossegor, as the resident wetsuit guru. They all laugh knowingly at this, sparking a string of similar observations, as if Hossegor is some parallel universe to their Torquay head office, inhabited by avatars of their Southern Hemisphere equivalents.

'When we go to Torquay, for me it was strange. It was like in Hossegor, the same feeling. I met a girl, she was like our Kiki,' says Mado. When Keke met former Rip Curl team manager Gary Dunne, he had the peculiar sense of meeting an Australian version of himself.

When the Rip Curl Hossegor Pro became part of the ASP world tour in 1987 the town was well and truly on the global surf map, and word of its dreamy beach breaks, cultured lifestyle, nude beaches and wild nightlife spread throughout the surfing world. French President François Mitterrand even attended the event.

The touring pros developed an instant fondness for the French lifestyle: the food, the wine, the women, the waves, the fact that they could sell their boards for a small fortune to local surfers hungry for the latest designs from abroad. Many a struggling trials competitor funded the next leg of the tour by selling off any spare boards in their quiver. In Hossegor, local bar Rock Food and its ebullient DJ Roland became an enormous hit. 'The first Rip Curl Pro was incredible – at Rock Food there was a party every night. Foster's was a sponsor, so we always drink Foster's at the comp,' Keke recalls.

THE CURRENS COME TO HOSSEGOR

The other monumental event in French surfing in the '80s was that Tom Curren met and married a local girl, Marie-Pascale, originally from Biarritz, and the couple moved to Hossegor in '89. They were the power couple of the pro tour, surfing's own JFK and Jackie, even if they appeared to care little for the public adoration.

Tom and Marie met during the 1980 world titles in France and married in 1983. If French surfing lacked a homegrown hero, Curren was the next best thing, married to a local and fluent in the language, and the French embraced him with open arms. What's less well recognised is that Marie-Pascale was a more-than-handy surfer herself, a three-time runner-up in the French championships and a runner-up for the European title.

'I grew up in Biarritz. As soon as surfing started there were always girls surfing. There were a few here in Hossegor, in Lacanau, Biarritz. We were like the pioneers for sure – now there's girls surfing everywhere,' Marie says.

Though Marie-Pascale and Tom divorced in 1993, Marie has remained part of the Rip Curl family and now works in the marketing department at the Hossegor HQ. She agrees that when she and Tom moved to Hossegor it had a profound impact on French surfing.

'At the Rip Curl Hossegor Pro, all the crowd were backing Tom up because he was married to a French girl,' she says. When I ask Tom whether he was aware of the impact he had on French surfing, he turns the question around. 'France made an impression on me,' he says. 'There were a lot of good days surfing with the local crew.' And he has a simple explanation for Rip Curl's rapid success in Europe. 'The demand for the suits might have had something to do with it. It gets really cold. If you had one you were surfing; if you didn't have a good suit you weren't that keen.'

Tom has fond memories of his time in France, and great respect for the man behind Rip Curl France and his business partner Fred Basse. 'Fred's like the most core guy in the water, I think. François has always been a really great friend. I think he's been an incredible contributor to the company because of his mind,' says Tom.

And Torquay made just as favourable impression on Marie. 'It was really cool, this time with Tom and Rip Curl. The company was always taking care of us. We could order the wetsuits we wanted with the colours we wanted. We were pretty spoiled,' says Marie. 'Claw and I used to go surfing together all the time with his son Daniel when he was 10 or 11, because we like surfing smaller waves, three to six foot, not going to Bells with all the guys. We would drive up and down the coast and he would show me all kinds of spots. We liked driving around checking the waves almost as much as surfing. We were on these little Search trips.'

THE CALIFORNIA OF EUROPE

Even as French surfing boomed, and windsurfing opened up new markets in largely surfless countries like Germany and Sweden, François had a vision that Portugal would be an important surf nation. The once great seafaring superpower had long been dismissed as one of the least prosperous countries in Europe, but its 1800 kilometres of coastline and the concentration of its population on the coast would see surfing flourish here.

Rip Curl's man in Portugal, José Farinha, started surfing in the '70s when there were about a dozen surfers along the vast beach of Costa da Caparica in southern Lisbon. Today there are that many surf schools, each ushering hundreds more beginners into the surf every year.

'When I started surfing, it's a huge beach, we look and we join the crowd just to have fun with the other guys,' says José. His father was into sailing and the family spent weekends and holidays at the beach. José starting riding a bodyboard when he was 12, when there were no surf shops in Portugal. His first surfboard was made in a friend's garage, a replica of a Gerry Lopez Pipeline gun, based on dimensions they copied out of an article in *Surfer* magazine.

That garage start-up became Lipsticks, Portugal's first surf-board label. José can recall his country's first surf contest in 1977, between some visiting Australian and English travellers and a handful of local surfers. 'It was not recognised as a sport, it was seen as an adventure, for druggies, beach bums,' he says.

In 1987, José travelled to France to watch the Lacanau Pro, where he met François and Fred. In the kind of impulsive deal-making that characterised Rip Curl's global expansion, the Frenchmen were impressed by the young Portuguese entrepreneur and offered him a job. 'They said, "We don't have anyone repping Rip Curl in Portugal and if you want to do it, let's do it,"' says José. 'I was working in Lisbon . . . I was selling art and working in art galleries, sitting in big city traffic jams, working from nine to five – not very good for surfing – so I quit.'

José was not the first or last to be swept up by François's infec-tious enthusiasm for the potential of the European surf market. 'He said, "Portugal is going to be a huge country, because 80 per cent of the country live near the coast, it has waves all year round, it will be the California of Europe,"' recalls José. 'He's a special guy, a natural leader, a party animal. It was really easy to deal with him because we had the same ideas. He's good at motivating people. He say, "Let's go to war," and everybody was following him.'

Peniche, just over an hour's drive north of Lisbon, was the logical place for them to launch the business in Portugal. José had long spent every weekend and holiday there because of its abundant surf. Its unique geography – almost an island, connected to the mainland by a narrow finger of land – means somewhere nearby is always offshore. 'Peniche was the best option – no crowds, surf in the morning, work a little bit and surf again,' says José. They sold a grand total of 80 wetsuits in their first full year of operation in 1989 but growth, when it hit in the '90s, was rapid.

'The business took off around '95, we start really doing some money. And we are growing naturally, more and more surf shops around Portugal. In every beach where there's good waves, we have a surf shop. Suddenly we end up with 40 surf shops,' says José.

Even so, it would have been difficult to imagine how profoundly surfing and Rip Curl would reshape the old fishing town of Peniche, and what an important part of the Rip Curl empire it would become.

TURNING JAPANESE

Peter Hodgart was a knockabout surfer and former electrician from Williamstown, a tough portside suburb of Melbourne, who'd spent 10 years travelling through Asia when he decided it might be time to return home in 1987.

'You learn how to turn your hand to a lot of things. I was just a hippie with a good tongue,' says Hodg.

Hodg had settled in Tokyo working as an English teacher but was getting homesick. He managed to land a job for the local Rip Curl licensee as part of a masterplan to score a job back at Rip Curl HQ in Torquay. Hodg got his chance when Brian came to Tokyo to dine with a suitor who was lobbying for the Japanese licence.

'We had geisha girls feeding us tidbits, Hodg and I on one side and these two Japanese guys on the other side,' remembers Brian. 'One of the guys started asking impertinent questions about how much money I made and then he started denigrating Hodg's wife.

Hodg got up and towered over this bloke and said, "Listen here, you fucking cunt, any more of that and I'll deck you." It got quite tense – I guess he didn't want to mess with Hodg.'

Hodg figured he'd blown his chances of a job back in Torquay but Brian admired his spirit. 'Hodg thought he'd blown it with me, but I was going quietly to myself, "Yes! Yes! Yes!" I don't think it was too long after that that we got Hodg back to Torquay,' says Brian.

'Brian said to me, "I don't give responsibility to people, they come and take it off me,"' says Hodg. 'I thought, this guy's just said to me I can come back to Australia and run his company.' It was typical of the way Brian operates – give someone an opportunity and see what they do with it.

But after 10 years in Asia, Hodg got off to a rocky start at the Torquay office. 'Brian said to me, "Fuck off, you're working for Claw." I thought, what am I doing wrong?' recalls Hodg. 'Ray Thomas said, "You're walking around bowing your head, and being subservient to everyone." I was three-quarters Japanese. I'd been there a long time.'

'Working for me at this point included a position with Rip Curl International communicating with and serving the needs of our overseas licensees,' says Claw. 'I'd been communicating with Hodg frequently for the previous couple of years in his position at the licensee in Rip Curl Japan, and recognised the clear and prompt communication, and that he obviously understood the position of the licensees far away on the other side of the world.'

Hodg eventually settled in to the new environment and found himself well placed. 'The cottage industry was about to explode. I was in the right place at the right time,' says Hodg. 'I never thought I'd be able to have a job being 100 per cent me. I'd lost jobs because of my long hair and surfing and dope-smoking.'

Hodg developed a warm affection for the eccentricities of the company's founder. 'There's Claw's Martian antenna, or Claw's curl, or Claw's halo,' he points out, miming Claw's trademark twirling of his hair with one finger. 'We all know we work for two fucking Martians.'

Hodg's favourite memory of Brian is being called into the boardroom for a meeting with some bigwigs from the ANZ bank who wanted to present Rip Curl with a business award. 'The guy from ANZ leaned over and said to Brian, "What's your secret? How have you done it?" Brian's answer was, "If I fucking knew I'd had have 10 of them by now." It was just one of those magical things that happened.'

Hodg eventually moved into product development, where his philosophy dovetailed neatly with the founders'. 'Making money is important but the best products make a difference, they have a reason for being,' says Hodg. His approach quickly earnt him the respect of his employers and a trusted position as resident mentor for new arrivals. 'For anyone coming into the business to learn the ropes, the best place to put them was with Hodg,' says Brian. Claw agrees: 'Hodg was always one of the best trainers in the company, particularly around product, communications and customers.'

But Hodg noted a worrying trend, as new business-school graduates started to displace the surfers who had grown the business. 'You hired street-smart travellers and then you've gone and hired guys who've been told what to do all their lives, from private schools and Melbourne Uni, with marketing degrees,' says Hodg. 'A couple left because they were lost in this. A couple got it.'

One of those old surfers who moved on was Pat Morgan, and Hodg inherited the new watch division from him. Pat had founded the division almost by accident, and much to the scepticism of his employers. 'One day I found a guy who was doing watches, an Australian guy living in Hong Kong. He took me to his factory, and I ordered 1000 watches and put them in the shop,' says Pat. While the watches sold well, they also came back just as fast because they weren't built to deal with the rigours of the surf. It would be left to Pat's replacement to tackle the problem of durability.

The new era of time and motion studies and sales meetings became a bit much for the old surfboard shaper but, fortunately for Pat, he had an exit strategy. He'd followed James Arness's advice all those years ago and had developed the land he'd bought for a song back in the '70s. 'I'd bought all this land so I knew I could step out,' he says. 'Christmas '89 we moved to the Gold Coast.'

Despite the stress and debauchery, Pat recalls his time at Rip Curl with genuine warmth. He's a fit and active 76-year-old, still surfing daily, and when I visit him at his luxurious home one block back from Rainbow Bay in Coolangatta, he's busy in the garage designing and building foils and devoting himself to learning the art of foilboards, still discovering new ways to ride waves.

These days Pat doesn't make it down to Torquay often, as he finds the cold too oppressive, but he enjoys catching up with the old crew on special occasions. Sadly, these days, those occasions are often funerals. 'I went to [local surfer] Joe Sweeney's service and saw Brian and thanked him for those years. It was a fun time.'

MOUNTAINWEAR

It was inevitable that Rip Curl would move into mountainwear, as its founders had been spending their winters in the snow for more than a decade. And customers had already starting wearing Rip Curl jackets on the slopes, even though they hadn't been designed for it.

'At that stage we saw a lot of people up at Mount Buller wearing Rip Curl surfwear jackets and they'd get back on the bus wet and bedraggled. We thought we'd better make some good stuff for them,' says Brian.

Their initial efforts were unspectacular, and that first range showed at the Canberra ski show to a lukewarm reception. 'It was so bad that we were embarrassed. We decided we're going to do this properly or not at all,' says Brian. Claw took on mountain-wear and a new range was developed with the sort of focus they'd applied to wetsuits, using themselves as test pilots. Soon after, Quiksilver decided to take its mountain-and-wave logo literally and moved into mountainwear too.

'Somehow or other we got into that ski show again up in Canberra, which was kind of a semi-closed shop,' says Brian. Their second effort shook things up, with a well-designed, functional product, and suddenly the major surf brands were a serious presence on the mountains.

Brian says there were several reasons for their success in the new market. 'One was we had a credible pricing policy. The other companies had a range of discounts that depended on how well you talked. Everyone said you've got to discount. We said, we don't do that, take it or leave it. They knew when they walked in they were going to get the same price as everyone else.'

The other obvious factor was their genuine passion for snow. 'And we manned the ski show with a bunch of knowledgeable people – the designers were there, I was always there, Claw was always there,' says Brian. 'We focused on the customer and I think the surf companies, through their intense competition with each other, were much better-run companies than many people had given them credit for.'

The surfers made an impact on the ski industry in other ways. 'The ski show was a fairly straight deal with people walking around in suits and ties. When we rocked up it's fair to say we were a bit different,' says Brian. 'We were always the last to leave the trade show and then we'd go out to a local restaurant.'

One unfortunate Japanese restaurant felt the brunt of the Rip Curl crew's taste for bedlam. 'It culminated in a huge food fight . . . where some of our people were well prepared and brought eggs. When they started throwing eggs, they went through the paper walls,' recalls Claw.

PULLING OUT OF THE NOSEDIVE

It was just as well Europe and mountainwear were flourishing, because at home and in the US, Rip Curl hit serious turbulence in the late '80s. Brian went to the US for three months to personally wield the axe, laying off staff and cutting costs. The incumbent management were moved on, and Butch Barr and Grant Forbes were relied on to steady the ship. 'It took a few years, but with Butch there we found our way out of the woods and I became experienced with being in a situation where the company had no money. I learnt a lot, and we buffaloed our way through,' says Grant.

Though stressful, the US was a great inspiration and provided Forbes with broad experience in the business. 'California was an absolute creative hotbed at the time,' says Grant. 'I started working on apparel development, and really enjoyed making stuff, and taking it to the trade shows and seeing people start lining up to buy it. And I bought the company's first Mac, a "Mac II" with the first versions of Adobe Illustrator and Aldus PageMaker, and learnt how to drive the thing.'

At home, the business hit a cashflow crisis. Australia was showing the early warning signs of the 'recession we had to have', as then Treasurer Paul Keating famously dubbed it. Interest rates skyrocketed, hitting a high of 17 per cent by June 1989, and

Australia experienced the most acute economic downturn since the Great Depression. Rip Curl wasn't immune. Team riders were asked to accept a suspension of payments, jobs were cut and some vigorous discounting was adopted to shift surplus stock.

'I think we got lazy, complacent,' says Brian. 'We had two external consultants we found through our accountants. We allowed ourselves, or I allowed myself, to become distracted. Meetings became focused on our sales and profit numbers and we lost sight of the main game, which was making good-quality stuff for surfers. It was at that stage that we nearly went bankrupt.'

The close scrape with financial disaster was a sobering warning of how easily they could lose everything. 'I would have got zero, not even a car. We didn't have any money outside of Rip Curl. Every year the profits were ploughed back into the business to finance growth. With high interest rates, the bank had us by the balls,' says Brian. The bank wanted them to sell the business for whatever they could get for it to pay off their debts, but Claw and Brian were determined to trade their way out of trouble. 'It was a bit stressful. That's the only time I'd wake up in the middle of the night, particularly when I thought we were going to go broke,' says Brian.

For world champion Damien Hardman, it became pretty obvious that the business was in trouble. 'I knew they were tight. When I won my first world title, for the time I had a pretty reasonable contract and it took them two years to pay me my incentive bonus,' he says. 'At one stage they said, "If we pay your incentive we might not be here." It was in dribs and drabs.'

There were lay-offs aplenty that saw many long-term staff shown the door, and upper management weren't spared. 'I got retrenched. They halved the wages of management. It was heavy,' says Shayne Paterson. 'It was killing Brian and Claw because they had to let go a lot of people that had been there forever.'

Their unlikely saviour was the sale of the troubled US business to swimwear label Raisins. 'We went through the negotiations with them, they paid half the money that they owed and it was that half of the money that saved our arse. Without that we might have gone down the gurgler,' says Brian.

The sale price was US$3 million, and the exchange rate was favourable at the time. But the Raisins lifeline did nothing to solve the persistent problems for the brand in the US. 'We never got the other half because they mismanaged it, so we bought it back for basically nothing,' says Brian. 'During that period, we got Butch to go over there again and run the US operation. He quickly turned it around . . . in the five or six years he was over there.'

Brian reluctantly took on their troubled surfwear division in collaboration with Grant Forbes and got it back on track. 'Our surfwear division was in a mess because I had waited too long to get involved, because I didn't think I knew much about apparel,' says Brian. 'I just knew wetsuits, but it's not too hard if you focus on the basics – what do the customers want?'

In the longer term, there was much good that came out of the brush with oblivion. 'If you stop being lazy and get off your arse, roll up your sleeves and just focus on making good stuff, that's the basics of it,' says Brian. 'That was probably my most satisfying period, pulling it out of the nosedive . . . making good stuff and customer relations. Developing clear terms of engagement with our retail customers that we could stick to. I think it's unfair if you treat one retailer better than another.'

'That's when Brian was at his absolute best, when the company was up against the wall. Brian was not afraid to make the hard decisions, take the bad medicine,' says Steve Perry.

Grant has mixed feelings about this period of rebuilding. 'It was a bit deflating to put four years' hard work into helping resurrect the USA operation, and then finally come back to Australia to find the centre of the universe as shaky as it was,' says Grant. 'At least I got to buy a new Mac, and one for Cambo [Neil Campbell], who'd taken over my old advertising job. There were all sorts of crazy things going on and it took a while before people stabilised a bit . . . There was a tight little group of really hard workers.'

It took about two years to salvage the business. In that time, Brian moved out of his big office into a pokey hole in the surfwear department. 'Our biggest problem was financing the growth for that period,' he says. He gives enormous credit to Forbes for the turnaround in their business fortunes. 'At that stage he was the most productive person working at Rip Curl. He focused on what the customer wanted and he didn't need an army of people working for him,' says Brian. 'And by this time with the company, and the people maturing a bit, there were fewer parties. Of course, when the crew get together telling stories it's always the fun times that get talked about; however, daytime was always for serious work.'

Brian credits in particular Rod Adams, who as CFO and accountant gave good, timely reports, along with Ray Thomas, Peter Hodgart and Grant Forbes. 'We had a very good team,' he says. 'Claw was focusing on having the right surfers on our team and running mountainwear. And we also had a great team of sales agents. That was probably the most enjoyable part of my job, visiting surf shops with sales agents. You were at the coalface, it was real. That was where the rubber hit the road. You learnt more about the business out in retail land and in the warehouse because that's where you see all your mistakes.'

The business crisis came on top of a testing time personally for Brian, who acknowledges that the demands of running Rip Curl had taken a toll on his marriage. 'On the personal side it was a fairly tumultuous time because my marriage wasn't working out, and Jenny and I separated again around '82,' Brian recalls. 'After a couple of years of the single life I met Leighanne, who was one of the crew working for Steve Perry in the retail store, and not long after we had a daughter, Jade, and she became a part of the Singer clan along with Samala, Naomi and Doji. Jade was born in late '88 and we got married later with Jade as flower girl.'

THE SEED OF THE SEARCH

In 1987, Cronulla goofy-footer Gary Green was rated sixth in the world when he abruptly quit the pro tour, citing disillusionment with the hectic contest schedule, dubious judging, substandard waves and the uncertain financial returns of pro surfing. Greeny was always a fun, irreverent presence on tour, with a fast, nimble style developed in Cronulla's punchy beach breaks and reefs. But the tour seemed to be sapping his spirit.

He gave it another crack in 1988, but 'my heart wasn't in it,' he says now. A fateful trip to Bells changed his life and expanded the career options of pro surfers well into the future. Greeny had been wearing Rip Curl wetsuits since leaving his old sponsor, Billabong, and was staying at Claw's house when Claw and Rip Curl coach Derek Hynd disappeared upstairs for a meeting. Hynd was an ex-pro surfer who'd lost an eye in a surfing accident and had become one of pro surfing's first full-time coaches.

'I was downstairs and I didn't even know what was going on but they were planning something,' remembers Greeny. 'And then they've called me up and gone, "What do you think about this?" and I've gone, "Is this a joke? This is unbelievable."'

What Claw and DH had been hatching was an innovative scheme to employ Greeny as a professional surf traveller, to be on call whenever they needed a surfer to go on a trip for film and photo shoots. The most immediate plan was to send him on a long, open-ended trip through Indonesia with filmmaker Peter Kirkhouse and photographer Ted Grambeau.

Greeny wasn't the first surfer to quit the tour at the peak of his powers to chase quality waves. Another Cronulla goofy-footer, Jim Banks, had pulled a similar move back in '81, but no one had been paying Banksy when he went tube-hunting through Indo and north-western Australia. Greeny was the first to be sponsored purely to travel and surf, and it would prove a portent of things to come in the decade ahead. 'The idea was brilliant because not everyone's into the competitive side of things,' says Greeny.

But Claw and Derek may have been dreaming up more than one surfer's freewheeling job description and a trip to Indo in that upstairs meeting. Hynd was a huge admirer of Greeny's surfing, from his days as a Billabong coach and also a Newport Plus teammate, when Greeny had migrated from Cronulla to Sydney's Northern Beaches to join the '80s super-club. 'For me, Greeny on his day was as insane to watch as Curren . . . He just could not be left to rot off the vine,' says Derek.

The '80s had been turbulent for Rip Curl, with geographic expansions, product diversification, spectacular growth and near-bankruptcy. As a new decade dawned, Rip Curl was ripe for fresh inspiration. Garish fluoro logos and big grandstand events at city beaches were about to give way to a whole new trip.

BRIAN'S OWN SEARCH

Amid the business CPR, Brian managed to do a fair bit of searching of his own. If he wasn't in the office, he was most likely skiing at Mount Buller or Chamonix, or sniffing out a surf destination somewhere along the way. Having been among the early arrivals at Bells Beach and Bali, Brian understood the value of being part of the first wave of surf migrants to a new wave region. In the late '80s he achieved that again when he visited the little-known Indian Ocean island nation of the Maldives.

'I'd been in Chamonix skiing and I was looking for a place to go surfing on the way home, and I'd heard that Alby Falzon [the filmmaker behind *Morning of the Earth*] had made a movie in the Maldives,' says Brian.

Brian contacted Rip Curl HQ to have his surfboards sent to Malé, the Maldivian capital, and arrived at the tropical atoll loaded down with all his ski gear. 'I go on this boat trip to an authentic fishing village and a guy there starts telling me about Tony Hussein,' says Brian.

Tony 'Hussein' Hinde was a salty old sea-dog from Sydney credited with pioneering surfing in the Maldives, after he and surfing buddy Mark Scanlon had been marooned there during a sailing adventure in 1973. The pair were crewing on a ketch called *Whitewings*, en route from Sri Lanka to Réunion Island, when it was shipwrecked on a reef in the dead of night. Having stumbled upon every surfer's paradise, Hinde never left. He converted to Islam and changed his surname to 'Hussein', married a local woman named Zulfa, and created the Maldives' first surf resort at Pasta Point.

Brian tracked down the legendary surf pioneer long before surf tourism had arrived in the atoll, and Hussein gave him a comprehensive tour of the local surf spots he'd discovered. 'He's got a zodiac, and him and I go around surfing all these breaks with no one there – Sultans, Pasta Point,' says Brian.

'He quizzed me about Tavarua [the world's first commercial surf camp], he said he wanted to start a surf camp. Not many years later, that's when he started the surf resort at Pasta Point,' says

Brian. The resort he founded, now known as Cinnamon Dhonveli, is one of the most luxurious surf resorts in the world, a long way from the simple life Hussein had initially created for himself. 'He lived very rough with his wife's family on the island that is now Pasta Point. He wore a sarong and in the evening he'd get up on the dining table and pull the sarong over him, and that was his bed,' recalls Brian.

Hussein saw his surf discovery transformed from a remote backwater to a hub of luxury tourism that hosts almost a million visitors a year. In May 2008, at the age of 55, Hussein was enjoying the waves of Pasta Point when he kicked out at the end of a ride, suffered a heart attack and was found floating facedown in the channel of the wave he discovered.

THE SALES AGENTS

The late '80s and early '90s were the heyday of the sales agents, when generous commission deals grew into sizeable fortunes. 'We had a great team of sales agents: Steve Jones in Sydney, Phil Bishop in South Australia, Mick Flynn in Victoria, Barry Young in WA. They were all highly motivated,' says Brian. 'The sales agents were earning so much, gradually they had to have reduced commissions. But I always gave them a year's notice of any reduction.'

The sums being made by the sales agents caused some angst for staff back in Torquay, who made a fraction of their vast riches. 'That was a bit of a bugbear for us in the engine room,' says Neil Campbell, who reckons he was earning roughly one-tenth of the most successful agents.

Rip Curl's first agent in Australia was Barry Young, who moved from Adelaide to Perth in '72 and started repping for the brand in '73. 'I'd made the decision to go to WA because I wanted to start my own business. I thought, if I really want to do something myself I saw WA as a new frontier,' says Barry. Initially, he only had wetsuits to show and there were only three surf shops in Perth. 'After I started they rang me up and said, "Mate, do you want to do a board short range? One of our partners has left and started this board short label called Quiksilver."' Barry became sales agent for both Rip Curl and Quiksilver. 'It was a slow process. Nothing really happened until five years later, when there was a sniff that this would develop into something,' he says.

When the boom hit in the '80s it was beyond anything he could have imagined. 'I knew something was happening when I started selling the product and people came back and said, "Everything you gave me sold." They thought I was some sort of god,' says Barry. 'You just could do no wrong. Everything these retailers were buying they were selling . . . We were getting paid on time because everyone wanted the product, they couldn't afford not to have the product and they would do anything to become an account.'

At one stage, Young employed eight people and had one of the biggest agencies in the country, and always hit or exceeded sales targets as the growth of the surf industry seemed unending. 'We always got the figures, that wasn't a problem. Everything was done on a handshake,' he says.

Young repped for both Torquay surf brands right through the '80s, until their growing rivalry made that untenable. He let Quik- silver go but continued with Rip Curl until 1996, by which time he'd done so well out of the surf business he could afford to retire to his beach house at Yallingup, at the age of 49.

Steve Jones was another agent who rode the great '80s surf boom – a former pro surfer who took shifts at the Newcastle steel- works to fund his travels on tour. 'I'd been on tour a few years when they offered me a job. I was one of the first to come from a surf-contest background to become a surf executive,' says Steve. He started in the Sydney office alongside Shayne Paterson and Belinda Hardman, working for both Rip Curl and Quiksilver initially, before moving into a role as NSW sales manager for Rip Curl, and eventually starting his own agency.

'Somewhere in the late '80s it boomed. Wow! T-shirts, clothing, everyone started making accessories. We basically couldn't keep up with supply,' says Steve. 'It really started from us as surfers, that was how the products were developed, for us surfers, then all of a sudden people were buying our lifestyle, our madness, as travellers and adventurers, and as hardcore people.' Steve did well enough out of his Rip Curl gig to semi-retire in 2000 at the age of just 43. For another 10 years he partnered in a Rip Curl store in Bondi with his old mate, former Channel Nine boss Dave Gyngell.

The sales agents were a colourful cast who proudly upheld Rip Curl's party culture, none more so than Queensland agent Dave Cross. 'A highly unusual guy, very smart, with an unorthodox selling approach,' recalls Brian. 'He didn't want to spend too much time working and he didn't have to because he was so intelligent.'

Crossy hailed from Victoria's Mornington Peninsula, had been a member of the East Coast Boardriders, and had ended up in Hong Kong working for the police force. He married a local woman, Violet, moved back to Australia and wound up selling hi-fi gear in Queensland. But the booming surf industry caught his eye. Crossy launched his own swimwear label, Wild, which Rip Curl bought a 50 per cent stake in, and he soon made an impact as Rip Curl's Queensland agent.

Brian stayed with Crossy, as he was universally known, all through the '80s whenever he visited the Gold Coast, and had finally met his match in the party stakes. 'He'd go on a bender for a few days at a time. He'd see a mob of bikies in a bar and challenge one of them to an arm wrestle and win – he just had that knack of getting on with people,' says Brian.

At a sales conference on Fraser Island with all of Rip Curl's agents, Crossy distinguished himself by being unable to deliver his sales report because he'd dropped a tab of acid prior to the meeting. Needless to say, Brian wasn't too happy about this. A business lunch with Crossy was just as likely to lead to a night-club in Surfers Paradise as a search for gold-top mushrooms in the Gold Coast hinterland. After days of excess, Crossy would spend just as long sleeping it off in extended periods of hiberna-tion before hitting the road ready to sell again. But it was a cycle that was never likely to end well.

In 1991, Dave took his own life, sending shock waves through the surf industry. 'I was shocked and then angry,' says Brian. In the search for answers, Brian recalled David talking about the suicide of two of his closest mates many years earlier, which he'd struggled with. 'Not even his close friends realised he'd probably been an alcoholic,' says Brian.

Crossy had gone on a massive bender then spent nine weeks determinedly drying out, but somewhere along the way, the battle had become too much. For many, it felt like a wild decade of surf industry excess had come to a sobering close.

CHAPTER SIX

THE BIRTH OF THE SEARCH: 1990–1994

In 1991, two Australian surfers who'd been gorging on the perfect waves and business opportunities of the great Balinese surf boom since the early '70s arrived in Torquay looking to make a deal. In an audacious move, Stephen Palmer and Robert Wilson had registered the trademarks of the major surf brands in Indonesia, hoping to use them as leverage to become legitimate licensees for the companies in a growing market.

The surf labels had been ravaged by counterfeiters and pirates exploiting their brands in Asia for years and were keen to find a solution. But no one was sure what to make of these two. Stephen and Robert were old mates from Parramatta in Sydney's Western Suburbs, dreaded "westies" in surfing parlance, who'd been inspired to travel to Bali by Alby Falzon's seminal '70s surf movie, *Morning of the Earth*. While they'd fallen for its idyllic hippie vibe and the mesmerising surf and exotica of Bali, they also exhibited an early entrepreneurial streak, a bit like the Rip Curl founders themselves.

To fund Robert's first trip to Bali back in 1973, they'd hired a copy of *Morning of the Earth* and a projector from the Silver Screen cinema in Manly, hung a sheet from the second floor of Stephen's parents' place and invited everyone they knew to come over. 'Remember this was the Western Suburbs so it was a mixed bag – we had revheads, bikers, surfers and your local pub crew. Word had gotten out and around 500 people showed up,' says Stephen. A liberal supply of weed ensured there were no issues between the rival subcultures in attendance. 'No problem finding the place from streets away – just look up in the sky for the big blue mushroom cloud above us illuminated by the projector,' says Stephen.

Robert spent six weeks in Bali before travelling through Java, Sumatra, Thailand and Malaysia. He returned home a year later and convinced Stephen to quit uni and join him. On their first few trips to Bali, the pair would buy up rayon shirts for a dollar each and sell them for $8 in Australia to raise the funds for their next trip. Robert went on to find work in north-west Australia and became a commercial diver to fund his Indonesian travels, while Stephen stayed in Bali and applied himself to learning the rag trade, eventually starting the OM Clothing Company. Rob returned to Bali in '78 and became a partner in OM, and they were successful enough to sponsor the OM Bali Pro-Am in '79 at Uluwatu, which evolved into an ASP-sanctioned tour event in '80 and '81.

But OM's Balinese-themed fashions went out of style in the '80s. Robert pursued his diving work and hooked up with pioneer surf explorer Martin Daly and a few mates. They chartered a salvage boat called the *Raider*, then skippered by Dave Barnett, to discover the waves of Panaitan, Enggano and numerous unnamed spots off the coasts of Java and Sumatra. Daly would eventually buy the *Raider* from Barnett and rename it the *Indies Trader*, pioneering the modern surf-charter industry. Robert later launched Australia's first outback motorcycle tours, Wild Bull Tours, while Stephen continued to work in clothing and eventually founded the brand Lost Boys, which became hugely successful in Bali in the '90s.

'That was with Phillip Hergstrom (RIP), from Beach Crew, and Rohan Robinson, now a fine artist,' says Stephen. 'It was going off and would have been a real contender, but Phillip was in a big hurry to grow it fast so brought in some very heavy local players from Jakarta. One day they told us they had registered the Lost Boys trademark in Indonesia and we could work for them now if we wanted to. Rohan and I did a moonwalk out the room saying, good luck, and never went back.'

Stephen retreated to his favourite eatery, Aromas in Jalan Legian, to lick his wounds, picked up a copy of *Surfer* magazine, flicked through pages and pages of ads by the major surf labels enjoying boom times in the US and Australia, and a lightbulb turned on. He grabbed some paper, traced the logos of the surf brands in black texta and went to see his friend, pioneering Balinese surfer Wayan Suwenda. 'I said, I'd like to get Robert involved with us, register these trademarks and go for the licence for as many as we could in Indonesia,' says Stephen. 'If we held the trademarks we would be in a good position to talk directly with the owners as opposed to going through the front-door hierarchy.'

'We would have returned the trademarks and scripts at cost regardless of becoming licensees or not – we were not planning on becoming pirates,' says Robert. 'What we were counting on when we approached the surf brands was that we had some credibility, given what we had achieved with OM.'

Stephen and Rob found themselves at the '91 Rip Curl Pro standing on the cliffs at Bells with Brian and Al Green. The initial reception was frosty, to say the least. 'Alan said, "So these are the pirates from Indo that have us by the balls. Let's throw them over the cliff,"' says Stephen. 'Fortunately, he was only joking. I think they respected our go-for-it attitude and next day we first met with Brian and Claw at Rip Curl, then Alan and John [Law] at Quik.'

The surf industry founders may have seen a little of themselves in these cheeky upstarts from Indo, and they agreed to grant them the licences. With their mission accomplished, Stephen and Robert jumped on a train north. Robert got off at Taree to speak to Hot Tuna founder Richard Meldrum, and Stephen went to the Gold Coast to meet with Billabong's Gordon Merchant.

The brands were all competitors, so Stephen and Robert divided them among themselves. They decided Wayan should take on Billabong. 'We thought Wayan would handle the visits to the Gold Coast much easier than to the colder Torquay,' says Robert. Stephen had a long history in clothing, so it made sense for him to handle Quiksilver and Robert to take on Rip Curl. 'I had always felt an affinity to the brand after getting one of their first wetsuits and loving to surf Bells and Winki,' says Rob.

The group had strong networks in Bali and quickly got stock into existing surf shops, launched their own branded stores and tackled the counterfeiters. 'By representing the international brands in legitimate trade, the Indonesian licensee had the legal right to prosecute counterfeiters, which we did on a regular and productive basis,' says Robert.

They understood cashflow would be a critical issue for many local stores so offered stock on consignment to ensure they held an adequate range of products, and maintained consistent pricing. 'Each week each store had to pay 70 per cent of their sales to the various suppliers, which meant great cashflow,' says Robert. 'No payment eventually meant no stock replenishment and everyone was doing well so there were no problems to speak of . . . This same system remains in place today.'

Robert and his Indonesian partner Fauziah quickly settled in to the business relationship with Rip Curl. 'Fauziah and I became the Rip Curl licensees and so part of the Rip Curl family, where we have ever since been treated very well,' says Robert. Robert and Fauziah's son, Lee Wilson, would go on to become one of Bali's best surfers and a two-time Indonesian champion.

Robert's first assignment as Indonesian licensee was to arrange a boat trip for senior management. It was an expedition that would have a far-reaching impact on the future of the business.

THE SEARCH

The brush with bankruptcy as the '80s came to a close gave Rip Curl's upper management cause to do a bit of soul-searching by looking back to their origins. 'The '70s was all about country soul, optimism, organic food, soft drugs, it was all that live-well idealism,' says Brian. 'Into the '80s, it became fluoro wetsuits and contests, Wall Street and "greed is good". You get to the end of the '80s and realise this isn't going to go on, and maybe the '90s was going to be a bit of a reversion.'

Claw agrees: 'We all got caught up in the greed thing. That was the main thing for Brian and myself, to identify a sense of change. It goes back to when we first started Rip Curl [surfboards] in '67, that first Summer of Love . . . There were some attitudes and a vibe abroad in the community, the restless youth.'

The founders had also begun thinking about the need for co-ordinated advertising campaigns. 'We had been thinking about what made us successful,' says Brian, 'and when we were young jumping in the back of a station wagon with a few mates, looking for waves, that spirit of 18-to-20-year-olds – having some nice, uncrowded waves, smoking a couple of joints, having a few beers, meeting some girls and then getting up the next sunny day and doing it all again.'

Brian and Claw met with a number of surf magazine editors in Australia and the US, who all responded enthusiastically to this image. Reader surveys always showed travel was the most popular feature of the magazines, so this was another indication they were on the right track.

Rip Curl convened an international management conference on a boat trip through Eastern Indonesia to brainstorm a new campaign, and this nostalgic mood became a talking point. 'We wanted to portray this feeling of going up the coast with a few mates. Someone just plucked out the word "search", which epitomises that feeling,' says Brian.

'We were always on the search in the beginning, long before the campaign and the famous boat trip,' says Claw. 'I think these things are the true values of surfers. They were the spirit of surfing long before us – get in the car and drive up or down the coast. We'd been doing a lot of that sort of searching. We were always travelling. I think it's a Victorian thing – you have to travel to find surf – but that existed right around the coast of Australia. We were always very nomadic, trying to find new and better waves.'

On board that floating management meeting were Claw and Brian, François Payot, artists Grant Forbes and Rohan 'Bagman' Robinson from Torquay, Marty Gilchrist from the US and Robert Wilson.

'We chartered Brett Beazely's newly imported 26-foot Kevlacat for fast transits and David Plant's yacht *Wyeema* to live aboard,' says Robert. 'Apart from the traditional Balinese outriggers and Brett Haysom's vessel *Anne Judith*, *Wyeema* was the first real surf-charter vessel operating out of Bali or Jakarta.'

The trip placed them at the leading edge of a new era of Indonesian surf exploration. Throwing your boards in the back of the station wagon and disappearing up or down the coast was soon supplanted by jumping on a plane to Indo and stashing your boards on a charter boat. The team headed east from Bali through Lombok and Sumbawa, surfing relatively recent discoveries like Scar Reef and Yo-Yos.

'Rip Curl have always combined business with pleasure and the Lombok–Sumbawa trip was no different – great waves, fishing and brainstorming. I'm not positive about who exactly came up with "The Search"; however, I have a feeling it was Brian, and I recall we all immediately agreed,' says Robert. Brian deflects the credit elsewhere. 'Marty Gilchrist might have come up with "The Search,"' he reckons. Claw says it was an idea he had been bouncing around for a while with artists Rohan and Cambo, which coalesced during that boat trip.

Regardless, the consensus in the midst of two weeks of good waves, beers, fresh fish and camaraderie was that they were onto something.

THE ARTIST

The newbie on board that boat trip was Rohan 'Bagman' Robinson, fresh from a stint working on the ill-fated Lost Boys venture in Bali with Stephen Palmer. Bagman was an old Geelong boy who'd been orbiting the Rip Curl galaxy since he'd been a grom. He'd entered a competition in *Tracks* to design a new Rip Curl logo as a schoolkid back in 1978 and had applied for a job in the retail store when he left school. But when he didn't get the job he went travelling, and had wound up in Bali as creative director for Lost Boys.

Like Stephen Palmer, he believes Lost Boys could have grown into a major international label. There were trade shows in Japan, exports to the US and a brief heady period based in Amsterdam where they sought inspiration in the infamous coffeeshop scene before the Lost Boys empire imploded.

When Rohan returned home to consider his career options, Stephen Palmer was in Torquay securing the Indonesian licence for the major surf brands. When Brian asked Stephen if he knew any good artists, Stephen dropped Rohan's name. After an interview with Brian, Rohan joined his old art school mate Neil Campbell in the Rip Curl art department. Only a few months after starting, Rohan found himself on board that fateful boat trip with the international management team.

I've tracked Bagman down to a secluded hinterland cabin near Mount Warning in northern New South Wales, where he spends his days painting in a ramshackle studio and soaking up the rural, subtropical ambience. It's a long way from the hubbub of Rip Curl head office, and his key role in one of the most enduring ad campaigns in surfing history.

'I see the whole Search thing as an extension of Lost Boys,' Rohan says, as he doodles in pencil on the old wooden table we are seated at on his front porch. Lorikeets screech in overhanging grape vines and banana trees, the hinterland looming over us as if it might reclaim the cabin if it were vacated for too long. With a quick flourish he recreates the original Search logo in pencil, and it conjures up memories of the era – Curren, Frankie Oberholzer and crew tripping through Indonesia and Africa and beyond.

Rohan's original Search imagery combined a stylised sun designed by Neil Campbell with Grant Forbes' Rip Curl diamond wave logo and what Claw dubbed 'the cosmic kiss', a red swirl that looked like a pair of lips. Rohan says the linework was inspired by New York street artist Keith Haring's iconic imagery, and he based the cosmic kiss on an image he found in a book of Aztec art bought from a second-hand store. 'It was bang, bang, bang. I don't think I mucked around with it too much,' he says. He, Claw and Cambo then built up a story around the Search concept.

'As an artist, having depth to something is what gives it longevity, building depth to the whole story rather than it just being on one level,' says Rohan. He has always suspected the retro musical tastes of the art department influenced the 'country soul' aesthetic of the Search campaign. 'We were playing a lot of Neil Young and we were playing it next to Claw's office,' he says with a chuckle.

TAKING IT TO THE BEACH

When the charter crew returned to Torquay, the theme was roundly embraced and a decision was made to bet the farm on it. 'We committed all of our advertising for the next year to it. It's like anything – if you're going to do it, you've got to do it full bore,' says Brian. 'We had the name, "The Search". We then needed to figure out a way to communicate this.'

Neil Campbell was a bit dirty that he hadn't scored a berth on the boat trip, but he dived into the Search campaign regardless. 'When Claw first came in and talked to me about the Search I thought, this is fucking brilliant. We were just frothing about it,' Cambo recalls. 'I just said, "Claw, that's genius." No one was interested in photos of surfers in contest vests. I want to see exotic places, and that's what most surfers are into, exotic waves.'

'We realised it was a big risk,' says Brian. 'There were even discussions about stopping the Bells contest at that time.' Fortunately, the contest survived, but in every other way Rip Curl's advertising and promotion were centred on the Search.

They first ran a teaser campaign featuring nothing but the new Search logo to build intrigue, a technique Claw and Brian had learnt from their early days road-showing Dave 'The Mex'

Sumpter's surf movies. 'For his film *Free Form* we went around sticking up little flyers saying, "*Free Form* is coming," a week before the actual movie posters went up,' says Brian.

The next stage of the campaign comprised empty line-up shots with Rip Curl and Search logos, a dramatic shift from the tight action photography and product shots that had come to dominate surf advertising. Cambo struck the mother lode when photographer Ted Grambeau presented him with a treasure trove of beautiful line-up shots from his recent travels. The Search campaign was away.

Brian was keen to test the reception out in the marketplace. 'I travelled up the coast on a shop trip three, four, five months after it kicked off and after the line-up shots were being used,' says Brian. 'Some people including MR were talking to me and using words exactly as we'd used them back in the office. Obviously it was communicating exactly what we wanted to communicate.'

Brian learnt another valuable lesson in resisting the overtures of his graphic artists to update or overhaul the campaign after 12 months. He was convinced they needed to hold their line. 'Another interesting thing is the artists are quick to say it's getting boring,' says Brian. 'Paul Neilsen [champion surfer and retailer] said it would be stupid to change, it's just starting to percolate through to the everyday surfer.'

The Search proved a far more enduring campaign than anyone could have imagined. 'Over time, it became a bit of a catchcry for the spirit of the business, that everyone at Rip Curl was on their own personal search and that the workplace should be a platform for them to launch their own journey of discovery – whether the goal be waves, career advancement, travel, or to find themselves,' says Rob Wilson. 'That might sound overly noble for a surf company but it is written into the company's core values.'

THE PHOTOGRAPHER

Around the same time as the Rip Curl management team were floating around Eastern Indonesia, a lone nomadic surf photographer named Ted Grambeau was traipsing about an island chain off the north-west coast of Africa. Ted had arranged to rendezvous with Tom Curren and Gary Elkerton, who were there to compete in an event. Ted hoped to drag them off on some serious surf exploration, which was more to his tastes.

Instead, Ted came down with a staph infection and spent 10 days in hospital, after which Curren and Elkerton were long gone, but the surf was pumping. Rather than cut his losses, without any surfers to photograph Ted roamed the islands, shooting the surf from every conceivable angle.

'Without surfers there, I got freed up to shoot line-ups because I didn't have an assignment,' says Ted. 'I'd be on the tops of hills and looking through valleys. There were incredible 10-foot swells back to back.'

Ted had no idea what he'd do with all these shots of stunning seascapes and empty waves. When he returned home he learnt of the Search campaign and realised he had a market for them. 'I thought, they've designed this for me. The Search was a combination of all the things I'd wished for in my photographic journey,' says Ted. 'The Search offered me a platform and a philosophy that was tailor-made to what I already believed in – show and don't tell. We were always at great pains to not reveal where we surfed, not to reveal places but to inspire people to go on their own search.'

Derek Hynd was hired as a freelance creative director for the campaign, despatching the Rip Curl team to the far reaches of the surfable world, and Ted became their lensman of choice. In the ensuing years Ted spent more time on Search trips than anyone, often with legendary surf explorer Martin Daly, skipper of the *Indies Trader*.

'One of the most significant moments was on one of the first trips on the Search when Brian and Claw came,' says Ted. 'Very rarely would you have the CEO or owners of a company involved in promotional activities on such a grassroots level. One of the images that captures that is of Brian and Claw and Curren and Sonny at the helm of the *Indies Trader* on the Search – you can just see everyone's beaming about being there. This is what it's all about. To me it sums up the Search. It runs through the whole company.'

Ask Ted to nominate his favourite moments on the Search and he rattles off a highlight reel of some of the most indelible sessions in surf travel history – Curren riding a Sunset-style right on a tiny Tommy Peterson fish or Curren's immortal first wave at Jeffreys Bay; discovering a perfect break in Mozambique with only a few local fishermen as an audience; pioneering surf missions to Russia, Iceland and Norway. Ted has a simple travel philosophy that made him the ideal anchorman on so many Search expeditions. 'The more challenging a trip is, the more valuable that trip becomes in the long run. Having shared difficult experiences with people becomes much more special than something that just goes to plan,' he says.

THE FILMMAKER

All these exotic surf missions were captured by Californian surf filmmaker Sonny Miller. Employing his artistic eye and enthusiastic work ethic, Miller's staggering body of work includes a feature length release every year for six consecutive years: *The Search* (1992), *The Search II* (1993), *Beyond the Boundaries: The Search III* (1994), *Feral Kingdom* (1995), *Tripping the Planet* (1996) and his magnum opus, *Searching for Tom Curren* (1996), which was awarded Video of the Year by *Surfer* magazine in 1997.

Sadly, Sonny Miller died of a heart attack in 2014 at the age of just 53. Only a year before his death, Sonny recorded a rare interview alongside Curren in front of a live audience for a US radio surf program, *Swell Season Surf Radio*, with host Tyler Breuer. It provides a rare insight into the inner workings of the Search program, and the dedication of Miller to its surf-adventure ethos. The occasion was a fundraiser for the Hurricane Sandy relief effort, and was the only theatrical screening of *Searching for Tom Curren*.

Miller thrived on the often chaotic and spontaneous nature of their travels. 'We were inspired by our opportunity to be given this glorious pathway,' said Miller. 'There's no Surfline [the surf forecasting service]. Our endeavours a lot of times were rewarded by our commitment to believe, like buying a lotto ticket. We didn't rely on guarantees: "You fly here for four days, you score." That's how it is today. We didn't have that.'

For Ted Grambeau, it was invaluable to have a kindred spirit on those trips, always ready to pull over to capture an evocative image. 'The times with Sonny driving around the countryside, stopping to take photos ourselves without the surfers, were always memorable,' says Ted. They also shared the purist's devotion to their craft, at a time when shooting on film meant you had to make every shot count.

'Not only do you have to be extremely precise in your technical aspects of exposure and shutter speed and how you stored the film, you only had a very limited amount,' says Ted. 'It was almost like bullets, and when you were out of film a trip was over for you. It really led to people understanding their craft to a much greater degree. Sonny was passionate about the craft of filmmaking, and incredibly experienced at documenting the world in interesting times.'

In the *Swell Season Surf Radio* interview, Sonny noted humbly, 'I was creating an illusion. That three and a half minutes [of film] might have taken three and a half months [to capture]. We were patient and we were lucky, it was a combination of the two.'

'I used to do camera support for Sonny on the beach quite a bit,' says Claw. 'We took one or two bottles of water, had no food, and we'd try and find places in the shade where you could cover the scene. Sometimes we had radios but usually not. You would just have to respond spontaneously, pick up the cameras and run up the reef. It was all a lot of fun. We were often befriended by people we hadn't even known were there, and they'd provide us with some sustenance, some rice or curried fish or tea or water. Sonny was fairly fair-skinned. He'd be burnt and parched, and someone would turn up with a coconut – "Here, white man, drink this!"'

'Sonny was probably one of the best people I've ever travelled with. He had the most upbeat nature. You could be in the most diabolical situation and Sonny is all happy and ready to go,' says Ted. 'That's just what you need on trips like the Search, when it's straining everyone's tolerance. He knew how to have a good time in life as well as get the job done in the most professional manner.'

Tom Curren goes even further. 'You know what held it together was Sonny's personality,' says Tom. 'He had this way of cheering people up when they're not feeling so good. That's what he was really able to do, and to look at the hilarity as opposed to looking at the hassle.'

THE ULTERIOR MOTIVE

There was another motivation for the Search that had little do with exotic waves on far-flung shores. Rip Curl team riders had enjoyed a stellar run through the '80s and early '90s. Aussie goofy-footers

Tom Carroll, then co-sponsored by Rip Curl and Instinct, and Damien Hardman had collected two world titles each, and Tom Curren had claimed another three, giving the Curl seven men's world titles in a decade. But they saw an ominous cloud on the horizon that suggested their run was due to come to an end. That cloud's name was Robert Kelly Slater, a hyper-talented Floridian. Kelly had ridden for Ocean Pacific and Rip Curl early in his career, just like his mentor Tom Curren, but in 1990 Quiksilver won the biggest bidding war in surfing history to sign the budding superstar.

'His manager Brian Taylor said, "You can start bidding at a million a year," but we didn't have the firepower to pay that sort of money,' says Claw. 'Our official line was, "We think you should take the Quiksilver deal. If they're going to give you a million a year, stop talking to us now and go over there and get the pen on the paper."'

Rip Curl knew they couldn't count on pro-tour success to put their surfers foremost in the public consciousness in the era of Slater. 'One of the many factors [for the Search] was that we thought Kelly was going to dominate for a period of time. We couldn't see any great surfers on the horizon to challenge Kelly and reach that level of intensity and excellence,' says Claw.

In that context, it made even more sense to create a non-competitive arena in which to showcase the dazzling talents, colourful personalities and wanderlust of the Rip Curl team. The idea of getting barrelled in Indo rather than schooled by Kelly in heats obviously had its appeal. No one could have predicted that Kelly would go on to collect an astounding 11 world titles over the most successful and enduring career in surfing history. With the benefit of hindsight, switching the focus from competition to travel seems like an act of genius.

CURREN ON THE SEARCH

The Search came along at the perfect time for Tom Curren. He'd become jaded with the world tour after his three world titles and had separated from Marie-Pascale in 1989. He was well placed to indulge the freewheeling itinerary of the professional surf traveller.

'It was presented to me as a filming-trip involvement,' says Tom. 'Sonny would be involved and the travels would take us here and there. Whatever it was called, the Search as a name, it's not an original name, per se, it's borrowed from other sources.' Tom points to Greg Noll's early surf movie, *The Search for Surf*, and Jack McCoy's classic '70s short film, *A Day in the Life of Wayne Lynch*, as likely inspirations.

'There were some major highlights and the quality of the waves we were getting. I was looking at some footage recently – we went all over, we went all kinds of different places. We were travelling and it was really fun. I had been competing and doing this was a complete change of pace,' says Tom.

After the structure and rapid travel of the pro tour, there was a glorious freedom and open-ended escapism in the Search program, but also a sense that the free-surfing path didn't offer career longevity. 'There was an uncertainty about how long that would go for,' says Tom. 'Rip Curl was willing to support this, whereas a company that was more mainstream wouldn't have. They went for it, they liked it, and they can look back and see if it was a good or bad business decision. I know a lot of people liked the films.'

Curren was the spiritual leader of an eclectic band of surf gypsies carefully selected by behind-the-scenes svengali Derek Hynd: relatively unheralded talents like Frankie Oberholzer and Byron Howarth from South Africa, Boris Le Texier from Réunion, and young Narrabeen rippers Chris Davidson and Nathan Hedge.

Frankie and Tom, in particular, hit it off with their similar silky-smooth styles and a penchant for free-form jamming on guitars. Hynd had talked up Frankie's abilities after discovering him at Jeffreys Bay, and the young South African didn't disappoint. 'Derek was like, "You've got to see this kid, he's the best surfer in the world," and he was serious. He meant it. He can only see out of one eye so he can't see that well,' Curren quips. 'But he's right, in a sense. [Frankie] was very good – very young but very good. He had all the new-school tricks, and he always had this really good technique. You can't get that technique without surfing a lot of waves, and he just surfed his brains out and he just got really good, and that's when I met him.'

For many, the Search will always be synonymous with Curren's epic first wave at Jeffreys Bay, the beginning of a long love affair and as timeless a piece of surfing synchronicity as has ever been captured on film. Tom reveals there was one quick take-off and kick-out before the celebrated 'first wave', but no one's quibbling.

'We had these great swells in South Africa, and we'd just be surfed out and it didn't matter because when the waves weren't any good we didn't have to go surfing,' says Tom. 'If it was a contest I would have had to try and prepare.'

The Search also inspired Curren's tastes for alternative surfboard designs. It was Derek Hynd who first turned Curren on to the thrills of a trawl through the dustbin of surfboard-design history.

'It was at Jeffreys Bay on that Skip Frye fish,' says Tom. '[Derek] was just saying, "This board's really good," and I remember looking at it and going, it will never work. It was very fast, and if you get used to it you can make it work. It worked back in the day so it still works. That culture, that vision of what surfing is, that's from kneeboarders. It's from the San Diego kneeboarders and other kneeboarders like George Greenough and Peter Crawford. That was when the impossible was made possible, and that's when people started trying to stand up on those boards. Even back when I was about nine or 10 years old, I surfed on a kneeboard standing up.'

That taste for alternative equipment, and shorter boards in particular, would feed into another one of the most memorable sessions of the Search.

THE FISH BOWLS SESSION

The story of Curren's mind-boggling lines in huge, Sunset-style rights on a tiny 5'7" Tommy Peterson Fireball Fish in 1994 is now the stuff of legend. But the raucous events leading up to that seminal session in the wilds of north-western Sumatra have never been fully told before.

Martin Daly's *Indies Trader* pulled into Nias, the famed right in Lagundri Bay, before hitting out to points further north midway through a three-week mission. The waves were four to five foot, but the crew hadn't come all this way to surf crowded, mid-size Nias. Instead, struggling with the early stages of cabin fever, Curren and Davo eyed a glimpse of civilisation on land, grabbed a couple of Claw's paddleboards and jumped over the side in search of entertainment.

'So, I jump on a board and follow them in, ride a wave in on the big paddleboard, and they are gone. I went, shit, where are they?' remembers Claw. 'I find them both in different places settled in with other surfers, having a good old time, just both completely off their guts, out of their minds.'

As the sun grew low and Nias's notorious mozzie hour approached, bringing with it the considerable risk of contracting cerebral malaria, Claw was eager to get his young charges safely back to the boat. But Tom's new playmates weren't so keen for the party to be over. "'What do you mean? Tom can stay here, we've got plenty of clothes and food for Tom," they reckoned. Davo found some Aussie ratbags,' recalls Claw.

Claw finally coaxed his star team riders back to the boat, but the mood for mischief remained. 'At dinner Tom and Davo are grinning like Cheshire cats, and they seem to have developed a good appetite,' says Claw. 'The boat's rocking, we've been feeling this sizeable swell. The sets on dark were five to six feet. The boat's rocking after dinner and it's six to eight feet by now.'

Now was the time for a session, the crew decided. 'So, they went night-surfing, taped flares onto their arms, reflective tape, waterproof flashlights. They got rigged up in this shit, dressed up looking like spacemen, and they went out and surfed for about three hours, at least, from 9.30 to 12.30,' says Claw. 'You could hear them giggling and screaming, see flashes of light and changes of direction in the tube. All the lights on the buildings on the beach are on, there's a crowd yelling and hooting. Then we got them on board and they were all really energised from being in the salt water and surfing. They had a few beers and finally went to sleep.'

The *Trader* motored through the night to a likely right-hand reefbreak to take advantage of the fresh swell. 'Early in the morning there's only myself and Martin Daly on deck and Bawa is like Sunset Beach, 15-foot barrelling right-handers,' says Claw. 'I tried to wake the boys up. "This is unbelievable, this is serious – powerful, amazing waves." But they were unresponsive.'

Claw was almost manic by this point, at the time and in the retelling, as he pantomimes the conversation with his slumbering charges:

"'You've got to wake up, guys, you've got to see these waves!"
"What's it like?"

"It's like Sunset Beach, but better shaped."

'All I'm getting is grunts and groans. So, we headed to Asu [a nearby left] and it's thick and powerful,' says Claw. 'One or two came up on deck and had a look and went, "That's shit." Then we went back to Bawa. We'd missed the big surge in the swell, but it was still magnificent. We get the boat perfectly placed, and they've started to go, "Holy shit, look at these waves." Davo's just bailed over the side, on a decent-sized board, a 6'10". He goes over and paddles into a wave that just turned inside out and got spat out.'

There was a flurry of action on board as surfers and film crews sprang into action, choosing equipment and jostling for lifts to the line-up in the tender, but Curren was in no hurry. 'Davo's grabbed Tom's 6'10", and Tom's only got a 7'10" Dave Parmenter widow-maker or the 5'7" Tommy Peterson fish to choose from, so he decides to wait for Davo to come in,' recalls Ted Grambeau.

Tom sat back observing the mayhem, watching the waves and taking his time over his choice of equipment. 'Everything kind of lined up. The swell lined up, it's a new spot that I hadn't seen before. Martin knew where it was. The waves were coming around the corner,' recalls Tom. 'Waves that were so perfect they looked like they weren't even moving. It was so perfect and no one was out.'

Claw had a different perspective on the session, having taken the boat around to the leeward side of the island, with Sonny Miller and Brian, to get Sonny's camera equipment on land, out of the brunt of the swell. 'Sonny, Brian and myself carried several cameras Sonny wanted to use from the land,' says Claw. 'It took us two hours, through a mosquito-infested, swampy island. We had half the inhabitants with us by the time we got to the other side.'

Meanwhile, Ted jumped in the tinny with Martin Daly and was shooting the rest of the crew feasting on stand-up barrels while Curren watched from the boat. 'Eventually Davo breaks his board, so Curren grabs the biggest board on the boat and comes out,' says Ted. He caught a set on the widow-maker, but wasn't happy with the board. Curren returned to the boat and seized on the Fish. 'He grabbed a board that Frankie had, a five-foot-something Fireball Fish – for most mere mortals absolutely the wrong choice of board if [the waves are] eight to 10 feet,' says Ted.

'I was pretty fascinated with that little board, I wanted to try it and it turned out okay,' says Tom. 'I'd only tried it a few days before that at Macaronis, head high, a foot overhead, but it felt solid and it held into turns . . . This is a board that was built for little waves, to zip around on, but it felt like a board that would be able to handle bigger and bigger waves, and actually feel like you were more in control than you were on a bigger board.'

Curren paddled back to the outside peak and scratched his way into some of the bombs of the day, rolling in on the foaming peak, carving wild lines on the tiny board and soaring through cavern-ous pits, in a display that confounded most assumptions around board design. 'Tom dispels all conventions and gets barrelled and reinvigorates the whole industry – and demand for fish surfboards and Tommy Peterson's shaping career,' says Ted.

Afterwards, the mood on the boat was euphoric. 'Everyone was on a high, experiencing this special moment of incredible surfing by the world's best surfers,' says Ted. 'It was one of the great experi-ences as a surf trip. You've just put it in the can, so to speak. There's a great vibe on the boat. Claw and Brian were beside themselves. It really shows why they understand what the whole concept of surf stoke is about. That trip went a long way to ensuring the longevity of the Search – it literally gave the early Search films cult status.'

There are other odd highlights that still stand out from the whole mad adventure. Claw recalls coming across a couple of young women camping out in a tent and a grass hut on an island in the middle of nowhere. They were invited on board and spent a memorable week on the Search before being dropped back at their campsite. 'There was one of the Search ads stuck on the wall of the hut,' Claw says, as if this was final confirmation that the campaign had hit its mark.

For Claw, the Search also provided the opportunity to observe the enigmatic ways of his star team rider at close quarters, and marvel anew at his uncanny rapport with the ocean. Claw recalls being anchored at a long left-hander in the Mentawais further south, waiting for a swell to hit, when Curren took Claw's 10-foot paddleboard out in tiny waves.

'On a certain swell this place can light up and roar down the line, with lots of different sections. It's not mechanical, not perfect, but we were anchored up there on a day that became great,' Claw recalls. 'Tom's got such an eye for surf. He studies the ocean constantly. He goes for a paddle on this paddleboard right out behind this break, as deep as you can go, and a four-foot set comes and he rides it from way behind the point, through all these crazy sections, in and out of the barrel, pig-dogging and kneeling and laying down and out into this blue-water channel, and comes out standing tall like the Duke [Kahanamoku]. The boys try to talk to him about the wave but he's very noncommittal, very deadpan. He just says, "I think the swell is coming up." It came up to six foot and was just all-time. All over the world I've seen that – he grabs a board, jumps over the side and gets these rides.'

Tom Curren later wrote an article on the Search trip for *Surfer* magazine:

Who are these children?: The mind ski generation

By Tom Curren

Priorities are changing rapidly for the children of today. I know three young surfers, Byron Howarth, Chris Davidson and Frankie Oberholzer, who can legitimately claim that by not going to school they have learned more than their peers. As surfers, they can also legitimately claim that by not competing they have ridden better waves. Ask yourself: What furthers a surfer more, a world amateur title or his best ever tube ride?

Recently I had the chance to surf and travel with these children and gain insight into what makes them tick. It's not the surf contests, and it's definitely not the pursuit of 'knowledge' in the traditional sense. In many ways, what they seek is simply beyond our ability to appreciate.

After a few days' travel, we pull up at a break the locals claim has never been surfed before. What's more, no one in the village has ever seen white people. It's the same as it ever was. How many places are left in the world like this? We exchange glances with natives still naive enough to be fearful and respectful of outsiders, without the peddling of wares that usually accompanies this sort of meeting.

We considered holding a surf contest with the canoe men as judges. We'd make score cards for them to hold up. Criteria? Subjective. Wipeouts would no doubt be the big score.

We're at a two-foot inshore Kaiser bowl pushing onto a sand beach. Davo rides the first wave so he gets to name the spot. Rivalry aside, he ponders a moment and comes up with Pit Stops. It sticks. It's a pit. Many of the places we've surfed remind me of other well-known spots and we start to name them accordingly. So far, we've been to Kaiser's, Little Drakes and St Leu.

Motor on to destinations unknown. Malarianoia keeps us high and dry on the ship St Larry. We inch past jungle islands, safe on our floating sanctuary, rarely venturing ashore to meet the locals. We wonder what we'd find. Would they be fans of Michael Jordan? MTV junkies? Headhunters?

These islands are mainly Christian. How this distant and foreign religion got here is unknown to me. People look different from island to island. The reason for this is not apparent. The islands themselves are slowly sinking back into the ocean. Trees on the shoreline without any nourishment finally fall, detaching themselves from the coral to which they cling. Coconut trees crowd and lean out over the water.

Equatorial flora and fauna, everything is growing. This is the sport of the world. Things unseen carry the Power of Creation and in turn are carried by the wind and sea to a final destination where they thrive or die. Oddest of all is the festering envy that many village people display toward foreigners. Out here, where there is little tourist traffic, this phenomenon is non-existent. Out here, the few locals we meet are more curious than anything. They simply want to know what we're about.

Travellers will save up for a vacation that will be spent under subhuman conditions and wonder how to manage not having to go back to the human race. Once you've given yourself over to a place like this, you can forget about western ways. Our values are shown to be nihilist and devoid of any use for past or future. We think we're living each moment to the fullest, when it's really just hollow entertainment. But we're very good at it, of course, all this slickly packaged stimulus. We make great cartoons.

Surfing's version of the caveman, meanwhile, has dropped from the world and landed here. He sets up camp and waits for months on end to stand in a cave for a 75-year stretch. Malaria stories are commonplace. But even more deadly and widespread are reported cases of hopelessness when faced with returning to Sydney, Tokyo or LA. Once home, they quickly rustle up enough quid to get back to these reefbreaks. Also remarkable are the Euros who just keep on backpacking on some kind of never-ending Euro pass. They come to take up surfing with their brethren, lolling about in the lineup, oblivious to the potential danger of collision. Ah, paradise as it was and never will be again.

A shift in local values towards materialism is accelerated by the many surfers who visit this new world on their own terms with their own toys. Because if there's a group of people with more extravagant needs, I've yet to find them. How will the surfers who come through here remain in the minds of the villagers? Like tourists? Worse? In any case, these people will soon see plenty of us; they live too close to too much great surf. It will be an amazing microcosm; once the hotels and surf camps are established, the scene will wander out to the next place on the periphery. And then the book will repeat.

In the local language, the word 'surfing' translates to 'mind ski'. Does this mean it's all in the mind, or is it because of the penetrating experience of riding your average wave here? Either way, the term works. Many surfers I know and grew up with chose surfing because everything else was boring. It was a way to escape a meaningless society. In doing so, we found our own internal balance and ultimately neglected the so-called important things and the ability to deal with the outer world. There was no way to change what was going on around us so we found a new place in surfing. It's happening all over the world and not just with surfers. Many young people these days are devoting all of their time and energy to their means of expression, their mind ski as it were, because humanity is too absurd to be a part of.

Even here, where thousands and thousands of perfect waves go unridden each day, sometimes you have to take steps to dodge the crowd. One night, while anchored near a 'resort' that all surfers dream of visiting, we went for a midnight session on a quarter moon, illuminated by our boat's search light and a beach bonfire. Flashlight surfing just to get a few waves after hours.

Soon we dropped anchor anew. Dawn revealed a dreamscape right. It was Sunset, Backdoor, Honolua and Haleiwa put together except longer, hollower, cleaner and no one out. Maybe 12 feet on the sets. Some great empty waves that will stay forever in the minds of everyone on the boat. Images of roundness, of wedges moving along a narrow track of reef down a huge point, gaining thickness and power the farther it went until the last explosion dissipated into a Sunset rip that swept down rather than out. Whoever made this wave must have known that it was ideal for surfing, or so it seems. I swear I didn't even want to look at it before paddling out for fear of being paralysed by the sheer beauty.

Two days later, we steamed south to an area that promised to have even better surf. It was hard to imagine anything as good as what we've just had. Our next spot was a long spinning left, like Jeffreys Bay in reverse, and we experienced both sides of the coin: epic barrels followed by epic thrashings. The name of the game was connect and collect. One day someone will possibly ride the best wave ever at this place on a 15-foot point day. Maybe it's already been done.

Today, no surf, so we spread the word of surfing to the native groms. Everyone was very enthusiastic about wave riding. Longboards, paddleboards and bodyboards were turned over to the locals to see how they'd take to the mind ski. Some of the kids found planks and took up the sport on their own.

For ages, the native children here have been playing in the breakers and going to sea with their fathers in dugouts to learn fishing. It makes me wonder what they think of the surfboards they're playing on now: a kind of mind machine for mind skiing, created by grown-up kids who still want to play in the ocean, refusing to surrender a childlike fantasy.

Will these children be like us? Will they be drawn away from their own people toward the empty blueness? From inertia to escape velocity – this is the mission of the mind ski generation.

THE COURT JESTER

Curren may have been the king of the Search campaign, but its quick-witted court jester was that same Cronulla goofy-footer who'd been handed the free-surfing gig back in '89 by Claw and Derek Hynd. Gary Green was already on the Search before it was called the Search and became one of its most regular and popular participants. Of the trips through Indonesia, the Maldives and South America, Greeny finds it hard to pluck out highlights but comes up with a few.

'Probably that first trip to the Mentawais, and the boat trip with Poto [the Tahitian-French surfer Vetea David] through Indo. Just perfect waves with no one out,' Greeny nominates. 'After that, where do you go next? You've surfed these perfect waves with just a few guys.'

Other high points included travelling with Brock Little to Morocco ('Brock was such a fun guy'), his first trip to the Maldives ('There wasn't anyone there then, just a few ab divers from Tassie'), going to Desert Point for the first time, and travelling with loose and always entertaining characters like Chris 'Davo' Davidson. 'There's a million stories,' he says. 'A lot of the breaks, they didn't even have names for them.'

Despite travelling at close quarters with Tom Curren many times, Greeny remains in awe of him. In many ways they were polar opposites: the quiet, stylish American regular footer and the raucous, hyperactive Aussie goofy-footer. 'Curren's totally eccentric to the max. He's a man of few words, but he's a funny guy,' says Greeny. He recalls one Indo boat trip when the Californian showed another side to his character. 'He was smoking ciggies and pumping beers at eight or nine in the morning,' says Greeny. 'It got to the afternoon and he's half-cut and he goes, "It's my birthday today." It's like he's been celebrating on his own.'

The next day, most of the crew were a bit dusty from the evening's antics, and Greeny swooped on an empty Macaronis line-up. 'They hit the beers and slept in, and I surfed it by myself with the cook.' Curren eventually made an appearance, skurfing through the line-up behind the tinny, still a few sheets to the wind.

Greeny says it was intimidating seeing his own surfing edited next to Tom Curren's otherworldly grace in the Search movies. 'The first Search movie, Curren's surfing at J-Bay, and then it goes to me and Dooma [Damien Hardman] surfing G-Land [in Indonesia]. I was going, why didn't they put us first? Because Curren makes you look silly,' he says. Even so, Greeny reckons his surfing peaked during that dreamy period of perfect waves, far removed from the exertions of the pro tour. 'The surfers you're with are the best surfers in the world. I think I was probably surfing better then, when you get to your 30s.'

Greeny revelled in the professional surf-traveller lifestyle for eight tube-laden years, but all good things must come to an end. 'It just gets hard as you're getting older and you're going on less trips. I got to 35 and I went, I can die now a happy man.'

These days, Greeny still lives in Cronulla, in a little two-bedroom apartment a stone's throw from the beach he grew up at, a new Force 9 thruster resting by the door waxed up and ready for action. He's surfing regularly and, fittingly enough, works as a baggage handler at Sydney Airport, lugging baggage for others going off on their dream trips, as if repaying his dues for all those years of unfettered surf travel. You couldn't wish for a more qualified person to be handling your precious board bag as you embark on your next surf trip.

It's years since he's been to Indo but Greeny's not in any hurry to go back: 'It's like remembering a beautiful girl. Do you really want to go back 30 years later, or would you rather remember them how they were?'

Greeny's got a rare boxed set of the entire Search DVD collection still in its wrapper but he's not about to spend his time reliving his glory days. 'They had a copyright thing with the music and they had to withdraw them from sale. My old girlfriend bought it before it got withdrawn,' he says, handling the boxed set like a sacred relic. He reckons it could be worth a bit one day, especially still in its wrapper, like those collectable Star Wars figurines.

'You go back into the normal world and you go, I did that? It's like another life. I'm eternally grateful to Rip Curl because I was living the dream.'

THE ICEMAN'S SEARCH FOR A NEW CONTRACT

Few anecdotes sum up the business style of Rip Curl through the early '90s better than the tale of Damien Hardman's contract negotiations. The Narrabeen goofy-footer had been pegged as a future champion before he'd even reached puberty, and had been wearing Rip Curl wetsuits since he was 12. Dooma went on to win world titles in 1987 and 1991 with a deadly vertical backhand attack and a ruthless competitive focus that had him dubbed 'The Iceman', and he became one of Rip Curl's most valued team riders.

Damien developed a well-documented love affair with the Bells Bowl, his backhand attack suited to its wide walls, and he took out the Rip Curl Pro twice, in 1988 and 1993. 'If you were a Rip Curl surfer that was what you aspired to do. The whole industry was there. It almost felt like it was Rip Curl versus Quiksilver at some of those events. It had a really good atmosphere,' he says.

Damien stayed with Brian at his acreage behind Bells for the first time in '88 and he's stayed there every Easter in the 30 years since. 'I didn't really know Brian well until I started staying with him, and he became like a father figure,' says Damien. 'One of my kids was conceived in his house, maybe a couple of them.'

Even so, there was no room for mateship when it came to business. 'What always amazed me about Brian was he was like two different people. He has the ability to switch off. You can have a meeting at 4.30 in the afternoon where he's kicking your arse and see him at 5.30 at the pub like nothing has happened,' says Damien.

That ability came to the fore when Damien's contract negotiations became bogged down in '91. 'My contract was pretty incentive-based. When it looked like I was going to win my second world title in '91, Claw came to me and said, "Your incentive's too high, we're worried if you win another world title we won't survive,"' recalls Damien. Remarkably, Claw managed to convince Damien to take a 60 per cent cut in his world-title bonus for the good of the business. Then, when it came to negotiating his new contract, Rip Curl's focus on the Search, and its investment in Tom Curren as the new, free-surfing face of the campaign, weakened Damien's bargaining position at a time when he should have been at the peak of his market value.

'They offered me a contract that was insulting,' says Damien. At the same time, amid great fanfare Rip Curl staged a press conference at Bells at Easter to announce their new signing of Tom Curren on a 100 per cent Rip Curl deal, worth a million dollars over four years. In front of the assembled media, Damien's close tour mate Rob Bain stood up and asked why they were throwing so much money at the American, while their Australian world champ's deal remained in limbo. 'It created a bit of a media storm,' says Damien.

The fact that Damien was staying at Brian's place at the time might have made for some awkward moments across the dinner table, but Brian's ability to compartmentalise his business and personal lives was up to the challenge. He left the contract negotiations to Claw but gave his business partner a gentle nudge to move things along. 'That hurried it up a bit. It was close to what I was already on,' says Damien.

'We somehow got Tom and Damien up on million-dollar contracts,' says Claw. 'They seemed to understand the economics of it when we explained it to them. Rip Curl's just a small backyard company that's punching above its weight. We're still a small, grassroots surf company that in some way has overachieved. Our surfers understood that.'

Damien's enjoyed a long relationship with Rip Curl ever since. 'During the period of the late '80s and early '90s Damien Hardman and Tom Curren were Rip Curl's two foremost surfers on the tour,' says Brian. In fact, Curren once told Claw that part of his reason for quitting the tour was that he was worn out from trying to overcome Damien's ruthless competitive act. 'I got to know Damien really well as he and [his wife] Belinda stayed at my place every Easter, and it didn't take me long to realise he was a pretty intelligent sort of person who asked all sorts of probing questions about our company,' says Brian. 'After he finished on the tour, we had no hesitation in appointing him contest director at the Rip Curl Pro.'

'Damien had been a surfer representative on the ASP Board, giving him further qualification,' says Claw. 'He set the blueprint for the current WSL [World Surf League] commissioners Kieren Perrow and Jessi Miley-Dyer.'

Damien owns several Rip Curl stores in New South Wales and was being groomed for senior management at head office after he quit the tour, but ultimately decided he wanted to return to his Narrabeen roots. He and Brian remain firm friends, and Dooma's quick to cop a tip on one of Brian's nags when it looks likely to get up. He reckons they've never forgotten the pay cut he took for the good of the business.

'Rip Curl have looked after a lot of people. I'm 52 and I'm still being paid a retainer, and I'm sure that's why I still get paid a retainer. That's one thing I always had in my back pocket,' he says.

THE SOUTH POLE

Brian's own search for the next adventure, meanwhile, showed no signs of abating. In December 1992 he embarked on a long-held dream to travel to Antarctica and climb its highest mountain, Mount Vinson.

Brian found himself in the tiny Chilean outpost of Punta Arenas, near the southern tip of South America, waiting for the weather to clear sufficiently to fly out on an old DC6. His fellow travellers included former Monty Python star Michael Palin and his entire film crew for the *Pole to Pole* documentary TV series; Peter Hillary, the son of the first man to climb Mount Everest, Sir Edmund Hillary; Qantas chairman James Strong and his wife Jeanne-Claude; and a Japanese crew who planned on riding motorbikes to the South Pole. 'A really eclectic mix of people,' says Brian.

Weather conditions were crucial because once you were over halfway there, if the weather closed in the plane had insufficient fuel to turn back and would have to attempt a landing in

Antarctica regardless. Brian recalls vividly the moment the pilot announced they were past the point of no return and a cheer went up on board. The DC6 landed on its glacier runway without incident and the crew settled in to the base camp of Quonset huts. From there they took a tiny single-engine Beaver, designed for short take-offs and landings in mountainous terrain, to the base of Mount Vinson. 'It was almost a crash landing – any harder and you would have hurt yourself,' says Brian. 'And we had to give [the plane] a push to get going again.'

The team had to set up tents in the freezing conditions before collapsing into sleeping bags. They awoke in their new, surreal environment of 24-hour daylight in a vast white, empty landscape. The expedition was to make its way from camp one to camp two and on to camp three before making an assault on the summit. 'By the time we got to camp three we were hit by a raging storm,' says Brian. The storm kept the crew holed up in their tents for a week.

'It was an interesting experience in dealing with yourself, wondering what would happen if this storm went on much longer, lying in the tent for hours awake,' says Brian. 'We were down to our last day of food. If it keeps going like this, what do we do?'

His companions proved ideal company in the testing conditions. 'It was so interesting, the stories Hillary told about his different exploits, particularly in the Himalayas, and James Strong had a lot of old aviation stories,' says Brian. 'After six days of storm everyone was getting worried because it was getting close to Christmas. Are we going to get home for Christmas? Should we abort the whole thing? Peter Hillary was lying back in his sleeping bag with his arms folded behind his head and just went, "I don't give a rat's arse about Christmas. We've spent all this time and money and effort to get here. I'm going to get to the top." I just went, I'm with you.'

The decision was made to make a break for it in a small window of favourable weather, and the team succeeded in safely getting to the top of Mount Vinson and back down in an arduous 14-hour round trip. 'The weather opened up on the way down . . . The scenery was stunningly beautiful and it was eerily silent,' says Brian. 'We had to do a lot of roped-up travel, in case you fell down a crevice.'

By the time they got back to camp three they had just enough energy to gobble down some soup and fall into sleeping bags. 'It was satisfying that you had done what you set out to do . . . We just wanted to get back home for a shave and a feed,' says Brian.

'We supplied quite a bit of the mountainwear for their trip and I recall James Strong was particularly taken by the slogan, "A product of the Search", which he noticed on some of the gear,' says Claw. Brian kept in touch with James Strong, a connection that would have a major influence on the business in the new millennium.

THE SKIPPING URCHINS

The Search took a strange and unexpected detour when Derek Hynd announced that he, Sonny Miller, Tom Curren and a loose collective of musicians would embark on a road trip across America, playing free-form jam sessions to Miller's movies at a series of small, intimate gigs. The whole mad enterprise was billed as the Skipping Urchins Tour, and Claw and Brian claim they knew nothing about it until the whole thing had very nearly spiralled out of control.

Claw recognises the huge contribution Hynd made to the Search but reckons there was a price to be paid. 'It's surfing folklore and it might never happen again. It was colourful and wild and loose,' says Claw. 'But he seriously fucked some things up with us by being so loose, just not paying attention to details, leaving things up in the air, skirting with disaster. Disaster caught up with us a couple of times . . . We got sued a few times with these things Derek did.'

'Derek Hynd was definitely a great inspiration but he was also a great headache,' Sonny Miller told Tyler Breuer in the *Swell Season* podcast in 2012. 'He was diabolically sitting back going, "How can I make this the hardest endeavour of their lives?" I think that was his ultimate goal.'

'You'd have to know the guy because he's very brilliant and very maddening at the same time, and if you're on the team he's in charge,' Tom Curren said during the same interview.

'I guess he had this picture, he had this plan of taking a movie across the country in a car and showing these movies with loud rock music, and we saw eye to eye on this – that this was something I wanted to do,' says Curren.

Hynd's personal goal was to drive across America – a dream not shared by his collaborators. 'Derek bought a car, a Chrysler Newport. He bought it in Pismo Beach [Central California, for $500 from the side of the road] and he told us all he was going to drive the car across America,' says Sonny Miller. 'And so, we told Derek, we love you . . . You have a great imagination, good luck. We met him in Rhode Island [on the US north-east coast]. He did pull off the drive, the car was there.'

'We had a little group of musicians, and one of the guys was sick of sleeping in Derek's car and eating pizza every meal so he left,' recalls Curren. They drove on to their next gig minus a bass player, and were setting up when a local musician named Chris Shaw wandered in off the street.

'He saw a few cars out the front of a place he used to play,' says Curren. 'So, he goes, "What's going on?" And we say we're looking for a bass player . . . We described our show . . . and he gets up and he basically tore the place up, and we were just going, "How can we get you to go to the next town?"'

Hynd was on some kind of mission to reclaim all that was real and true and pure about the surfing and music lifestyle, like the Blues Brothers with surfboards, and knew he was testing the tolerance of his employers. 'One thing about Brian and Claw, they're just fucken classic individuals. I love those guys,' says Derek. 'But they weren't at all happy with the Skipping Urchins road trip and ordered me to pull the plug halfway through but . . . the show must go on,' he declares, defiant to this day.

But Rip Curl management became concerned as Chinese whispers drifted back from the US about the chaos on the road. 'I think I was trying to shut it down then, sensing that it was so loose and out of control,' says Claw. 'The Skipping Urchins tour was completely unauthorised.'

'The tour fell apart in a one-car garage at Ocean Beach, San Francisco, one bloody cold November night, and I guess this freaked out Brian and Claw with good reason,' says Derek. 'Over 100 people in a one-car garage with Tom on drums pressed to the wall and Arno doing Hendrix proud wasn't exactly Woodstock but to my mind [was] incredible, honest, unbeatable. The stuff of word of mouth . . . Couldn't beat it.'

Even when the rest of the crew refused to join the gruelling cross-country itinerary, Derek fronted at every scheduled gig to explain their non-appearance, and the band eventually boarded a flight and reconvened at Rhode Island to continue the tour. 'The Urchins tour made it to the East Coast and thank god for that. Core surfing and core surf attitude ruled over there. I reckon Tom felt it too,' says Derek. 'In all my time travelling as a surfer, nothing beat the Skipping Urchins Tour. Every bit of it, I wouldn't have missed it for quids.'

Tom also cherishes those memories, and believes Derek was prescient in his bold punt that surfing would branch away from competition into more of a cultural exploration. 'Derek saw that, he knew it was going to be like that in the future,' says Tom. 'He also did it in a way that it was more of grassroots event. The band plays and they show some movies and people have fun. It's kind of rowdy, there's food fights between the band and the audience. At the end of the day those are lasting friendships that are formed at those times. They're important to me.'

CHAPTER SEVEN

GROWING PAINS: 1995–1999

As the halfway mark of Rip Curl's 50-year history, the mid-'90s were a time of intense global expansion. Forays into new markets, growth in established ones, the increasingly bold excursions of the Search, the irrefutable economics of offshore manufacturing and a major restructuring of the business into a single global entity saw Rip Curl evolve into a truly international brand. The arrival of the internet meant the world was more connected than ever, and trends and influences spread more quickly across borders.

'We went more committed and more sophisticated with the Search, and the business was becoming more international, more established in Europe, the USA, South America,' says Claw.

The expansion proved a formidable challenge for all involved. 'We were growing so fast that we had to learn more skills every few months, because there were more and more people in the company every week,' says Grant Forbes. 'Flying by the seat of the pants is okay in a Tiger Moth but not in a 747.'

Ensuring that Rip Curl's free-spirited essence survived was an inexact science. 'We spent a huge amount of time defining what

Rip Curl was about, all the corporate-speak brand-values stuff, just trying to capture what had come naturally to a like-minded small group earlier in the piece,' says Grant. 'So, the culture, to me at least, started to feel a little artificial later in the game. It became almost impossible to pick up a good idea for something in, say, London, put it into my sketchbook, have samples knocked up a few weeks later in Shanghai, and bang it into the range a couple weeks after that. In fact, I'd have half a dozen staff looking at me in horror if I tried. That's not a criticism of the company, it's just a fact that management of multi-million-dollar product ranges isn't that easy, and you need a bunch of reliable, conservative people to keep it together.

'New crew join the ship and have their own personal goals and ambitions, and professional ways of working, and they bring skills that we hadn't needed previously, but in that very process I think a lot of the creativity gets diluted.'

Respecting regional differences while ensuring some continuity across the globe was another delicate balancing act. 'In some respects, our very naivety and innocence in the fashion industry gave us a fresh edge,' says Grant. 'I had a great working relationship particularly with Fred Basse in France, and also licensees in Brazil and Argentina, who continually cranked out exciting product, often unsuitable for Australia, but steeped in creativity nonetheless. USA ranges were fabulous sometimes and dreadful the next. Efficient management demands homogenous global product design and sourcing, I'm told, so a lot of that diversity had to go. The politics of the international game are difficult, and the skills necessary to balance the egos of such a loose and crazy creative group, the kind of people who identify most with Rip Curl, are hard to learn.'

Still, Australian and New Zealand sales increased tenfold over the '90s. In 1996, Rip Curl was nominated as one of 'the world's greatest brands' by the global Interbrand group, and was one of only two Australian brands to feature, along with Qantas. In 1998, Rip Curl was voted *BRW* magazine's Australian Manufacturer of the Year.

THE WETSUIT PROGRAM

Neil Campbell reckons the heart and soul of the business could always be found in the wetsuit division, where stalwarts like Ray Thomas and Sparrow still held sway. 'Ray Thomas, I think he was the holder of all the knowledge,' says Cambo. 'Sparrow . . . was so anal, which I loved . . . He was focused on total function . . . He was all about cut and fit. He was just a freak. I used to love going in the cutting room with Sparrow. They'd knock out a wetsuit and you could put it on and go for a surf.'

Ray was in charge of the wetsuit program for many years, a huge bestowal of trust by the founders, and he never let them down. 'We were always pushing to make wetsuits freer and freer. The old rubber was like cardboard. I was pushing the Japanese supplier to make it more and more stretchy,' says Ray. 'It wasn't off the shelf, but it was usually good for them too because later on everyone else got it.'

Damien Hardman remembers a trip to Bells always began with a visit to Sparrow to get fitted for the latest wetsuit and hear his swell forecast. 'He'd have all the charts out, and he'd go, "It's going to be like this." He was a forecasting guru,' says Damien.

Two of the biggest innovations in wetsuits came out of Rip Curl in the mid-'90s: the Ultimate, a top-of-the-line suit with a high price tag that combined all the latest features with contoured panels for improved fit and flexibility, and Elasto, a new super-stretch neoprene for added comfort.

'I wanted to bring out the Ultimate wetsuit and I talked to Ray

Thomas about it – let's see if we can make the best wetsuit in the world, and put it in the shop and see what happens,' says Sparrow. 'I said, "Everybody wants a Rolls-Royce but not everybody can afford it. If we can produce a product that no one can buy everyone will want it." But we couldn't make enough of them.'

Ray Thomas would also take the product out to market and explain the virtues of Rip Curl innovations to the retailers. 'We used to go on these roadshows and Gary Crothall used to come with me, and it was like a rock show,' says Ray. 'We were in town for one night, had all this product knowledge stuff and then we'd have a party. They were quite legendary among old retailers.'

Ray's retired now, but still very much a part of the Rip Curl family. 'The wetsuit part of the company is still the soul of the company and even though the other product areas are worth much bigger bucks, the wetsuit team is where you will find the real Rip Curl spirit even today,' he says.

TIME AND TIDE

One of the great success stories of the '90s was Rip Curl's watch division. Peter Hodgart set about overhauling Rip Curl watches from the moment he took over from Pat Morgan in '89 and his first priority was making watches that could be worn in the surf with confidence. That meant coming to grips with the monumental challenge of creating a truly waterproof surfing watch.

'I've taken over this department and they were making these kiddies' watches that couldn't perform in the water,' says Hodg. 'Almost half the watches we sold came back. It was a bit of a hard start.'

'The watches were shithouse. They were coming back because they weren't waterproof. We decided we're either going to do this properly or stop,' says Brian bluntly.

Pat Morgan had found an old Victorian surfer from Gunnamatta, Rod Payne, who ran a watch factory in Hong Kong, and he proved the perfect collaborator. Together, Hodg and Rod left no stone unturned in their quest to research every aspect of the watch business. 'We went through the Swatch factory in Switzerland with an early miniature camera,' says Hodg. 'Together we went through training to learn what we were doing. After Switzerland we realised it came down to buying the best stuff you could afford and then testing it every way you possibly can.'

At one stage, Hodg was immersing crayfish pots full of watches into the turbulent Southern Ocean to see how they fared. 'We started testing every watch in multiple ways – air, water, heat, cold – and if they failed one of those tests they didn't go into production,' he says.

Hodg was a great believer in every product having a compelling reason for being; that it must perform some practical function that enhances the surfing experience. When he turned that principle to watches, it wasn't long before the logical approach emerged.

'There was a brainstorming session and the tide-watch idea came up. Butch Barr said, "I've got one but it's no good." So, I de-engineered this watch and we found out who made it, this sailor from New York,' says Hodg. 'I contacted him and explained the engineering properties of what I wanted to do. We worked with him for 15 years until we got knowledgeable enough and bought him out of the program.'

Rip Curl management backed the concept of the tide watch with a serious R & D budget, but the sales agents were harder to convince of the concept's merits. 'Brian Singer said, "It's all just beer money to them. You've got to go and convince them that it will sell,"' Hodg says. 'So, Ray Thomas and I went out on the road to sell them. We went to surf shops and told them we had watches that could predict the tides. The surf shops all had tide charts on the wall, so I'd say, "Pick a date and I'll tell you what the tide will be." And after we'd done that three times they were like, "I want that. Give me that!'"

Rip Curl applied for a patent for its tide-watch technology in 1992 and it was eventually granted in 1996. In the same year they brought out the first analogue tide watch, the Tidemaster, having found an old Swiss watch-master working for a French company. Together they developed the first Swiss movement watch, with full tidal and moon phase information.

Every step of the way was a learning process. New types of hinge had to be developed to withstand the rigours of the surf. Bodyboarders lost more watches than anyone, as the force of wrist straps pulling against the watches relegated many of them to the bottom of the ocean. 'We still get returns . . . It's a continual evolution of things going wrong and fixing them,' says Hodg.

'Once we were happy with how waterproof our watches were, and learning customers were confused by the term "water-resistant", I started marketing our watches as waterproof,' he says. 'This caused a huge stir in the watch world, as the controllers of the industry had decided "water-resistant" was how they could hide from water-problem warranties. Net result was a big upswing in sales, and customer and retailer confidence. We were hurting the traditional watch-sellers and they didn't like it.'

Before too long Rip Curl had been reported to the Australian Competition and Consumer Commission (ACCC) over their use of the term 'waterproof' and, after several increasingly strongly worded letters, were summoned to front a member of the ACCC's ominously titled 'enforcement committee'.

'I was very prepared for the meeting, as we had been told in no uncertain terms this was very, very serious and they wanted us to stop the use of the term "waterproof", says Hodg. 'Well, they'd never had to deal with someone like me. Usually, the lawyer and company spokesman did all the talking and giving of exhibits, etc., but in our case I wasn't just a spokesman, I was the guy that built the program, and no one knew more about watch-testing than me and Rod Payne ... We gave a two-year, full waterproof warranty. No one else did that either. We had the best service and repair centre in Australia. Still do!'

In the meeting, accompanied by Rip Curl lawyer Tony Roberts, Hodg bamboozled the experts with his knowledge and the thoroughness of Rip Curl's watch-testing program. 'The ACCC boss man was blown away as I dismantled his team one by one. He threatened me with a fully blown court case at which I would be liable as well as Rip Curl,' recalls Hodg. 'I said, bring it on ... In the end, he told me he had to have a win to take back to the enforcement committee. They don't lose, and things were going to blow up! I said okay, and I put to him we would continue to use a new term, "waterproof tested", in all marketing and on our watches. He agreed that was a reasonable compromise as I could prove we tested for 100 per cent waterproofness and warrantied it and other aspects fully. Tony and I left on a big high! To this day we are the only company allowed to use this term – 100 per cent waterproof tested.'

It was a great example of the business backing itself and its people. 'I pushed ahead as I knew immediately we had cracked the code and were willing to fight all comers for the right to say what we believed in,' says Hodg. 'It was a heady time in my office, and for those around me. I loved the fact Brian let me take on the ACCC.'

Watches quickly grew from around $125,000 in sales in 1990–1991 to nearly $12 million by 2003–2004. Of that, they sold $10 million worth of what they called 'fashion' watches and only $2 million worth of tide watches. But their development was a potent lesson in how the functional product lent credibility and appeal to everything else they did.

THE TED AND TOM SHOW

On their Search missions, photographer Ted Grambeau had developed a rapport with Tom Curren, which made Ted the perfect candidate for a difficult, some would say impossible, assignment on the North Shore of Oahu. Rip Curl had just released its new tide watch and Claw had a vision of Curren in a Backdoor barrel, his front arm protruding from the tube with the watch on it, showing off his new board shorts. The challenges of achieving such an image amid the crazy hustle and bustle of a North Shore surf season, and a packed Backdoor line-up, were considerable even before you factored in Curren's mercurial nature.

Ted recalls the morning of the shoot. 'Off I go, checking the surf, walking down the track at Off the Wall, this little lane with perfect light coming through the foliage, and through that framed track is Tom Curren in the barrel. That's the shot! I've missed it. I've blown it.'

Ted sprang into action, grabbed his gear and set up in a rush, hoping he'd be lucky enough to capture a similar moment. As Ted was shooting on film, he only had 36 exposures to work with on each roll. 'I decide I'll keep a full roll the whole time, so if I shoot half a roll I'll change rolls, just to make sure I have enough frames to capture an entire ride,' Ted explains.

'Tom's all over the place, up to Off the Wall, and back to Backdoor. There's two or three waves when he went in and out of the barrel, but nothing epic. I keep changing rolls and moving up the beach and back to Backdoor,' says Ted. Trying to keep track of Curren in the busy line-up was hard enough, let alone frame him through a viewfinder. And then the wave of the day rose out of the horizon.

'Tom drops in and I just put the finger down, and Tom's in this barrel on the foam ball. The board is like a rodeo ride, but he's still going and I don't know if I've ever shot a full roll of film on one sequence before. He finally came out of this barrel and did a jelly-armed shake. It was the most perfectly ridden wave that I've ever seen at Backdoor. And then I have the suspense of the roll of film going to town to get processed,' says Ted.

'He came in after that wave. He said, "I was going to change boards because this board was feeling a little too long." The board put him deeper than he would have liked but I don't know if any other surfer could have handled that situation – it was the best tube-riding I've ever seen in my life. I went up to the Rip Curl house and said, "I've done that. What else do you want me to do?"'

MEDIA NIGHT GOES NEXT LEVEL

One antidote to the dangers of corporatising Rip Curl's free and wild culture was the annual media night each Easter, which reached new levels of decadence and debauchery through the '90s.

'Media nights were pretty epic. They had a dwarf-throwing contest at one. Another time they had army tanks in the car park. One year, Claw and Brian came in on camels,' recalls Damien Hardman. 'They had guys jumping out of choppers, guys doing dick tricks. It was pre–[mobile] phones – you couldn't do that these days.'

Brian's brief for these events was succinct: 'classy bizarre' was how he defined the desired ambience, a description that might be also applied to director David Lynch's cinematic style. And one could have been forgiven for feeling like they'd wandered into a

David Lynch film as fire twirlers, dwarves, magicians and classical violinists entertained the crowds, or mock gun battles raged in the Rip Curl car park, or helicopters buzzed over the Bells line-up as surfers rode in fluorescent wetsuits in the inky darkness.

For Brian and Claw, media night carried on a tradition of outrageous behaviour in Torquay that they'd inherited from their elders. 'It was really an extension of the early Rip Curl Pro days, when crews from Narrabeen would travel down and make it an extended trip. They were quite wild periods. But even they were just apprentices to the earlier Boot Hill crew,' says Brian.

The task of organising media night fell to Rip Curl stalwart Gary Crothall, whose qualifications for the role seemed to comprise having played in several prominent rock bands as a drummer through the '70s and '80s. 'There was no budget. A few days before the event Brian would say, "Have we got enough elephants? How many dwarves have we got? How many clowns have we got?" They had to be memorable, and they always were,' recalls Gary. 'I played in bands and worked at Rip Curl, came and left twice when I toured and made albums,' says Gary. He appeared on *Countdown* with a band called Redhouse in the '70s, was a regular with local outfit Shadowfax, and wrote the title track for David 'The Mex' Sumpter's '70s surf film *On Any Morning*.

Gary eventually had to choose between Rip Curl and rock-and-roll. 'I came back to Rip Curl the second time and was asked to join this band, Goanna. I did one and a half years with Goanna but I was firmly committed to Rip Curl by then,' he says. Goanna exploded in popularity in 1982 with a huge hit single, 'Solid Rock', one of the first great Australian anthems of the Indigenous rights movement, but by then Gary was ready to settle down to a steady job. 'I've had 50 years of Rip Curl and rock-and-roll – I've been blessed, mate. I can't say any more than that,' he says.

Though he's witnessed immeasurable change since landing on Rip Curl's doorstep as a teenage kid back at the old bakery, Gary reckons Claw and Brian have provided a continuity of spirit. 'I don't think they've changed in their mindset since day dot. They created products so they could do what they wanted to do. That's all they wanted the company to be about.'

(ON)BOARD MEETINGS

Another key strategy to focus on their core mission was the floating international board meetings, the first of which had given rise to the Search campaign. That trip was considered such a success, and such a desirable way of doing business, that the international management team convened on boat trips annually through the '90s.

'Meetings and surf were the only activities,' says the Frenchman Fred Basse. 'It was sometimes intense, but after a surf we were able to continue. I did enjoy them a lot. We went on the [*Indies*] *Trader 1* at the beginning of its activity and so many times in the Mentawais. Claw was always coming with maps researching the next good left for the crew and him. We went also in Costa Rica and several times in the Maldives.'

Those boat trips continued into the 2000s and were highlights of the year for new members of the management team. Steve Kay remembers running into one of the Rip Curl boat trips when he was still at *Tracks*, and their own boat had broken down in the Mentawai port of Sikakap.

'The *Indies Trader 1* comes steaming into the port like the *Queen Mary* compared to what we were on,' says Steve. 'They moored up beside and asked what's going on, and we told them. They ran downstairs and ran up with a carton of super-cold VB.' Steve never forgot that act of kindness to a bunch of marooned fellow surf travellers. A few years later, Steve was enjoying the rather more opulent Rip Curl boat trips himself.

Brian recalls one boat trip that would have ended in disaster if not for a late nocturnal wee over the side of the boat by his co-founder. 'We were on one of our May budget meetings on board the *Huey* [a converted ex-Japanese customs patrol boat] up in the Mentawais. We were quite far north heading back south, and the Indonesian skipper had been on a long stint', says Brian. 'We heard the engine stop and then rev really loudly. We all came up on deck and there was a reef right in front of us, and we'd nearly crashed right into it. Claw had got up to have a piss, saw the white water in front of us and warned the skipper. We wouldn't have drowned, but crashing into a deserted island at night with a solid six-foot swell would have been inconvenient.'

TURNING OFFSHORE

The Australian Government, under Labor prime ministers Hawke and Keating, had been steadily reducing tariffs and protectionist policies throughout the '80s and early '90s to increase Australia's global competitiveness. Industry and Commerce Minister John Button drove the policy, which was widely regarded as a necessary modernisation of the Australian economy, but led to many redundancies in Australian manufacturing and caused much angst in Labor's union base.

Rip Curl was not immune to the sweeping reforms. Little by little, an increasing proportion of products were manufactured offshore, beginning with accessories and clothes, though the company still prided itself on manufacturing its own wetsuits and providing a dedicated customer service.

Rip Curl had long been manufacturing wetsuits in its key markets because import duties were too high. 'The reason why we licensed various countries was twofold – there were often high import duties so you had to manufacture in the country, and we often didn't have the capital or management to open subsidiaries,' explains Brian. As a result, wetsuits had been manufactured in the US, France and Argentina, as well as Australia.

The slashing of import duties in Australia meant that it became dramatically cheaper to manufacture in Asia. Rip Curl tried to keep manufacturing locally for as long as possible but eventually the economic realities became irresistible.

'The Australian clothing industry was going through dramatic changes, with customs duties changing from 35 per cent to less than 10 per cent. In fact, the Australian Government decided they were no longer going to subsidise clothing manufacturing,' says Brian. 'The Labor Government got rid of protectionism, so at that point we decided to get our surfwear made in China. Aussies were voting with their wallets not their hearts. I was in a shop one day watching women buy clothing, and one said with obvious disdain, "All these clothes are made in China." She looked at the price of the Australian-made stuff and bought the Chinese stuff.'

Nonetheless, Rip Curl was wary of allowing outside contractors to make its wetsuits. 'We needed a good wetsuit factory in Asia. We'd had wetsuits made with other companies in other factories, but we had developed all sorts of technologies that we didn't want to share with others so it was better to put it through our own factory,' says Brian.

Eventually, the problem was solved by buying their own wetsuit factory in Thailand, OnSmooth Thai, which was owned by Butch Sadikay, the owner of the Jetty Surf retail chain. There they could control all aspects of production, ensure quality and protect their own technologies. 'I met [Sadikay] and, over an hour's conversation, did a handshake deal for a million dollars and bought the factory from him, and didn't have a moment's drama subsequently – a real gentleman to do business with,' says Brian.

Sadikay had bought the wetsuit factory in 1994, after the previous owner had gone broke and the factory wound up in the hands of receivers while it still held a large order of his prepaid stock. 'We negotiated with the banks and took it on, the whole operation worldwide,' he says. 'We doubled the size of the factory, got it pretty efficient, and started to make wetsuits for people who supplied our retail group.' They had been making wetsuits for other surf brands and their own Jetty Surf shops until 1997, when Butch proposed selling the factory to Rip Curl. 'Brian's similar to myself – he shoots from the hip and he's honourable,' says Butch. 'The reason people don't do handshake deals is that people don't honour them but we old-timers do . . . After a number of lawyers' meetings, it was consummated as per the handshake.'

In France, Rip Curl embraced offshore manufacturing reluctantly, given a European sensibility that valued local production. 'Around '92 we started to produce in Asia and slowly we had more and more done offshore,' says Fred Basse. 'The Hossegor factory saved us from difficult situations several times during this learning curve [about] Asian production. Several times we had Asian wetsuits with production faults that we could fix in the factory in Hossegor.'

Inevitably, the day came when the Hossegor factory fell idle. 'When we stop the production in '95 we kept most of our workers. When they were leaving there were no replacements but we maintained the machinery and most girls. Lucky we did it as today one of the strengths of Rip Curl is its aftersales service,' says Fred.

Many staff mourned the closure of the wetsuit factory. 'I'd say, "I go to work at the factory," and it was a real factory. Now it is the office – the smells are gone,' says Mado Ustarroz, the finance manager.

Patricea Dohen, the long-time wetsuit manager, admits she cried when the factory closed.

'It was difficult for us and for the girls, for everybody. The factory for us was like the heart of the company,' says Mado.

But business continued to boom in Europe. In '97 a new sales manager, Henri Colliard, joined Rip Curl from mainstream athletics brand Reebok and brought a new level of profession-alism to operations, while François Payot took a step back from the day-to-day business. Fred Basse balanced his growing work responsibilities with a headlong dive into the new frontier of tow-surfing in big-wave discoveries off the French and Spanish coasts.

THE DREAM TOUR

In 1998 former world champ Rabbit Bartholomew took over as director of the ASP (Association of Surfing Professionals) and ushered in the Dream Tour era. In a raft of sweeping changes, Rabbit supported a doubling of contest prize money, new loca-tions came on tour and existing events were encouraged to move into prime surf season, with mobility to chase the best waves, or risk losing their spot in the schedule.

In the short term, the bold changes posed the dilemma of moving Rip Curl's highly successful event at Hossegor from August, at the end of summer, to September or October to take advantage of the more reliable autumn swells. François Payot was not happy.

'When ASP decided to move the dates to late October, I disagreed because I was thinking that some events must be done in front of the public and not only for TV or internet, as our public need to see their heroes and live action,' says François. 'We already had some events in Fiji or Tahiti which had nearly no public at all.'

Rip Curl had played an active role at ASP meetings before Rabbit's tenure, with Claw and François serving as event and regional representatives at various times. 'Claw was recognised as founding father so he had every right to be there. Rip Curl was the first to invest in pro surfing,' says Rabbit. 'François was very strong and very vocal at the meetings. He was full on. This is before I ran it.'

When Rabbit took the top job at ASP, the previously friendly dynamic between him and François shifted. 'When I used my casting vote to double the prize money he called it Rabbit's Putsch,' says Rabbit, a reference to Hitler's Munich Putsch, when the Nazi leader tried to seize power in Germany in 1923. 'He was way off it. There were six surfer reps and six event reps and he saw me as the seventh surfer. We could agree to disagree, but he was very professional and accepted the referee's decision. He wanted pro surfing to succeed.'

But when François refused to agree to changing the dates of the Hossegor event, ASP offered the licence to Quiksilver, who jumped at the chance.

Quiksilver had always held its event in Biarritz, and François says Quiksilver asked his permission to build a secondary contest site at Hossegor. But because of the superior waves, Hossegor soon became the primary site.

François stood his ground and found other ways to maintain Rip Curl Europe's profile on the tour schedule. 'We held a WQS [World Qualifying Series] in Hossegor at the same date as before, and the government of Portugal and city of Peniche offer us a golden deal to come and organise a WCT [World Championship Tour] over there,' says François. 'I was more than pleased, and with two WCTs, Rip Curl maintained a high presence on the tour.'

There was some scepticism that Rabbit's gambles on prize money and scheduling would work, or that the cash-strapped ASP could afford to alienate its major sponsors. He recalls, 'I remember walking into this Rip Curl meeting in Hawaii and we had this folder with all the minutes from the AGM, and Payot had the folder and he's going "Tick, tick, tick, tick."' François's inference was that the ASP was a time bomb ready to explode. 'He could definitely intimidate people if he wanted to,' says Rabbit.

The new scheduling did not get off to an auspicious start, with the European events cancelled due to travel safety concerns following the September 11 terrorist attacks in 2001. But in the longer term, the Dream Tour concept proved itself. 'That late September–October date proved to be very successful,' says Rabbit. 'You have the lows come across into the Bay of Biscay and offshore autumn conditions and the best beach breaks in the world. We had the Andy [Irons]–Kelly rivalry. François Payot came to me and said, "I demand you give me back my contest," but the event licences had to be honoured.'

The loss of the Hossegor event would ultimately open up new opportunities for Rip Curl. 'For compensation they accepted the new concept I had, a contest which will change location every year – the Search contest was born,' says François.

AMERICAN RESCUE

One of the toughest gigs at Rip Curl, reserved for its most trusted and valued generals, was running the US business, a perennial burr in their saddle blanket. In '97, it was accountant Rod Adams' turn to try to stem the losses.

'I'd been grizzling to Brian about the CEO over there and he said, "You go and do it then," so I went over there and did my job in Torquay as well,' says Rod. From '97 to '99, Rod divided his time between Torquay and California, acting as CEO in the US and CFO in Australia. It was a huge workload, especially as he had a wife and kids back in Torquay.

'The Americans thought that they knew best and all I simply did was replicate what we did in Australia,' says Rod. 'It was taking the Australian product and adding some US product. In wetsuits it was taking the Australian range and adding some thicker wetsuits for New England along with hoods and thick booties. Same in apparel – it was, grab two-thirds of the Australian range and add a third of American. Skiwear it was just one range, not separate ranges for the Southern and Northern Hemisphere. It was simple. As a foreigner you can look from the outside in and you can see things more clearly.'

Rod's pragmatic approach did not always please his American staff. 'That pissed off a lot of people in America and it was really tough for me,' says Rod. 'In a time of full employment, if they didn't like what I was doing they could go and get a job elsewhere.' He subscribed to Brian's view that you learnt most about the business in the warehouse and in surf shops. 'I would spend 25 per cent of every day talking to customers or in the warehouse,' says Rod.

After three years, with the US business out of the red, Rod considered it mission accomplished, but Rip Curl's woes in the US weren't over yet. 'When it was a bit above breaking even I came back, and the new guy promptly took it back into losses,' he says.

Rod returned to Torquay to a business transitioning into one global entity to better manage its growth.

ALL IN THE SAME BOAT

By 1999, it was becoming apparent that Rip Curl's piecemeal international expansion and varied business structures were becoming a liability in an increasingly global marketplace.

'We had a somewhat disparate ownership of Rip Curl internationally with some different shareholders owning the operating companies, Rip Curl USA, Rip Curl Australia and Rip Curl Europe,' says Brian. 'For two reasons we wanted to combine everything. We wanted all the shareholders or owners in the same boat rowing in the same direction, without their own individual agendas. And we had concerns that, with different ownership, brand fragmentation could occur, or the way the brand was portrayed could vary around the world.'

The process of forming one global entity required a cast of experts and advisors who assessed the relative valuations of the different companies and the tax implications for the shareholders. 'We put all the companies together so we each now held a somewhat smaller share of a bigger company,' says Brian. 'The process began in 1999 and culminated in 2000, and we celebrated at Le Parisien restaurant in Geelong with a 1990 award-winning Grange, claimed to be the best vintage at that time.'

Though they worked closely with international business consultants like KPMG, Brian reckons they received their best guidance from a local lawyer in Geelong who had a family connection to their business. 'We voted Ken Andrews from Harwood Andrews our outstanding advisor of the process and got him a dozen bottles of the 1990 Grange,' says Brian. 'He was my old school friend, whose son, Justin Andrews, worked at Rip Curl for a while for Hodg and now is the CEO of Oakley/Luxottica in North America.'

Cultural differences endured between Rip Curl's constituent countries. Fred Basse developed his own candid way of defining the traits of the global family members.

'The Americans consider they are the centre of the world, they know nothing outside their country . . . Having the biggest market in the world, if they are successful there, they believe there are no reasons it should not work outside,' says Fred. 'Their market is competitive and we found often their product good.'

Fred didn't spare his compatriots. 'The French have a strong personality and are certainly arrogant. They like to give lessons. They have difficulties with Americans and get on well with the Australians,' he says. 'I believe finance was not our priority and luckily Australia was providing the balance and forced us to improve.'

Fred appeared to have a good grasp of the Australian psyche. 'The Aussies are competitors. They refuse to lose and they have to always compete with the USA,' he says. 'Claw was certainly the hardest of the Aussies, especially in surfing teams and contests. To make him change his opinion, the Americans or the French had to be better by at least 20 per cent . . . Brian was much more open-minded.'

Fred's candour may have ruffled some feathers, but it was typical of the kind of frank discussions that allowed the various Rip Curl members to work productively. 'During the time I did work on the globalisation, the sentence I heard the most [began] "In my country . . ." As soon as somebody was starting his sentence by these words, there was an argument, no verified facts and mostly emotional perception. We lost hours of discussion due to ego questions,' says Fred.

The globalisation of the business inevitably came at the expense of the independence of each region, as local cultural characteristics gave way to a more unified brand message. 'Rip Curl gave a lot of autonomy to their big licensees like Europe, USA and Australia at the beginning,' says Fred. 'When globalisation came with a form of authority, it was hard to change the mentality.' But the arrival of the internet and a more international online media meant trends, fashion, content and tastes became more global. Rip Curl's timing seemed spot on.

ARGENTINA

One of Rip Curl's most surprising growth markets arose in the late '90s in Argentina, a country that had hardly been renowned for its surf culture. Today, Rip Curl is the dominant surf brand, accounting for around 50 per cent of total surf retail in the country.

Rip Curl's Argentinian licensee, Cristóbal Colón (the Spanish name for Christopher Columbus), was founded by wife and husband Viviana Pallocchini and Alejandro Amicola in 1978. They aimed to cater to the emerging sports of surfing, skateboarding and snowboarding with three multi-brand stores in and around Buenos Aires, and they stocked Rip Curl products right from the start.

'We bought Rip Curl clothes for our stores from De Leonardis, a guy from Mar del Plata. Only a few core surfers wore these clothes,' recalls Viviana, a passionate advocate for the brand.

'One day, he came and told us that we were the only ones who understood the values of the brand and that, as we were already buying everything that he produced or imported, he wanted to introduce us to the board in Australia, so he can transfer the licence of Rip Curl in Argentina because he has health problems,' says Viviana. 'We were so happy that we said yes immediately, without even thinking. It was a really exciting moment because since the beginning we had been putting our soul into the brand, selling the products at Cristóbal Colón. Also, we had taught everyone already the pronunciation of Rip Curl, the meaning of the name and values of the brand. That's how we started . . . very carefully, with a lot of hope, leaving behind our own brands that we produced, to dedicate entirely with devotion to develop Rip Curl in Argentina.'

Soon after, Claw travelled to Argentina to meet the new licensees. 'We remember we went to buy a formal dress to give a good serious first impression,' says Viviana. 'And so, we went to the small airport next to the river to pick them up, and we saw Claw walking to us with his long hair and his Reef Mundaka sandals, not a formal look at all! Always very true, fresh, natural and spontaneous.'

They went to lunch at a smart riverside restaurant to impress the Rip Curl co-founder, where Claw felt moved to cool off with a wade in the river. 'Claw took his sandals off and went into it and got stuck in the mud, thinking that it was the sea,' says Viviana. 'You need to know that no one here swims there. At that moment we felt identified with his spontaneity, and we felt we could build a strong and long relationship.'

In a nation where surfing was a fringe sport and the economy was volatile, progress was slow initially. 'At the beginning, the brand was only known in Mar del Plata and the development was almost zero,' says Viviana. 'We start developing big ranges, almost all local designs because Australian ranges were very focused on neoprene, some t-shirts and board shorts ... Mar del Plata is a city by the sea, but [much] of the Argentinian population lives in Buenos Aires. So, we had to adapt ranges to the city lifestyle and local demand, with an inspirational theme based on surfing. That's how we started selling dreams, the dream of the feeling of freedom when riding a wave.'

As Rip Curl became a more unified global business, the Argentinian licensees wholeheartedly bought into the strategy. 'They're smart people in Argentina. They don't try to change anything, they just faithfully execute the brand,' says Steve Kay, who now oversees international licensees. 'They are really early adopters of all of these selling points.'

The result has been a remarkable uptake of the brand, despite often challenging economic and political realities. 'Argentina is a very difficult country. Every three or four years politics change,' says Viviana. 'Our major goal is to keep Rip Curl exclusive, and that aspirational feeling of the brand. We don't want to make it popular. Popular things in Argentina have a short life.'

THE BLUE BOOK AND THE YELLOW BOOK

As Rip Curl's business modernised, Claw and Brian realised they wouldn't stay on much longer as full-time executives. They decided the company's founding principles needed to be defined, so they wouldn't get lost along the way. 'I'd read a book called *Built to Last*, by two Harvard University people [James C. Collins and Jerry I. Porras], and that had quite a big impact on our thinking,' says Brian. 'It showed that those companies that had a set of values and talked about them often did a lot better than those companies that didn't.'

During winter in Mount Buller, the two founders wrote out the company's values, among which were a focus on the customer, creativity and innovation, honesty and integrity, and community and environment. The philosophy of the Search was also enshrined as central to the company. These values became the basis for the 'Yellow Book', which also articulated how employees could conduct business in accordance with Rip Curl's principles, and recognised the key role of 'the crew', Rip Curl staff around the world who embodied those ideals.

At the same time, the 'Blue Book' defined the brand: that is, how Rip Curl was perceived externally by its customers and consumers. A research company was engaged for this purpose and its findings confirmed what management had thought, and formed the basis of the Blue Book. It identified brand values like technology and leadership, respect and reliability, as well as fun and irreverence.

Communications director Gary Dunne, in close consultation with Claw and Brian, was tasked with pulling the yellow and blue books together, with new creative director James Taylor. These two internal documents have become vital to the way Rip Curl does business to this day.

Brian recalls that various people within the company tried to articulate what Rip Curl's vision was or should be. 'Many of the suggestions were quite altruistic, with us trying to be all things to all people,' says Brian. 'And Hodg came along and thumped his fist on the table and went, "What is all this shit? We're just a fucking surfing company."'

This frank outburst resonated, and the vision to be the 'ultimate surfing company' was roundly embraced. It's easy to be cynical about the creation of corporate mission statements and brand visions, earnest framed mantras that are hung on walls and expected to motivate the troops daily to dig deep for the collective good. But at this stage in Rip Curl's evolution, the exercise seemed to fulfil a real need to define and explain the curious, organic process they had all been a part of for the past several decades.

Far from gathering dust on bookshelves, the brand books are referred to daily, brought to meetings, used as ammunition to pitch new ideas and provide a touchstone for major decisions. 'You can just do things here . . . if you've got the money and you've got the responsibility and it matches up with the brand values,' says Neil Ridgway, international marketing chairman. 'I use those books as a green-light ticket to so many things – if it's in the book I can do it, so let's go.'

RIP CURL SIGNS MICK FANNING

By 1998, Kelly Slater had collected a record six world titles and Rip Curl hadn't had a world champion since Damien Hardman in 1991. It was a bitter pill to swallow after the glory days of the '80s. Despite the marketing success of the Search campaign, Rip Curl liked having world champions and team riders on the podium, and there was a sense that the Search might have started to lose its impact.

'Our very private mantra was, only recruit a surfer who can beat Kelly Slater,' says Claw. 'We had plenty of surfers. We did a lot of good things with them, and they did a lot of good things for us. But there was clearly a top dog – if you wanted to get on the top step of the podium you had to beat the top dog. And we saw those qualities in Mick Fanning. We saw a surfer who we thought could beat Kelly Slater.'

In 1998, that was a bold prediction. Mick Fanning was a spindly 16-year-old from Tweed Heads with a few good junior results, still largely in the shadow of his Coolangatta mates Joel Parkinson and Dean Morrison. Rip Curl had earlier made a play for Parko. 'I think Joel was sponsored by them for about a month but he never signed the contract and went back to Billabong,' says Mick. Fanning may have been their second choice, but Claw saw something in his whippet speed, lightning reflexes and strength of character that he felt sure would take him places.

'I saw him surf in the semifinal and final of the Australian titles at Bells Beach. Mick just streaked them, his first clearly dominant contest performance,' says Claw. 'In the final, at the 19-minute mark he was last, and in the last 11 minutes of the final he just blew them out of the water, and it was a very strong field, so that was a breakout performance. I'd seen film of him surfing old Kirra, the last year of the great old Kirra [before the Tweed River sand-pumping shifted the bank]. I knew this was something different, something new. The speed and acceleration, it was remarkable.'

Rip Curl's marketing man Michael Ray had first spotted Mick's talent in a Quiksilver video and drew him to Claw's attention. 'Mick had this tiny two-minute segment, but he had that whole

Mick Fanning speed whip going,' says Michael. 'I said to Claw, "Have you seen this guy?" Claw went to a junior contest and saw him surf and said, he's the guy.'

Mick hadn't even competed on the World Qualifying Series and was still at school, but had come to attention in Gold Coast, Queensland and national titles as part of an impressive talent pool in Coolangatta known collectively as the 'Cooly Kids'. Mick and his older brother Sean were riding for Quiksilver on fairly modest deals when Mick got a call from Michael Ray.

'I went to the Gold Coast to see my grandparents and rang up Mick. We knew he was on about $10,000 [a year with Quiksilver]. Let's offer him $100K over three years. Let's make him an offer he can't refuse,' recalls Michael.

'It was pretty funny. I'd just got home from school, and the phone rang and this voice goes, "Is Mick there?" and I go, "Yeah, speaking." He goes, "This is Michael Ray from Rip Curl. We're just ringing up to offer you a contract."'

As Mick recalls it, Michael didn't beat around the bush. 'We'd like to get you on the team. I'll get straight to the point. We want to offer you $35,000 [a year],' Michael told him.

Mick was typically self-deprecating. He said, 'You're kidding me, right? Have you seen me surf?' He suspected it was one of his mates playing a prank. 'I said, "Why don't you ring back when my mum gets home?"'

But it wasn't a prank and Rip Curl weren't kidding. Mick was the youngest of five kids, brought up by a single mum, Liz Osbourne, on a nurse's salary. Mick's parents split when he was just three and living in Campbelltown, in the working-class Western Suburbs of Sydney, a long way from the beach. You'd have got extremely long odds back then that he'd one day become a professional surfer, let alone a three-time world champion.

Liz takes up the story. 'I came home from work and he said, "Mum, Rip Curl have spoken to me on the phone. They want to sponsor me for 35 grand,"' recalls Liz. 'I thought, I don't have to buy him any more clothes.'

Mick was still a minor, so Liz had to sign contracts on his behalf and quite organically became Mick's business manager. 'I wrote to Quiksilver . . . I was very nice. I said, "We were loyal to you and we want to stay with you but we expect $35,000,"' says Liz. 'And they just said no. I was shocked . . . Craig Stevenson at Quiksilver, every time I see him he shakes his head and says that was the biggest mistake of Quiksilver's life.'

Michael Ray spoke to Quiksilver team manager Andrew Murphy to offer to pay out Mick's contract. 'Murph was like, "I love Mick but we can't match that offer. We'll let him out." We paid out his contract to Quiksilver. Mick had quite strong loyalty to them,' says Michael.

Liz and Mick met with Gary Dunne, who'd become Rip Curl team manager, to sign contracts. 'After it was all signed, Gary Dunne said to me, "Well, now we own Mick Fanning the surfer," and I thought, oh my god, what have I done? I've sold him out. But it was the best thing that's ever happened to Mick,' says Liz.

This was early '98, so when Easter rolled around Mick made his way down to Bells Beach for the first time as a Rip Curl team rider. 'I went down and hung out in the Rip Curl house, this 16-year-old kid with all these guys like Hedgey [Nathan Hedge] and Byron Howarth. I already knew Raff [Darren O'Rafferty] and Zane [Harrison],' says Mick.

'Walking into the office was a bit daunting for me. I walked in with Hedgey and he was the golden child who knew everyone's name,' Mick recalls. 'When I first met Claw, he was as excited as he is today. Claw was super engaging, Brian was a bit more reserved.

I always thought Brian was a bit harder. Claw was the one who would sit there and talk to you about surfing. As time went on I figured that Brian didn't really want to be intrusive. He was just there for support, where Claw was super involved, always ringing up and seeing how things were going, just really interested, really frothed out on surfing.'

It didn't take Mick long to realise what a student of the sport Claw was, and how carefully he'd selected their latest recruit. 'He looks at the backgrounds of surfers and what their attitude is like ... To sit down and watch a contest with him is pretty amazing. Even to this day he'll get out his notepad and write down scores. He's really clued up.'

Mick made just as powerful an impression on Claw, who saw something beyond Mick's gangly frame and self-deprecating humour. 'You could see he had a big future, combined with these personal qualities: inner strength, determination, humanity,' says Claw. 'When we first saw him, he had a brashness and heart, but it was the speed – white lightning – and then he's got all these deep, powerful personal qualities which he could take on to the field of battle.'

CHAPTER EIGHT

SALTS AND SUITS: 2000–2004

As the New Year ticked over and the world finally got to party like it was 1999, as computer nerds everywhere anticipated a cataclysmic collapse of society courtesy of the Y2K bug, Claw and Brian were contemplating a step back from their full-time, hands-on roles at the Curl.

On the lookout for a new CEO to guide the brand into the new millennium, Brian called in James Strong, his travel companion from that Antarctic expedition almost a decade earlier. By this time, Strong had completed an impressive stint as CEO of Qantas, overseeing the merger of Qantas and Australian Airlines into a single entity and its floating on the Australian Stock Exchange. He had become something of a legend in the Australian aviation business and was hugely respected as a business leader, philanthropist and patron of the arts.

Strong's appointment as chairman of the Rip Curl board in 2001 was widely seen as a sign of the surf brand preparing to follow in the footsteps of its competitors Quiksilver and Billabong by going public. 'I knew the prior chairman of Qantas, Gary Pemberton, had become chairman of Billabong. James was a fairly obvious choice,' says Brian.

Sadly, James Strong died in 2013 at the age of 68 from complications following surgery, and is warmly remembered as a giant figure in the Australian business scene, with his trademark bow tie and sense of adventure. His wife, Jeanne-Claude, says it was the bond forged between him and Brian during their Antarctic adventure, and the qualities her husband saw in Brian, that drew James to the position. 'Brian was very solid and a good team member and very supportive of everyone in the team – a very clear thinker, very confident in the snow and very fit,' Jeanne-Claude recalls from that trip. 'He was very impressed by Brian as a man and an individual. He liked his vision and his sense of fun . . . James was asked to join the boards of several companies around Australia and many of them far larger than Rip Curl. He would have been loath to join any private company had it not been for the quality of Brian and Claw.'

Strong's first job as chairman was to attend a meeting in California. 'We were staying in a house in Carlsbad [north of San Diego] when we were woken by an early morning phone call from a mate of mine to say the 9/11 terrorist attacks were happening, on the very first day that [James] started with Rip Curl,' says Brian. 'I raced into the room where James and Jeanne-Claude were sleeping to break the news and we spent the next two hours glued to the TV before we set off for our annual Rip Curl International meeting. It certainly had a very sobering effect on the meeting, particularly for the Americans.'

One of Strong's first tasks was to help recruit a new CEO. Strong's pick was David Lawn, a highly regarded senior executive who came from a background in apparel with Jeans West, Country Road and Myer Grace Brothers. He was also a non-surfer, which caused some gnashing of teeth among the salty old-timers at Rip Curl. Initially, David would take on responsibility for Australia and New Zealand while Brian continued as CEO for a 'settling-in' period.

David Lawn was a huge admirer of both James Strong and Rip Curl, and jumped at the opportunity. 'Who doesn't want to be interviewed for the job as CEO of Rip Curl?' David says today. 'I still say James is one of the most influential people in my life. I still miss him. He was a wonderful human being, he just had so much time for you. I was very attracted to the opportunity to work with Brian and Claw and the magic of that brand, and to be in a project with James where the goal was significant growth, it wasn't a difficult decision. I still think very fondly about the time I had there.'

The new CEO came with the clear goal of expanding the apparel side of the business. 'I was a bit of a student of the brand. My background was in apparel retailing,' says David. 'I thought we had a terrific brand but not an apparel sensibility. We were much stronger in technical product, but in apparel Quiksilver and Billabong were much better at that than Rip Curl.'

In Torquay, there were some fears that the appointment of a non-surfing CEO and the reduced presence of the founders would spell an end to their old, informal ways: the bare, sandy feet in the office, the long lunch-time surfs, the proudly salty workplace culture. But they needn't have worried.

'That stuff is the charm, not the problem. I found that part of it really easy,' says David. 'The toughest part was that they didn't really have the people and infrastructure to cope with the growth ... The tension of having a company in the hands of surfers and then people with experience outside of surfing bringing change to the organisation, that was the hardest part.'

David's agenda for the business was clear-cut. 'The company

had three things to do,' he says. 'Grow the apparel business – apparel was a much smaller percentage of the company than it needed to be. We were not good retailers, we didn't have many stores. And we had to get the four companies to work together. It was a bit like Star Wars, it was run by a whole lot of fiercely determined and passionate people in other parts of the world making decisions in isolation. To get the company to operate as one company, that was hard. And we had a business in America that just wasn't working. They were the major projects of the CEO coming in. We had some success, but not total by any means ... There was a fair bit of internal resistance. It's human nature ... If we kicked goals everywhere they probably would have backed off more, but we did hit some bumps.'

Chief among those bumps was the ongoing underperformance of the US business. 'America was just fucking hard work the whole time. I ended up going over there and living there. I felt I had to, but I don't think I was successful at that. I joined a long line of people,' David says ruefully.

David found allies in some of the newer arrivals at Rip Curl who were eager to learn the ways of the modern business world, like creative director James Taylor and marketing chairman Neil Ridgway. Among the wins, David says a more unified global brand and marketing message, under one consistent logo, were major achievements. 'Neil and JT did a great job globalising the marketing,' he says.

He also developed a deep respect for Rip Curl's enigmatic founders. 'They are the real thing, in terms of authentic brand leaders and owners,' says David. 'Claw is the soul of the company and his spirit is the spirit of the company and surfing ... Brian, in contrast, is a hard-headed, strong, detail-oriented warhorse. And he's tough and he's very strong-willed.'

David believes the founders should have accepted an offer from the VF Corporation, owners of Vans, North Face, Reef, Lee and Wrangler, to buy the business in 2006. 'We had an offer for the company – it wasn't quite what they wanted but it was at least double what they'd get now,' says David. 'To be integrated with a machine that can take things to volume, I wanted to lead the company in that direction to operate as a global company. That's very easy to say, very hard to fucking execute.'

THE BEAN COUNTERS

As part of the process of globalising the business, CFO Rod Adams hired a young accountant named Michael Daly, also from Price-waterhouseCoopers, who would come to play a huge role in the business. Michael had been working mainly with international mining companies but was feeling the need for a change of direction. 'I was looking for a company that was smaller, that I could really feel engaged and passionate about, something more in line with my way of life,' says Michael. 'I had made a list of five companies that interested me, largely branded sporting companies. I was lucky enough that one of those companies was Rip Curl and I got the call from the headhunter one day – would I like to meet with Rip Curl about a role?'

'I knew Michael had the temperament, and his good technical accounting skills were going to be perfect for Rip Curl in the transition to what was foreseen to be a public company,' says Rod.

'I took a pay cut, indeed a significant one, and my colleagues at PwC all thought I was mad, but I was happy with the decision,' says Michael. 'One of my first tasks was to prepare a financial result for the month and year-to-date to the end of May. Unfortunately, I had to report that the result was nowhere near what they thought it was. I think I was asked to check it five times. I assured them I knew what I was doing and it was right. It was certainly a baptism of fire, but Brian, Rod and all the founders took the news well and gave me the autonomy to do what I needed to do to get the finance function working better around the world.'

Michael arrived at Rip Curl as a range of new appointments were made. 'The Brazilian subsidiary was set up with a new CEO, a new CEO was appointed to replace François as European CEO [Olivier Cantet], a new Group CEO was appointed to replace Brian [David Lawn], Stephen Kay was appointed to be the General Manager of Australia, a new USA CEO was appointed [Jimmy Olsson], Neil Ridgway was appointed to be the Global Advertising and Promotions Manager and I could list out another 50-odd major changes,' he says. 'It was a crazy time in the life of Rip Curl.'

There was much to get used to about Michael's new workplace. 'Sand footprints through the corridors were always a novel one,' says Michael. 'In my first year, as well as Group Finance Manager I was also jack-of-all-trades including overseeing our cleaning. The cleaners were always complaining to me about people being barefoot and walking sand through the place. I initially found it frustrating as cleaners would try and follow the footprints to find the culprit and point them out to me. Now, I just love seeing sand footprints in the carpet as it means our staff are living to our vision.'

Michael came on board with the understanding that he would eventually move into the role of CFO to replace Rod, but when that didn't transpire after three or four years he nearly walked. 'I aired my concerns to Rod and our HR manager at the time. Before I got my arse into gear about looking for another job, essentially Rod offered himself up and ultimately departed the company.' It was a selfless move by Rod, who'd been a faithful servant of the business for many years, and one that Rip Curl would be grateful for in the years ahead.

TO FLOAT OR NOT TO FLOAT

In 2000, Gold Coast–based surfwear brand Billabong created a sensation on the Australian Stock Exchange with one of the most successful floats in recent history. Its initial public offering was massively oversubscribed as Billabong's staff, retailers, surfers of all stripes and serious investors clamoured to get in on a brand that appeared destined for unending growth. Billabong floated at $2.30, and by 2007 had risen to a high of $17.19. After the successful float of Quiksilver, and the vast fortunes made by many of their senior management, going public looked like the smart thing for Rip Curl to do, to cash in on the years of hard work spent building a brand.

'We toyed with the idea. In fact, it was one of the reasons we hired James Strong, in case we decided to go down that road,' says Brian. 'A lot of our retail customers had shares in Billabong so I figured they were more inclined to buy from Billabong than from us, which did occur. Surf was running hot at that time.' Brian says they considered the downsides to going public. 'What it seems to me is you're forced into more short-term thinking, because of all the masters of the universe, I mean analysts, looking for annual and quarterly improvements. So, it forces the company into short-term thinking because they're focused on the share price. It's not necessarily a great way for a company to behave. Going public is an exit strategy.'

For these reasons, and because continuing challenges in North America in particular made it a less-than-ideal time to float, Claw and Brian proceeded cautiously. In the longer term that caution appeared well founded, even though floating had vastly increased their competitors' financial resources. 'At a point in time before the GFC it had our two main competitors flying, and we couldn't fly like that,' says Claw. 'They had financial horsepower we didn't have. They had four times the resources that we had to launch initiatives.'

They've never regretted the decision to not float. 'Being a public company has not been good for the surf industry. How can you have long-term strategies? You can spook the market quickly,' says Claw.

Rod Brooks, by this time firmly entrenched at Quiksilver, admired the way his old friends stuck to their guns and retained ownership. 'I wish Quiksilver had have done that,' says Rod. 'It was very hard for Claw and Brian. They nursed that company through some very difficult times.'

Mick Fanning had not long joined the Rip Curl team, and had quickly leapt to the upper echelons of the pro rankings, and he remembers being uneasy with discussions of Rip Curl going public. 'As an athlete it was sort of scary because I could see what was happening with the other brands,' Mick says. 'I'm glad they didn't, and they stuck to their roots.'

That feeling was shared by many at Rip Curl. 'Claw and Brian have always wanted Rip Curl to be a soulful surfing company,' says Ray Thomas. 'Even though they got out on a few tangents, they stuck to the core products – making stuff for surfers . . . They put their nuts on the line quite a few times.'

'There was nearly this perception that they'd been left behind, left on the shelf. In fact, they were the ones who weren't left on the shelf,' says Rabbit Bartholomew. 'Not having to listen to the bottom line of a public company and still having that control of their own destiny and not have to make targets, they can play a longer game and handle the dips. They've really killed it there.'

At the time, the intense competition between the brands, and between old friends Al Green and Brian, made it tough for the Rip Curl founders to watch their peers cash in so spectacularly. When Quiksilver USA purchased all the company trademarks from Quiksilver International for an astronomical sum, Brian recalls Greeny showing him a cheque with more noughts on it than either of them could have imagined when they'd begun their businesses back in 1969. 'It was a competition – you wanted to win. Greeny came around with the cheque – it was a pretty sizeable amount and we certainly did have a good celebration,' says Brian.

THE NEW CREW

As part of a program of generational change, Rip Curl began to attract a new cast of senior staff who would help propel them into a new era. Rather than having to choose between salts and suits, they discovered a new generation of eminently qualified young professionals who also happened to be dedicated surfers.

At Rip Curl, they had always been big on the idea that they were their own customer, and James Taylor was a perfect example of this when he walked into their Torquay store cashed up with English pounds after a few years working in London, looking to purchase a top-of-the-line Elasto wetsuit. JT had been working as an art director for a high-end magazine called *How to Spend It*, a glossy aspirational supplement to the *Financial Times*.

'I was working with this freaky, genius art-director guy. He had a breakdown and the head of the *Financial Times* said, "You've got the job if you can do it,"' says JT. 'I was art-directing shoots for Stella McCartney and Marco Pierre White [a Michelin-starred chef].'

But JT always knew he'd return to his beloved Victorian coast. 'After a couple of years working in London and dragging flatmates down to Cornwall to surf, I was ready to come home,' says JT. 'I walked into Rip Curl with heaps of pounds for the first time in my life and bought an Elasto.' By chance, he ran into an old mate from university days who told him there was a job going in the art department.

JT met Ray Thomas and got the job. 'That was 1999. I just saw an opportunity,' says JT. 'I'd come from a really high-end art department delivering monthly deadlines. There was a real opportunity to structure how creative was delivered. I came in to do advertising and product design for wetsuits. It was such a different time. From there it was just like an awesome lucky journey of having really great people to work with.'

One of JT's first jobs was to establish a modern and consistent brand identity, for which he enlisted the help of renowned British designer Alex Willcock and his agency, The Nest. The collaboration resulted in the new red-wave logo to provide a cohesive visual identity across all marketing and products. 'He was amazing, he has an incredible mind – he really helped us,' says JT, of Willcock. 'He taught us how to do that, to be able to articulate a brand point of view. That's a big part of why it looks all considered and tight.'

When JT talks about the opportunity to work with great people, he points to the roster of A-grade photographers he's collaborated with on campaigns. 'The people I've been lucky enough to worth with is the magic of the place – Jon Frank, Ted Grambeau, Trent Mitchell, Corey Wilson, Dave Sparkes.' The close collaboration with marketing chairman Neil Ridgway is also key. 'Neil isn't an artist but the way we work together the art comes out really well, and he loves branding.'

JT has helped orchestrate some groundbreaking campaigns. When Rip Curl was planning the launch of the H-Bomb, the world's first heated wetsuit, Ted Grambeau alerted them to a location in Iceland where ice flows into the ocean, and where there were waves. JT was convinced but needed to sell the idea to Neil. It was an expensive, untried and high-risk venture, but Neil gave it the green light, with one qualifier.

'Neil said, "If this shoot doesn't work, things won't be that comfortable for you here at Rip Curl,"' recalls JT. But Neil needn't have worried – the campaign set a new standard for wetsuit marketing. 'He told me later, "I needed to get the best out of you,"' says JT.

The campaign for Mirage board shorts was conceived to announce what Rip Curl billed as the world's most technical board shorts, which felt 'like wearing nothing'. The bullet-time, multiple-GoPro-camera set-up, as used in the movie *The Matrix*, reflected the product's innovative nature. In collaboration with Timeslice Films, they used up to 50 GoPros mounted in a row to shoot surf action sequences.

'The stuff we did with the 50-camera array was a completely new way of showcasing surfing, which was unique, and that was hard, that was so fucking hard to do,' says JT. The first 'bullet-time' shoot was in the Sunway Lagoon wave pool in Malaysia with the Rip Curl A-team: Mick Fanning, Owen Wright, Matt Wilkinson and Stephanie Gilmore. Four hours of torrential rain halted the complex shoot, drowning several laptops and cameras. Once the rain cleared, they required a night shoot under floodlights. The results, though, were extraordinary: dynamic surfing sequences frozen in time and examined seamlessly from multiple angles.

Mick Fanning urged the Rip Curl team to take the technology to the ocean, adding a whole new set of variables to what was already a monumental logistical feat. Mick suggested a wave in Fiji called Swimming Pools, off Namotu Island, which proved ideal. 'When I talk about great people to work with, he's one of them,' says JT.

For all the high-tech image-making and bold new technical frontiers, JT reckons he still relies on the company's founders for guiding principles. 'Working with the founders is great because they see the fundamentals. They're all about simplicity,' he says. 'We're not discounting because we're a premium brand. The dream is white sand and blue water.'

The enduring surf-first ethos has also helped draw the right people to the business. 'It's attracted surfers to the company. You walk into the workplace and you instantly have a bond because everyone is equally excited to go for a lunchtime surf,' says JT. 'I'm really keen on all my crew getting in the water. I've got to be attentive to who I bring into the business, and who is the customer? That's how we stay on point with our messaging.'

Another prime example of this generational renewal was Milan Thompson, an industrial designer and the son of long-time Torquay shaper Kym Thompson. 'To say I was born into the industry is pretty correct. I grew up with the sons of the founders and knowing the founders,' says Milan. 'I studied industrial design with the intention of going off overseas. There was no real intent to get back involved in the surf industry.'

But Rip Curl recognised that the talented young designer could be an asset at a time when they were keen to inject more youth into the brand, and offered him a traineeship. 'I worked with Grant Forbes on apparel and then watches with Hodg. I was fortunate to work under that original crew,' says Milan. 'They'd been through a massive explosion – anything they put their name on was a success. When I came on there had been a bit of a slowdown, and there was a push to bring on a bunch of young crew like myself to put some new ideas on the table. I wasn't formally trained in apparel design and was thrown in the deep end. There was a lot of trust . . . from those guys.'

Milan has since grown into a senior role as creative director of technical products and mentor for a generation of younger crew. In 2006, along with Mick Ray and Peter Hodgart, he helped form a technical group within the organisation to bring together designers from different product divisions. 'We were trying to bring a strong DNA across product groups and build a more collaborative environment,' says Milan.

Milan is focused on balancing that youthful influence with the fundamentals of the brand. 'We're all pretty fortunate, you don't have to do your 10 years here. You're given a fair bit of responsibility pretty quickly,' he says. 'It's a really youthful environment, but there's still a knowledge base around to make sure we don't slip.'

But when I interview him, what Milan's most excited about is a looming swell that's promising to deliver a week of classic winter waves. 'The next few days it's going to be pumping and we'll definitely get our share of waves,' he says. 'You don't build a successful company without discipline and structure, but it's balanced with time at the beach and time in the marketplace.'

THE MAGAZINE MEN

In the new millennium, a well-worn path developed between the offices of *Tracks* magazine, in inner-city Sydney, and Torquay. The first to make that trek was former *Tracks* editor Gary Dunne, who had joined Rip Curl as national team manager and communications manager in 1994, and became international team manager in 2002. *Tracks* publisher Steve Kay followed in 2000, and soon recruited one of his *Tracks* ad salesmen, Nichol Wylie, to join him. And in 2003 another ex–*Tracks* editor, Neil Ridgway, made the journey south to become international marketing chairman.

'For some years Steve had been coming down at Easter trying

to sell me the next 12 months' worth of ads and I realised he was a pretty shrewd operator and consummate salesman,' says Brian. Steve started as the global head of promotions, but titles never held a lot of sway at Rip Curl. Steve laughs when I ask if there was any formal induction process. 'There is now. At the time when I joined it ran on more simple guidelines,' says Steve. 'My first day when I arrived there was no desk, no phone, no computer, and none of the people who reported to me knew I'd been employed so it was an interesting first day. You had to look after yourself in those days.'

One of his first official duties was to hand out the trophies at the Rip Curl Pro, which had been moved, somewhat controversially, to a semi-secret beach break west of Cape Otway. 'I figured out they probably got me to do it because there was a very large chance of me being killed by the locals,' says Steve. 'Fortunately, it was won by Sunny Garcia – he was the person who stopped me from being killed.' A prominent local had threatened to throw Steve off the cliffs. 'Sunny looked at him and he walked away. There was a big shit-fight after that, and we certainly agreed never to go down to that area again.'

After that start, the transition from publishing to the surf industry was fairly smooth. 'In some ways business is business, it's all about meeting deadlines and achieving goals,' says Steve. '2000 marked the turning point for the magazine business. It started going down, whereas the next 10 years at Rip Curl were a very exciting time.'

Nichol Wylie didn't need too much convincing to join his old boss at Rip Curl. Wylie had got to know Claw and Brian working on the ski patrol at Mount Buller and selling them ads in *Tracks*. He moved to Torquay with the aim of landing a job in the surf industry and it paid off when he got a call from Claw requesting a chat.

'I'll never forget the conversation. He said, "We don't know what you're going to do but we really want you to join Rip Curl," recalls Nichol. 'They gave me the job of product manager of mountainwear and footwear.'

Nichol benefitted from working under Rip Curl veterans like Ray Thomas, Peter Hodgart and Rod Adams, while learning much from the modern management style of the new millennium under the mentorship of Steve Kay. He worked his way up through roles as national sales manager, general manager of men's and women's surfwear, general manager of Rip Curl Australia and New Zealand and, ultimately, group general manager of product.

He recalls new CEO David Lawn asking to be taken for a surf down the coast so he could better understand the spirit of the brand. 'Mother Nature was not kind to him. It was a flat day but a wave came out of nowhere and cleaned him up,' says Nichol. 'I had to grab his legrope because he was paddling towards a patch of bare reef thinking reef was safety, but he would have been completely smashed if he'd paddled over there.' Lawn sat on the beach to catch his breath, where he was promptly set upon by march flies. 'He drove home with march fly welts and red, raw skin because we kept surfing,' says Nichol.

The incident serves as a neat metaphor for the corporate managers struggling to come to terms with Rip Curl's business style. 'Though the corporates contributed significantly to the business, they never really became accustomed to Rip Curl's way,' says Nichol. 'They've come in and we've listened to them, taken on the good bits and tried these new ways, but we'd always revert back to the Rip Curl way.'

Nichol recalls Claw drumming into him the importance of their founding principles of risk-taking and experimentation. 'He got me in a bit of a headlock about the state of the surf industry,' says Nichol. 'He gave me a spiel about how he always wanted to challenge the norm when things got a bit boring, not to listen to the metrics of retail, to keep trialling things and not to fear failure, to have a crack. He said, "What are you going to do to take things to the next level, because the surf industry has always been a leader."'

The speech was so impressive Nichol asked Claw to address his team of designers. 'For two hours he had 10 or 15 people in the boardroom and you could have heard a pin drop,' says Nichol. 'He talked about the different times he had to shake things up, how he might have had one success to 10 failures and left a lot of mess along the way, but he spoke to people about not fearing failure, to always agitate for change . . . I love that stuff, it's why I'm here.'

From Brian, Nichol reckons he learnt the importance of treating all retailers fairly and equally, and the value of acting quickly. As Brian was fond of saying, 'If you make quick decisions you can spend less time in meetings, less time chained to your desk looking at emails, and more time surfing the Bowl.'

Neil Ridgway trod the same path to Rip Curl in 2003. Neil had some reservations about the move south based on his experience of Torquay's ferocious social life each Easter. 'I'd said to [then *Waves* editor Vaughan] Blakey, "If I ever go to Torquay to work for one of the surf companies, shoot me before I get to the border," because you know what it's like at Bells over two weeks. It's just two weeks of carnage, and you leave pretty wrecked.' Neil has never regretted the move to Torquay.

But Neil had also walked into the corporatising era at Rip Curl. 'David Lawn had a whole lot of new ideas about merchandising and how the company should be run, which was probably good for me because I knew nothing about [that],' says Neil. 'I thought I was coming down from Sydney and I was going to buy a few ads and go surfing. The first six months of my time here I shat myself because I found myself in meetings about product and about fabric and segmentation and retail and racking and swing tags and all these things I had absolutely no idea about. I always thought in those first six months, if they ever find me out they'll get rid of me pretty quickly, but I learnt a lot really fast.'

The new catchcry was a unified global message and branding across all regions, and implementing that philosophy formed a big part of Neil's job. He also worked closely with Gary Dunne in a concerted effort to regenerate their team of sponsored surfers. 'One of our mantras has been recruiting the next generation. The team does a lot of that for you. Generations always attach themselves to a generation of elite surfers,' says Steve Kay. 'When I joined the company, there was a concern at that time around 2000 that the brand was ageing. We had a fear that Rip Curl was beginning to be regarded as an old man's brand ... We really attacked that for probably 10 years, and then after that I think between better products and really good marketing, great team, the comment sort of disappeared. It's not the issue that it was 17 years ago.'

'And it took 10 years, it absolutely took 10 years to change that,' says Neil. 'For many years we had a team that was pretty good, but they weren't world champions. We didn't have a world champ for 16 years. And since then we've had 10 in 10 years, but it takes 10 years to build that generation, and fill in the generation behind and change that perception.'

'In a way, Rip Curl has to be a perpetual adolescent, and so how you create that perpetual adolescence is by reinvention, by having successive generations of elite team members, great events, and then obviously products that are relevant to that generation,' says Steve. 'The way you do that is to make sure people who are designing product are actually the customer. A lot of the staff have to be young and relevant to the generation who are surfing at the time.'

And it's here Neil admits they might have missed the mark with some of the design heavy-hitters brought in from outside surfing.

'That's where some of those guys from Nike and Puma ... just didn't understand what it feels like to be a surfer and why you'd get up at five in the morning when its freezing and put yourself through all sorts of things to get to a wave,' says Neil.

Over in Europe, meanwhile, where Rip Curl's original rebel spirit had been embraced with such enthusiasm, there were some serious misgivings about the new corporate direction. 'The spirit of the company changed. Some of these new managers had no surfing culture,' says Fred Basse. 'James Strong required Claw, Brian and François to back away from the business and they were not as much in contact with the crew ... For me they cut themselves off from the reality of the market and their company.'

'James didn't want myself, Claw and François communicating directly with the executives,' explains Brian. 'He had concerns there would be mixed messages, that the executives would listen to the founders rather than the CEO.' Despite some reservations, the founders accepted the strategy of their new CEO and chairman, though Brian admits, 'The systems that we built up over a number of years he kind of dismantled too quickly, and there was a lot of confusion.'

Fred Basse kept the company's core surf credentials strong with his big-wave tow-surfing antics, with expat Aussie Todd Lee. In March 2003, Todd whipped Fred into a wave at the newly discovered big-wave outer reef of Belharra that was estimated at 60 feet. Fred was likely the only senior surf executive to be nominated for an XXL Big Wave Award, finishing second behind Hawaiian charger Makua Rothman.

In many ways the story of the modern surf industry is of this tug of war between modern corporate business culture and the old maverick surfing spirit, a game of push and pull that may have sometimes gone too far one way or the other before finding a sensible middle ground. 'Salts and suits,' as esteemed surfing writer Phil Jarratt summed it up in his book of the same name. The outcome of that tug of war would have huge ramifications for the future of the business and the entire surfing industry.

THE ART OF THE SEARCH

The new corporate approach also meant that some of the mainstays of the company increasingly felt out of place. But the restless spirit of the old surf crew provided the ballast that ultimately helped keep the good ship Rip Curl on course.

Creative director Grant Forbes was one old salt who managed to parlay his itchy feet into a bold trans-American motorbike journey with Ted Grambeau that formed part of the Search campaign. 'By that time, I'd moved away from the creative design field and left it to a younger crew,' says Grant. 'I was responsible for the licensees and importers around the world, but really, I was starting to feel just like a travelling salesman, which is not what I ever wanted in my life . . . I had a huge backlog of holiday pay and long-service leave accrued, and could afford a year off.'

Grant harboured a long-held dream to ride a motorbike from Los Angeles to Patagonia, at the frigid tip of South America, and he knew Ted well enough to know it wouldn't be too hard to convince him to come along for the ride. Ted jumped on the project despite several considerable obstacles. 'I said, "I don't have a bike, I don't have a licence. I've only ridden in Bali on those little motor scooters and I don't have any money but I'm interested,"' recalls Ted.

The pair managed to secure sponsorship from BMW, which loaned them two top-of-the-line road bikes. They pitched the concept to Rip Curl as a bold and open-ended addition to the

Search program, and Neil Ridgway backed them. 'The only condition was I would have to ride the bike into media night at Bells,' says Ted. 'I pulled it off, then I just had to get a licence.'

Over eight months, they scored incredible waves through Mexico and Central and South America, but for Ted the highlight was the wild scenery of Patagonia. 'Patagonia on motorbikes is an experience you'll never forget . . . It was easily one of the most amazing journeys I've ever taken,' says Ted.

The trip so deeply affected Grant he decided he wouldn't return to Rip Curl, and opened a small surf shop and art gallery called Tigerfish in Torquay upon his return. Grant eventually sold the business and immersed himself in a new obsession, sailing, and he and his wife set sail to Darwin and then on to Thailand, where they can still be found today. Like many others before and since, Rip Curl has provided a platform for Grant's own Search.

'As for my time at Rip Curl, I'd have to say that I'm just incredibly lucky to have had that experience. Not many people could have had the opportunities that I did or had a career that was so wild, exciting, fun, mad and satisfying,' says Grant. 'A powerful thing indeed is the Power of the Curl. I'm proud to have been there. My family has all been part of Rip Curl at various stages, and yes, despite all the debauchery and madness, I've somehow managed to stay married for 40 years. I once said that I'd choke before wearing another surf brand, and here I am 12 or 13 years after I've left and there's still no other surf brands in the cupboard.'

Asked where the spirit of the Curl resides these days, Grant nominates one of its first employees. 'I guess that, to me, it's people like Gary Crothall who typify the best of Rip Curl. Solid, loyal, dependable and a certain make-up that just fits the company. Gary would know every single retailer in Australia. There's lots of other people there who fit perfectly, quietly do their stuff every day, enjoy the company of their co-workers, go nuts at media night and the Christmas party, laugh about what Brian and Claw get up to, and make the place very special.'

AUSTRALIAN RULES

The mounting rivalry between Quiksilver and Rip Curl played out in many ways, none more spectacular or with a greater chance of serious physical injury than the annual Australian Rules football match.

The Rip Curl crew has enjoyed a long love affair with Aussie Rules. The first wave of surfers who moved in to Torquay integrated with the local community by bolstering the ranks of the local footy club, the Torquay Tigers. If the farmers and fishermen of established Torquay society were suspicious of these long-haired layabouts, their attitudes softened if the newcomers could fill a hole on the half-back flank or lay tackles on the burly farmers' sons of the western districts. It was probably only a matter of time before Rip Curl and Quiksilver decided to bring their competitive instincts to the footy field.

AFL stars with an interest in surfing were soon attracted to the annual grudge match as coaches; Dermott Brereton, Gary Ablett Snr, Billy Brownless, Gary Lyon and Greg Healy all took turns. Professional footballers would suddenly appear with jobs in the warehouse of both companies a week before the game.

Neil Ridgway had come from New South Wales, so Australian Rules was a new culture to him. He took to it with more enthusiasm than finesse. 'It was great because you trained for eight weeks and I met guys who worked in the warehouse or worked in Sourcing or worked wherever, [so] we wouldn't have ever known each other except for them going, "There's that prick in Marketing with the soft, cushy job while we're packing boxes,'" says Neil. 'You got to know people really well and you got to play against Quiksilver, which I liked because I wanted the opportunity to cream someone from Quiksilver.'

The matches were fierce, bruising, often bloody encounters. The annual grudge match peaked in the early 2000s, when an estimated 10,000 spectators turned up for the occasion. Local police were filthy that no one had alerted them to a major event in town and that there were no adequate toilets and traffic control, but no one at either company had anticipated the huge turnout.

'I'd never played a game of football in my life. I was at fullback, and I watched the ball go over my head all night as they kicked goal after goal after goal,' says Neil. 'Dermott Brereton was our coach and Gary Lyon was Quiksilver coach, and I did win Tackle of the Match. I've still got the ball.'

Steve Kay has a more grisly recollection of the matches. 'I can remember being on my hands and knees looking for people's teeth . . . They'd find them, we'd wrap them up in a tissue and drive them up to the dental hospital to see if they could put them back in,' he says.

The tradition was eventually ended in 2004 due to the growing injury toll. 'We canned it and went back to a surfing contest, which was much nicer and way better. It just brought it back to what the companies were about,' says Neil.

WHITE LIGHTNING

In the early 2000s, Kelly Slater was back on the ASP world tour after a three-year break, at the top of his game and engaged in the fiercest rivalry of the modern era with the Hawaiian Andy Irons. Taj Burrow and Joel Parkinson looked set to lock in places in the top five as serious world-title contenders for years to come. At a glance, the skinny kid from Tweed Heads might have looked out of his depth. Mick Fanning had faced devastating hardships in recent years, with the death of his beloved brother Sean in a car accident, and a severe case of scoliosis, or curvature of the spine, that had threatened to cut short his career.

Yet there were early indications that Claw's judgement in betting on the speed and personal drive of Michael Eugene Fanning was spot on. 'When he landed on the pro tour he landed on the back of Kelly, Andy, Joel, Taj. Mick immediately rose up to the next in line,' says Claw. 'What a cauldron to step into.'

In 2001, Mick repaid that faith with the greatest competitive roll of his young career, and the greatest domination of the Australian leg of the pro tour since another Gold Coast uber-talent, Michael Peterson, 30 years earlier. At a time when Mick was trying to manage his scoliosis through rigorous training and stretching, in quick succession he won the WQS event at Margaret River, made the final of the Quiksilver Pro at Snapper Rocks, and won the Rip Curl Pro at Bells as a wildcard on his first attempt. Even he was stunned.

'I was just coming off a win in WA. I was just pumped on that and trying to qualify, and I ended up getting to the end of it and won the Bells. It was so surreal,' says Mick. 'And for the party we ended up going to Claw's place with all the Rip Curl crew. I was just sitting there talking to Claw and Brian . . . At that stage it was 10 grand for a win and it was the first time it had run through in the first four days, and they went, "It was such a great weekend we're going to give you another 10 grand." I was tripping.'

Mick's mum Liz threw in her nursing career to become Mick's full-time manager and quickly proved she was no pushover. With a master's degree in hospital administration, she mixed it with

Rip Curl management in the boardroom without ever taking a backward step. 'I had to go down to Torquay to sign a contract. I'd just given up nursing because that's what Mick asked me to do,' says Liz. 'I put the suit on and I grabbed the briefcase and I walked into this boardroom with all these blokes and they just looked at me. I was a bit intimidated in the beginning. I might have been director of nursing at a hospital but I was in a power position there – with this I wasn't in a power position. But I never felt that they used that. They were always willing for me to negotiate a win-win situation. They'd mumble and grumble about what I'd suggest but, in the end, they'd agree. I always felt an equal.'

A strong Irish Fanning family trait is a readiness to speak their minds, and it's served mother and son well. 'Being his mum, there was so much more emotion there,' says Liz. 'Will Swanton [a newspaper journalist] said to Gary Dunne, "Liz is a bit of a mother hen," and he said, "No, she's a lioness!" I thought, that was really what I wanted to be ... Of course, I'm going to try and get the best for my boy.'

Mick showed the same forthright manner in dealing with his major sponsor. 'I've always found when people are sponsored they think they've always got to say thank you, but it's a partnership. We've got to work together. It's not just a one-way street,' Mick says. 'If things weren't right I'm never one to hold back my opinion. There were times when they wanted me to go on Search trips and I had contests coming up. It's like, what do you want? You can't do both – you're either on the Search or you're winning world titles.'

Yet negotiations have always run smoothly. 'It's pretty easy. They put a contract in front of you and you say yes or no,' says Mick. 'That's one thing with Rip Curl. I never really had to sit there and argue over money. We never got to the end of contracts – we always agreed, let's just get it done.'

Rip Curl had high expectations for their young star, and Mick quickly lived up to them, qualifying for the world tour on his first attempt and rising to a solid top-five fixture. 'He became the highest-placed rookie ever . . . I think he really tried hard to do it because he's that loyal,' says Liz.

RIP CURL GIRL

One of the major movements in surfing in the new millennium was the influx of women into the waves, and the surf industry's collective realisation that it had been underserving a large and potentially lucrative market.

'Girls were starting to buy surf stuff that was made for men, tank tops and tees. So, it was women's decisions to become consumers of surf brands before we realised there was a market for it,' says Brian. 'That's how we got into making stuff specifically for women . . . It was women who demanded it.'

Quiksilver had been first to recognise the opportunity with the launch of its women's label, Roxy, in the early '90s, with four-time world champ Lisa Andersen as the brand's figurehead. Billabong had a smart, articulate and media-savvy ambassador in seven-time world champ Layne Beachley. But since Pam Burridge had won the title back in 1990, Rip Curl had gone without a women's world champ and had perhaps been the slowest to embrace the women's market. They soon made up for lost time.

Rip Curl famously recruited a natural-footer from Kingscliff, New South Wales, at the age of 12, such was the unearthly grace and early promise of Stephanie Gilmore's surfing talent. Apart from Gilmore's well-documented rise to greatness, Rip Curl also took a punt on a powerful goofy-footer from Sydney, Jessi Miley-Dyer, who has gone on to an influential career of her own.

'Neil [Ridgway] brought me over from Roxy when I was 15. Steph rode for Rip Curl already,' says Jessi, now the commissioner of the women's tour for the World Surf League. After a stellar junior career and a high point of fourth on the world tour, Jessi stepped into the key role with WSL to help create pathways for the next generation of women's surfers.

Steph and Jessi signed with Rip Curl when it was swinging the focus squarely back to success on tour after the original Search era, and they were at the vanguard of a new generation of high-performance women's surfing. 'When I look back I really appreciate how much they did for us, because they paid for every-thing,' says Jessi. 'Steph and I, they sent us to Hawaii for six weeks. They sent us to Maui to watch the title go down and they paid for everything, and they gave us a per diem. I thought this was the best thing ever, US$50–$60 a day. It was actually really smart because they sent us to watch the world title, and it was where Steph won the world title and I won the event the next year.'

While ex-pro surfer Matt Griggs was hired as 'pit boss' to support the men's team on tour, the women weren't forgotten. 'They put on [former pro surfer] Kate Skarratt as pit boss and she was epic. They were definitely first. Having Kate was a big thing, flagging that they supported the program,' says Jessi. 'All the contracts were around your performance. I think that's something they've done really well. That's always been their brand DNA, to be their best.'

Jessi also appreciated the fact that Rip Curl never pushed any particular line around body image or conforming to a beach-girl stereotype. As a strongly built power-surfer, Jessi was valued for her surfing. 'Rip Curl never, ever talked to us about anything like losing weight,' says Jessi. 'I definitely had a stage when I was about 18, heaps of girls have that little blowout. I think they do a really good job of understanding what surfers are about at a young age . . . They do a fair bit of sussing you out when you're young, and understand what makes you tick.'

A LEGEND RETURNS TO THE CURL

By the end of the '90s, Tom Curren and Rip Curl had drifted apart. The Search program was seen to have almost run its course and it was becoming increasingly difficult to pin Tom down to sponsor commitments. Tom had always been elusive, but this time he seemed to drop off the radar all together.

'He drifted and drifted this time and dropped out, and he just wouldn't communicate,' says Claw. 'We've always had a good relationship. I said, "If we're going to pay you money, you've got a free slate, but somehow it's got to relate to our business and to our customers. Like, if you're a musician going on tour, you've got to play some of your best-known songs. You've got to give them a bit of what they want. Get Al [Merrick] to make you a modern-day Black Beauty [one of Curren's most celebrated boards] and go out and ride it at Rincon [Tom's home break in Central California]." But he couldn't respond or turn up to anything.'

At Rip Curl, there were agonised debates about what to do with their most high-profile team rider. Ultimately, Claw had to make a tough call. '"We've had a lot of discussions about this. The only thing we can do at this point is stop sending you cheques," Claw recalls of the conversation. '"You haven't met any of our requests. It's terrible. We hate this. We've had a long and wonderful relationship, but we guess it's over."'

'He had become too difficult post–the Search of the '90s for even Claw to deal with,' recalls Neil Ridgway. 'He would do stuff like turn up to the airport and chuck his passport in the bin so he didn't have to leave home.'

Curren rode for a couple of small, short-lived, fringe surf

brands, The Realm and North Shore Underground, but he remained largely absent from the public spotlight. 'He explored other options but not much happened. It just fell into an abyss. He needs a certain amount of structure, that's why it's always worked with Rip Curl,' says Claw.

Tom had split from his first wife, Marie-Pascale, back in 1993, and remarried to a Panamanian woman, Makeira, in 1995. 'It was Maky coming to us and saying, "I think Tom's lost, he's lost his way. What do you think about Tom?"' recalls Claw. His response was candid: '"We love him and respect him, but I don't think we can send cheques because he wouldn't respond to any of our requests. We didn't ask him to go back on tour or do a tour of TV talk shows."'

But Curren had a staunch advocate in Neil Ridgway. As a surfer growing up in the '80s, Neil had long admired Curren and jumped at the chance to get him back on the team. 'I had only been in my job for about a year and I used to look at Tom doing ads for a bunch of brands where he was often depicted doing gimmicky things that I thought made him look bad,' says Neil. 'This is *Tom Curren*, right? He shouldn't be made to act like a trained monkey to make a buck . . . So, I brought him back on the team – with some resistance internally about the same old dog and the same old tricks – but I didn't care. We got him on for footwear first and sent him on a Search trip with Ted Grambeau to Russia and that went well. Then we just set about putting a plan around him and he really got involved. Product, the kids, Search trips – the whole deal.'

Neil even had a plan to encourage the notoriously skittish surf star to turn up to his sponsor commitments. 'He had these four "commercial incentives" in his contract, where if he turned up at the trade show or did the sales conference or played a gig somewhere or other, he could earn a bonus on top of his base retainer and that worked well for focus in his new deal,' says Neil.

But, of course, Curren's greatest value was always in the ocean. Neil recalls Curren paddling out at Pipeline after the 2005 Rip Curl Pro Pipeline Masters had been called off for the day because it was too big and dangerous. 'He got one insane left from Second Reef and then backed it up with a drainer at Backdoor, which eventually made the cover of *Surfer* magazine that winter,' says Neil. 'I was standing with Luke Egan at the Pipe Tower sort of arguing/debating about why they should surf that day, and Luke saw Curren's waves too and I just went, "Well, there you go . . ." And Luke said, "Well, that's *Tom Curren* . . ." Like, that was different or supernatural. I saw Tom as he walked up the beach after the Backdoor wave and I said to him, "Don't worry about the commercial bonuses for the rest of the year, mate. You just earnt them all!" He paddled back out for more.'

The Rip Curl team thrived on spending time with a surfer they'd idolised as grommets. 'I went on a boat trip in an offbeat place with him once and purposely put him and Steph Gilmore in a cabin together so Steph could pick up some "Curren Magic",' says Neil. 'She only had one or two world titles then, but she freaked out because she was too in awe of him and bunked in with photographer Dave Sparkes instead, which would have been weirder, in my view.'

Mick Fanning was stoked to have the opportunity to rub shoulders with a surfer he'd studied in old Search videos. 'He's so eccentric. Between him and Frankie [Oberholzer] they were the cornerstone of the Search, those two guys are the ones who brought it to life,' says Mick.

SEARCHING FOR TOM CURREN

These days, Tom lives in a quiet, leafy street in a hillside suburb of Santa Barbara, California, in a Spanish Mission–style cottage behind a picket fence with his wife, Maky. Curren has always been a tough interview subject who can appear by turns wise and profound, scattered and delusional, or simply uninterested. This time he's been characteristically tricky to pin down, and is away in Israel on unstated business when I arrive in California from Australia specifically to gain an audience with His Eminence. But I need not worry. He returns soon after and devotes several days to our interview – over an excellent meal with him and Maky at a local Japanese restaurant, and long, rambling backyard chats about everything from the future of competitive surfing to the important role fashion plays in his life. Who knew?

At age 54 Tom is still fascinated with alternative surfcraft; his recent experiments involve paddling into solid beach breaks on a thick paddleboard before leaping off it onto a skimboard, like an aquatic Challenger space launch. He's still exploring the synergies between surfing and music and, at the time of writing, is heavily involved in two film projects and the near-completion of a new album.

Their home is simple and comfortable, set on a large block with a makeshift music studio out the back and a self-styled irrigation system which appears designed to imbue the house with the soothing sounds of running water while diverting greywater into the garden. Lengths of hose are run between a series of buckets and barrels: from the washing machine, water is pumped up to a bucket on the roof, where it cascades from a small bamboo pipe into a 44-gallon drum at ground level. Yet another hose directs it into a smaller bucket and then the garden. When a wash cycle releases a deluge of greywater into the system, Tom expertly sucks on the end of the final hose, as if siphoning petrol, releasing the flow into his veggie patch. It's the kind of homespun tinkering he applies to surfcraft: ignoring orthodoxies and aesthetics, cobbling things together intuitively and somehow making it all work.

Though his disdain for interviews is legendary, and I wince a little at shoehorning him into a conversation with my little voice recorder running, he's in an expansive mood. Unprompted, he launches into an animated discussion of his love of fashion.

'I follow fashion, I love it. They have to be aware of where fashion is going,' he tells me seriously, as if imparting advice for me to pass on to head office. 'Paris was and still is the top of fashion. Paris has a reputation for luxury . . . If you just like shoes, some people like to have a lot of pairs of shoes.' I'm left unsure if he's taking the piss, or if he imagines I hold some sway with his employers and is making the case for his employment as a fashion consultant.

If so, he needn't have been concerned. Simply being Tom Curren is enough to warrant Rip Curl's continued support. Curren's job description is pretty loose these days: a roaming brand ambassador available for a few surf trips and appearances a year, with enough time and freedom to pursue his own projects. 'It's fairly breezy. I like to represent Rip Curl,' he says. 'The identity I feel I most enjoy is in the team that does the product-testing.'

He praises Rip Curl's long-term commitment to its team. 'They're striving to have the best team. That tells the story that the team is important. It is more important than quality product.' Tom pauses after this bold declaration, ponders it for a moment, before looking doubtful. 'That might not be true,' he concedes.

He'll occasionally remind the surfing world of his abilities, such as at the 2014 Heritage Heat at Jeffreys Bay with his old sparring partner, Mark Occhilupo. Curren won the day with one extraordinary tube ride, a testament to his uncanny rapport with the world's great waves. 'It was pretty emotional,' says Tom.

Tom's four kids have all followed in his footsteps, as keen surfers with finely tuned creative instincts. Son Nathan is a documentary filmmaker whose first feature, *Biarritz Surf Gang*, captures the raucous blossoming of surf culture in France in the '80s. Lee-Ann is a sponsored travelling free surfer and musician, gigging regularly with her band, Betty the Shark. Younger sons Patrick and Frank, from his second marriage, still live with their mum and dad in Santa Barbara and, having flirted with competition, are now more inclined towards their father's taste for travel and free surfing.

It's been a remarkable journey for a surfer who changed the sport of wave-riding like few others yet remains as humble as ever. 'I have a lot of people to thank. People had confidence in me when I didn't. I do have to thank Rip Curl,' he says. 'I just want to be a part of what they do, somehow . . . because it's not about the legends of the sport, it's about these young men and women pushing the boundaries of the sport of surfing, and somehow they've given me that space. They did right by me, so I definitely wish them well.'

GOING BIG IN BRAZIL

In 2002, Rip Curl bought out its Brazilian licensee and moved its offices from the teeming metropolis of São Paulo to the popular beach town of Guarujá, in a bold gamble on the future of Brazilian surfing. Despite a volatile economy and political climate, Brian was convinced the country's surf culture was ready to flourish, with a population of nearly 200 million people, the majority concentrated close to the coast, and a generation of inspired young surfers ready to burst onto the world stage.

'I saw that the beach culture there was at least as strong as in Australia,' says Brian. 'I came back convinced that we had to go through with this buying-out of the licensee and I ran into some objections at the board level, particularly from James Strong, who didn't like the idea of doing business in this volatile country in South America. It took me quite a bit of convincing to get him and a couple of the others to agree, but to me it was a lay-down misère.'

The man who has led Rip Curl's expansion in Brazil is former pro surfer Felipe Silveira, who competed on the world tour in the early '90s. Felipe surfed through the old trials system on the ASP tour and finished as high as 56th in the world, before deciding to study business administration and forge a career in the surf industry. He joined Rip Curl as a sales rep before moving into the role of brand manager for Rip Curl's Brazilian licensee. 'That's a really visionary thing about Brian Singer,' says Felipe. 'He's been my mentor, he used to teach me a lot of things about business. I learn a lot from 2000 to 2002 – I learnt about the financials and doing budgets, the Rip Curl way to do business. Brian ask me to build a business plan for the brand in Brazil.'

One of Felipe's first initiatives was to move the office to Guarujá. 'I talked to Brian: "We need to move to the coast. There's no way to run a surfing company in the city. We need to live surfing. We need to live the brand values,"' says Felipe.

Some doubted the wisdom of moving the business from Brazil's commercial centre in São Paulo, but just like Torquay and Hossegor before it, Guarujá has proven the ideal place to run a surf business. 'A lot of people say it is too risky. "Guarujá is 70 kilometres from the city, there is no industry, are you crazy moving a company to the coast?" But he supported the decision,' says Felipe. 'The crew can surf every day and test products, have a more informal business and guys can surf in the middle of the day when the waves are good and keep the spirit good.'

In 2007, Felipe was appointed CEO of Rip Curl Brazil at the age of 39. 'We improve a lot the business since then. Rip Curl has a unique position,' he says. 'We are not the biggest brand because we're a private brand. We didn't go to the madness of buying other brands, going public. At one time we thought we were behind. Now we laugh about it.'

TIME TO STUMP UP

On Boxing Day 2004, a region that had become synonymous with perfect waves and dreamy surf trips was devastated by one of the greatest natural disasters in human history. The Boxing Day tsunami was triggered by a 9.2-magnitude earthquake off the coast of Sumatra that displaced 30 cubic kilometres of water. An estimated 230,000 lives were lost across 14 countries, including 166,000 lives in Indonesia.

In Bali, Rip Curl licensee Robert Wilson decided he could not just sit back and do nothing as the nation that had given him and surfing so much reeled from the devastating aftermath. Robert wrote a forthright email to Rip Curl offices and senior management around the world, spelling out how much Indonesia had meant to surfing and to Rip Curl, and prescribing what he thought would be reasonable contributions to the relief effort from each territory.

'It was a combination of a request and a demand, where he had put the amount he wanted from each office and each of the founders and senior executives,' recalls Claw. 'He basically said, "We've all had a great time surfing in Indonesia and the Indian Ocean and now it's time to stump up." Everyone responded accordingly.'

Rather than waiting for the large aid agencies to coordinate their relief efforts, Robert flew to Padang, in West Sumatra. 'After attending a meeting with various parties in Padang, we decided to circumvent bureaucracy and go it alone,' he says. With the funds he'd raised, Robert chartered a pair of timber trading ships, bought emergency supplies and headed out into the worst-affected areas. On board were 116 generators, 116 water pumps, 400 water tanks each holding 20 litres, jerry cans, tarpaulins and building tools.

They headed towards the epicentre of the earthquake, to the island of Simeulue and the town of Calang, on the North Sumatran mainland. 'There had been a lot of media attention and international aid directed toward Banda Aceh and Meulaboh so we decided to direct the bulk of our attention toward Calang which was only accessible by sea, given the coast's bitumen road had for the most part been flipped over by the tsunami,' says Robert. 'The foothills of Calang had also been a guerrilla stronghold for fighters from the Free Aceh Movement (GAM) since 1976 so, besides the coastal town probably copping the biggest free-standing waves, we figured they might not be getting too much love from the authorities.'

In Simeulue, the locals had known to race to higher ground when the ocean receded and casualties were remarkably few, but in Calang, Robert's crew discovered an apocalyptic scene. 'We found complete devastation. Three-quarters of the population had been killed and all houses and infrastructure utterly destroyed, from the beach to the foothills two to three kilometres inland,' says Robert. 'The locals described a wave like an *ular sendok* [cobra] and as tall as the coconut trees. I later measured the high-water mark at 25 metres. The locals also described the sea water as being very hot; indeed, besides scalded bodies, the leaves and grasses seemed to have been scorched.'

By 20 January, less than a month after the tsunami struck, the boats had made four trips to Calang and delivered 350 tonnes of relief supplies, mainly funded by Rip Curl's contribution. Rip Curl then set up a foundation to allow its staff and customers to contribute to the ongoing relief effort and funds were directed to the Maldives and Sri Lanka, as well as Indonesia, to assist in their recovery.

'Indonesia and the Indian Ocean have been very important to Rip Curl. The early surfing in Bali, we were there early on, and all over Indonesia we were early adopters,' says Claw. 'The Maldives, we were there early . . . It was our corporate duty and our spiritual duty on the Search to stump up. But Robert Wilson's effort was just heroic. I know it gave me and everyone else a really good feeling that we were able to do something decisive and immediate where and when it was most needed.'

CHAPTER NINE

THE WORLD-CHAMP FACTORY: 2005–2009

By 2005, the great Kelly Slater–Andy Irons rivalry was in full swing and Rip Curl surfers hadn't claimed a world title for 14 years. And after the focus on exotic travel with the Search in the '90s, there was now a clear goal at Rip Curl HQ to produce world champions. Slater and Irons were powerful figureheads for their respective sponsors, Quiksilver and Billabong, both booming as public companies, and Rip Curl wanted a spot on the podium.

Rip Curl's star-studded team of today is the result of decades of work by many hands: Claw the perennial talent-spotter, former team manager Gary Dunne wrangling surfers as they tripped about the world, and Neil Ridgway's vision in recruiting another former *Tracks* magazine colleague, Matt Griggs, to become a 'pit boss' for the team.

'I went to West Ham Stadium once just to watch the soccer and I saw their West Ham Academy, and I thought, we're paying all these surfers and they're not galvanised and focused,' says Neil. 'We really started in about 2006 running them towards world titles and really putting effort in, not just giving them money and opportunity but asking, how can we help them be the best they can? And so, we've run it sort of as a world-champ factory, and winning world titles for a pro surfer is the most important thing they can do round here.'

Central to that mission was recruiting former pro surfer turned writer turned high-performance coach Matt Griggs. Neil created the role of 'pit boss' after his West Ham epiphany to oversee and support Rip Curl team riders on tour, with the specific goal of winning world titles.

'Pick up their singlet, look at the conditions, make sure the media was handled the right way, make sure the ASP knew what they were doing, make sure [the surfers] didn't fuck up in their heat, make sure they didn't get too pissed, pull them out of trouble if they were in trouble,' says Neil of Griggs's job description. 'Some you couldn't do that for, but that's okay because that's what we love about surfing. We love that there's a bit of an edge to it. It should remain somewhat *outlaw* even as it grows on the world sporting stage.'

Mick Fanning welcomed the greater focus on preparation and training that Griggs brought to the Rip Curl team. 'It changed the game a bit. We had such a good team but it always seemed like we were struggling to get continuity with everyone,' says Mick. 'Neil would sit there and always ask, "Is there anything you need?" and a lot of times it's just to have someone there to help out.'

The results were immediate. Mick made a celebrated return from a devastating hamstring injury to claim his first world title in 2007, and backed it up with his second in 2009. Fellow Gold Coaster Steph Gilmore was even more dominant, racking up four consecutive titles from 2007 to 2010. Neil's world-champ factory was spectacularly productive.

'When Steph and I both won was amazing. It was a powerful time for Rip Curl. It's like the whole office won,' says Mick. 'It's really cool to go into the office and every person is so pumped. The whole office is watching it on TV and cheering.'

There was also an emphasis on cultivating a team culture in which surfers supported each other, an ambitious approach in an intensely individual sport like surfing. 'It's always been that way, we always bounce off each other,' says Mick. 'We've got so many different personalities but everyone gets along really well. It's not like you have to hang out with them, you enjoy hanging out with them.'

Rip Curl's approach ushered in an era of greater attention to athlete welfare on the tour, which was soon populated with entourages of coaches, managers, trainers and support staff. The approach reached its zenith at each season's end in Hawaii, when the Rip Curl team were cossetted in a luxurious beachfront house, their every need catered to so they could fully focus on charging massive Pipeline.

'They all need different things. Some need a coach, some might need a sports psych, some might need a physio, some might need a chef,' says Neil. 'When we put them in at Pipe and we've got that house and we've got two or three guys running for a world title, we just look after them . . . It paid off in spades in world titles. It was great. There's nothing better than being on the beach with three horses in the race, and it's like the Melbourne Cup of surfing at Pipeline. You feel like Bart Cummings, and they're coming down to the line and they win a world title – that's a pretty good feeling.'

'Claw has always had an incredible eye for surfing talent. He is a freak,' says Steve Kay. 'And the other thing that he was a great proponent of was to find groups of kids and take them through the experience together . . . It's a bit like a football team. If you have one person who's really successful it rubs off on everybody else, or it inspires them to work harder to reach greater heights.'

Determining a surfer's worth to the brand remains a vague science at best. 'I've got plenty of ways to value the effect of the wins on the brand and sales – mostly that the wins increase the brand's equity,' says Neil. 'CEOs and accounts boffins will say product managers make the product, and Sales or Retail sell the product; and in Marketing you spend all the money, you don't make any money, and I say, without the brand and without the ambassadors and the marketing stories you wouldn't sell any of your fucking product at the price you do.'

'The truth is, you'll never know from a dollar point of view. It's so intrinsically a part of who we are,' says Steve. 'If we didn't want to have world champions and have the best elite team in the world we just wouldn't be Rip Curl. That's what we do. It reminds me of that adage – ships weren't made to stay in harbours. Companies like Rip Curl, it's actually how you stay relevant. If we woke up one day and found that we weren't passionately interested in our team and how they were going and whether they were going to win a world title, you'd know that Hang Ten time or Lightning Bolt time wasn't far away,' says Steve, referencing once popular surf brands that wound up as generic department-store labels.

DAVID LAWN DEPARTS

David Lawn stepped down as CEO in 2006 after five years at the helm, leaving behind a more unified global brand. But it had not been all smooth sailing. 'In the end, I guess we felt there was too much change too quickly,' says Brian, who felt they needed to reassert their founding principles.

'It was a fascinating five years. I feel very fondly towards the people and the brand. There were some wins but I wouldn't call it a complete win, by any means,' says David. 'There was a bit of a revert back to the founders doing things the way they used to do it. It might be what saved them. That's a big thing for me to say.'

David concedes that his expansionist vision for the business could have backfired once the GFC hit in 2008. 'The fact they decided to play defence – from 2006 to 2010 they played pretty defensively – may have saved the company. It allowed them to be in a stronger position than they may have been,' he says.

James Strong brought another corporate heavy-hitter, Ahmed Fahour, on to the Rip Curl board. Fahour would eventually replace Strong as Rip Curl chairman, and later held CEO positions for National Australia Bank and Australia Post during a decorated career.

'I remember James Strong approaching me when I was living in New York, telling me about the company and these guys and the history,' says Ahmed. 'I said, "Are you serious?"'

But something about Strong's passion for the brand piqued his interest. 'My first ever board meeting, I turned up from an NAB board meeting and I still had my suit on,' says Ahmed. 'There they were in flip-flops and shorts and t-shirts. I remember straight-away François saying, "If you're going to be with us you're going to have to lose that tie, lose that shirt, go down to the shop and get some stuff."'

Although they didn't always see eye to eye, Ahmed likes to think he brought a greater level of sophistication to their financial management systems, particularly during the GFC. 'In that first couple of board meetings I said, "What's your working capital like?" They looked at each other, and they looked pretty stern, and I thought, oh it must be pretty bad. They said, "What's that? What does working capital mean?"' recalls Ahmed. 'But what they lacked in knowledge of accounting language they made up for in their understanding of the business and what makes the customer tick. When we went through the GFC and people were falling over left, right and centre, I'd like to take a little bit of credit for de-leveraging the balance sheet and insisting that they not put on any debt.'

Ahmed recalls board meetings, 'always at a beach somewhere', when someone would notice the wind had swung offshore or the swell had picked up, and the meeting would be swiftly adjourned. 'I'd just think, fucking hell, this is unreal. Just living life to its fullest is the way these guys operate,' he says. But that very informality carried the risk of them being underestimated.

'For me, coming from the corporate end of town, you see these guys, you think they're nice guys, you might even think they're simpletons, but they're three very sharp men,' he says. 'Claw is one of the sharpest marketing minds I've ever met. François is very, very smart and involved in a lot of businesses. Brian is a business genius, he's one of the smartest people I've ever met. The under-standing of how the branding industry works and how to make it click, his deep understanding of the business, is phenomenal.'

There was one other element to their way of doing business that left a lasting impression. 'How well they wanted to treat the other private shareholders – it didn't matter if you had 100 shares or 60 per cent of the company, they wanted everyone to know what was going on, they treat everyone the same,' he says.

Today, the founders look back on this period with mixed feelings. 'I regarded it as a really good learning experience,' says Brian. 'I loved the way you could have a really vigorous discus-sion with Ahmed without any offence being taken. He was great to bounce ideas around.'

'We learnt a lot from those folks from the business world and we had good ones – smart, experienced, well educated. Con-sequently, they all understand and value the brand,' says Claw. But the corporate heavyweights were never a natural fit at Rip Curl.

'I think it's a fair generalisation that these folks are more short-term, goal-oriented than us Rip Curl long-gamers,' says Claw. 'I guess many of them worked for public companies and were in various incentive schemes which rewarded fast and big results . . . Our business is very diverse and I doubt whether any of the expert managers who have come on board have got their arms around all that complexity and diversity.'

One senior manager who came to grips with the complexity of the business during a time of great change was Michael Daly. 'I served as CFO under David Lawn until his ultimate departure in September 2006. At that time François Payot was appointed as the Group CEO, essentially as a caretaker, for a few years,' says Michael. 'François was not your traditional CEO, and I think he would even agree that in those years as CEO he relied on me heavily to execute on the vision that he laid out. It was in these years, 2006 to 2009, that my role started to evolve more to Chief Operating Officer.'

'François managed with a very hands-off, collegiate, family style and developed a close working relationship with [Michael],' says Claw. 'Michael really grew during this period while doing most of the hands-on management, while François focused on big-picture issues.'

One legacy of David Lawn's reign was the expansion into single-brand flagship retail stores. Rip Curl's ability to launch their own stores with a broad product base became critical as many major surf retailers began struggling in the lead-up to the GFC. 'From about 2006 onwards, well before the GFC, the warning lights started to flash in some areas of surf,' says Steve Kay. 'In Australia, it was the retailers like Brothers Neilsen, Shady Haze, Wild in Newcastle who had big stores based in premium shopping malls. The malls kept ratcheting up the rent and the sales weren't going up to the same extent, and it got to a point where the economics didn't work anymore and they started going broke.'

With a shrinking retail distribution base, Rip Curl made the decision to roll out a series of flagship stores at a time when many were warning that bricks-and-mortar retail was in serious decline. 'We started opening stores and they were succeeding. And then we started opening stores in airports and they did really well for us, and it all just mushroomed from there,' says Steve.

Steve attributes the success of their single-brand stores to that broad product offering they'd developed over decades. 'Most companies can't run successful single-brand stores ... because their breadth of product is too narrow to sustain the kind of sales to pay the big rents you have to pay, because they just don't have the watches and footwear, that big travel luggage/backpack/accessory market that we have,' says Steve.

The success of the flagship stores has sparked an epiphany in the way Rip Curl sees its business. 'I think the milestones are the stores – our own network of flagship stores around the world. When I joined there was probably five in Australia and fuck-knows-how-many around the world, call it 10 to 15. There's well over 350 now,' says Neil. 'If they said to me 10 years ago, here's two million dollars, I would have said every time I'd find another Mick Fanning and do another event. But five years ago, my opinion changed completely. If you gave me two million dollars now, I'd open another flagship store at a prime surf location every single time, because you can tell the brand story so many different ways ... all in one place. Mind you, I would kill for another Mick Fanning.'

Opening their own stores was never going to be popular with existing retailers, but Neil reckons that when they open one of their flagship stores, their sales increase in nearby multi-brand stores as a result, despite an initial backlash from retailers. 'You

Left: Brian: 'Happy as Larry at the beach, Redcliffe, Brisbane, in 1949.'

Claw: 'Early holiday at Torquay campground in 1958 with (from left to right) Uncle Tom, Aunty Ivy, my father Arch, mum Jean, myself, my Queensland cousin Denise, sister Laurel, Aunty Rubie, Uncle Jim and cousin Raymond (flexing).'

Claw: 'My own studio bedroom in the family home in Brighton around '59/'60 in my beatnik period with (on left) the Vic Tantau 9'6" we acquired from Terry Wall after Arch snapped the nose off it, and a brand-new balsa George Rice nine-footer.'

Brian: 'Myself, Claw and our mate Butch Fuller with a couple of summer holiday-makers we recruited for the photo shoot at Claw's surf shop at Lorne in 1965.'
Trevor Lemke

Brian swinging off the bottom on a nice day with a stiff offshore at Bells, in the semifinals of the 1967 Bells Easter Classic. *Barrie Sutherland*

BELLS BEACH SURF SHOP

Sydney custom boards
keyo, bob mctavish plastic machines;
platt and spencer models; peter clark,
keith paul happenings, and our own
rip curl models

surfwear and accessories

repair, hire-board and surf
school services

top surfers advising —
terry wall, brian singer and doug warbrick

42 bell street, torquay

Left: The original Bells Beach Surf Shop business card (front and back).
Right: The first Rip Curl surfboards logo designed by Simon Buttonshaw,
with a suitably cosmic aesthetic.

Claw: 'From left, Sue Brown, Charlie Bartlett and a young John Law hamming it
up, with me watching on, out the front of the Zeally Bay Road flats.' *Andy Spangler*

Brian: 'Myself, Spange (Andy Spangler), Claw, John Law, Nigel the dog and some fairly progressive shapes for the times, outside my garage where it all started in winter 1969.'
Andy Spangler

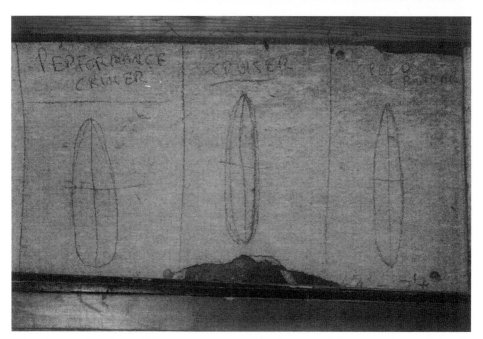

Claw: 'Some rough scribblings of cutting-edge designs of the times from the wall of the old garage at Boston Road once we'd moved to the bakery in 1970. There's a cruiser, a performance cruiser and a speed cruiser.'

The first Rip Curl ad, in *Surfing World* in late 1969, with some prophetic words: 'We know what we're doing and we will be around for a long time.' *Photo of the Bells dawn line-up by Barrie Sutherland.*

Scenes from the old bakery:

Claw: 'Hanging around out the front of the shop with (from left to right) Brewster Everett, myself, Terry Goldsworthy, Little Tony and Gary Crothall.' *Hugh Webster*

Claw: 'The glassing room set up in front of the original old bakery oven.' *Hugh Webster*

Claw: 'The old garage, the shaping and ding-fixing bay.' *Bob Smith*

Claw: 'After the old fibro house out the back was available for lease, it became our office and wetsuit factory. It is still standing today, though sadly the old bakery is long gone.' *Bob Smith*

The early wetsuit crew. Back row, left to right: Lesley, Sparrow Pyburne, Claw. Front row, left to right: Sjarn Garner, Magooer the Gluer, Sue Muller and Nancy Millikan. *Barb Graham*

The first two Rip Curl Pro contest posters showed a rapid advance in prize money but not so much in graphic design.

If you can't Rock 'N' Roll

▼

Don't fukkin come!!!

The now infamous party
invitation that became a
Quiksilver advertising slogan
and led to some revellers
enjoying a lengthy rehab at the
nearby Hare Krishna farm.

RIP CURL

SUMMER VESTS

Summer is fun time, fun waves and fun surfing. There's always been plenty of colour in the boardshorts and summer surfing, but not in the wetsuits. This season we have a whole new range of colours for our Summer Vests and wetsuits: Yellow, Sky Blue, Navy, Tango Orange, Brown and Green, as well as our standard Red, Green, Blue, Purple and Black. We have all these colours in our new super-lite neoprenes. They look great in our new Summer Vests and suits, and we'll be using them for coloured gussets and panels in our Steamers and Springs.

Put some colour in your surfing — RipCurl's new coloured lightweight vests and summer-suits.

All RipCurl wetsuits are guaranteed for six months.
Made by surfers for surfers.

Two early Rip Curl icons
with contrasting personal
styles: the enigmatic and
reclusive Michael Peterson
and the always flamboyant
and outspoken Terry
Fitzgerald, in an early ad
for Rip Curl summer vests.
Courtesy Rip Curl archives

The first issue of *Backdoor* magazine with soon-to-be 1978 world champ Wayne 'Rabbit' Bartholomew on the cover. *Dick Hoole*

Brian: 'We were about to depart by boat from Point Lonsdale for a staff party at Frankston, across the bay from Queenscliff. Here myself, Ray Thomas and a local copper are taking a keen interest in the festivities.' *Bob Smith*

Brian: 'Myself and Butch Barr in our new purpose-built wetsuit factory on Geelong Road in 1976.' *Courtesy Geelong Advertiser*

Brian, Skyhooks lead singer and keen surfer Graeme 'Shirley' Strachan, Claw and 1966 world champ Nat Young enjoying the celebrations at the grand opening of the new premises in 1980. *Courtesy Rip Curl archives*

The new shop created quite a buzz and drew a large crowd to the opening. *Courtesy Rip Curl archives*

The launch of the new segmented wetsuit range in the early '80s shook things up with bold colours and graphics. Rabbit (left) was Mr Dawn Patrol, while Cheyne Horan and a young Tom Curren represented the competition model, the Aggrolite. *Courtesy Rip Curl archives*

The first Californian Rip Curl store, photographed from the site of the old Richard Nixon Museum, which Rip Curl acquired, near Trestles in Southern California. *Courtesy Rip Curl archives*

Brian: 'Nick Wood wins Bells and becomes the youngest ever winner at 16 years of age. Claw, Nick and myself enjoy the post-presentation celebrations on the Bells foreshore in 1987.' *Courtesy Rip Curl archives*

Judging from the top deck of the old double-decker bus parked on the Bells clifftop in the '80s. *Dick Hoole*

Brian: 'Myself with Rip Curl staff Belinda Hardman, Andrew Egan and Meredith Marshall in a party mood at our office in Collaroy in the mid-'80s.' *Courtesy Rip Curl archives*

Claw: 'We've enjoyed a long association with 1964 world champ Midget Farrelly, and it was fitting that he was a co-sponsor of the Rip Curl Pro in the early days. Here Midget and I are getting into the party spirit in the mid-'70s, and below, 25 years later Brian and Midget share a beer at the opening of the new office extension.'
Courtesy Rip Curl archives

Brian, Graham Cassidy and Claw at Bells in the early '90s. Cassidy was one of the key architects of pro surfing in Australia and shared a vision with the Rip Curl founders. *Courtesy Rip Curl archives*

Gabriel Medina wins in the gaping barrels of Teahupo'o in 2014, en route to claiming his first world title. *Courtesy World Surf League*

Wild scenes on the beach at Pipeline in Hawaii as Gabby secures the title in front of an adoring Brazilian throng. *Corey Wilson*

Ted Grambeau

Tyler Wright has become equally famous for her hard-charging courage in waves of consequence as her steely competitive resolve when she sets her eye on pro surfing's greatest prize. *Neil Ridgway*

Mick Fanning right at home in the funnelling barrels of his home break, Kirra.
Ted Grambeau

Mick says goodbye to a huge crowd at the 2018 Rip Curl Pro at Bells Beach, after coming agonisingly close to a fairytale farewell, finishing second to Brazilian Italo Ferreira. *Rose Ridgway*

open a store in Huntington Beach, you get kicked out of Jack's [Surfboards], which is the biggest surf store and the biggest account,' says Neil. 'They kick you out and then 12 months later they ring you up and say, "Do you want to come back in?" Because all these people are coming into their store and going, "Have you got any Rip Curl gear?"'

THE SEARCH EVENTS

The Rip Curl Search events were designed to marry the Search marketing campaign with elite competition. It was an ambitious plan to bridge the abiding cultural divide between so-called soul surfing, with its unquenchable thirst for new frontiers, and the commercial world of professional surfing contests, with its big-name stars, sponsors' banners and towering grandstands. The task of finding suitably exotic surf spots and staging events in new, often remote locations each year proved a massive logistical feat.

'As soon as the hooter goes for the final and you've dished out the trophies you've got 365 days to find the next place, the next government, the next wave, deal with all the fucking graft and corruption along the way,' says Neil. 'I sent guys like Scott Hargraves and Andy Higgins and Brooke Farris into the middle of nowhere just to try to find the right place and then run the plan. Inevitably, when we get there, to the outside world they all looked like epic travel adventures, which they were, but on the inside, there was often a lot of trouble you had to deal with because you were in a new place and they had you over a barrel. You couldn't speak the language and you had to pay your way upfront.'

The first Search event was held in 2005 on Réunion Island at the bowling lefts of Saint-Leu, best known for a 22-year-old Occy's devastating free-surfing attack in the 1989 Billabong movie *Pump*.

Mick Fanning cemented his return from the hamstring injury by winning the final against fellow Aussie Phil McDonald. And the concept of Rip Curl's roaming 'licence to Search' was greeted with enthusiasm by surfers and fans alike.

'It was all François Payot's idea,' says Neil. 'It was brilliant, captivating thinking, but to this day I can't recall him ever attending one contest. Which is completely in line with his style.'

SOMEWHERE IN MEXICO

In 2006, the Search event headed to a secret location in Mexico, a stunning sand-bottom, right-hand point break that looked like Snapper Rocks on steroids, delivering possibly the best waves ever seen at a pro contest.

'I reckon at the time it was the best surfing contest I'd ever watched, because it was this new wave, it wasn't like watching Pipe for the 30th time,' says Steve Kay. 'It was a fricken incredible wave. I couldn't believe I hadn't heard of it before. The surfers were just frothing, the standard of surfing was really high; it was just an unimaginable success from any level.'

'Higgo [Andy Higgins] found that one. He came back with a video of it at two foot,' says Neil. 'I said, "What's Plan B, mate?" He said, "There's no Plan B. This place is incredible."'

The secret location blew the tour's collective minds. Neil recalls trying to paddle out for a free surf with pro surfer Danny Wills. 'We stood there and we counted ... over 40 waves, bang, six-to-eight-foot waves, without a break. Of course, Willsy went straight through it but it took me three goes to get out.'

The event ran through in three straight days, and Andy Irons won the final against Taylor Knox in a dominant display of flawless tube-threading and one monster air in the final for good measure.

Despite the epic conditions, or perhaps because of them, Rip Curl copped a pasting from surfing's online commentariat for exposing the once-secret surf spot. Even though they never named it, the location was always going to get out.

'We got smashed for ages about that,' says Neil. To rub salt in the wound, promised support from the local government never eventuated. 'It was another place where we got ripped off. We never got a cent and we just got shitcanned for not building a medical centre or something . . . Truth is, Andy Higgins stuck to his word and paid the village the $10k they asked for and he did everything they wanted in regards to food and local supply, so they capitalised and benefitted and he respected their home. In the end, I believe that angst was generated by expats who just wanted to buy up the land for themselves anyway.'

TROUBLE AT EL GRINGOS

Those travails were nothing compared to what the next Search location had in store for the Rip Curl crew. The original plan had been to return to Réunion every second year of the Search event series, but after the freight-train barrels of Mexico it was decided that it would be an anti-climax to revisit the user-friendly lefts of Saint-Leu. The decision was made to take the Search to South America and scour the wave-rich Chilean coast for a worthy venue.

'We ended up at Arica [a northern port town] in Chile. We were going somewhere else in Chile but these expats were firing up the world about how Rip Curl were going to expose the place and hurt the environment,' says Neil. 'They wanted us to give money to their organisation so they could shepherd things through.'

Pesky expats warning of environmental Armageddon were nothing compared to the threats posed by the Chilean mafia when their leader decided he wanted in on the action. Neil tells a story about the Search's arrival at the heavy, slabbing peak known as El Gringos, in Arica, that sounds like something out of *The Sopranos*.

'Chile was probably the most hardcore [of the Search events] where the mafia had found their way into it,' says Neil. Rip Curl had negotiated about US$400,000 worth of sponsorship of their event from three levels of government – local, provincial and federal – but none of the funds had been forthcoming when the mafia boss stepped forward offering to fix the impasse. Neil was summoned to a meeting at his walled compound in the Chilean desert, patrolled by armed guards.

'When we got in there it's just him and us and the translator . . . He was, like, clapping his hands and a little waiter came out and got us a drink,' says Neil. 'He basically said [through the translator] . . . "If you want your sponsorship money, you have to pay him five grand in cash." . . . I said, "We can't do that, we don't do bribes." Neil suggested instead they pay a 'finder's fee' for his help and the mafia don seemed happy. 'And with that, he basically clapped his hands and the meeting was over. We got out and got in the car, and the translator said, "I'll meet you outside," and he walked outside. And Higgo and I drove out and the translator said, "I'm smarter than you, I thought the car might go boom."'

The next day, Neil and Andy met the mafia boss at his apartment in town. The asking price had gone up overnight to $10,000. 'And I think, oh fuck, this is going to be the never-ending story. So, I said to Higgo, "We're out of here," says Neil. 'We walked out and he was yelling and screaming at us. We got back and we only had a day or so to go and we got everyone together and I said, "Righto, the flights are all booked, we're out tomorrow. We're not taking any equipment, nothing. We'll get it later, we're out." And

I'm trying to keep the contest rolling with KP [World Surf League commissioner Kieren Perrow] and those guys not knowing any of this. They're going, "Oh, the wind's a bit iffy. Let's go another day." And I'm like, fuck, let's get this thing over. It was lucky that we had the Chilean Navy with us. I told this Navy lieutenant and he said, "We are the Chilean Navy, we are more powerful than the mafia. You don't have to worry about anything." I was still worried but we got it done and Andy [Irons] won, of course.'

After the presentation, Neil was walking back to his hotel and realised he was being followed. 'I thought, this is the end. But I got back to my hotel and got into my room, had everything packed and we were all out of there the next day,' he says. 'So, I didn't pay the bribe but we didn't get a cent [in sponsorship]. When I came back it was like, I've got to tell the board I haven't got the money. This is going to be horrible. And they just laughed. Literally just laughed. "What did you expect? This is South America. We knew you probably had Buckley's chance of getting it anyway."'

BACK TO BALI

After that experience, the Rip Curl crew were understandably keen to run an event a little closer to home in 2008. They explored Lennox Head, on the NSW North Coast, as a venue but were met with staunch resistance from the locals. Gnaraloo, a remote cattle station in north-west Western Australia, was explored as an option by the state's Rip Curl rep, Mike McAuliffe, and the initial reception from the local pastoral leaseholder and Tourism WA was promising.

The Western Australian Government put $500,000 of funding on the table for the event and the owner of Gnaraloo Station, an eccentric Irishman named Paul Richardson, was happy to host the event and house the surfers and event staff. A Search event in a mystical Australian reef break seemed like a perfect fit. Rip Curl threw a formal dinner at Steve Kay's house with Glen Hamilton from the WA Government, and Stomper MacAuliffe and Tim Thirsk, to celebrate the signing of contracts with the relevant government departments, and gushing press releases were sent out.

There are few, if any, local Gnaraloo surfers as such, but there is a hardcore band of long-time regulars who regard the wave haven as a sacred site and were not thrilled at the prospect of a pro contest coming to town. The future of the area was already a hotly contested topic as leaseholders pushed for more tourism development to supplement the dwindling returns from livestock, while surfers and environmentalists called for greater protections.

A coordinated campaign was launched in opposition to the event, with online petitions and impassioned arguments about the threat to the fragile coastal environment, on the edge of the Ningaloo Reef. 'It just went absolutely pear-shaped,' says Neil. 'I got death threats, Mike McAuliffe's kids got hassled at school. There was a very factional fight over the coastline that we didn't know was going on. There was a lot of hypocrisy, just like Chile, but there were also some solid WA surf crew who were protective of their lifestyle and in the end that was that. We just had to call it off.'

Running out of time and options, Rip Curl turned to the tried-and-tested waves of Bali, though that now came with its own set of challenges. Horrific terrorist attacks in Kuta in 2002 and Jimbaran in 2005 had claimed 222 lives, and cast a pall over one of surfing's most beloved playgrounds.

Neil and Scott Hargraves met with ASIO security advisors in Canberra, who warned them off the idea. 'A lot of those terrorists were still at large and the Bali bombings were still pretty fresh in everyone's minds,' says Neil. 'There were these three spooks, one straight guy, one hard guy and one funny guy, and basically they were telling us in three different ways, you can't do this, we don't want Australians to die, this is a real risk for terrorism. I said, "Are you telling us we can't do it? And they said, "No, but these are the risks."'

Neil sat down with Claw, Brian and François to weigh up their options and received an unexpected response. 'I thought, well, they're going to tell me no, and where am I going to have this contest? Because we had a licence with the ASP that could not be broken. I said, "There could be an attack, and you could lose the whole company in my opinion if that happened." They said, "We're not going to let them stop us going surfing. We're not going to let this stop us holding an event, so if you want to go to Bali, off you go."'

Surfers had been among the first to return to Bali after the terrorist attacks, keen to support the local communities who had always welcomed them so warmly. Rip Curl's decision to go back to Bali was another confirmation that surfing would stand by the Balinese people who relied on surfing tourism for their livelihoods.

'Bali was hardcore, the secret police we had to have in there and the security plan,' says Neil. 'David "Woody" Wood [head of security for the contest] and an undercover guy I should not name would bomb-sweep the whole place before everybody got there. The AFP were there in civvies wearing backpacks with machine guns in them mixing with the fans. There was a real fear that they could drive a boat into the Uluwatu cave and blow the whole place up. That was pretty scary.'

The event was billed as 'Somewhere in Indonesia', to add an element of mystique to the location, but almost everyone knew exactly where it was. Happily, the event ran without incident, and was won by Bruce Irons in his final year on tour over fellow Hawaiian Fred Pattachia in quality waves at Uluwatu, after early rounds had run at Padang Padang. The Bali event had proven a success but, even so, Neil and the crew were relieved to have it wrapped.

'There's a great picture of the stage and there's François and Claw and me and Jeff Anderson [Rip Curl Indonesia's CEO] and Higgo, with the gamelan orchestra playing – this great stage and the two pro surfers. We'd swept it that morning for bombs and the dogs had been through, but I could not get off that thing quick enough,' says Neil. 'That's the Search, that's what it's all about – it's an adventure, it's fun and it's part of the spirit of it. That's why they said, go to Bali. They love it.'

Steve Kay reckons not many companies, surfing or otherwise, would even consider such high-risk ventures in today's environment of terrorist threats and legal liabilities. 'These guys were classic products of the '70s,' he says. 'They flew by the seat of their pants.'

'I wouldn't say there was no concern for risk assessment, because that was our job – to manage the risk. But that's what I love about working for Rip Curl,' says Neil. 'It was a wild place. When you came down for media night it was a gathering of the tribe where surfers went wild, like they always went wild.'

Even so, the accumulated stress of those pioneering Search events led Rip Curl to look for a more permanent home for its roaming event licence. They found it in a Portuguese fishing town that was desperate for new economic opportunities.

'When you do that for so many years, we just needed a breather,' says Neil. 'It's pretty hardcore doing that for five or six years straight, on top of everything else. You have to rekindle your appetite for risk.'

HOW SURFING TRANSFORMED A FISHING VILLAGE

Peniche, there can be no doubt, is a fishing town. If the all-pervasive aroma of sardines is not enough to convince you, there are the fleets of trawlers ploughing through the harbour entrance each day, the scores of waterfront seafood restaurants displaying the day's catch on ice in their windows, the sprawling cannery that dominates the harbourfront.

But in recent years, as catches declined and quotas tightened to encourage a sustainable harvest, the town's economy teetered on a precipice. Peniche's gregarious mayor, António José Correia, decided that the tiny town – perched on a rocky outcrop, linked to the mainland by a narrow peninsula, its historical centre still encircled by an imposing fortified stone wall to repel invaders – would need to open itself up to modernity.

Since the late '60s, travelling surfers from the UK, America and Australia had begun rolling into town in dilapidated vans on their great transcontinental surfaris. The surfers copped a bad rap, with their long hair and strange clothes, and the great mushrooming clouds of pungent smoke hovering above their car park campsites. Yet they kept coming, in ever-growing numbers. Enthusiastic young locals swelled the numbers. Surf shops sprang up and surf schools flourished, attracting an increasingly international clientele.

Correia sensed that surfing might hold the key to his town's economic future. The mayor was already a convert to surfing, having witnessed a surf clinic for people with disabilities in 2001 that he describes as a 'surf baptism'. When he was voted in as mayor in 2005 he already had a vision for Peniche as an emerging surf capital to help bolster the economy.

In November 2008, when Correia found himself invited to meet with local representatives of an Australian surfing company and its garrulous marketing man from head office, he was all ears. Neil Ridgway, with his boundless bonhomie, rounded, smiling face and stocky physique, could have almost passed for the mayor's long-lost son. Neil spoke through an interpreter to the mayor, who appeared to be on the verge of hugging him as an enthusiastic bridge to the language barrier. After being shunned in his homeland from one coast to the other with equal venom by surfing tribes 3000 kilometres apart, Ridgway appeared to have found a kindred spirit on the other side of the globe who shared his conviction that a surfing contest could be a force for good in the community that hosted it.

Mayor Correia had chosen an unusual venue for their first meeting: the church of the Fortress of Peniche. The old fort was built in the sixteenth century, when the port of Peniche was of great strategic importance to Portugal as a major maritime power, and served as a political prison from 1934 to 1974, during the Estado Novo dictatorial regime. 'I chose the church because of the ambience – tranquil – and we present our reasons and our spots and then we have a dinner at a restaurant with the gastronomy of Peniche. At the end of the dinner I think that we win this', recalls Correia.

The decision was quickly made to stage the 2009 Search event in Peniche, with a view to making it a permanent fixture on tour. The local Rip Curl licensee, José Farinha, found himself staging a major world-tour event at the last minute.

Rip Curl's people in Portugal were well connected, and Portuguese Tourism was supportive. 'When we went to Tourism of Portugal, the president said, "I don't want a one-year competition, we want at least a three-year deal. We want to do big events,"' recalls José. '[He] has a lot of surfers in the family so he understood surfers are not just drug people and junkies.' Portugal's major telco, PT, gave access to cutting-edge technology that has set the standard for events on tour. 'They bring all the knowledge they have about technology and we give a lesson to the world in technology,' he says. 'We were the first to give live transmission in 3D . . . We bring a lot of innovation to this contest.'

Rip Curl Portugal's young head of marketing at the time, a suave, confident entrepreneur named Francisco Spinola, was a driving force behind the event and was more or less thrown the keys to the family car to make it happen. 'I really thought there was potential to do a WCT [event] here so I went to Neil and, in his way, Neil always gives me quite a bit of empowerment,' says Spinola.

The Rip Curl team in Hossegor was mobilised to help pull the event together at short notice. Rip Curl Europe's communications manager, Marie-Pascale Delanne, was handed the massive task of coordinating media for the event. 'It was a huge responsibility to organise it, men's and women's events. We were all in Peniche for months,' she says. 'It was a big event, I invited 50 to 60 media from all over Europe. It was a mobile event, changing sites. It was so fun and we worked so hard.'

The first Rip Curl Portugal Search event was centred on the muscular but fickle beach breaks of Supertubos, with a licence to go mobile in search of the best waves in the region. But it almost ended in disaster before it even began. A huge storm and wild seas inundated the event site the night before the first day of the waiting period, and the crew awoke to find the contest structures awash.

'There were waves running all through the site,' remembers Mayor Correia. 'We had crisis meetings at five o'clock [in the morning], and we had to start up again everything.' But the near-disaster only galvanised the crew. 'We had all the workers and the equipment to the beach to cooperate. When the media arrive, they see what we do to rebuild the contest, the capacity of Peniche to respond to a problem.'

With no event to broadcast on day one, the webcast and the media's attention was turned towards a tow-in session at nearby Baleal, where Mick Fanning and Taylor Knox used a jet ski to whip each other into the huge waves. 'The first day the event site was destroyed but the media and the broadcast TV for the first time see big waves in prime time. It was very, very important,' recalls the mayor.

They took the Search philosophy literally, using four locations throughout the waiting period to make the most of a challenging surf forecast. When they moved to a fairly remote beach break out of town without road access, organisers wondered whether any of Portugal's famously enthusiastic surf fans would show up. After a massive relocation effort just as the contest got underway, they were stunned to see a human tide of thousands of fans marching kilometres up the beach to witness the day's competition.

The event finished back at Supertubos in front of huge crowds in quality waves, and was won by Mick Fanning en route to his second world title. The jubilant contest presentation validated the mayor's vision. 'The ceremony when Mick Fanning made his victory speech, I was behind him and he turn to me and say, "Mayor, Peniche has the best waves to receive a WCT," and seeing that by the winner, Mick Fanning, that was important for the WCT to keep going,' says Correia.

The mayor has a magnetic personality that has endeared him to all in the pro-surfing community, and a poetic sensibility rare in a politician. 'It makes an ambience for us, each one of us. This ambience, it's the result of the interactivity between all the members of the team: surfers, coaches, workers,' he says. 'This good ambience, I think it reflects on the good relationship that we have between me, Farinha, Spinola. At the press conference [in 2017], Farinha remark that we start in 2008 and all three are present.'

The Rip Curl Pro Portugal has provided some epic moments as the penultimate event of the pro tour, influencing world-title races and reliably delivering quality waves. 'In 2011 we ran the event in two and a half days. It was really a shock,' says Farinha. 'It was a magic three days in a row, rights and lefts, a magic event and a magic party after that. All the surfers were so happy. We rang the bar – is everything ready for the party tonight? And they organise the party in two hours and it was magic.'

It would be difficult to overstate the impact the event has had on the town. 'The mayor is very clever, there were so many people who came from all over Portugal,' says Marie-Pascale. 'Everybody loves going to Peniche. The sardine industry was really falling apart and now surfing is what feeds everybody out in Peniche – restaurants, bars, hotels. The surf schools only close for Christmas and New Year. People from Russia and Scandinavia come to Peniche to learn to surf.'

'There's an impact on the economy of families with local lodgement. Now we have around 500 homestay hostels with a capacity of 3000 beds,' says Correia. 'Before it was summer, it was very seasonal, and now it's all year round.'

Since that first event, three hotels have been built or substantially upgraded in Peniche, at a total investment of around 20 million euros. Economic impact studies put the total value of the event to Peniche at more than 10 million euros annually. A new Rip Curl flagship store towers over the squat harbourfront shops and houses of Peniche, a monument to the surf commerce transforming the town.

'It was a long-time dream of François's. We have a discussion with the mayor and say we need a prime location to do a proper shop here, an office and showroom. We went to city council and we find the land,' says Farinha. 'We did a concession on the land for 25 years and today this is the biggest surf shop in Europe. It's one year now, we are up more than our target by 30 per cent.'

'We have created the conditions for this and knew this is an important store for the municipality. It was unanimous to approve,' says Correia. 'I propose to the municipality to honour Rip Curl with a medal of merit for the economy, to recognise its importance.'

'There is Peniche before the event and after the event,' says Spinola. 'You come to this city after nine years and it's a different city. The five-star hotels are here because of the contest.' Spinola himself is a great example of Rip Curl giving people the freedom to pursue their own Search. He was only 29 when he helped pull together that first event, and was then granted the autonomy to take over management of the event through his own company, Ocean Events.

'We made an agreement with Rip Curl that they will keep up the sponsorship of the event but I would run it under my own company. That was a very smooth transition,' says Spinola. 'I always felt the event was mine and ours. I never felt like an employee.' He now applies the same philosophy to his own business. 'My people, they work with me, not for me. You put trust in people.'

Now 37, Spinola spends his days at the event ushering politicians around the contest site, introducing them to pro surfers, schmoozing his vast network of contacts. He believes surfing can be a source of real prosperity for his country. It is a point not lost on nearby coastal towns – Nazaré has become a global focus of big-wave surfing, and in 2011 Ericeira was officially declared a World Surfing Reserve, the first in Europe, for its stunning coastline studded with quality point breaks. At lunch in an opulent VIP dining room at the event, two other mayors requested meetings with Neil to discuss the possibility of Rip Curl stores in their towns, as if they are a badge of prosperity in this new surf economy.

'We have a really strong connection with the ocean, with the discoverers back in the 1500s,' says Spinola. 'And we realise it's a little bit like Australia. I studied in Sydney for an MBA and I could really feel that it's kind of the same beach culture. You can live in a big city and still surf every day.'

The entire city of Peniche is the first surf region in the world to be formally assessed as a sustainable surf tourism destination. Dr Jess Ponting, the director of San Diego State University's Center for Surf Research, founded STOKE Certified to evaluate sustainability among surf tourism operators. STOKE bench-marked Peniche against a criteria of 84 measures of sustainability and designed a road map for the town to achieve a certification of sustainability, a goal they are now working towards.

Of course, with all this attention, the waves of Peniche have become more crowded. It is still possible to find uncrowded waves along this coast, but not all the locals are happy. 'My son included. Sometimes in winter time I can find some spots by myself even in front of my house, but I won't tell you where I live,' José Farinha says with a grin.

THE BIG CRASH

The Portuguese event also provided a much-needed shot in the arm for Rip Curl Europe, which had nearly fallen victim to the GFC. Jobs were shed and the directors didn't draw a wage for three years, during a tumultuous rebuilding plan.

'From a business point of view, it was the most stressful time,' says François.

His staff in Europe recall it as a traumatic time, as the rapid boom of surfing's mainstream cool quickly evaporated and left the business exposed. About 30 jobs were lost in the Hossegor office alone. The mainstream department stores slashed their orders of surf brands dramatically, recalls Gilles 'Keke' Darque: 'We had to fire people. I think that was the worst moment for Rip Curl.'

François could have walked into a plum job with any other surf brand in Europe, but he never considered it: 'To me if one day you can work for Rip Curl and the next work for Billabong, that is business. For me it is a passion. I can have different women but I have only one brand.'

Fred Basse is scathing in his assessment of the surf industry as a whole for losing its core focus. For the publicly listed brands, he says the pressure of trying to maintain constant growth and rising share prices took a toll. 'Around 2005 some signs started to ring, drop of sales, shops closing, but most board members of the surf industry refused to listen to this bell ringing,' says Fred. 'The increase of sales was done through expensive acquisition. On top of this, most of the CEOs were having a big part of their wages in bonuses. One of the big consequences of this situation was huge overstocks starting to appear in the warehouses. For the company on the stock market, it became dramatic. Not able to pay back their debts, their values started to drop to nearly end up bankrupt. A lot of shareholders lost their assets.'

As a private company Rip Curl was better placed to accept the inevitable downturn, but there was still much soul-searching. 'As the president of EuroSIMA [the Surf Industry Manufacturers Association], I was in the middle of all the problems happening,' says Fred. 'Most CEOs who were surfers lived the hard times. The other ones, from other industries, went to rebound elsewhere. They didn't care much anyway – surf for them was a good line for their résumé and the GFC was an excuse for the failure. I strongly believe we could have reduced the impact by listening better to the signals of the market. All companies in Europe reacted too late.'

And because the founders were now a step removed from day-to-day business, some of their simple business principles were overlooked. 'François had one rule: don't go faster than the market. Brian had another rule: your expense can't go up if you don't progress, and if you go down your expense has to be reduced two times more. Unfortunately, these simple rules were not applied,' says Fred.

Back in Torquay, they were riding out the GFC in better shape than a lot of their larger rivals. It ended up being a blessing in disguise for Rip Curl when the surf industry tanked, before they'd had a chance to go public. For Neil Ridgway, that meant being able to go hard when everyone else was reducing their marketing spend.

'When everyone else was saying, "Cut back on marketing," Claw and Brian and François were saying, "Here's a seagull,"' says Neil. The marketing man was unfamiliar with this bit of business terminology and asked the obvious question: 'What's a seagull?'

'It's like a seagull flies over and drops a big shit, and it lands somewhere and splatters,' Brian explained. 'Well, we're going to drop a big shit full of money and it's going to land and splatter. Where do you want the money to go?'

'And so, when you drop the seagull into the market, when everyone else is pulling back, you're going harder and in three to five years' time, when it starts to come back, you reap the rewards because you're already there and people trust you. So, they're pretty visionary about that sort of stuff,' says Neil.

GETTING IT RIGHT IN THE USA

The counterpoint to all the GFC doom and gloom was that Rip Curl's US business was on the upswing under a new, carefully selected management team. After innumerable missteps and restarts, and a revolving door of senior managers, by 2010 Rip Curl seemed to have finally got things right in the world's biggest surf market.

The key recruitment of Kelly Gibson from O'Neill gave them stability and credibility in the market, and a core team of senior personnel soon gelled around the mission of giving the US business an 'American flavour'. Kelly had come up through the NSSA, winning a men's national title under the tutelage of expat Aussies Ian Cairns and Peter Townend, and had gained a valuable insight into the Australian psyche that prepared him well for working at Rip Curl. 'I learnt to deal with Australians being very blunt and brash and to the point, and that's just the way it is,' says Kelly. 'I say to people, Australians don't understand Americans because we beat round the bush.'

Gibson finished a career-high 41st from a couple of years chasing the then ASP tour, and peaked at 16th on the US domestic circuit, the Professional Surfing Association of America (PSAA), at a time when Californian surfing was just coming out of its anti-competitive doldrums. The home of his future employer proved a particularly happy hunting ground for Gibson, as he made it through the old trials system into the Rip Curl Pro at Bells twice, in '85 and '86. But he was cluey enough to realise that scraping into a few main events didn't make for a sustainable pro-surfing career.

'I figured I needed to get a job. I started off as a sales rep,' says Kelly. He went on to run apparel at O'Neill for six years, and his recruitment was seen as a major coup for Rip Curl. 'I knew Claw from years ago. I was a shop grom when I was 15, 16. We would drive from Hermosa Beach to San Clemente to order custom suits. One day they said, "This guy Claw wants to go surfing with you," recalls Kelly. 'I met him at Bells a few times. He started ringing me up in '05 and just having chats about the brand. I didn't think much of it.'

But Rip Curl had picked their mark carefully and Claw, Brian and François met with Kelly in Newport Beach in 2006 and 'made him an offer he couldn't refuse', according to Brian. 'When your beliefs as a person and a surfer align with a brand like the ultimate surfing company it's hard to say no,' says Kelly. 'I stayed with Claw in '06. I'm a huge surf fan and we could really talk a lot about surf. He's a wealth of knowledge, obviously. He thinks a lot about the customer and the brand.'

'It started working about a year and a half after Kelly took over . . . That team got apparel to click,' says Bob Mignona, former publisher of *Surfing* magazine and now a consultant to the industry.

What impressed Mignona over Rip Curl's long, often painful journey to success in the US was its ability to persevere through the hard times. 'I used to track businesses year on year. Twenty-five per cent of the businesses that were around were gone the next year. There was a turnover of almost 100 per cent over four years,' says Bob. 'They all fell by the wayside: Counter Culture, Catchit, Gotcha. Look at a mag from 1974, only two per cent of the business are still around . . . Rip Curl's had more CEOs [in the US] than anyone. I would say they've had three restarts since the start. And this time the failing is over.'

I've flown to California to try to understand why it took Rip Curl so long to find its feet in the US, and why it's worked this time. I head out to Costa Mesa to meet Kelly and get a tour of the spacious office and warehouse premises Rip Curl opened 10 years ago in the surf industry hub known as Velcro Valley. The sheer scale of the operation is impressive: vast warehouses full of stock, large offices for each division of the company, a central bar and entertaining area with beer on tap and a kaleidoscope of Rip Curl memorabilia on the walls, including sepia shots of the old bakery, classic boards, signed contest jerseys and posters. The Costa Mesa office is one of three global design hubs for Rip Curl, along with Torquay and Hossegor.

'It was definitely a case of "build it and they will come" when they opened this place. Luckily it paid off,' says Kelly. Revenue has more than doubled in 10 years. 'We're going to do $75 million in North America. Ten years ago we were doing $35 million, and some of those sales we would call "shit sales". That's $75 million of quality sales,' he says. They employ around 100 staff at their Costa Mesa HQ and many more across 30 Rip Curl stores they have opened throughout North America.

Kelly has been heavily influenced by François. 'He had a European flavour to the brand, and I really took that to heart, to make sure we gave it an American flavour,' says Kelly. 'Now things are globalising more, trends are closer all over the world.'

He recalls going to his first sales conference soon after joining Rip Curl and getting a taste of how the Europeans did things. 'It was in Spain and I went straight from the airport to the party, and they were on fire. And then they had a great conference ... I've travelled a tonne with Rip Curl – work hard, play hard, get your surf on, enjoy your nights.'

At a conference in Bali in '08, the international crew took a break from meetings to make the most of the swell on the Bukit Peninsula and were confronted with triple-overhead Balangan. 'Everybody paddled out. I thought, this is a bitchin' company. It's pretty rare where everyone's giving it a go,' recalls Kelly.

Chief among his challenges when he came to the helm was expanding Rip Curl's reputation for quality beyond wetsuits. He reckons the Mirage board shorts ('like wearing nothing') were the turning point for making inroads into men's apparel. In women's they focused on swimsuits and garnered attention with their high-profile US team riders Alana Blanchard and Bethany Hamilton.

Kelly says Rip Curl has benefitted from the spectacular growth and catastrophic falls of its rivals Quiksilver and Billabong, and its own slow start in the US. 'We're in a really good, healthy spot. We're not an old brand here. For a lot of kids wearing Rip Curl, it wouldn't be perceived as old. We're not a dad's brand over here,' he says. 'We've been that alternative to the traditional brands that really have a much broader reach.' He says they have more in common with snowboard brand Burton or outdoor label Patagonia, deeply rooted in functional and essential equipment.

Central to the success has been a core senior management team who have brought stability and garnered respect: Dylan Slater, who began as team manager and has risen to president of Rip Curl North America under Kelly's mentorship; Mary Miller, women's global chairman; Shawn Peterson, men's global chairman; and Paul Harvey, vice president of North American sales.

I meet the team during a lunch break from a management meeting, and gather around the central bar area to chat over sandwiches and salad.

'We built a pretty great US crew,' says Dylan. 'The people we're working with, the crew we recruited, there's a lot of US talent that knew the market well.'

'Authenticity is a big thing – they appreciate that we are committed to surfing and we are not trying to be every little trend that comes up. That gets a lot of respect from our industry,' says Paul.

'We're super proud of the fact that we're privately owned by Brian and Claw. That comes out of our mouths on a weekly basis,' says Dylan.

'The consumer all over the world is changing, that's the most exciting thing,' says Kelly. 'But we haven't really changed. We're making product for people who go surfing. How you talk to the customer and how you distribute your product to the customer, that's changing. The old-fashioned way, word of mouth, is still your number one.'

All the hard work culminated in Rip Curl picking up five awards at the SIMA Image Awards in 2015, for the year's best swimwear, board shorts, wetsuit, accessory – for the Search GPS watch – and women's marketing campaign for 'My Bikini'.

'Ten or more years ago, the brand was not at a respected level – the wetsuits were, but the thing that makes me most proud is the brand is still respected by the customer,' says Kelly, who's now transitioned into a role as a non-executive board member.

The US crew got a taste of just how loose its founders can still get when they visited in 2015 to celebrate the turnaround of the business. 'François and Claw and Brian came over for it, and Brian was in a very good mood,' says Kelly. 'He was drinking out of these kegs of light beer, but in the US, "light" means low carbs, not low alcohol.'

The party moved to a bar in Laguna Beach called the Dirty Bird, and culminated with Brian somehow being locked out of his hotel room naked. Brian reckons he got up in the middle of the night to take a leak, opened the door into what he thought was the bathroom but found himself in the hallway outside his room, stark naked, as the door clicked shut behind him. He sheepishly made his way to the lobby to request a spare key. 'That was my first introduction to Brian Singer. I thought, wow, the owner of this company is still going this hard. We're not selling insurance here,' says Shawn.

'I've been with the company 11 years now. We don't have as much face time with those guys as we'd like, but I still get on a plane and go over there thinking, I'm going to sit in a room with these guys who started this brand from nothing,' says Kelly. 'And they're still really being stewards of the brand. They keep us honest.'

CHAPTER TEN

THE ULTIMATE SURFING COMPANY: 2010–2014

Rip Curl's grand experiment with mainstream business executives had produced mixed results. As with some of their early road trips in a cantankerous old kombivan, their copilots sometimes steered too far onto one side of the road, perhaps overcorrected, but thankfully had avoided rolling the whole thing.

By 2010, there had been a deliberate shift to promoting internally. 'I see this really starting when François was CEO in 2006 to 2009,' says Michael Daly. 'At the time I headed up HR and therefore I ensured we executed the vision on all recruitment and appointment decisions.'

But after four CEOs in seven years, it seemed the top job was a hot potato no one was too keen to handle. After François stepped in as caretaker CEO upon David Lawn's departure, another Frenchman, Olivier Cantet, was given the job. He lasted three years, before Brian reluctantly took on the job in 2012 to steady the ship, also in a caretaker role. Claw says this return to leadership from the company founders helped get the business back on track. 'We had terrific performance with François's couple of years,' says Claw. 'Brian knows his shit and he's fast on his feet and he's a great public speaker.'

But neither François nor Brian was up for the demands of the role in the long term. Eventually, it was the relatively young accountant, Michael Daly, who had quietly and effectively performed the CFO's role for a decade, who was given the top job. Michael had been passed over for the CEO's role in 2009, but figured he was young enough to get another shot at it, and set about learning everything he could about the business.

'I loved Rip Curl and my work, so I got over it really quick. I figured at the time I should make space for Olivier to make his own mark as CEO,' says Michael. 'I seriously considered leaving but loved it too much.'

Instead Michael spent two years in the US, and played a major role in turning around the North American business. 'Kelly and I worked well together, and I certainly think the combination helped accelerate our earnings improvement in the USA,' says Michael. But he was always intent on returning to Torquay. 'In November 2012 I got the call from the board to come home as I was to replace Olivier Cantet as CEO in six months, after Brian served as interim CEO ... There was no interview, no process, just a phone call to say the job is mine and [to] come home. I returned to Australian in January 2012 and formally became CEO in July 2013.'

'Claw, François and I always thought you can't have an accountant running the business, but fairly soon I realised he'd put himself in the position where you couldn't choose anyone else,' says Brian. 'Michael moved himself around the company and worked in every department. He moved to the US as Chief Financial Officer, and Kelly Gibson's right-hand man. Because Claw was living on the Gold Coast and François was based in Bali at the time, it took them a while to realise this, but I'd seen firsthand the sorts of things he'd done to prepare for the position.'

'Obviously, we've got a lot of faith in Michael Daly, making him global CEO, and he runs everything on a day-to-day basis,' says Claw. 'While there were some good learnings while we had traditional corporates on the board, and across senior management, none of those people lasted. I can't think of one who's still in the organisation today, and from my point of view they were as counterproductive as they were productive.'

Today, senior management have almost all been with Rip Curl for a decade or more, and have been mentored by predecessors whose history with the brand goes right back to the early days. 'I regard one of my main functions as identifying talent and people that I thought could go a long way in their lives and in our business,' says Claw. 'Today's leading managers and stars are all successive generations of the first group that we picked up from the surfers around the Torquay, Bells Beach, Surf Coast region.'

'Senior management nearly all surf. Michael can't surf for peanuts, but he snowboards, loves the outdoors and loves a beer, and is in touch with the crew and he will go with us to any beach in the world. So he carries the torch for non-surfers in the company,' says Neil. 'The surfers have all stuck because you can work in a great international brand and company, live in an awesome place, be a surfer and act like a surfer, have a great time and still do really good business and still have a proper professional career.'

Neil points to the regional CEOs around the world to underline his point. 'You look at the people who run the company around the world. Felipe Silveira in Brazil was on the WQS, Kelly Gibson in the US was on the tour and made the top 16 [of the PSAA], Mick Ray runs Indonesia, and Wilco Prins heads up Europe. The surfers are definitely in control,' he says.

BALI AND BEYOND

There is no better example of the surfers being in charge than Michael Ray, a Rip Curl stalwart for over 25 years and a fourth-generation surfer, a rarity in Australia surfing. Mick's great-grandfather J. J. Ray stopped off in Hawaii on his way home from World War I and learnt to surf in Waikiki in 1917. Mick's father and grandfather were both keen lifelong surfers, and his brother Tony was a top-line pro and big-wave charger of the highest order.

Michael's career at Rip Curl had suitably salty beginnings. He was 21, studying at uni, and had just come in from a surf at Bird Rock when he noticed Claw had left his wetsuit behind and dropped it off to him. Mick reckons Claw gave him the 'Claw Questionnaire', and the next day he received a phone call from Rip Curl HQ. 'Doug Rogers called me up and said, "We're looking for someone to look after the team part-time," so I started looking after the national team two days a week,' says Mick.

A couple of years later he was offered a full-time gig helping out with international licensees and marketing. It was an ideal position to learn about the business and work closely with the founders: 'Marketing with Claw, licensee stuff with Brian,' says Mick. He got a firsthand look at how the founders worked together. 'Brian and Claw used to put together the ads. It was interesting to see Brian and Claw's synergy. Claw had the creativity and Brian had the clarity on who the customer was,' says Mick. 'They used to clash. Claw would word it really obtusely and Brian was like, "No, we've got to hit them between the eyes." That yin and yang, the balance, was somewhere in the middle.'

Mick moved into wetsuits and spent 15 years heading up the division, learning the ropes from Ray Thomas as part of the process of generational renewal. When Rip Curl's South-East Asian manager, Jeff Anderson, resigned to spend more time with his family, Mick was ready for a new challenge. Jeff had done a remarkable job growing Rip Curl's business in Indonesia and Mick had big shoes to fill.

'It was a good opportunity career-wise and it was Bali,' says Mick. The business in Bali still runs along the lines established by those two westies who snapped up the big surf brand licences back in the '90s, Rob Wilson and Stephen Palmer. 'The model's like nowhere else in the world. It's 80 per cent consignment. We own all of the stock in all the stores,' says Mick. 'Once the shop's sold stock to the customer they pay us the wholesale. The whole consignment thing is a dirty word but those shops didn't have the capital to buy the stock, so it actually works pretty well.'

In such a sprawling, diverse, majority-Muslim nation, there are profound cultural differences to be understood. When Rip Curl started in Indonesia, almost all their business was in Bali. Now 60 per cent of it is outside Bali, from high-end malls in Jakarta to corner shops in remote surf outposts. 'Outside of Bali there's not a natural link to surf culture. You've got to try and teach them stuff. You've got to convince mainstream Indonesia that surfing's cool,' says Mick. 'They're a flighty market. Next week they can think something else is cool.'

But there are advantages that make the potential rewards worth the effort. 'Rents aren't that expensive and salaries are a lot cheaper,' says Mick. 'Total sales aren't as high, but you can generate more profit. And it's growing fast. There are 260 million people in Indonesia. There's more middle class in Indonesia than the whole population in Australia.'

SELLING THE DREAM

During the tough times post-GFC, when other surf brands were licensing the production of doona covers and home furnishings to try to boost their bottom line, Rip Curl doubled down on its commitment to the core surf market. The mantra and mission statement, 'The Ultimate Surfing Company', became a vital compass in pitching seas.

'What we used to call the surf industry is under threat of failure now. They're just another bunch of apparel manufacturers. We don't want to wash too much of the true spirit of surfing out of it, all that stuff that comes with real surf culture,' says Claw.

'How could we have created a more sustainable industry? Grow really slow,' says Bob Mignona, the former *Surfing* magazine advertising manager, now a consultant to the surf industry. 'In Japan the corporate philosophy is slow growth. The old adage is, the faster you grow the faster you fall. What goes up too fast will come down. The Rip Curl guys have in one sense avoided being greedy. They weren't taking a whole lot of money out of the business, they weathered some really tough times.'

Sam George, that American teenager Claw picked up hitchhiking on the Gold Coast 40 years ago, is now a screenwriter living in Malibu, but he's never forgotten the spell that first Australian road trip cast over his surfing life. 'The fact that Rip Curl didn't go public, they at least maintained that thread,' says Sam. 'Sometimes it got a little tenuous, but they maintained that thread to their product, which is dreams. What they're selling is dreams. They're selling driving up the coast. That was the dream that they sold me. It was Australia, Bells, new sights and people who were totally dedicated to surfing. That was a dream that Rip Curl sold me and I bought into it.'

That philosophy extends to allowing surfing during office hours, as long as the work gets done, as a touchstone to resist creeping corporatisation. There was a point at which non-surfing staff began asking why they couldn't take time off to go shopping, pointing out that the surfers were able to come in late or disappear for long lunches whenever the waves were good. The company organised surf lessons for the non-surfers so they wouldn't feel left out.

THE FLASH BOMB

The Flash Bomb wetsuit, launched in 2012, was the perfect product for the company's sharpened focus: their heritage product, an essential piece of functional surfing equipment, in a new and improved form.

The Flash Bomb was developed with the goal of creating the world's fastest-drying wetsuit, an innovation that would mean going for a second surf on a cold winter's day didn't involve wriggling into a cold, damp wetsuit – an ordeal that had long tormented cold-climate surfers. This bit of product development was, in part, an act of self-interest for its creators.

'Very rarely do you have a product that actually does exceed the expectations of the customer,' says Steve Kay. 'And anyone who's tried to put on a wet, clammy wetsuit would know that if you could give me a product that was much easier to put on after I'd been using it I'm going to like it. The Flash Bomb did that. The proposition that we were able to use in our advertising and in stores actually taught us a lot about what we do with a lot of other product launches since then.'

The world's first GPS watch, the world's lightest travel luggage, the Mirage board shorts and the Anti-Series of outerwear are all examples of this approach, to own a product category with tangible improvements on what was previously available.

'We had this succession of what we called "products with unique selling propositions" that all had incredibly powerful and emotive marketing, that really spoke to that underlying principle of exceeding the customers' expectations,' says Steve.

'And getting the whole world on board with a product like that, because when a product like that goes around the world in a full cycle for a year and everything Steve says happens around the world, the second year going through it's like, pheeeewwww, it really takes off,' says Neil, making the sound effect of a rocket launching into the stratosphere. 'But if you get halfway round the world and one region goes, "We're not going to back that," and it breaks that chain of product marketing and messaging and word of mouth, it really puts a halt on things. So being united on that message behind great products, there's been 10 years of that sort of stuff.'

THE BRAZILIAN STORM

The task of broadcasting their message around the world was made easier with the addition of an extraordinary new talent to the team from the fast-rising surf nation of Brazil. The world tour has seen an influx of Brazilian surfers in recent years: freakishly talented, hungry for success, some rising from impoverished backgrounds, often providing for extended families with lucrative sponsorships.

Rip Curl was quick to embrace the movement, signing the leader of the Brazilian Storm, Gabriel Medina, in 2009, when he was just 15. Medina dominated junior surfing globally before bursting onto the pro tour in 2011 with two contest victories, in Hossegor and San Francisco, before claiming his first world title in 2014.

Gabby, as he's known to his Rip Curl teammates, distinguished himself for his wild and creative aerial manoeuvres. 'I'm completely bamboozled by how Gabby does it. Gabby's just going into a new zone, some new, instinctive zone. I don't think you can teach it, though,' says Claw.

Mick Fanning has been one of Gabe's staunchest defenders against critics of his steely competitive streak, which often ruffles opponents' feathers. 'The first year he got into the Pipe event, he was just so eager to learn. He's actually a really sweet kid, he's very family orientated and has a really big heart,' says Mick. 'I think the media only see what happens during an event, and in an event he's a stone-cold killer. He. Does. Not. Give. A. Fuck. Away from the events, he's the nicest kid on earth.'

It's difficult for non-Brazilians to appreciate the level of fame and attention Gabe attracts in his homeland. 'He's a superstar over there. It's scary. He says, "Sometimes I can't even go surfing because there's people waiting out the front of my house." He lives on the beach but still has to jump in his car to go surfing some-where else,' says Mick.

For Gabriel, the chance to join the same team as his idol was a big part of the attraction in signing with Rip Curl. 'It was a dream come true to be in the same team as Mick Fanning and be part of one of the best surf brands in the world,' says Gab. 'I had just become 15 years old, my contract with Volcom was about to finish and Felipe Silveira [Rip Curl Brazil's CEO] invited me to come to Guarujá, where Rip Curl office is in Brazil. I remember well that day, when I went with my dad and my mum.'

Silveira remembers watching a young Medina take out the Rip Curl GromSearch in 2009, going from fourth to first in the last few minutes, and realising he was witnessing a rare talent. 'It was a really good left close to the rocks and the other three guys were locals, putting a lot of pressure on Gabriel,' says Felipe. 'In the countdown, everyone got a wave and left Gabriel outside with 30 seconds to go and he got a set wave, took the last wave and the kid surfed with abandon like it was the last wave of his life, like he was surfing for his life, surfing with no limits. He scored 9.5 on his last wave. I was shocked with the way the kid surfed that wave. I said . . . "We need to sign this kid."'

Gabe signed with Rip Curl and a week later won a six-star WQS, still the youngest male surfer to win an ASP (now WSL) event. 'I was searching for the next world champion. The brand that had the first Brazilian world champion would have a point of difference in the market so we took it very seriously,' says Felipe.

The Rip Curl founders liked what they saw from the get-go. 'During the finals for the Rip Curl Pro at Johanna [in 2010] we watched him surf for eight hours on an adjacent left and he clearly demonstrated surfing at the level of Kelly Slater and Mick Fanning in the final,' says Brian. 'Kelly beat Mick in the final with one huge alley-oop but Gabby had pulled off many more outlandish aerials during his marathon free surf.'

Gabriel walked into a Rip Curl team on the rise, and a culture and support network that cultivated success. 'The cool thing about it was to meet my idols. I met Mick that I've always watched in surf movies, who always inspired me,' says Gabriel. 'I met Owen [Wright] that is a great friend on tour, super-nice guy. Wilko [Matt Wilkinson] also is an incredible guy, funny, cool to travel with. And Mason [Ho] is a very funny bloke. I had the opportunity to meet not just surfers, but also people that work at Rip Curl, guys like [former team manager] Gary Dunne, a guy who helped me a lot, really a lot. He gave me all support and took care of me. I'm really grateful to meet him. Keke in France, and today [current team manager] Ryan Fletcher . . . All the guys from Rip Curl in Brazil and internationally treat me so well and today I feel like I'm part of their family.'

For Gabriel, it also meant stepping up to challenge his hero, Mick Fanning, in the most intense competitive environment, vying for a world title at Pipeline while staying together at Rip Curl's beachfront team house. 'Two years we've been fighting for the world title, in 2014 and 2015, but in 2014 it was a more direct fight. I didn't know how it was going to be,' says Gabe. 'He is a guy who knows where to put himself in those moments. He was focused on his job and I was focused on mine . . . He taught me a lot.'

With Mick now retired from the tour and on the Search, Gabriel is hungry to fill Mick's imposing shoes. 'It's a big responsibility to substitute him and be the number-one surfer of the team, but with Mick's retirement I want it,' Gabe says. 'I want to assume the responsibility and be the guy that he was, to inspire people . . . I'm ready and I like challenges.'

In December 2018, Gabe secured his second world title and took out the Pipeline Masters with a whole new level of backhand tube-riding, after an intense three-horse race against his compatriot Filipe Toledo and Australian Julian Wilson. At just 24, Gabe showed he was ready to claim the mantle of Rip Curl's number-one team rider on tour, and he is acutely aware that one more world title would put him in the illustrious company of three-time world champs Andy Irons and Rip Curl icons Tom Curren and Mick Fanning. Even in retirement, Mick's presence loomed large over the title race. Having just signed a new 10-year deal with Rip Curl, Mick played a valuable support role. 'Mick turned up at the team house and was a very strong senior presence in giving the surfers advice as they required. He's been a strong and positive influence on Gabby,' says Claw.

It would be hard to overstate Gabe's impact on Brazilian surfing. His 2014 world title and innovative aerial surfing have inspired legions of grommets across the country. He's also opened his own surf training facility, the Gabriel Medina Institute, together with his parents, Charlie and Simone, to help produce the next generation of Brazilian champions. The institute features classrooms, a swimming pool, gymnasium, trampoline and museum, all right on the beachfront at Maresias, where Gabriel learnt to surf.

'The institute was an idea from my dad, my mom and mine. We wanted to give back all that the surf gave us to these children, to try to give them the support I had or even more,' says Gabriel. The institute can cater for up to 60 students at a time, from the ages of 10 to 16. As well as surf training and coaching, it offers computing and language classes, medical care and dentistry, and is all funded by Gabriel.

Felipe Silveira doesn't see the Brazilian Storm passing any time soon. 'The influence of Gabriel in the market in Brazil is huge,' says Felipe. 'After Gabriel Medina was world champ, the success that he was having, every kid that surfs wants to be Gabriel Medina. They see surfing as an opportunity to become famous and make money, like soccer. Brazilians used to lack confidence. Their goal used to be to make the trials, now the kids want to win the event. Gabriel showed them.'

Now Gabe's younger sister, Sophia, is making a name for herself as the next big thing. 'She just won GromSearch in under-16. She is only 14, she is following in the footsteps,' says Felipe.

MICHAEL PETERSON'S LAST FAREWELL

As new Rip Curl surfers emerged in the modern era, the original rebel surf star left the building. No surfer better captured Rip Curl's early maverick spirit than Michael Peterson, the rangy, long-haired natural-footer from Coolangatta, with his hyperactive energy in the water and his enigmatic, reclusive ways on land.

When Michael passed away in 2012 from a heart attack, there was an outpouring of grief and tributes throughout the surfing world. Michael's family chose to spread his ashes at a handful of his favourite surf locations, and his younger brother, Tommy, had the solemn duty of scattering a portion of Michael's ashes in the Bells line-up during the 2013 Rip Curl Pro. 'It would have been a privilege for Mick to know he had his ashes scattered at Bells,' says Tommy.

Michael had been living a shadowy existence for many years, suffering the effects of electroconvulsive therapy in the '80s, and his own efforts to self-medicate his undiagnosed schizophrenia in the '70s. MP lived with his mother in a small flat in South Tweed Heads, rarely venturing out publicly, but was still revered by all who had witnessed his freakish surfing feats. The fact that many of those feats were performed on the wide-open walls of Bells during a period of unparalleled dominance in the '70s, all while wearing Rip Curl wetsuits, earnt MP a special place in the pantheon of Rip Curl champions.

Claw reckons there are three surfers who have represented the Rip Curl spirit most potently over the decades: Michael Peterson, Tom Curren and Mick Fanning. When I mention this to Mick, he seems slightly nonplussed for a moment. For a surfer who's received just about every honour there is in the sport, this one seems to matter. 'That's a huge honour. You think of those guys and they were so true to themselves, and Rip Curl supported that. That's really cool,' says Mick.

Claw and Brian never forgot the boost that MP's endorsement gave their wetsuits in those early days. 'They looked after Michael Peterson until he passed away, and in fact the family's still associated,' says Neil Ridgway. 'And they're still associated with Curren, and [with] Mick I think the same thing will continue. I've always admired that about them, particularly with the Petersons.'

'They don't need to ring up and ask us for anything. They can use the Peterson name for marketing, that's no problem,' says Tommy. 'We've always been loyal, we've never left. I always say to

Singer, I found something good and I stuck to it. Our sponsorship contract was a handshake with Claw when Michael got sponsored. I ring Ridgway and say, "I'm going down the shop. Let them know I'm coming." They still honour the handshake, 47 years later. That's not bad.'

THE FANNING FACTOR

It's stating the obvious to say that Mick Fanning has become a powerful figurehead for the Rip Curl team. But he's also expanded the role of a sponsored team rider, not just by endorsing the brand but also in advocating for his fellow surfers and challenging management when he doesn't agree with decisions.

'There are times when things aren't feeling right. If the marketing plans don't feel right you just speak up. What are we doing this for? You get in there and try and give your two cents' worth, ask how we want to be portrayed,' says Mick. 'I think that's filtered down to Wilko, Owen, Alana, Tyler, Nikki – you can have a marketing plan but you've got to support the individual and who they are.'

Of course, Mick has risen to his position over the course of a decade, with three world titles and the unrivalled affection of the surfing public. But it was his 2015 encounter with a great white shark at Jeffreys Bay in South Africa, in the midst of a world-tour final, that brought him a whole new level of mainstream public recognition. Later that year, while Mick was competing in the Pipeline Masters in Hawaii in pursuit of a fourth world title, his eldest brother, Peter, died from a heart condition. During these crises the relationship between the brand and the surfer has come to the fore.

'They're amazing. Every time something's happened, the shark thing, Neil was the first one on the phone to Mum. When Peter passed away, Neil was the first one Mum spoke to and he sat with her all night,' says Mick. 'It's a lot more than business. If the stickers and contracts disappear we'll still be friends.'

Mick's mum, Liz, agrees. 'It took us a little while to get used to Neil, specially Mick. There wasn't a bond there in the beginning and now Mick tells Neil things he wouldn't even tell me,' says Liz. 'He's been such a wonderful person. He's a very, very good friend and he's been a confidant of mine. He's never let me down and I've never let him down.'

Neil vividly recalls watching the webcast of the Jeffreys Bay final between Mick and Julian Wilson while speaking to Liz on the phone. 'I pretty much speak to his mum every heat, or we text every heat, and I was talking to her on the phone – "It's about to start, Julian just got a wave. Okay, alright, I'll call you back when we win."' Neil and Liz always text each other the phrase 'Keep the faith' during critical moments in tight heats, but those words took on new meaning on this occasion.

The shark encounter – most experts agree the incident didn't constitute an 'attack' as such – was broadcast live around the world, with millions watching as a large dorsal fin surfaced next to Mick and began thrashing around, the shark knocking him from his board. Liz remembers those agonising protracted seconds when Mick was floating in the water with a large white pointer coming at him, and he became obscured by a wave in front of him. Liz says she jumped out of her seat and physically grabbed the television screen as if trying to rescue her son.

'The wave went up and you couldn't see him and I went, he's dead. How are we going to deal with him being dead tomorrow?' says Neil. 'And I was freaking out and the wave went down, and he was still swimming and I rang Liz straightaway and she was screaming and I went, "He's on the jet ski, Liz, he's on the jet ski.

Look, his arms are moving, his legs are moving. Look, he's okay, he's okay."'

Later that year, Mick was locked in a five-way battle for the world title, coming into Pipeline in one of the closest finales to the pro-surfing season in history. Mick was sleeping soundly in the master bedroom of Rip Curl's beachfront team house with no idea of events unfolding back in Australia.

'When Pete died, and I knew because I was on the phone when the girls found his body, I didn't know what to do,' says Liz, who was in Hawaii to watch Mick compete. 'I just called Neil and he came around and sat with me and we discussed how we were going to tell Mick. It was on Facebook in two hours.' They made the decision to let Mick sleep and tell him the tragic news first thing in the morning. 'It was 10 or 11 at night. I said, "I want to get around there at four in the morning because he needs to hear it from me,"' says Liz.

Neil recalls the scene in the pre-dawn darkness as they woke Mick and broke the terrible news. 'He went, "What the fuck are you doing here?" and I go, "You've got to talk to your mum,"' Neil says. 'Throughout the course of the morning, word got around the house what had happened and he was very upset, and then at some point he started going about his routine and someone asked him about his brother and he just started telling all these nice stories about his brother. I said, "You don't have to surf, you can go home. You don't have to prove anything. You can quit." And he said, "I'm going to surf. I'm not surfing for points. I'm not surfing for the title. I'm surfing for Pete, because that's what he would have wanted me to do. Look after Mum." And he was off.'

On an epic day at 10-to-12-foot Pipeline, Mick prevailed against some of the greatest Pipe specialists in the world: Jamie O'Brien, Kelly Slater, John John Florence. On one memorable ride in his stacked round-four heat against Kelly and John John, he burst out of a long tube ride, raising his arms and gazing towards the sky as if saluting his brother. 'He beat them all . . . Kelly, John John. It was only that they ran out of light that day, he would have won. We woke up the next day and it was two foot and the wind was out of his sails,' says Neil.

Mick couldn't rekindle the fire of the previous day in the mediocre conditions and Gabriel Medina knocked him out in the semifinals, allowing Brazilian Adriano de Souza to claim his first world title. Liz was almost relieved. 'I don't know how we would have dealt with all the attention if he'd won,' she says.

'His strength of character is good for the brand to be aligned with . . . He's true to his word, and that's a nice thing to be associated with at every level,' says Neil. 'When the whips are cracking, you may have the world's best surf team but there's only one horse that you can rely on every time to be there in the end, and it was him.'

THE TEAM

Rip Curl has had some experience supporting team riders through trying times. That same December in Hawaii, Owen Wright was dominating the biggest days at Pipeline in preparation for the event, with an outside shot at the world title himself. But the hard-charging goofy-footer copped a flogging by a huge set of waves and was washed in suffering from concussion. Lapsing in and out of consciousness, he was rushed to hospital and diagnosed with a traumatic brain injury and bleeding on the brain. His recovery took a year, but he signalled his return in the best possible way by winning the season opener, Quiksilver Pro, at Snapper Rocks in 2017.

'We keep him on the books and we pay him full whack and we look after him, because we think that's the right thing to do for the surfer,' says Neil.

'Their support throughout that was amazing, and to see me back and healthy and smiling, that's why they support you,' says Owen. 'They were in my doctor's meetings, all the help I could get I got . . . They were just so proactive to get the right help.'

Owen's sister, Tyler, paused her own career while she nursed her big brother through his recovery, then she went on to win the first of two world titles in 2016. 'Tyler put her life on hold to the point where her coach and myself were going, "Just go and do your thing." You don't want to see them stop doing what they do. The best thing she could do was what she did, and it inspired me,' says Owen.

'With how injured he was, it was very hard to know what the right thing to do was at the right time,' says Tyler. 'I was still highly stressed by the whole situation. I didn't think he should be competing . . . Even winning the title, I was still very much stressed.'

And the rest of the Rip Curl team played an important role in Owen's recovery. 'I had Wilko come to check in and Mick was there, and I was going up and visiting Mick and having chats,' says Owen. 'I had Rip Curl guys, Fletch [Ryan Fletcher] and Neil, just everyone checking in. That really plays a big part in it when you're injured. It was just huge support emotionally.'

When Mick took time off the tour in 2016, after the trials and tribulations of 2015, and with Owen out of action, Matt Wilkinson stepped up to fill the breach. The NSW Central Coast goofy-footer, previously better known for his novelty wetsuits and sense of humour than his contest results, won the first two events of the year and finished 2016 at a career-best fifth in the world, and repeated the result in 2017. 'When Mick wasn't there, there was a lot of oxygen there for everyone to stand up and say, okay, it's my time now,' says Neil. 'As much as Mick's still the leader of the pack, him having time away was great for those guys.'

Wilkinson has been with Rip Curl for 20 years, since sending them a video his dad, Neal, shot of him when he was nine years old. 'My first contract was, like, $1500 wholesale worth of clothes, and I just remember getting stickers for the first time and being so fricken' happy,' says Wilko.

Since then, he's risen up the ranks to join the Rip Curl A-team, and has enjoyed the close-knit environment of mutual support they cultivate. 'The way they do it is, the groms kind of get to connect to the older guys,' says Wilko. 'When I got a wildcard into the Réunion Island comp, they put me in a house with Hedgey and Mick, and I was the little dish pig but I felt like I was becoming friends with those guys. On the Search you become close to those guys. It's pretty inspiring to be hanging with guys like Mick, and see his work ethic and his professionalism towards surfing.'

Owen agrees. 'It was pretty cool to be nurtured as a surfer and an athlete. You had Mick there leading the way and all the grommets were pretty stoked,' he says. 'They were very accommodating of all their grommets. I was at the Pipe Masters at 16, I was at their Search event at Uluwatu at age 17. That's unheard of these days. That nurturing of youth, I think that repays tenfold. They book houses and we all get to stay together. We've been doing this since we were 10 years old, Wilko and myself and my sister.'

The only time team harmony seems threatened is when multiple team members are in contention for the world title at season's end while sharing the same house in the pressure-cooker environment of the Pipeline Masters. 'They are very strong-willed characters, and of all the guys Mick and Gabby are the most strong-willed of all,' says Claw. 'I recall one occasion when Gabby was on the rise and the two of them were having some great fun trying each other out in play-fighting or wrestling, which resulted in a few squashed hedges and other damage, and started to look more like a UFC title fight than boys having fun.'

Certainly, Claw's eye for talent has stood the test of time. In 1976, the first year of the pro tour, 13 of the top 16 were sponsored by Rip Curl, and they've supported a procession of legendary surfers since. 'There are too many great surfers to name, but we remain grateful for all their efforts,' says Claw. 'Modern pro surfing is the sum total of what thousands of surfers have contributed.'

Claw gives particular credit to their world champions: Rabbit Bartholomew, Tom Carroll, Tom Curren, Damien Hardman, Mick Fanning and Gabriel Medina in the men's, and Pam Burridge, Stephanie Gilmore and Tyler Wright in the women's.

'Pam is a lady with many talents and dimensions, only one of which is surfing,' says Claw. 'She joined the Rip Curl team in her very early teens, and came very close to winning the world title on numerous occasions, was runner-up six times, and at Rip Curl we were all over the moon when she won the world title in 1990.'

Rip Curl had to wait another 17 years for its next women's world champ but then the floodgates opened. 'Possibly the most remarkable female talent to appear on the Rip Curl roster was Stephanie Gilmore,' says Claw. 'Steph turned pro at an early age and immediately won the world title, dominating the field. She won four world titles back to back with Rip Curl before moving to another sponsor. That caused a lot of angst at Rip Curl but she was a powerful contributor to the Rip Curl brand, particularly in the two years when both Mick and Steph took out the world titles for us.'

Tyler Wright is now flying the Rip Curl flag on the women's tour, with two world titles and counting, and groundbreaking free-surfing performances in heavy conditions. 'She is setting new standards for females in power-surfing and big barrels, her only issue there being sometimes she goes too hard. She seems fearless and gets hurt like her big brother, Owen,' says Claw.

Brian nominates a handful of team riders he believes have most powerfully represented the brand through the decades. 'In particular the regular footers Michael Peterson, Tom Curren and Mick Fanning, along with the goofy-footers Tom Carroll and Damien Hardman. These surfers have all been instrumental in helping define that indefinable magic of the brand.'

THE TROUBLE SHOOTER

Many great female surfers have ridden for Rip Curl over the years, but one woman who has had a huge impact on the brand is less well known. Brooke Farris was a young aspiring pro surfer from Perth having a crack at the World Qualifying Series when she befriended world champ Layne Beachley. Layne offered her a job as her personal assistant, which led to Brooke organising Layne's own pro event, sponsored by the Commonwealth Bank. (An event won by a 14-year-old Tyler Wright, still the youngest female winner of a pro event.) From there, the ASP offered Brooke a job as the women's tour manager, then Rip Curl recruited her as its international events manager. In July 2016, she took on a new role as general manager of digital marketing and ecommerce.

As events manager, Brooke coordinated the Search events, a role that involved everything from negotiating with gun-toting soldiers to safely couriering large amounts of cash through foreign cities. 'It's hard building relationships because everyone knows you're only there for one year. There's some reluctance to engage. It requires a lot of good communication and having to go into your wallet,' she says.

Brooke spent three months in Puerto Rico in 2010, living in a hotel that was a converted hospital, and basically pulling the event together from scratch. The event site included a 20-foot tower behind the dunes, but when local authorities saw it they wanted it pulled down. 'When they saw the structure, they freaked out. They choppered in with gun belts on,' says Brooke. 'We managed to talk everyone around . . . English isn't their native language, so we had some pretty interesting conversations.'

The whole contest site flooded a few days before the event and the tour judges were robbed at gunpoint after a surf, requiring a major upscale in security. But those challenges were nothing compared to the anguish of three-time world champ Andy Irons' tragic death in an airport hotel room in Dallas, Texas, as he tried to fly home to his pregnant wife, Lindy, in Hawaii.

Andy had been unwell since arriving in Puerto Rico and missed his first-round heat. 'We got started at Middles and he wasn't there and we sent a doctor to see him, and the doctor had set up blood tests for him on the way to the airport,' says Brooke. But Irons, desperate to get home to Kauai, never stopped for those tests. Instead, he boarded a flight to Dallas, missed his connecting flight to Hawaii and checked in to the Grand Hyatt Hotel at the Dallas/ Fort Worth International Airport. Hotel staff found him dead in his bed the next morning. An autopsy found the cause of death as a heart attack due to coronary heart disease and 'acute mixed-drug ingestion'. As with the assassination of John F. Kennedy, almost every surfer can remember where they were when they heard news of Irons' death.

'[His uncle] Rick Irons told me out the front of the hotel that Andy had passed away,' says Brooke. 'Neil was the first person I called and we just pulled in the key stakeholders . . . We all got in a war room in the hotel and discussed how to manage the situation. We called a lay day, held a paddle-out for the surfers, and for the rest of the week we had a Hawaiian flag at half-mast. It was crazy how it all happened and went down. The night before we had all been celebrating Stephanie [Gilmore] winning her fourth world title.'

The pro-surfing family pulled together and supported each other through their grief. 'The surfers needed each other and they could share stories and grieve,' says Brooke. Irons' death caused profound soul-searching among the pro surfers – their bubble of invincibility abruptly burst, even as Kelly Slater racked up an outlandish tenth world title.

But for Brooke there was little time to grieve. She was already exploring the next Search venue. She'd earlier carried out reconnaissance in Barbados, but on-ground logistics looked too hard. In Puerto Rico she'd met with the world's foremost surf forecaster, Sean Collins, along with Claw and Neil, to assess options. His recommendation took them by surprise – not some distant tropical reef or exotic point break, but a pounding beach break in the midst of a sprawling metropolis: Ocean Beach, San Francisco. 'We went there to scope it out, how accessible it was, would we have access to permits. We have this whole document that we fill out for the Search when we reccy places,' says Brooke.

They committed to Ocean Beach. Brooke and a small contest crew rented a house in the Haight-Ashbury district, where the whole Summer of Love had converged in 1967, and got to work. When a permit fee had to be lodged in cash to meet a deadline and staff per diems were due to be paid, she found herself withdrawing US$37,000 in cash from a downtown bank. With then ASP Australian manager, Matt Wilson, and a couple of contest staff, they devised a plan to get the cash safely back to the house. They bought a transportable safe so they could keep the money under lock and key when they got it home. Matt wheeled the empty safe down one side of the street, providing a decoy for would-be robbers, while two young women carried the cash in their handbags on the other side of the street. 'All of the neighbours must have wondered what we were doing,' says Brooke.

The event was most notable for Kelly Slater winning his 11th world title ... twice. A tabulating error meant the ASP awarded Slater the title while Owen Wright still had a mathematical shot at it, an error picked up by a surf fan who crunched the numbers himself and pointed out the mistake on an internet forum. 'ASP looked at their numbers and went, this person is right,' says Brooke. 'Renato [Hickel, ASP tour manager] called me up and said, "There's a problem. Kelly hasn't won yet, he has to surf one more heat because Owen is still in contention."' Slater eventually secured the title, but ASP CEO Brodie Carr took responsibility for the embarrassing blunder and resigned.

The Search events have always thrown up the unexpected. 'You could never prepare yourself for those types of things. It was all-consuming,' says Brooke. 'They're the most rewarding events for everyone involved including the athletes ... The Search brought something super special to the tour.'

Despite the hair-raising adventures and generous concessions for surf time, Brooke takes her career at Rip Curl seriously and is wary of people misreading the barefoot, surf-first culture of the place. 'I'm pretty protective about how we're perceived,' she says. 'They say no one ever got fired for going surfing at Rip Curl but you can get fired for not doing your job. There's a fair bit of trust and autonomy.'

THE KAUAI GIRLS

While Tyler Wright has led the charge for Rip Curl on the women's tour in recent times, a couple of surfers from Kauai have had just as great an impact from outside the competitive arena.

Bethany Hamilton and Alana Blanchard were long-time

surfing buddies enjoying a blessed grommet-hood on their island paradise when they soared to stardom for different reasons. The pair were surfing together as stoked teenagers when their revelry was abruptly shattered. Bethany was attacked by a tiger shark and had her left arm bitten off just below the shoulder.

The subsequent events – the nightmarish panic in the water, the spreading tide of blood, the desperate paddle to shore, the efforts to stem the bleeding with a makeshift tourniquet, the frantic ambulance ride to hospital and her gradual and inspiring recovery – have been well documented. A Hollywood feature film, *Soul Surfer*, and a book of the same name took Bethany's story to millions around the world, inspired a flood of fan mail and made her a household name, a byword for courage and resilience.

'I was only nine when I first came on the Rip Curl team. I think my dad had a friend that worked for Rip Curl so they were supporting the local grom,' says Bethany. 'I'm 29 so that's 20 years. I was just doing all the local contests. I was just like your super-frothed surf grom, super stoking just to get sponsored, for clothes and bikinis and stickers.'

The shark attack curtailed, but ultimately didn't derail, those youthful dreams of a career as a professional surfer. 'Already that was the plan, and then I think it didn't take too long to continue the dream,' says Bethany. 'Two or three months later – it happened in October and my first contest was in January – I made a final in one of the events. I didn't really limit myself in my thoughts. I put my head down and went hard at it. I look back and go, I was crazy and kind of innocent in an awesome way. In my life I've had this continual thing where people doubt me more than I doubt myself.'

What Bethany has achieved since is truly extraordinary. Never mind getting back in the water and overcoming her fears; she claimed a national title just two years after the attack, competed again at the highest level on the world tour, defeated world champions in perfect tropical island surf, married and had two children, and has continued to surf and travel and inspire legions of young girls to embrace their dreams. All this has made her one of the most admired surfers in the world.

'I feel like I've accomplished a lot and I feel really good. The drive is still going,' says Bethany. 'It was really cool for Rip Curl to give me some wildcard opportunities.' Bethany has made the most of her wildcards, beating world champs Steph Gilmore and Tyler Wright in perfect reef surf at the 2016 Fiji Pro, shortly after becoming a mum.

'Fiji was super rad, coming off post-partum recovery, and being a mum and pushing myself competitively,' says Bethany. Rip Curl also gave her a wildcard into the Rip Curl Cup Padang Padang in Bali, where she humbled more than a few big-name pro surfers in perfect barrelling lefts. 'I made a couple of heats at the Padang Cup, that was a really fun memory. I remember the guys not liking me too much.'

But perhaps her greatest surfing achievement has been surfing Jaws, first towing in with a jet ski and then paddling the huge Hawaiian outer reef. 'I'd always dreamed of towing it and then guys started paddling it,' says Bethany. 'Towing it was so much fun but it's such a different sport. Paddling it was really fun in a really crazy, psycho way. The adrenalin pumping through your veins all day is next level.'

Married to husband Adam Dirks, and with two small boys, Tobias and Wesley, Bethany's focus for now is on motherhood. 'I love it so much. There are no words to describe the feeling of bringing life into the world. Taking care of them day after day is so magical, teaching them about the ocean, camping and having fun.'

A 2018 feature documentary, *Unstoppable*, has taken her story and influence to millions more. 'It started off as more of a surf edit and we ended up making this big, old, long documentary,' says Bethany. 'It's just the story of me going from a little girl to motherhood and surfing along the way.'

Brooke Farris recalls being in the Mentawais in Indonesia on a Rip Curl boat trip in 2011 when Bethany suffered a serious fin chop to her arm. 'A woman who's lost one arm, with the other arm cut, in the middle of nowhere,' recalls Brooke. 'Alana was on the boat and she had been in that situation before so it was pretty traumatic.'

Their skipper, Albert Taylor, stitched up the wound, but Bethany had lost feeling in her hand so the decision was made to cut the trip short and get her to proper medical care.

'[Albert] was so steadfast in his approach, he said he thought he was going to have to clamp her arm it was bleeding so badly,' says Brooke. 'She and Alana and I went to Singapore to see a doctor and they said, "So, you've already seen a doctor." We said, no, someone with a first-aid certificate stitched it up. They were amazed at the astounding job he had done. They said it was one millimetre away from hitting a major artery.'

Alana Blanchard has taken a more traditional path as the talented model/surfer girl, so perfectly fitting an ideal long revered by marketers that her endorsement has helped launch some of the most successful product lines in Rip Curl's history. She has been criticised for trading on her looks, for being more model than surfer, and for a less-than-stellar competitive record. One senses it is water off a duck's back for Alana, who is too busy following her own dreams to worry about the critics. Married to Australian pro surfer Jack Freestone, and with a young baby boy, Banks, she too is moving into a new phase of life.

'Being able to share motherhood with Alana, we've got such a special bond. We talk mum-talk together. I can't wait to share life with her as mums, have our little guys grow up together,' says

Bethany. But Bethany still has more goals to achieve in surfing. 'I just keep pushing myself and planning surf trips, working on the progressive side of my surfing. I look forward to pushing that. I don't feel like I've accomplished my full potential,' she says.

THE GPS WATCH

By 2012, Rip Curl had enjoyed 20 years of healthy sales for its tide watch, but when Shane Helm took over the watch division he was already thinking about what might propel Rip Curl watches into a new era.

'My pitch was, the tide watch had been fantastic for the past 20 years, and we had to give the next generation a reason to put a watch on their wrist,' says Shane.

Shane's story is classic Rip Curl: yet another young surfer who didn't want to have to go off to the city to pursue a traditional career, and who dared to dream of a vocation based around waves. 'I was working in the warehouse, with the tape-gun packing boxes, while I was studying architecture in Geelong,' says Shane. 'I did a standard year away in Indo, came back and needed a full-time job. I got a job in customer service, then a job in sales, then as a sales rep.'

In 2006, Peter Hodgart offered Shane a job as his understudy and as Australian product manager, and six years later Shane inherited the watch division from Hodg. 'I always wore a tide watch but nobody really knew how to set them. It seemed to be the biggest fault with the watches,' says Shane. 'I had this idea already for a GPS watch. With GPS you could set the time and tide for people if you could triangulate their location.'

Shane travelled to Hong Kong two to three times a year to visit their long-time watch supplier, Rod Payne. 'We've had one supplier who made our first watch, right the way through, for more than

30 years', says Shane. 'He knew what it took to make a watch for surfers, and he was also a keen snowboarder.'

On a visit to Hong Kong in 2012 with a group of designers, the team adjourned to Rod's ski chalet in Japan for a bit of powder-riding to round off their meetings. The fateful excursion was a potent example of why time in the field is so valuable.

'The iPhone 3GS had just come out, the first one with tracking, and there was an app called Ski Tracks, which tracked your elevation, how many lifts you did, how fast you went', recalls Shane. 'I made everyone download this Ski Tracks app. We were all on the lifts looking at how fast we'd gone. The week-long trip turned into a competition. We were so excited by what we could do, this new evolution of technology. That's where the idea of the GPS watch was born.'

Shane returned to Torquay convinced he had found the incentive for a new generation to strap on a watch. He convened a small focus group that met each week for three months to develop the concept. 'It was all top secret. We'd go through how this thing would work, the key features – length of ride, time on wave, how fast you go.'

He took the concept to the board of directors, including Claw, Brian, François and CEO Michael Daly, with high hopes of attracting some serious development funding. 'It was a really big and expensive project', says Shane. 'I've got a certain amount of budget, but if there's a crazy idea Claw and Brian will always entertain it. There's an extra pool of money you can access if you've got an innovative idea.'

Shane made his pitch and Brian, ever the pragmatist, cut to the chase. 'Brian asked me two questions – is it possible, and how much is it going to cost? My two answers were, "I don't know." But he was determined to find out. Shane travelled to Sydney, New York, Berlin and Taiwan, visiting app developers and suppliers, coming to grips with the complexities of the project.

'We had another board meeting and I had the answers,' says Shane. But he wasn't sure Brian was going to like them. 'It was more than a million dollars just to make one. And this was in a pretty tough time in the surf industry when most meetings were about trying to cut costs.'

Rip Curl had recently paid the enormous development costs of the world's first heated wetsuit, the H-Bomb, and though it provided great marketing value, sales had been sluggish. Development costs for the GPS watch were almost identical. Shane sat down after his presentation and waited to see if his idea would fly.

'François hadn't said anything . . . He stands up after this has been going on for a while and he said, "Do you want to know what I think?" He's got the blue brand book in his hand. I'm sitting there hoping this thing gets off the ground,' recalls Shane. François paused for dramatic effect and looked around the table, before announcing in his emphatic French manner: 'I think we either do this or we shut the fuck up about being the ultimate surfing company and we all go home.'

'Brian looks at Claw and goes, "You know he's right." Claw goes, "We're doing it, aren't we?"' says Shane. And just like that, the decision was made to allocate a million bucks for development of a product no one was sure would find a market.

'I don't think it would have got over the line without François. None of them had smartphones, so it was a leap for those guys,' says Shane. 'It was going to take a momentous effort. We worked with partners in Sydney who were incredibly keen to do an amazing job with this product, which has got them a lot of new work subsequently – VML, a global agency . . . They built the website and the app. Rod Payne made the outside of the watch. We had another company making the GPS components and software that goes inside the watch. Everyone was passionate about the project.'

Testing had to be exhaustive before the watch went to market. 'We had about 200 watches out in the world, in the wild, catching data, coming up with different algorithms, making sure this all worked,' says Shane. 'We had the first version in the water to get them on people and start testing them. Owen Wright was down for a photo shoot, the surf was four or five foot, and JT [creative director James Taylor] brought him over and said, "Owen has been asking about a fitness watch." I said, "Let's go surfing. Here's a watch. Put it on your wrist." In the car I explained what it did, and how it worked. He was really excited.'

Out in the water, Owen's competitive instincts came to the fore. 'He got a few waves and paddled up to me – "I've gone 31 kilometres an hour." I said, "I've got 33." Straightaway there was this competitive thing. He got in a huff and paddled straight out to sea, a six-foot bomb came straight to him, and he rode this wave all the way down to the valley and paddled back up with this grin on his face. He was yelling out in the line-up, and this is my top-secret project, he's yelling at me, "38, I've got 38." That was one of those moments – when those guys get excited, you know you're onto something.'

A soft launch at Bells in 2014 provided the first real indication of the market response to the concept. 'We didn't actually have the product, it was coming soon, our production wasn't due until September. We had orders coming in to the Torquay store, had 140 people on a waiting list. That's when we knew there's real customer demand here.'

The moment of truth arrived when the product landed and orders shipped. For Shane, the trajectory of his career with Rip Curl would be largely determined by the market's response to his ambitious gambit, and whether that $1 million in development would ever be recouped. 'The product arrived and we'd ordered a lot,' says Shane. Would the surfers of the world share his fascination with how fast and far they travelled on a wave? Damn straight they would. 'It paid for itself and then some. It's been a fantastically successful product,' says Shane. 'We've been selling it at a really strong rate ever since.'

And he's not done yet. 'We're working on GPS2. We're adding more features to the watch and bringing some of that technology to our more basic tide watches,' says Shane. 'There's areas we're working on which are not watch-based – how we can get into tracking surfing, bringing communities of surfers together more. It was good to get a success with the first one, so when I go and ask [the board] they're more willing to listen.'

The fastest speed so far recorded on a wave is 46.7 kilometres an hour by Bruno Santos at Skeleton Bay, the mystical African freight-train left, closely followed by Mick Fanning with 46 kilometres an hour at the Snake, the mysto right featured in the Search in 2017. Shane reckons Jeffreys Bay is consistently the fastest wave in the world, followed by Cloudbreak in Fiji.

One customer bought a GPS watch specifically for a trip to Chicama, Peru, widely regarded as the world's longest wave, with the express goal of logging a one-kilometre ride. 'He got a couple of 700s and a 750. On his last day he got a 960-metre wave. That's the longest one I've heard of,' says Shane.

The GPS watch also brings up some topical issues around user data. 'The app's like a social network. We have a lot of data from 50,000 users all over the world, surfing all kinds of waves. We're very careful with that,' says Shane.

The statistics are mind-boggling. Since its launch, GPS watch users have logged over a million surf sessions. They've paddled over 5,000,000 kilometres, the equivalent of 133 times around the world or 14 times to the moon. They've ridden waves over 1,000,000 kilometres – 32 times around the world, or 3.3 times to the moon.

THE WORLD SURF LEAGUE

In 2013, with the publicly listed surf brands on the ropes, a US-based consortium – a group known as ZoSea Media, headed by a former Quiksilver exec Paul Speaker – made an audacious takeover bid for the ASP. The big three could no longer afford to carry the considerable costs of running multiple events each, so Quiksilver and Billabong were receptive to the bid.

Rip Curl was a staunch hold-out to the deal that promised to save the surf brands millions while granting ownership of the tour to ZoSea, funded by billionaire investor Dirk Ziff. The new tour would be known as the World Surf League and promised big things such as unified media rights, consistent webcast quality and production, and big non-endemic sponsors, in a bold new era that would elevate pro surfing to the mainstream.

'We voted no to the WSL,' says Neil Ridgway. 'I was on the board of the ASP for 10 years, Steve was on the board, Claw and François had both been on the board. We didn't give up the tenure on the ASP easily. And if you think about it, Claw and Brian and François, as a private company, they would have spent $50 million on pro surfing, hands down, and more if you roll all the team in from all around the world.'

But Rip Curl was outvoted, and the Association of Surfing Professionals and its 36 years of pro-surfing history was handed to ZoSea. All that has been widely reported. What's less well known is that Ziff, pro surfing's new cashed-up benefactor, and his wife, Natasha, were introduced to the world of surfing through Tom Curren.

'There's one school of thought that says Tom Curren is responsible for the WSL,' says Claw. 'Somehow, somewhere, sometime, this truly unique character . . . met a woman called Natasha Ziff, a highly creative person with a very interesting background. She was so enamoured with Tom's outlook on life and the quality of his music. My understanding is she started a small record label for the purpose of producing this bizarre, unique, deep musician.'

That connection resulted in the release of the most polished musical offering the world had seen from Curren, a smooth, bluegrass-tinged pop/folk EP called *Summerland Road*, which was catchy as hell but somehow failed to win a wide audience. 'I met the Ziffs through a friend, a Florida connection,' says Tom. He'd been on tour with Sonny Miller and Derek Hynd when they met a rapper named William Kimble. Tom ended up opening for Kimble, at whose concert Natasha Ziff heard him play and launched a record label, Wolf Bomb, to record him. And Dirk Ziff actually played guitar on the record.

Curren remains deeply grateful to the Ziffs, and upbeat about their patronage of professional surfing. 'I'm just blown away at their love of surfing, I really am,' says Tom. 'When you think about it, what they did is going to have such influence long into the future . . . My wish is for competitive surfing to go on and with the WSL, competitive surfing has been able to go on and rise to new vistas and far-reaching impacts into the future.'

Even so, Tom's not blind to the risks involved, for professional surfing and its new owners. 'Pro surfing, you can relate it to the ocean, it's capricious, it's misty and mystical, and so you have to deal with that stuff,' says Tom. 'Obviously, if you're going to commit to something like that you've got to know what that commitment means. You have to study pro surfing. It's an investment . . . You have to think about what people watch, [like] the NBL and the NBA. What if they start losing the viewership? The WSL, they're still tinkering with that. You get the sense the WSL's not out of the woods yet.'

LIBERATION MANAGEMENT

Wilco Prins is another case study of Rip Curl's success in bringing young business talent up through the ranks. If you'd told a young Dutch surfer living in a tent in Hossegor while he interned at Rip Curl that he would one day be CEO of Rip Curl Europe he would have laughed in your face.

'François Payot somehow or other identified and mentored a crazy Dutchman, Wilco Prins, who is doing a fine job of running our operations in Europe,' says Claw. 'Plus, he really gets the brand and is a true believer in our brand values and principles, and a real leader of the culture.'

Growing up in the Netherlands is not the ideal pedigree for a surfer but Wilco has managed to pursue his passion all the way to the top job in Europe. He seems a little incredulous himself, sitting in his vast office at Rip Curl's Hossegor HQ, surrounded by vintage surfboards and memorabilia from the brand's storied past.

'At one point, you're at a crossroads and you have to go left or right,' he says. 'I lived in Holland until I was 18, windsurfing and skateboarding. I started surfing at 13. We get waves, like once a month. There's a lot of surf in Holland,' he claims.

The young Dutch surfer dreamed of a job that would allow plenty of surf time, so when he saw an advertisement for a business school in Bordeaux, not far from Hossegor, he jumped at it. He landed an internship at Rip Curl that was meant to last four months but stretched out to nine. He lived in a tent at a beachside campground, surfed his brains out on the dreamy Hossegor beach breaks and met the girl who would become his wife.

When the internship finished Wilco travelled to Bali, where he was chasing surf and weighing up his next career move when he overheard a French accent in a bar. It belonged to a former colleague from Rip Curl who suggested there might be a permanent job for him in Hossegor. Wilco headed back and made a pest of himself about the place for a few weeks, hoping to score an audience with sales manager Henri Colliard or the boss-man himself, François Payot.

Wilco was beginning to question if that casual job offer over a beer back in Kuta was really worth cutting short his holiday and flying halfway across the world for, when he was finally offered a gig in Marketing. He worked his way up through footwear and wetsuits, and rose to head of sales to the core network, independent surf shops. 'Jean Grandy was in charge of footwear and he was a real character as well. He lives in Bali now. He was my guru in terms of product management,' says Wilco.

In 2012, at the age of 35, with 12 years' experience at Rip Curl, Wilco had a fateful meeting with Michael Daly, who was visiting from Torquay. 'He said, "What do you want to do?" I said, "I wouldn't mind running Rip Curl,"' Wilco recalls, with disarming candour. 'They got me into some management training programs, and two months later I was offered a job as CEO.'

Some months prior to this, with Olivier Cantet acting as European and global CEO, François had nominated Wilco Prins as the best candidate to take over as European CEO. Wilco underwent an intense two weeks' personal tutelage under Brian Singer, learning every aspect of the business. 'For 10 days, every day I met with Brian. The first few days it was like, "The way things are done in Europe are fucked. This is the way things should be done. What do you think?"'

He learnt a lot from Rip Curl's co-founder in those 10 days. 'You need to be involved, you need to be present in the stores, in the warehouse, not sitting in the office at a desk. It's about going into the warehouse and having a coffee with the guys and knowing what's going on,' says Wilco.

Like François before him, Wilco sees part of his role as being proactive in developing European surf culture. He is President of EuroSIMA, and hopes to see a European world surfing champion during his tenure. The development of local surfing talent is personal, with his own son an aspiring pro surfer. 'There's a lot more kids that surf all year long. There's a whole lot of 11-to-14-year-olds absolutely ripping. Kids start surfing a lot younger,' he says. 'I spend all my spare time at grom contests with my son, Hugo.'

Still, that core mission of catering to surfers is more challenging in a diverse market like Europe, where many countries have very little surf. 'Some areas you have to be a bit more creative, places like Croatia,' says Wilco. 'The rich thing about surfing is it's the mother of all action sports. It's pretty easy to be involved in a country where there's no waves if there's kitesurfing or windsurfing. Surfing is at the top of the pyramid for water sports. You adapt it to the different countries, but the umbrella is still the same.'

The Rip Curl party culture melds comfortably with the European sensibility and Wilco delights in upholding the tradition of his Torquay forebears. 'Rip Curl definitely had the wildest parties and still do, and sales meetings and releases,' he says. 'We are forced to do our parties here at the office because nobody wants to have us.'

Wilco's rise is a classic example of what he calls the 'liberation management' style – a term first coined by business writer Tom Peters – that has been Rip Curl's way of doing business since the beginning. 'Where Rip Curl Europe is special is the way François managed it from the start as an *"entreprise libérée"*,' Wilco says, giving the business buzz term a far more romantic tone in French. 'François would give you a mission and you would execute it the way you wanted. The job was not restricted but there was a framework. There's a lot of opportunity at Rip Curl to evolve and take initiatives.

They really like pushing people to be entrepreneurs. Now that's the trendy thing, a lot of big companies are trying to adopt that kind of system, which was already here built up from the ground.'

Peters' term neatly summarises the Rip Curl philosophy. 'Crazy times call for crazy organizations,' he writes in *Liberation Management*. 'Free the human imagination . . . Get close to and serve the customer . . . Customize products and services . . . Create teams that allow people to express their personalities.'

Peters says HR people operate by this unwritten rule: 'Thou shalt not hire a person who has an unexplained nanosecond in their life past the age of three.' Peters argues for the opposite approach. 'Hire a few genuine off-the-wall types. Collect weirdoes,' he writes. 'This is coldly logical stuff . . . How are you going to conquer weird markets with stuffed shirts?'

Claw agrees they stumbled on this way of doing business almost by accident, in pursuit of spending as little time in the office as possible. 'We've loved operating that way. A lot of the corporate world is quite interested in Rip Curl,' says Claw.

Steve Kay admits it took him a while to get used to the hands-off approach of his employers. 'There were times in the old days when Brian was up at Buller all winter. He comes back from one stint up there and someone had moved him out of his own office,' Steve recalls. 'For a while I misunderstood that as disinterest and just leaving the running of the business to other people, but in fact it comes right back to that vision and ambition that they had, to be a really serious global company and succeed over a wide range of products. But on top of that they have another layer – you have to do all that as quickly as possible so that you can actually maximise the amount of time you spend having fun.'

CHAPTER ELEVEN

THE SEARCH NEVER ENDS: 2015–

LAST TO LEAVE

Though the founders might be pulling back from the business, I can report firsthand that the notorious Rip Curl party culture they helped cultivate is alive and well, and showing no signs of abating.

'They never said no to a party at Rip Curl,' says Neil Ridgway.

'They started the party and were the last people there most of the time,' adds Steve Kay.

To prove their point, I'm invited to a soiree to celebrate the retirement of two long-time servants of the brand – former NZ CEO Paul Muir and South Australian sales rep Phil Bishop, both departing after 30 years with the Curl – and the 25th anniversary of Queensland sales rep and store owner Martin Sonja.

'We're older and we have more sense when it comes to executive behaviour – the world's changed, but it's still a great place,' says Neil. 'You'll see tonight, we'll go down there and have a great time and it won't be dry.'

Neil is not lying. Revellers gather at local restaurant and bar Growlers, and hit the ground running. I'm staying at Brian's place, and as thanks I'll be his designated driver for the evening, though he insists he's having a 'quiet night'. A new generation of Rip Curl crew have other ideas, relishing the chance to blow the froth off a few with the founders. There are raucous speeches, tall and true tales swapped at the bar, and cackles of mirth arising from scrums of old mates. Fun and irreverence are key brand values, after all, and this lot seem like sticklers for the dictates of the blue and yellow books.

I join Brian in a huddle with one keen young bean and Brian asks him where he'd like to go in the business. 'I'd like to run the place one day, to be honest,' the smooth 20-something says. Brian seems impressed and I imagine there's a fair chance he might just do that one day.

I estimate that Brian has had five 'last beers' by around midnight, when I gently suggest it might be time to bring that 'quiet night' to a close. No one else seems at all keen for Brian to leave. I eventually acquire a troop of extra passengers who each attempt to drag us inside for a nightcap when I drop them home, before I finally get us back to Brian's acreage hideaway.

This legendary stamina seems to have served the brand well. 'If you think of Rip Curl starting in 1969 . . . you had things like Lightning Bolt, Katins, Hang Ten and Platts, and the reality is that none of those brands were able to maintain the rage in terms of reinvention and staying relevant to successive generations of youth,' says Steve Kay. 'Think back to our magazine days and you had Kuta Lines, Hot Tuna, Mambo, Hot Buttered. I mean, 95 per cent of surf companies have failed at some point to continue to remain relevant to successive generations of youth. How did it succeed when so many other companies have failed?'

I'm regaled with one outrageous story of a company bus trip up to the MCG for the State of Origin rugby league match a few years ago that ends with Brian inviting the entire busload and a few hangers-on back to his place for a post-match party. Perhaps this is one way you remain relevant to successive generations of youth.

SPARROW HONOURED

In 2017, John 'Sparrow' Pyburne was honoured by the Surf & Boardshorts Industry Association (SBIA) with the Service to the Industry Award. It was a fitting recognition for Sparrow's almost 50 years of dedication to the mission of making a better wetsuit.

Sparrow's never been one to court the limelight and the honour came as a complete surprise. 'I had no idea what was going to happen. I thought they were going to present the Rip Curl team with an award,' says Sparrow. 'I never cared about winning anything. The only important thing in my whole life was being in the water . . . That's why I'm still here, so I can go surfing.'

Sparrow can still be found deep in the rabbit warren of the Rip Curl HQ at the cutting table or manning a sewing machine, as he has since the old bakery days, puzzling over more efficient ways to wrap the human body in neoprene. He's obsessive about pure function, occasionally clashing with the marketing or design crew over matters of aesthetics like the placement of logos. 'I'm a function person. I'm not into cosmetics. My priority is, is it working? If it's not, I'm going to fix it,' says Sparrow. 'The important thing was, if you make the best wetsuit, people are going to come back and get another one.'

Sparrow recalls having to wedge a broom through the door-handle of his office in the old days so surfers couldn't get in until he was ready to see them. 'I used to have a queue of people out the front door of the factory . . . right through the factory to my room,' he says.

'I've known Sparrow since he was 16 or 17. He's a real classic, he's a fanatic,' says Ray Thomas. 'He's got some really extreme ideas, which is good. If you just used Sparrow's ideas you might not come up with something commercial. He's got his heart and soul in the rubber, that's for sure.'

At the 2017 SIBA Awards, Rip Curl took out another four awards, for best wetsuit, best board shorts, best swimwear and best customer service. Steve Kay sees it as further confirmation that their global approach is working. 'It amazes me that, by and large, despite what some of our regions say, a really good product sells really well everywhere,' says Steve. 'As I travel the world looking at all these places it does give you that sense – holy shit, we've got to produce good product here because there's a lot of mouths being fed by the sale of Rip Curl products around the world now.'

MICK FANNING CALLS STUMPS

In late February 2018, Mick Fanning announced his retirement via Instagram. The surfer who's been synonymous with Rip Curl since he won Bells as a wildcard in 2001 would make the Rip Curl Pro his farewell event.

It was massive news, but no one close to Mick was surprised. His confrontations with mortality – the infamous shark incident and the death of his brother Peter in 2015 – had reordered Mick's life priorities. He had taken an extended break in 2016 and returned to the tour in 2017 to see if he could rekindle that famous competitive fire, but by his lofty standards a 12th-place finish was a fate he couldn't abide.

I had always been going to head to Bells for Easter 2018 to witness the spectacle that the Rip Curl Pro has become. From a folding card table on the beach at the very first Bells Rally to the famed double-decker bus on the clifftop in the '80s, the contest infrastructure has grown into a sprawling prefab city of grand-stands and competitors' lounges and judging towers. There's a whole boulevard of food vans and two enormous video screens in the car park that beam the action to those who can't find a clifftop vantage point amid the Easter throng.

In Torquay, conversation appears to be about little other than Mick's imminent retirement. I pick up some supplies at the local IGA, where a middle-aged woman is chatting to the check-out girl. 'I'll be sad to see him go but he's tired. He needs a break,' she reports knowingly, as if discussing her own kin. Handpainted signs decorate picket fences along the Surf Coast Highway calling out 'Good luck Mick' and the ubiquitous #cheersmick hashtag.

A gala retirement dinner is held at the grand RACV Resort for several hundred of Mick's closest friends and significant figures from his career. It is the same site as the old Torquay Golf Club, where the very first Surfing Hall of Fame presentation dinner was staged back in 1985, when surfing pioneer Snowy McAlis-ter and Mark Richards were honoured. That was a low-key affair compared to this evening's glittering occasion.

Rip Curl has spared no expense, with Mick Fanning bobblehead figurines for every guest and facsimiles of its legendary Search trophies as the centrepiece for every table, each named after a surf break where Mick has won events or secured world titles. There's an entire hallway of Mick's surf magazine covers on display. In many ways the evening showcases how far surfing has come since 1985. But keeping it real at our table of surf journalists in a corner of the vast room is Tommy Peterson, younger brother of the great Michael Peterson, loudly heckling, necking beers, haranguing bar staff and threatening to spark up joints throughout the night.

On the main stage, however, it's all heartfelt tributes, hilarious anecdotes and warm reminiscences from a cavalcade of Mick's nearest and dearest. 'The world needs role models, and I'm sure it's not easy being a role model, but you have become a role model for many kids around the world,' Brian says to him.

Neil Ridgway gives thanks for the huge contribution Mick has made to Rip Curl's business over the past two decades, in contrast to the fortunes of some of their competitors. 'We ain't going broke, brother,' Neil assures him, before pausing for dramatic effect, 'thanks to you.' The crowd laps it up. 'Tonight, we don't want you to do anything because this is your night, and we're all here for you,' says Neil.

Kelly Slater pays tribute to Mick's competitive spirit in the water and fundamental decency on land. 'I've really enjoyed my time surfing with you. You always bring the best out in me. I don't get nervous because I know I can't surf nervous. I have to be on my game,' says Kelly. 'In the water he's like, "Don't fucking talk to me," and when he comes in he's just happy Mick. I really appreciate that.'

Childhood mate Joel Parkinson speaks poignantly of the year they went head to head for the world title. 'Two thousand and nine was probably the hardest time, the most pressure on our relationship we ever had,' says Joel. 'Everyone from our area wanted us to do well and win world titles, and . . . we were walking around town and we had two football teams, and you had to take sides.' Joel recalls the pain of losing that world title, hobbled by a mid-year ankle injury and forced to watch his friend blitz the back half of the season to chase down Joel's commanding ratings lead. 'We both went for our dreams and they happened to run into each other,' he says.

The crowd are then entertained by Grinspoon frontman Phil Jamieson, whose band performed at Mick's first world-title party in the car park of the Kirra Pub back in 2007, as the Coolangatta crowd went wild. A collage of images from that raucous party is projected onto large screens: Mick joining the band on stage; his mum, Liz, crowd-surfing; and throngs of locals moshing in honour of their hero. 'That's the most Australian thing I've ever seen,' quips the MC for the night, Rosy Hodge.

Tonight, Jamieson smashes out a spirited version of Grinspoon's old hit 'More Than You Are' on acoustic guitar, ending his performance standing atop Mick's table and bellowing:

> Were you neurotic as a child?
> Did they come around and watch your style?
> Did you have plans to be a star?
> Did you have plans to become more than you are?

With the entire surfing world and a huge Easter crowd willing him to victory, Mick surfs all the way to the final but falls short of the fairytale finish, coming second to the rampaging Brazilian Italo Ferreira. Mick doesn't appear to mind a bit, smothered by Italo in an affectionate bear hug as the hooter sounds, and swamped by family, friends and wellwishers when he returns to the beach.

In his farewell speech Mick says simply to the Rip Curl founders, 'Thanks for believing, thanks for trusting and thanks for the guidance and the vision. It's been a fun journey.'

THE RETURN OF THE SEARCH

While Rip Curl's world-champ factory had been running at full steam, the Search had taken a back seat. By 2015 a decision was made to relaunch the celebrated campaign, which had been quietly bubbling away in the background.

'The Search has come up and down in spikes over the past 15 years to really good effect,' says Neil. 'We say you can't have a Search without going on the Search. The exploration, the time and effort and money it takes to do it properly – the company is committed to that. Things like the Snake with Mick [a remarkable secret right-hand point Fanning surfed alone in mid-2017], they're not easy to find, and when you do they're hard to get to, but they're really worth it.'

It was the ideal time to restart the Search, as another three-time world champion approached the end of his competitive reign and contemplated life beyond the pro tour. 'When we first did the Search, there was Curren, sick of the tour, and Frankie [Oberholzer]. We want to bring that back for a once-in-a-generation surfer retiring,' says creative director James Taylor.

They've teamed up Mick with another laidback free-surfing phenom, Hawaiian Mason Ho. Mick and Mason make a great double act. Mick's been known as a disciplined competitor, and is ready to throw off the shackles by experimenting with board design and discovering new waves and horizons. Fun-loving Mason is all about loose, stylistic flourishes in his surfing.

'I'm just really excited to get on the Search. Mason and myself are similar to Frankie and Curren 20 years later,' says Mick, who loved the old Search videos as a grommet. 'I just want to go and . . . [create] a good chapter and legacy. That's sort of where my goal-posts are now, creating something timeless. Hopefully in 10 years' time some kid goes, "I watched that."'

SAME AS IT EVER WAS

I've brought my 12-year-old son Alex along for Mick's swansong at Bells and he's in grommet heaven, surfing before and after the event each day, delighting in his coloured wristband, feasting on the VIP catering, meeting many of his heroes. The surf's pumping in the perfect autumn weather, and Alex catches the biggest wave of his life out at Bells. After a week of it he wants us to permanently relocate to Torquay from our home on the balmy, subtropical Gold Coast. 'Tell him to come back in August,' Neil suggests.

With Alex frothing for maximum ocean time, I decide to test that old adage: 'No one at Rip Curl ever got sacked for going surfing.' My in-depth research during the event consists largely of surfing Winki Pop with my boy while the contest is on at Bells, switching to Bells when the contest moves to Winki, and scouring the surrounding reefs on the lay days. I rationalise that in some way the Rip Curl story needs to seep out of those ancient cliffs and reefs and illuminate to me the spirit of place that fuelled this whole outlandish adventure. No one at head office seems to mind a bit.

One afternoon, when an onshore sea breeze springs up and the contest's put on hold, Alex and I lob at Claw's place, intent on borrowing longboards to tackle Cosy Corner, a gentle kiddy wave protected from the breeze. Claw grants us the pick of his extensive quiver of longboards lined up neatly in racks in the garage, all with immaculate wax jobs. Claw says Cosy Corner is where he does a lot of his surfing these days when he's in Torquay, and we reflect on how a surfing life eventually comes full circle. He seems charmed by our father–son excursion as we trot off carrying the boards in tandem, Alex with the nose of the boards under each arm, me carrying the tails. We soul-arch across the tiny peelers through packs of learners, yahooing like loons.

Another day, we scout out a less popular reef that requires a mountain-goat descent down a steep, muddy hillside, and Alex makes for a little hollow right dubbed Sparrow's after Rip Curl's resident rubber guru, who pioneered it. My boy paddles out to join a gang of local groms and is welcomed into the fold, trading hoots and tubes, and comes in eyes agog, his post-surf debrief a high-pitched euphoric babble.

After a late session at Winki Pop with only a handful out, including Kelly Slater and a couple of Brazilian backpackers, we reach the beach on dark, barely able to drag ourselves away from the empty waves. The setting sun lights the western sky in a psychedelic blaze of orange and pink, while a full moon rises in the east, its reflection dancing on the inky swells. I am gripped by a powerful surge of emotion, clasp my boy in a hug and insist neither of us will ever forget this moment. I feel like more is revealed to me now about the allure of this coast than any number of interviews could.

Some claim Torquay's charm has been sullied by the modern era of crowds and commercialism. I can confidently report, however, that through the eyes of a child the magic remains the same as it ever was.

THE BIG THREE

There's been a seismic shift in the surf industry landscape in recent years, and in many ways Rip Curl is the last man standing. Quiksilver and Billabong, after rising and falling spectacularly as public companies, are now both owned by investment firm Oaktree Capital Management, under the umbrella company Boardriders Inc. Quiksilver is in the process of moving its Australian headquarters from its traditional Torquay base to share the cavernous and sparsely populated offices of Billabong on the Gold Coast. Far from celebrating the tough times of their competitors, Claw and Brian seem genuinely saddened by the changes wrought on their industry.

'I think it's really sad that a company that started in Torquay will no longer be there, along with about 100 people in Torquay being out of work,' says Brian. 'It gave people added experience to be able to swap jobs between Quiksilver and Rip Curl.'

'We had the glory days of the surf industry particularly in the '70s, '80s, '90s in Australia,' says Claw. 'Ourselves along with Billabong and Quiksilver were termed the Big Three. Collectively we built the industry, fuelled by the nine-to-five competition which was fierce, week in, week out, year in, year out. That fuelled the strength, growth and viability of the industry. I'm pretty much of the view those two immediate competitors of ours in their original form in Australia were managed and operated in a manner very similar to Rip Curl. It might be something about surfing that rubs off on the way you do business. It always seemed that Al Green at Quiksilver and Gordon Merchant at Billabong were very much our equivalents and contemporaries, having similar goals, similar personal skills and facing the same challenges.'

Because Rip Curl's success grew out of that fierce competition, Claw says he'd like to see his old competitors strong and trading according to their roots, as a buoyant surf industry, like a rising tide, floats all boats. 'I'd probably be dreaming to think it would be just like the good old days once again; however, if Billabong and Quiksilver return to some of their age-old management practices and business style I'm sure things would be better, and perhaps it is not too big a stretch to think that a re-emergence of the good old tried-and-true ways would help those companies and our industry enormously. I believe that we can prosper better together than we can alone,' he says.

Claw's enough of a realist to know that the goal of those brands' new owners might vary from Rip Curl's. 'If you're owned by private equity the charter is very clear, to improve the company and onsell it for a profit,' says Claw.

In this new world order, Claw feels more affinity to brands in different, though allied, sectors. 'There are enormous parallels with Patagonia – [a] fairly large, privately owned company successfully operating in an ever-changing world,' he says. 'Other core companies have transitioned from their original roots to reach a wide range of customers and success, two examples being Vans and North Face. Vans has been a really long-term cultural constant of skateboarding. It shares a lot of similar branding principles and initiatives [with Rip Curl]. North Face are strongly focused on technical functional products similar to Patagonia and Rip Curl. Both Vans and North Face retain a lot of product and brand integrity, even though they have now grown to annual sales in the small billions.'

At the time of writing, the Rip Curl founders are courting offers to buy the business. With the next generation of the founders' families showing no signs of taking over the reins, and the founders well into their 70s, there is a need for a succession plan or exit strategy. But they insist they're in no hurry.

'We had a couple of people interested about three years ago. At this age you're always for sale at the right price,' says Brian. 'There's no imperative to sell, but all our eggs are tied up in the one basket. The three of us are very keen that any buyer really looks after the brand and our crew into the future. We are prepared to forgo dollars to ensure it does go to the right home.'

'Taking care of the brand and the crew, continuing to be the ultimate surfing company, it's the way we want it to be,' adds Claw.

Ex-chairman Ahmed Fahour agrees. 'The most important thing is, now these guys are getting to an age where they're not going to be there forever, to ensure whoever owns that brand into the future manages it not as a business but as a whole-of-life experience,' says Ahmed.

The founders are now non-executive directors on the Rip Curl board, with Brian acting as chairman, and the board meets several times a year in their various global headquarters. 'Brian, François and myself virtually agree on everything. We've appraised things from different standpoints and express them in different ways, but at the end of the day with anything serious we always agree,' says Claw.

CEO Michael Daly generally leads the meetings. 'We proceed with a day of meetings called the "founders meetings", where the founders interact with leading executives,' says Claw. 'Then we go into board meetings and have leading executives as guests, have one of the regional CEOs attend board meetings or parts of the board meetings on certain subjects, which works very well, very harmoniously.'

Kelly Gibson is transitioning from his role as CEO of Rip Curl North America to a new position as a non-executive board member. 'Kelly's changing his lifestyle and he's become a more-than-welcome board member to represent . . . the surf industry in the US,' says Claw.

It's fair to say these are not your average corporate board meetings, and it's not uncommon for Claw or François to lie down and take a sly kip in the midst of proceedings. 'It's certainly true of both François and myself, but it's only true when we've had people holding the floor and waffling on about all and sundry, but nothing of real relevance to Rip Curl's business or brand,' says Claw.

Just when startled consultants or guests are questioning whether they still have an audience, Claw or François will pipe up from the floor with a pertinent observation. 'We've definitely used it strategically,' admits Claw. 'François is very sharp with numbers. He's a fabulous card player and played in finals of the world bridge championships on a number of occasions. So, from time to time, François completely blows these experts away by requoting their own numbers and throwing them back at them with a totally different conclusion . . . The impact of this is all the more dramatic when for some period of time preceding this François not only appeared to be disinterested, he in fact looked like he was asleep. This is a tactic I've often used myself.'

On occasion, the slumbering executives might have simply succumbed to exhaustion. 'Time out in our meetings is sometimes more a result of a few big nights on the party program that we engage in with our staff, crew and customers when we're on the road,' says Claw. 'We spend 15 to 16 hours of the day together, including lunch and dinner, so there's lots of reminiscing, there's lots of having fun.'

For CEO Michael Daly, the board meetings have been the biggest culture shock about joining Rip Curl. 'I had presented to boards of listed companies before – very formal, very official, very structured,' says Michael. 'I always find our meetings a riot, the complete opposite to what I was used to. For years I watched the likes of James Strong and Ahmed Fahour come in as formal directors in large companies and deal with Brian, Claw and François. You would think that such types would walk all over the founders. It was certainly not always that way. Even today, not a meeting goes past when I don't get a laugh. I watched Brian, Claw and François all try on a pair of size-34 walkshorts in one board meeting. It was the same pair in succession and all three of them were standing there in the boardroom in Europe in their jocks, comparing notes on whether these shorts were a true size 34 or not. James had gone to the toilet and walked back in and just had sheer shock in his eyes, seeing the three guys standing around in their underwear.'

There are other little eccentricities of the company founders that continue to make life interesting. 'François and I were in a café in Torquay one day and we both had Rip Curl t-shirts on,' says Michael. 'We finished our meal and the server asked whether we would like to put that on the Quiksilver account. We looked at her and François, as sharp as ever, just said, "Yes, of course, madam, that would be great." We still owe Quiksilver that $30.'

THE SECRET SAUCE

At the start of this book I made the bold claim that I'd somehow unearth deep and revealing secrets to Rip Curl's success: how exactly this humble garage start-up had managed to not just survive for half a century, but also thrive as the prosperous, global business it is today. Twelve months on, after hundreds of hours of interviews with dozens of characters across six countries, I'm rather less confident that there is a neat, easily articulated answer. There remains some unfathomable mystery to Rip Curl's success, a wild heart that defies capture or replication. It's tempting to revert to Rip Curl stalwart Peter Hodgart's summation: 'It was just one of those magical things that happened.' Or as Brian told that ANZ banker all those years ago, 'If I fucking knew I'd had have 10 of them by now.'

John Witzig, that key chronicler of surfing in the late '60s and early '70s, puts it down to the characters and the times in which they were drawn together, as Australian surfing found its self-belief and a new generation rejected their parents' conservative values. 'I think it's happenstance – the combination of individuals in a particular time that encouraged adventurous behaviour and curiosity, and people who weren't afraid to challenge whatever the prevailing orthodoxies were,' says John. 'If you thought of something, it wasn't, "Why can't I do that?" It was, "How could I do it?" You could just do stuff. It was utterly conducive to us thinking we could do whatever we wanted to. It was a fabulous period.'

As a flag-bearer for surfing's counterculture roots, I'd suspected John might be cynical about the rise of the big surf brands, but

I couldn't have been more wrong. 'The surfing world could do a hell of a lot worse than having people like Claw and Brian in charge of a major surf company,' says John. 'These are people who kept their commitment to surfing really strong and that strikes me as being impressive.'

Nat Young, the 1966 world champion and test pilot of the shortboard revolution, agrees. 'They always had a surfers' attitude to it, which is what I really liked about it,' he says. 'I think it's important for surfing that we have people like that involved.'

'Claw and Brian are two very different men,' says Steve Kay. 'A reason why the company has been so successful is that their skill bases are very different but very complementary, so they're not fighting each other for control of areas of the company. There's a natural division between the two. Claw is brand and marketing, team and events. Brian has an outstanding record of judgement in more of the business affairs . . . But then at another level they both have a very similar vision for the company.'

Gary Green, the original Search surfer, has a simple explanation for why the brand continues to resonate with successive generations of surfers. 'I think because they've kept it rootsy, because it's been Sing Ding and Claw, and they've got this core vision of how they wanted the company and they've stuck true to that,' says Greeny.

It's a view shared by former NSW sales manager and ex-pro surfer Steve Jones. 'Brian used to always say in the meetings there was an in-built culture at Rip Curl – "Keep your feet in the sand" – and I think to this day Rip Curl was the hardest core out of the trio [Rip Curl, Billabong and Quiksilver],' says Steve. 'I think Rip Curl did the right thing resisting the siren song [of going public]. Keeping it tidy and in-house, they didn't have to go through that boom and bust. They just stayed true to their formula, kept it on a nice even keel, with integrity intact.'

Rod Adams, the sober-headed bean counter, reckons there are simply good business practices behind the wild parties and sandy footprints through the corridors of Rip Curl HQ. 'What's different is that there's not that many good businesses. It's not that Rip Curl's unique, it's the way that business should be run,' says Rod. 'To listen and adapt to change, adapt to meeting customers' expectations, ensuring the product was the best, the quality was the best, delivery was the best, the relationships were fair for all the stakeholders.'

For Brooke Farris, it's those surfing-based brand values that keep the business on track. 'It's authentic. We've got the founders still a part of the business, so they have a guiding hand. They remind us of why we're here and what we're doing. They stop us looking over our shoulders and keep us paddling to the next peak,' says Brooke. 'We always want to make the best-quality surf products . . . sticking to what we're good at is why we continue to prosper.'

Two-time world champ Tyler Wright reckons it's the close relationships and continuity of ownership that allows the connection between athletes and the brand to flourish. 'Good people run it. I think they're very particular as to who they've got working for them,' says Tyler. 'They've stuck to what they're good at. I have zero idea about business, but for the athlete growing up we know the owners, we know who we're working with and dealing with. I think that is something special, that is something for them to be proud of . . . I know who my bosses are.'

Fred Basse believes it's the perennial youthfulness of the brand, and its geographic diversity, that has allowed it to survive challenging times. 'The capacity of the brand to not become old with its consumer base and being able to renew it with every new generation, I believe a big part of it comes from our team and events,' says Fred. 'The other point is the international approach of the surf industry. Rip Curl is in so many countries that it allows it to balance the performance. When USA was having a hard time Europe was supporting, and vice versa a few years after. Australia was always consistent and all the small licensees have performed well, with some of them getting bigger and bigger, like Indonesia.'

Ahmed Fahour still marvels at the eccentric business smarts he at first struggled to recognise at Rip Curl. 'Initially, I was like, what the fuck have we got here? But very quickly I was thinking, holy shit, there's a secret sauce here,' says Ahmed. 'The financial return was always the last thing we ever talked about. It was, how authentic is what we're doing to our brand, our purpose, what we're all about? It really taught me very, very quickly one of the real reasons why they're successful is they always had the end customer in mind. They always wanted surfers to know that everything was built with purpose and value, not for the purposes of making money. But by doing that you make money by building a product that everyone wants and values . . . They gave me an inordinate amount of understanding of how a global consumer business in little old Torquay can take on the rest of the world and win. Their business acumen is as shrewd as [that of] any other businessperson I know.'

Steve Kay says Claw and Brian were always more ambitious than their casual, surf-for-the-day attitudes suggested. They had two main ambitions: 'They wanted to have a global company to follow their customers around the world. Coming from Australia, it was really exciting for someone to have that global vision,' says Steve. 'And the second one was that they were very ambitious about the breadth of products they wanted to do after they got over the idea of just being a wetsuit company. And their capacity to do both really has been quite remarkable . . . They worked on those two great ambitions and they did more travel than most owners and spent time in product-related meetings here just grinding things out.'

Another defining feature was the deep and abiding loyalty of long-time staff, whom Claw terms the 'true believers' and 'heavy lifters'. Rod Adams credits Brian with innovative ways of remunerating senior staff, ensuring loyalty and performance. 'He's happy to put innovative bonus arrangements in place, innovative equity arrangements in place,' says Rod. 'We would have still been there even if he didn't put them in place.'

Ray Thomas is one of the Curl's 'heavy lifters', who took on various roles and could always give the founders honest feedback. 'Brian was like the Prime Minister and Claw was like the Minister for Propaganda,' says Ray. 'I could always really argue with them, they'd never take offence. They liked it that I'd go hard and put in 100 per cent and take ownership of it.'

Terry Wall, their old business partner in the original Bells Beach Surf Shop, has a deeper insight than most into the nature of that relationship. 'Sing Ding and Claw's personal and professional relationship has lasted longer than their marriages, and longer than most rock bands – which is probably closer to their business relationship,' he says. 'How and why? They overlap in their core driver of living with the freedom required for a surfing life, but differ in their skill sets so they can contribute to complementary bits of their business, so fewer arguments. Both rascals, they share wild sides, and thrive in the company of other surfing rascals. Yet they are both "great blokes" – one of Brian's common descriptors of others. At the end of the day, the business was a means to an end, and they stumbled into and through it, like most of us stumble through life. They just happened to bump into each other at the right time, when they were both at a loose end.'

I'm no business expert, but for me there are two defining traits of the Rip Curl story. One is what Europe CEO Wilco Prins terms 'entreprise libérée', or 'liberation management', as espoused by business writer Tom Peters: granting staff the freedom to take risks and back hunches, and rewarding them for an entrepreneurial approach. The Rip Curl founders worked out early that it was not only more efficient to back their people and allow them to use their own judgement and initiative, but that it also freed up more time for surfing, skiing and travel.

Which leads me to the other defining trait: that simple urge to build a life around the beach and the vagaries of the swells, the tides and the winds. As any surfer knows, the drive to get in the ocean when all the requisite earthly variables align is a magnetic and addictive force. At the core of the overarching Rip Curl narrative is one recurring story, of a surfer who didn't want to have to head into the dark heart of the city to make a living, who dared to dream of a life close to the light and sea spray and rumbling energy of the coast, and was moved to do whatever it took to make that dream a reality.

That dream continues, from Claw and Brian's original fumbling forays into surf commerce to François forgoing careers in medicine and architecture to stay at the beach in Hossegor, from José Farinha growing fed up with traffic jams in Lisbon while his heart yearned for the waves of Peniche to Francisco Spinola tiring of the office-bound corporate world, from Peter Hodgart plotting a way to transition from the teeming metropolis of Tokyo back to his beloved Torquay to James Taylor fleeing London's pressurised media world for the freedom and escape of the Victorian coast.

While that restless surfing impulse has been blamed for laying many careers to waste, at Rip Curl it served as the great motivator to get the job done then reap the rewards: that 'secret sauce' Ahmed Fahour puzzled over.

Brian Singer has given plenty of thought to the reasons for their success. 'We were definitely customer focused and worked hard, but timing did play a role in our success,' says Brian. 'Many people look back to the time of their youth with great memories; however, I do think the late 1960s and early 1970s were a special time of social change. It was a melting pot of the civil rights movement in the US, the advent of the contraceptive pill, the Vietnam War and increased economic freedoms, and surfing rode this new wave of music, sex, drugs and rock-and-roll. This was the world into which Rip Curl was born.

'I feel we were really lucky, like many others, to have lived our life in the surf industry. We lived and worked in the lifestyle we loved. The early days were special – on the road selling to surf shops and meeting great people are some of my best memories. Certainly, the surf industry is in a different place today, as is surfing itself. No longer rebels of society rejecting many of the values of the previous generation – parents are now actively encouraging their kids to surf. However, surfing and the industry is still a wonderful way for young people of today to live their life.'

SLIDING DOORS

Brian's adamant he and Claw have never been motivated by wealth. 'Our western system places too much emphasis on money as a measure of success,' says Brian. 'Things get more complicated, there's more stuff to worry about and be responsible for. It doesn't necessarily change your life or create happiness, but it does allow the . . . means to spend more time with your kids and grandkids, which is probably the best thing.'

Brian's well aware that there are those who resent their success and wealth. 'It's great that lots of ratbag surfers have done well out of the surf game,' he says. 'You do hear people being jealous of that. For those that surfed a lot more and cruised around a lot more it

373

may well be that people who worked harder could be jealous of them. I never got to surf J-Bay, for example, and that's a pity.'

In a reflective moment, Claw reminisces about his last visit to San Francisco in 2017, and a chance encounter with an old participant in the original Summer of Love, a colourful character known as Diamond Dave. A rapper, poet and advocate for the homeless, Diamond Dave Whitaker is regarded as a spiritual leader of the Haight-Ashbury hippie scene.

'This small old guy started talking to me – a real hippie, quite well educated,' recalls Claw. 'I was having a great old time talking to this fella a couple of years older than me for two or three hours wandering around Haight-Ashbury ... He explained all about the Summer of Love, the dancing and singing and concerts in the park, explaining the values to me. He said, "I've been living by that value set ever since. I'm a believer in that." He said, "We talk to our people over in Australia and we know about Nimbin. I've held true to it, and that's why I don't have a lot of money." I explained our Summer of Love. He said, "I can see you're a fellow traveller, but you would have been better off if you had stuck with it."'

Diamond Dave can still be found spouting his free-form Beat poetry around the Haight-Ashbury scene in rapid-fire, staccato bursts, as if the Summer of Love never ended. It's fascinating to contemplate what might have happened if Claw's own surfboard business founded that summer had never taken off. For Claw, the chance encounter with Diamond Dave was a kind of sliding-doors moment where he glimpsed what an alternative life might have looked like.

In the lead-up to their 50th anniversary, Rip Curl has been engaged in a determined search for any surviving surfboards from their early days, fashioned in Brian's garage or the old bakery. Those late-'60s and early-'70s models, mainly gunny single-fins, are exceptionally rare as they weren't doing huge numbers and, pre-legropes, they took a pounding on the rocky shorelines of Bells Beach and its surrounds.

'We're desperately looking for them now, there might only be 30 or 40,' says Claw. 'We'd love to get our hands on any of those early vee bottoms shaped by Shane Stedman in Brookvale with the original Rip Curl logo. Bob Smith [Rip Curl's resident archivist] drove up to Portarlington on the Bellarine Peninsula to look at one, but the son had stripped the glass off it and reshaped it. Bob was nearly crying when he told me that story.'

Claw remains as surf-obsessed as ever, with an encyclopaedic knowledge of the sport, an enviable collection of historical boards and an insatiable appetite for watching, discussing and analysing wave-riding in all its forms. He divides his time between Torquay, where even the hedges in his garden are trimmed into the shape of waves, and a modern beachfront pile on the Gold Coast, with a weather station on the roof.

His kids are all accomplished skiers and recreational surfers. Eldest child Daniel, after an elite skiing career cut short by a brutal knee injury, has become a nature and landscape photographer. Daughter Ava is a New York–based filmmaker and artist, Tanya is a mother to four kids, and Lisa is studying to be a doctor with a specialty in natural medicine. Youngest daughter Millie has just qualified as a ski instructor.

Brian is kept busy monitoring the progress of his latest Melbourne Cup prospects under legendary racehorse trainer Lloyd Williams, as part of a syndicate that includes his old Quiksilver pal Al Green and Mushroom Records founder Michael Gudinski. Together they've won the 2016 and 2017 Melbourne Cups: Almandin won the race that stops the nation in 2016, and in 2017 they snared the quinella, with Rekindling first and Johannes Vermeer second.

'Watching them come up the straight, they could have dropped an atom bomb and I wouldn't have heard it,' says Brian.

These days, most of Brian's time is spent at the beach or in the mountains. 'As chairman of Rip Curl, I attend about six or eight board meetings a year, but otherwise I'm surfing the easier breaks around Torquay or northern New South Wales, and on boat trips surfing with my kids and grandkids,' says Brian. 'Winters are spent skiing at Buller, with an annual heliski trip to Canada.

'I'm lucky to be the proud father of four kids and see them all get on really well with each other. Watching my grandkids surfing is like reliving my own youth. Although all my kids have worked at Rip Curl at some point, only my youngest, Jade, is currently working there. My other two daughters are great mums – a much-underrated profession – and my son has his own business.'

François Payot, meanwhile, divides his time between his farm in Hossegor, an apartment in Paris, a rustic surf retreat in Madagascar and a rural acreage in Mullumbimby in northern New South Wales. Towards the end of my time in France, I'm invited to lunch in Paris at one of François's favourite restaurants with him, his ex-wife Marianne, their adult daughter Dune and his current girlfriend Lisa, a statuesque African-French woman in her 30s.

Dune has brought her pet beagle, who curls up under the table on a newly purchased canine bed as we enjoy classic French bistro fare, fine wine and wide-ranging conversation in French and English. At one point, Marianne and Lisa step outside to smoke a cigarette together, apparently the best of friends, and I can but marvel at this delightfully French scene. 'With all the wives and girlfriends, he's the only person I've ever met in my life where every girlfriend and every wife is still his best friend,' Maurice Cole had told me earlier. 'When we had his 60th birthday here a couple of years ago they were all there. They all talk to each other. He's a freak.'

Rip Curl has delivered lifestyles its founders could never have imagined as impoverished surf vagabonds and dharma beach bums in the heyday of surfing's counterculture era. Or perhaps they could imagine it, and that is their secret.

THE 50-YEAR STORM

It's the middle of July, deep into another southern winter, and the same intense weather system that is bombing the Surf Coast with a powerful groundswell is dumping snow on the Victorian Alps. In Torquay, the 50 Year Storm Invitational – a special one-day big-wave event to honour local surfer Shaun Brooks, who took his own life in 2012 after a long struggle with mental illness – has been put on standby. The event galvanises the local surfing community in memory of one of their own, and anticipation is high to see if the swell will deliver the required 10-to-12-foot surf. Competitors are flying in from as far afield as Queensland and Bali.

This is Torquay in its natural state, long after the Easter crowds have gone home and turned their minds to Australian Rules football. As I look around the surfers gathered in the Bells car park, pulling large surfboards out of the back of four-wheel drives, I note many members of the Torquay surf industry's second generation: the sons of the industry pioneers and their contemporaries.

Shaun was a former world junior champion and renowned big-wave charger, the son of Rod Brooks and brother of ex–world tour surfer Troy, who has flown in from the Gold Coast for the swell. Among the other invitees are an array of familiar Torquay family names: Shyama Buttonshaw, Jack Perry, Jeff Sweeney, Carlo Lowdon, Adam Robertson, Mick and Tony Ray.

Perhaps this is the great legacy the first generation has passed on to the next – that they wouldn't have to choose between surfing and career. Among their number are IT specialists, designers, surfboard shapers, young entrepreneurs of many stripes. As a group, they are probably more worldly and well travelled, with greater career and life options ahead of them, than most surfers living in regional Australia. And I start to appreciate that this isn't really the story of one surfing company and its unlikely business success, but rather that of an entire community staking a claim to a lifestyle it dared to believe was possible. 'That's the way I always thought it should be – a broader, ongoing, multi-generational love and commitment to surfing, and the culture, community, industry and lifestyle it fosters,' says Claw.

At Rip Curl HQ, Neil Ridgway seems delighted by the absenteeism the latest swell has inspired. 'There'd be 20 of our guys out there – JT, Helmy, Mick, Johnny, my two art guys, watch guys, wetty guys . . . then the older guys would have been out at Torquay Point or Tubes or Point Impossible,' he boasts. The job description at Rip Curl appears to include a responsibility to partake generously of this great natural elixir and bring that good energy into the workplace, like bees carrying pollen back to the hive.

Late that afternoon, I visit Butch and Chris Barr, who live next door to Brian at Addiscot, the historic home of the original Bell family, after whom the beach is named. When the Barrs moved here in 1974, not long after Butch began as Rip Curl's first accountant, they'd still get visits from Girly Bell, a daughter of the pioneer family, who was by then an elderly lady, checking on her family's old homestead. Chris helps curate a local online history project, the Museum Without Walls, and its quarterly newsletter, *History Matters*. Torquay's rich history feels palpable around these parts.

Chris takes me for a cruise out to the back paddock in their little golf buggy they call the 'speed machine'. Rolling hills stretch eastwards towards Bells Beach. Kangaroos graze. A meandering creek and a gully of gum trees wind their way through a fold in the hills to the ocean. 'We used to have great parties out here, just park a flatbed truck at the bottom of the hill and get a band to play. They were great times,' says Chris. They must have been – a tight-knit community of idealistic young surfers at the peak of surfing's 'country soul' era feasting on uncrowded waves, starting businesses that would give birth to an entire industry, staging mini-Woodstocks in the back paddocks, snapping up coastal real estate for a song.

All this land is still owned by Claw, Brian and Butch, and remains undeveloped, combining with the Bells Beach Surfing Reserve to ensure the foreshore around Bells retains its rural charm. Standing here on this grassy hill, swell lines stacked out to sea, a stiff offshore whistling about my ears, storm clouds gathering in the powerful west, I'm struck by the sheer audacity of their dream: to come to this place and build a life, a community and, ultimately, an entire industry around the frivolous play of riding waves. The success of this particular mission can never be captured in *BRW* rich lists or share-market prices.

The next morning, organisers of the 50 Year Storm Invitational are gathered on a timber walkway overlooking Bells in an earnest huddle, gazing at mobile phones and analysing buoy readings and swell forecasts. Finally, the decision is made to call the event off. Though the swell is a solid six-to-eight feet, ruler-straight and stretching to the horizon, there have only been a couple of the requisite 10-foot sets all morning. But there is no sense of anti-climax. This will not be a day for the history books – just another epic day of waves for the local crew. 'The event is officially off,' an organiser announces through a megaphone. 'Go surfing, the waves are pumping.'

And that's just what they do. A new generation paddles out to meet yet another swell.

ACKNOWLEDGEMENTS

I owe a lot of people a tonne of gratitude for opening up their lives and stories to me to allow the Rip Curl story to be told. Thanks to Neil Ridgway for giving me the opportunity, and Claw and Brian for being so generous with their time and trust.

Thanks also to the many members of the Rip Curl family around the world who extended their hospitality, especially François Payot, Fred Basse and Maurice Cole in France; Tom and Makeira Curren, Kelly Gibson and all the crew in the US; Monica Little, Aimee Susol and archivist Bob Smith at Torquay HQ; Meagan Patterson for organising my travel; Chris Barr for historical perspectives; and Ted Grambeau for the rich insights and imagery.

I always say you never really finish a book like this, you just run out of time. Thousands of people around the world have contributed to the Rip Curl story and to those I never got to, my apologies. I hope this book inspires more sharing of the Rip Curl folklore, those stories that didn't make it into print and are best shared over a few cool beverages with good friends.

To Alison Urquhart at Penguin Random House, this marks our eighth book together over 20 years (as Ali points out, we started young!) – thanks for the faith and opportunities and wise counsel. To my first-time editor Tom Langshaw, thanks for finessing the manuscript so adroitly and picking up my overuse of the term 'salt-encrusted'.

As always, deep gratitude to my family for putting up with the absences, the deadline-induced grumpiness and the endless retelling of choice anecdotes.

Discover a
new favourite